Principles of Irish Law

(FIFTH EDITION)

BRIAN DOOLAN

GILL & MACMILLAN

Gill & Macmillan
Goldenbridge
Dublin 8
with associated companies throughout the world

www.gillmacmillan.ie
0 7171 2839 3
Print origination by Carole Lynch, Dublin
Printed by Biddles Limited, England

A catalogue record is available for this book from the British Library.

1 3 5 4 2

To my Son
Cristian

and

In memory of my late parents
Paddy and Emily

CONTENTS

PREFACE TO THE FIFTH EDITION

The need for a fifth edition of this book which has established itself as the standard introduction to Irish law arises from the changes in our law which have occurred since the last edition was published. In the preface to the fourth edition the hope was expressed that that edition would remain relevant until the close of the millennium. That expectation has not been realised because of the sheer volume, variety and effects of the legal changes have occurred in such a short period. Consequently, the time-span between this edition and the last one has been reduced from five years to three years, a trend that is very likely to continue. To this author the necessity to quickly respond to the legal changes is not a source of complaint. Indeed as one who has criticised our institutions of government for failing to understand the ramifications of independence and relying for too long on old laws based on out-dated ideas, such a trend is most readily welcomed.

This edition incorporates the constitutional amendments, the various statutes and statutory instruments and cases which have brought about changes in the law since the fourth edition. However, there is one matter on which I cannot definitively state the law. When going to press the amendments to Articles 2 and 3 of the Constitution, enacted in a referendum consequent to the Belfast Agreement (or the Good Friday Agreement as it is invariably referred to), and conditional upon the full implementation of its terms, have not been brought into effect because of the lack of political progress on the matter. In the expectation that peace on this island will be maintained and that the agreement will be fully implemented, the new articles are included in the text. Of course, should the political process break down the original versions of Articles 2 and 3 will stand.

In other respects, I have endeavoured to state the law as of 31 December 1998.

Brian Doolan
Vilnius
6 January 1999

TABLE OF STATUTES

TABLE OF STATUTORY INSTRUMENTS

TABLE OF CASES

Table of Cases

IR = Irish Reports; ILTR = Irish Law Times Reports; ILRM = Irish Law Reports Monthly; SC — Supreme Court; HC — High Court; CCA — Court of Criminal Appeal.

Part One
THE IRISH LEGAL SYSTEM

Chapter 1

THE NATURE AND HISTORY OF IRISH LAW

Nature of Law

Jurisprudence is the science of law, though unlike the natural sciences which have immutable laws, legal laws are the product of human endeavour. Laws are rules of conduct imposed by a state upon its members and enforced by its courts. These rules of conduct constitute the law of the land, the domestic law. The purpose of these laws is to maintain a certain standard of behaviour amongst its members in the interest of the common good.

Law and Morality

There is a connection between legal laws laid down by a state and certain other norms of behaviour known as laws of morality. From a legal perspective the essential difference between these two sets of rules exists in their respective enforcement. Legal rules are enforced in the courts. Rules of morality depend for their observance upon the good conscience of the individual and the force of public opinion. In any society it is usual to find the rules of morality observed by the majority of its members reflected in the legal laws of that society.

Classification of Law

Law is classified in different ways. One distinction is made between public law and private law. Public law is that portion of the domestic law governing the relations between the state and the individual; constitutional law and criminal law are examples of public law. Thus, public international law governs the relations between states. Private law is that portion of the domestic law which controls the relations between individuals within the state; contract law and property law are examples of private law.

Law is also divided into criminal law and civil law. The objectives of both, though closely connected, are clearly different. Criminal law defines a variety of actions forbidden by the state. In order to protect itself society disapproves so strongly of such actions that it permits the state to punish those who depart from the standards set. Punishment is the ultimate sanction: the purpose of criminal law is to punish the offender, rather than compensate the victim. The purpose of civil law is the orderly resolution of disputes between individuals. It provides a remedy, usually a financial one, to the wronged party against the wrongdoer. Compensation of the aggrieved party is the aim, rather than the punishment of the wrongdoer.

The law also draws a distinction between the rules of law, referred to as substantive law, and the machinery by which these laws are enforced in the courts, which is known as procedural law.

Law and Fact

Our law draws a distinction between the rules of law governing any particular case and the facts which must be proved before a verdict can be reached that the law has been breached. In the crime of assault it is a question of law as to the precise definition of assault and whether the conduct amounts to assault in the eyes of the law. It is a question of fact as to whether an assault has been committed and whether the defendant was the culprit.

Nature of Irish Law

For historical reasons, explained later, Ireland has not an indigenous body of laws. Instead, we have a foreign system of laws implanted after a conquest which obliterated the highly developed native Brehon laws. Following military and political domination came common law, a product native to England which was applied in the colonised countries such as the United States of America, Canada, Australia and New Zealand.

Meaning of Common Law

Common law is the ancient unwritten law of England so called because it was made common to the whole of England and Wales after the Norman Conquest in 1066. Thereafter, over generations, this ancient law became embodied in a wide variety of judicial decisions. With the passage of time common law came to mean judge-made law as opposed to statute law, or the law enacted by parliament.

Meaning of Irish Law

'The common law is an integral portion of our jurisprudence', commented Gavan Duffy J. in *Cook v Carroll* (1945). Currently, Irish law draws on many different sources such as a written constitution, the laws of the European Union, statute law and judicial decisions. A body of law thus exists which can be styled as distinctively Irish. The simplest definition of Irish law is that body of legal rules administered in Irish courts.

THE HISTORY OF IRISH LAW 1170–1918

Introduction of the Common Law

Although Strongbow, or Richard FitzGilbert, Earl of Pembroke, led the Normans into Ireland in 1170, the reception of the common law was a slow gradual process. King John, on a visit in 1210, ordained that the laws and customs of England were to be observed, though this decree merely extended the common law to English settlers living mainly in the Pale around Dublin. The remainder of the country was subject to the Brehon laws and by 1331 the Irish were generally entitled to the benefits of the common law.

The development of common law courts in Ireland closely followed the English system. The Court of King's Bench was established after the visit of King Richard II in 1394–95. The judges were English born and on service here. A court system was not universally established by 1556 because in that year the Privy Council of Ireland ordered a dispute involving title to land to be decided by the Brehons, though by 1570 the Commissions of Assize were travelling the country, hearing both criminal and civil cases. By 1614 there were five circuits embracing the whole country.

Poynings' Law

Many attempts were made to introduce the statute law of the Parliament of England into Ireland which had a parliament of its own. The validity of such laws was denied by the English judges in the reign of King Henry VI. In 1484 the opposite conclusion was reached in the case of the *Merchants of Waterford*, a decision reinforced in 1494–95 by *Poynings' Law*, a statute of the Irish Parliament, which declared that all statutes previously passed in England should have full effect in Ireland. This statute did not give the English Parliament any right to legislate for Ireland, though it did fetter the future freedom of the Irish Parliament to legislate. It provided that the Crown's representative in Ireland and the Irish Privy Council should decide on the legislation it deemed desirable to lay before the Irish Parliament. Drafts of these proposed measures were to be sent to England for the sanction of the Crown and the English Privy Council. When this consent was obtained, the draft laws were then laid before the Irish Houses of Parliament. While this procedure did not subject the Irish Parliament to the English Parliament, it did effectively render the Irish Parliament impotent unless the Crown in London approved.

For hundreds of years the Irish Parliament legislated by this process. For the purposes of legal uniformity between the two islands the Irish Parliament passed many statutes which had been previously enacted in London. For example, the *Statute of Frauds* passed by the English Parliament in 1677 found its way into an Irish statute, similarly entitled, in 1695.

Supremacy of the English Parliament

The English Parliament declared, in the *Dependency of Ireland Act 1719*, that it had the right to legislate for Ireland. Until that year the Irish House of Lords had served as a final court of appeal for law cases in Ireland; this function was transferred to the English House of Lords. This statute is known in history as the *Sixth of George I.*

Legislative Independence

In the wake of American Independence and the rise of the Irish Volunteers, a campaign was mounted by Henry Grattan for the restoration of legislative independence for the Irish Parliament. This was granted by the *Dependency of Ireland Act 1782* which repealed the *Sixth of George I* and *Poynings' Law.*

Henceforth an Irish law would pass through the Irish Parliament in the same way an English Bill passed through the English Parliament. When enacted by both the Commons and Lords it would be sent to the Crown for royal assent. The Irish Parliament was thus subordinate only to the Crown. The appellate jurisdiction of the Irish House of Lords was restored.

Constitutional and Legal Integration

The legislative independence of the Irish Parliament was brief. Two years after the 1798 Rebellion, the *Act of Union 1800*, enacted by identical statutes in Ireland and England, brought total constitutional and legal integration. The 'United Kingdom of Great Britain and Ireland' was created with a single parliament at Westminster, to which members from Ireland were elected. For the next 120 years all statute law applicable in Ireland would be enacted at Westminster and the English House of Lords would be the court of final appeal for law cases from Ireland.

MODERN LEGAL HISTORY FROM 1919

Constitution of Dáil Éireann

Following the general election of December 1918, the elected Sinn Féin members met in Dublin on 21 January 1919 and constituted themselves as Dáil Éireann. It drew up a document known as the 'Constitution of Dáil Éireann' containing five short articles, and promulgated a 'Declaration of Independence' and a 'Democratic Programme' which reaffirmed the sentiments expressed in the Proclamation of the Irish Republic of Easter 1916. These documents, although of historical importance, had no subsequent constitutional or legal significance.

Government of Ireland Act

The British Parliament reacted to the establishment of Dáil Éireann and the continuing War of Independence by enacting the *Government of Ireland Act 1920* which partitioned the island into Southern and Northern Ireland with separate parliaments and all-Irish institutions. For reasons explained later this statute was never effective in 'Southern Ireland'.

The Anglo-Irish Treaty

The Articles of Agreement for a Treaty between Great Britain and Ireland was signed in London on 6 December 1921. Southern Ireland was to become the Irish Free State (Saorstát Éireann) and was to have dominion status within the British Empire.

Constitution of Saorstát Éireann

The *Constitution of the Irish Free State (Saorstát Éireann) Act 1922* was enacted by Dáil Éireann sitting as a constituent assembly on 25 October 1922. This Constitution was innovative in form and content; it was a written composite document establishing the organs of government and declaring fundamental freedoms. Most importantly, it was the yardstick against which all other law was to be tested, and if any inconsistency was found, the provisions of the Constitution were to prevail.

This Constitution declared that all authority comes from God to the people and, in turn, all powers of government come from the people. The power to make laws was vested in the Oireachtas which consisted of the King, the Senate and Dáil Éireann. The Crown was to be represented by a Governor General.

The executive authority, that is, the branch of government entrusted with carrying the laws into effect, was vested in the King who was aided and assisted by an Executive headed by a President. The Executive Council was responsible to Dáil Éireann.

Justice was to be administered in public courts by an independent judiciary. To the courts fell the additional task of deciding whether any law was repugnant to any provision of the Constitution. From the Supreme Court of Justice an appeal lay to the British Privy Council.

The Constitution contained a declaration of rights and social principles. Rights such as the inviolability of the person and dwelling, the right to trial by jury, and freedoms of expression, association and religion were guaranteed.

For obvious reasons this Constitution could not provide a totally new system of laws to come into effect with the new Constitution itself. It therefore provided that 'subject to this Constitution and to the extent to which they are not inconsistent therewith, the laws in force in the Irish Free State at the date of the coming into operation of this Constitution shall continue to be of full force and effect until the same, or any of them, shall have been repealed or amended by enactments of the Oireachtas.'

Dismantling Saorstát Éireann

The Constitution of the Irish Free State never met with the approval of all political groups and, inevitably, with the passage of time it was dismantled by ordinary laws. The Oath of Allegiance, the Senate and the office of Governor General were among the deletions. The abdication of King Edward VIII in 1936 provided an opportunity to remove the Crown almost completely from constitutional affairs.

Constitution of Ireland

Early in 1937 a new Constitution — Bunreacht na hÉireann — was published, debated and enacted by Dáil Éireann. On 1 July 1937 it was adopted in a plebiscite by the People as the fundamental legal document: 685,105 voted in favour; 526,945 voted against. It came into effect on 29 December 1937 and in the intervening years has been amended a number of times by the People by either the addition or deletion of articles. It has been applied by the courts in a large number of cases, many of fundamental importance to our law.

While the 1937 Constitution radically altered our constitutional philosophy and law it could not, and did not, introduce a totally new system of laws. Instead, the practical approach of continuing the laws which were in force in the Irish Free State immediately prior to the coming into operation of the new Constitution was adopted, though only to the extent that they were not inconsistent with any of the articles of the new Constitution.

Republic of Ireland Act

Ireland did not completely sever its relations with the British Crown until 1948. Until that year the executive function in relation to external affairs was performed by the British Crown on the advice of the Government. This power was repatriated with the passing of the *Republic of Ireland Act 1948*.

Membership of the European Union

In 1972 Ireland joined the then European Economic Community which had been established by the Treaty of Rome in 1950. An amendment of the Constitution was necessary so that laws enacted outside the State could have application within the State. Ireland has played a full and active role since joining. Legal, political, social, economic and cultural activities emanating from our membership of the European Union (see Chapter 7) have had a profound effect in shaping the modern Ireland.

Amendments to the Constitution

Since the Constitution was enacted by the People, amendments to it must be enacted by the same method. Every proposal to amend the Constitution must be initiated in Dáil Éireann and be passed, or deemed to have been passed, by both Houses of the Oireachtas (see page 27). Every proposal submitted to the People in a referendum is approved if a majority of the votes cast are in favour.

There have been various proposals to amend the Constitution. Some have been rejected and some have been approved. Indeed, in recent years amending the Constitution has been done almost annually. The most relevant changes are discussed in the appropriate place in the text.

The Supreme Court decided in *McKenna v Ireland* (1996) that once a Bill to amend the Constitution had been submitted to the People, the People were entitled to reach their decision in a free and democratic manner and the use by the Government of public money to fund a campaign designed to influence the voters was an interference with the democratic process and the process for the amendment of the Constitution. To further this principle of equality, the *Referendum Act 1998* established the Referendum Commission, the primary role of which is to explain the subject matter of the referendum to the population at large, as simply and effectively as possible, while ensuring that the arguments of those against the terms of the referendum and those in favour are put forward in a manner that is fair to all interests concerned.

Belfast Agreement

The latest amendment to the Constitution incorporated the agreement reached in the multi-party negotiations with regard to Northern Ireland, signed in Belfast on Good Friday, 10 April 1998. While a major part of that agreement is concerned with Northern Ireland, two matters agreed therein had constitutional implications for this part of the island. The first was the changes made to Articles 2 and 3 of the Constitution (see page 8), which abandoned the legal claim to the territorial area of the island of Ireland, and the second was changes to Article 29 of the Constitution, which allowed the State to be bound by the Belfast Agreement and to recognise institutions established thereunder which may exercise jurisdiction over the whole of the island.

Chapter 2

NATION AND STATE

Ethos of the Constitution

The ethical and moral values on which the Constitution is based, enacted and amended as it is by the People, will naturally reflect the broad values of Irish society. These values will, of course, change from time to time and will prompt changes in the Constitution. The Preamble acknowledges the Christian God and seeks to promote the common good with due observance of prudence, justice and charity. Kenny J. in *Ryan v Attorney General* (1965) spoke of the 'Christian and democratic nature of the State'.

Popular Sovereignty

The Constitution declares that all powers of government derive under God from the People, whose right it is to designate the rulers of the State and in final appeal to decide all questions of national policy. In constitutional theory the People are the sole organ of government possessed of unlimited powers. The People, the first and primary authority, created the State, the institutions of government and declared fundamental rights.

The Irish Nation

A nation is defined as a body of people recognised as an entity by virtue of their historical, linguistic, religious or ethnic links and without regard to political or geographical boundaries. The People, the primary law-makers and the ultimate source of authority, under God, are the Irish nation. The Irish nation claims an inalienable, indefeasible and sovereign right to choose its own form of government, to determine its relations with other nations and to develop its life, political, economic and cultural, in accordance with its own genius and traditions. It is the entitlement and birthright of every person born in the island of Ireland, which includes its islands and seas, to be part of the Irish nation. Furthermore, the Irish nation cherishes its special affinity with people of Irish ancestry living abroad and who share its cultural identity and heritage.

The National Territory

The Irish nation inherits, and rightfully possesses the territory of the island of Ireland, which includes its islands and seas. The Constitution recognises the political partition of Ireland and provides that, pending a united Ireland, the laws enacted by the Parliament established by the Constitution shall have the like area and extent of application as Saorstát Éireann (Irish Free State) (see page 5). The Constitution then states that it is the firm will of the Irish nation, in harmony and friendship, to unite all the people who share the territory of the island of Ireland, in all the diversity of their identities and traditions, recognising that a united Ireland shall be brought about only by peaceful means with the consent of a majority of the people, democratically expressed, in both jurisdictions in the island.

The State may exercise extra-territorial jurisdiction in accordance with the generally recognised principles of international law. The right to legislate with extra-territorial effect was exercised when the *Criminal Law (Jurisdiction) Act 1976* was enacted which permits the arrest and trial in this State of persons alleged to have committed certain offences in Northern Ireland and Britain. The Supreme Court, in *Article 26 and the Criminal Law (Jurisdiction) Bill 1975*, held that the Oireachtas could legislate in such a manner.

The State

A state is defined as a self-governing political community occupying its own territory. The People created the State called Ireland which is declared to be a sovereign, independent, democratic state. The Supreme Court decided, in *Byrne v Ireland* (1972), that the State is a juristic person which can be sued for the wrongful acts of its public servants. An attribute of sovereignty, according to the Supreme Court in *Webb v Ireland* (1988), was the State's entitlement to claim items of antiquity found without an owner in the State.

The name of the State is Éire, or in the English language, Ireland. The *Republic of Ireland Act 1948* states that the 'description of the State shall be the Republic of Ireland'. Speaking of this statute in *Ellis v O'Dea* (1990) Walsh J. in the Supreme Court said: 'It does not purport to change the name of the State nor could the Oireachtas do so even if it so wished. An amendment of the Constitution would be required for a change in name.'

The national flag is the tricolour of green, white and orange. The Irish language is the national and first official language, with English recognised as a second official language. Where there is conflict between the texts of the Constitution the text in the national language is to prevail.

Nationality and Citizenship

Nationality is a legal status based on allegiance. Fidelity to the nation and loyalty to the state are fundamental political duties of all citizens. Citizenship is the legal concept which binds the individual to a state. It determines the rights and obligations of a person within the domestic law. The Constitution declares that a person who is a citizen of Saorstát Éireann is a citizen of Ireland and no person is to be excluded from Irish citizenship by reason of sex. The future acquisition and loss of citizenship is to be determined by law. The *Irish Nationality and Citizenship Acts 1956 and 1986* provide that:

(i) Every person born in Ireland is a citizen from birth. Pending the reintegration of the national territory, a person cannot obtain citizenship by birth if born in Northern Ireland after 6 December 1922, the date on which the Constitution of Saorstát Éireann was ratified by the British Parliament, unless a declaration of citizenship is made.

(ii) Every person is a citizen where either parent was a citizen at the time of that person's birth.

(iii) Citizenship on marriage can be acquired should the non-citizen lodge, not earlier than three years from the date of the marriage, a declaration accepting citizenship as post-nuptial citizenship. The marriage must be subsisting at the date of the declaration, the couple must be living together as husband and wife, and the citizen spouse must submit an affidavit to that effect when the declaration is being lodged. The non-citizen lodging such a declaration becomes a citizen from the date of the lodgement.

(iv) The President may grant citizenship as a token of honour to a person, or his or her child or grandchild, who in the opinion of the Government has rendered signal honour or distinguished service to the nation. One such honorary citizen was the late Alfred Chester Beatty who bequeathed a library to the nation, and another is Dr Teide Herrema who was a kidnap victim. Others include Tip O'Neill, retired speaker of the American House of Representatives, and Jack Charlton, the former manager of the Irish soccer team.

(v) The Minister for Justice may confer citizenship by naturalisation. The applicant must be of full age; be of good character; have lived in Ireland for one year immediately prior to the application; intend in good faith to reside here after naturalisation; have given one year's notice, and have made a declaration of fidelity to the Nation and loyalty to the State.

The acquisition of another citizenship, whether by marriage or otherwise, does not automatically lead to the loss of Irish citizenship; a declaration of renunciation must be made.

Aliens

A person not a citizen is in law an alien. The *Aliens Act 1935* reserves to the Minister for Justice control over aliens. Their entry to the State may be prohibited or restricted; they may be deported; they may be required to reside in a particular place; and registration, travel and employment within the State may be regulated.

An aim of the Treaty of Rome is to secure freedom of movement for workers within the member states of the European Union. This freedom allows a worker to accept employment in the other member states. But a worker who avails of this freedom does not change nationality or citizenship. A French citizen who comes to work here remains an alien under our law, though the full rigours of the *Aliens Act* would not be used in those circumstances because of the obligations imposed by the laws of the European Union.

Domicile

Though not mentioned in the Constitution, domicile is an important legal concept. Domicile is the place in which a person has a fixed and permanent home and to which, whenever absent, he or she has the intention of returning. Domicile may be altered without any formality. Citizenship and domicile are separate and distinct concepts. An Irish citizen may have a French domicile and, conversely, a French citizen may have an Irish domicile. The relevance of domicile is considered on page 279.

THE SEPARATION OF POWERS

An Important Constitutional Principle

The doctrine of the separation of powers advocates the distribution of the powers of government among different institutions of the State. 'The Constitution of Ireland', according to Ó Dálaigh CJ. in *In re Haughey* (1971), 'is founded on the doctrine of the tripartite division of the powers of government — legislative, executive and judicial.'

The legislative power to make laws is reserved to the Oireachtas. The executive power entrusted with carrying the laws into effect is vested in the Government. The judicial power of applying the law to disputes is reserved to the courts.

The theory of the separation of powers does not favour the three functions of government being distributed between three independent institutions without some overlapping or co-ordination. Such an arrangement would prevent good government. By separating the organs of government, limited power is conferred on each; thus no organ is possessed of unlimited power. Abuse of power by one can be checked by the others and tyranny, hopefully, is prevented. This doctrine is more than a mere political theory; it is one which has considerable constitutional importance. The following sample of cases illustrates how jealous each organ of government is of its respective powers, and will repel any invasion from the other organs, and will refrain from trespassing into the domains of the other institutions of government.

Encroachment by Legislature in the Judicial Domain

In *Buckley v Attorney General* (1950) the Oireachtas passed a statute concerning a case then being litigated in the courts. The Supreme Court declared the legislation to be unconstitutional. The plaintiff, in bringing the action, was exercising a constitutional right and was entitled to have the matter determined by the judicial organ of the State. The effect of the statute was to have the dispute determined by the Oireachtas and that was an unwarrantable interference by the legislature in the judicial function.

Equally, the courts are mindful not to stray into the legislative domain. The Supreme Court, in *McGrath v McDermott* (1988), refused to condemn tax avoidance which was not prohibited by statute. 'To do so', as Finlay CJ. said, 'could only constitute the invasion by the judiciary of the powers and functions of the legislature, in plain breach of the constitutional separation of powers.'

Encroachment by Executive in the Judicial Domain

The case of *Murphy v Dublin Corporation* (1972) had to decide whether the Government could claim executive privilege and thus be excused from producing essential evidence in pending litigation. The Supreme Court ruled that since the courts were charged under the Constitution with the administration of justice, they alone could decide what evidence was to be produced.

The making of executive policy is strictly for the Government and cannot be reviewed by the courts. This principle was clearly applied, in *Boland v An Taoiseach* (1974), where the Supreme Court refused to intervene in a matter which was then at the policy-making stage. Once the matter has moved beyond that stage, and the Government acts in contravention of the Constitution, the courts may then interfere: *Crotty v An Taoiseach* (1987) (see page 37).

Encroachment by Executive in the Legislative Domain

The Supreme Court ruled, in *Article 26 and the School Attendance Bill 1942*, that it was for the legislature and not the executive to define the expression 'a certain minimum standard of education' contained in Article 42.3.2° of the Constitution (see page 292).

Encroachment by the Legislature in the Executive Domain

The Supreme Court, in *Attorney General v Tribunal of Inquiry into the Beef Industry* (1993), upholding the doctrine of the separation of powers, refused to permit a tribunal of inquiry established by the Houses of the Oireachtas to inquire into discussion at Government meetings, though, following an amendment of the Constitution, these discussions may be disclosed where the High Court rules that either the administration of justice, or the needs of an inquiry established under the authority of the Houses of the Oireachtas, so demands.

Chapter 3
THE OIREACHTAS

National Parliament

It was noted in the previous chapter that the powers of government in our Constitution are divided threefold: legislative, executive and judicial. The legislative power, concerned with making laws, though not exclusively so, is the province of the National Parliament (Oireachtas) consisting of the President and two Houses, Dáil Éireann and Seanad Éireann.

THE PRESIDENT

Office of President

The Constitution establishes the office of President of Ireland who is head of State and takes precedence over all other persons in the State, though subject to the law. The President must exercise all the powers and functions conferred on that office both by the Constitution and statute law.

Eligibility, Selection and Election to Office

Citizens over the age of thirty-five years are eligible for election and a candidate, except a retiring or former President who may self-nominate, must be nominated by not less than twenty members of the Oireachtas or not less than four county councils or borough corporations.

The President, who must be elected by direct vote of the People, holds office for a term of seven years and may be re-elected once. While retaining this office, the President cannot be a member of either House of the Oireachtas or hold any other position of emolument.

On entering into office the President subscribes publicly to 'maintain the Constitution of Ireland and uphold its laws'. The President has an official residence in Dublin and is paid a salary which cannot be reduced during office. The President might be intimidated by either the Government or the Houses of the Oireachtas in the exercise of constitutional and legal functions, should a reduction in salary be permitted. The President cannot leave the State without the consent of the Government.

Powers of the President

Dáil Éireann is summoned and dissolved by the President on the advice of the Taoiseach. The High Court, in *O'Malley v An Taoiseach* (1990), refused to place any impediment between the President and the Taoiseach in this important matter by declining to grant an injunction to restrain the Taoiseach from advising the President to dissolve Dáil Éireann. However, the President may refuse to dissolve Dáil Éireann on the advice of a Taoiseach who has ceased to retain the support of a majority in Dáil Éireann.

The President, on the nomination of Dáil Éireann, appoints the Taoiseach. On the nomination of the Taoiseach, with the approval of Dáil Éireann, the President appoints the other members of the Government. On the advice of the Taoiseach, the President accepts the resignation, or terminates the appointment, of a Government member. The President appoints the Attorney General on the nomination of the Taoiseach, appoints the Comptroller and Auditor General on the nomination of Dáil Éireann and appoints judges on the nomination of the Government.

The President may, after consultation with the Council of State, convene a meeting of either, or both, Houses of the Oireachtas and may communicate with them by message or address on any matter of national or public importance. All such messages or addresses must receive the prior approval of the Government.

The right of pardon and the power to commute or remit punishment imposed by a criminal court is vested in the President. The Constitution permits such power, except in capital cases, to be conferred by statute law on others. *The Criminal Justice Act 1951* confers like powers on the Government who may delegate these to the Minister for Justice.

The President is Supreme Commander of the Defence Forces and officers hold commissions from the President. The control of the Defence Forces rests with the Minister for Defence by virtue of the *Defence Act 1954*.

All Bills passed by the Houses of the Oireachtas require the signature of the President for their enactment into law. The President's role in the legislative process is discussed on page 29.

The Republic of Ireland Act 1948 provides that the President may, on the advice of the Government, exercise certain functions with regard to our external affairs. The sole function conferred is the accreditation of diplomatic representatives abroad.

Immunity from Action

The President is not answerable to either House of the Oireachtas, or to any court, for the exercise and performance of the powers and functions of that office. This is not an immunity from having to observe the ordinary law.

Removal from Office

A President may be impeached for stated misbehaviour in either House of the Oireachtas. Such a motion must be signed by at least thirty members of the House of the Oireachtas in which the motion is moved and must be adopted by not less than two-thirds of that House. The charge must be investigated, or be caused to be investigated, by the other House. The President has the right to appear and be legally represented at such a hearing. Where the charge is declared proved, and is of such a nature as to render the President unfit to continue in office, a resolution of not less than two-thirds of that House removes the President from office.

A President found to be permanently incapacitated to the satisfaction of at least five judges of the Supreme Court may be removed from office.

Presidential Commission

When the President is absent from the State, or incapacitated, or has died, resigned, been removed from office, or refuses to carry out the functions of office, a Presidential Commission exercises all such powers and functions. This Commission is composed of the Chief Justice, the Chairman of Dáil Éireann and the Chairman of Seanad Éireann.

The Council of State

The Constitution establishes a Council of State to aid and counsel the President. Prior to the performance of certain constitutional functions the President must consult the Council of State, which is an advisory body.

Membership is drawn from three groupings. The Taoiseach, the Tánaiste, the Chief Justice, the President of the High Court, the Chairman of Dáil Éireann, the Chairman of Seanad Éireann, and the Attorney General are *ex-officio* members. Every former President, Taoiseach and Chief Justice, able and willing to act, is also a member. The President may appoint not more than seven other persons to be members. These seven hold office while the President who appointed them holds office. They can resign at any time or have their appointments terminated by the President. Meetings are convened at such times and in such places as the President decides.

THE HOUSES OF THE OIREACHTAS

Duties of the Oireachtas

The Houses of the Oireachtas must sit in or near Dublin city unless otherwise decided. One session must be held annually. Sittings are in public but in cases of special emergency two-thirds of the members present may agree to a private sitting. Each House makes its own rules of procedure to ensure freedom of debate.

Nominations to constitutional offices, such as the Taoiseach, the other members of the Government and the Comptroller and Auditor General, must be approved by Dáil Éireann before appointment by the President.

The right to raise and maintain military forces is vested in the Oireachtas. The Houses of the Oireachtas must elect a Chairman and Deputy Chairman from among their members and prescribe their duties. All questions for decision in each House are determined by a majority of the members present and voting. In cases of equality the Chairman has a casting vote. But there are constitutional exceptions to the majority vote rule. One, discussed earlier, requires a two-thirds vote to remove a President from office.

The Government must prepare estimates of the financial affairs of the State for submission to Dáil Éireann (see page 36). International agreements to which the State is a party must be laid before Dáil Éireann (see page 37).

Privileges and Obligations of the Oireachtas

Official reports and publications of the Oireachtas, and all utterances made in either House, are privileged, which means that members cannot be prosecuted or sued for things said within the precincts of either House. This constitutional protection exists to encourage freedom of debate and an abuse of this privilege may be punished by either House itself. Members are free from arrest, except in certain criminal cases, while going to, within, and coming from, either House of the Oireachtas.

By virtue of the *Ethics in Public Office Act 1995*, members of the Houses of the Oireachtas must make public disclosures of certain personal and business interests and must, before speaking or voting on a measure, make certain declarations where he or she has actual knowledge of a material interest in the subject matter of the proceedings. The *Electoral Act 1997* imposes an obligation on members of the Houses of the Oireachtas to make an annual return of certain donations received.

POWERS OF THE HOUSES OF THE OIREACHTAS

Concurrent Powers of Both Houses of the Oireachtas

In some instances both Houses of the Oireachtas have concurrent powers. Each House may, by resolution, remove from office the President, the Comptroller and Auditor General, and any judge. The declaration of a state of emergency, and its termination, must be made by both Houses. Legislation must be passed, or be deemed to have been passed by both Houses. Ordinary legislation may be introduced in either House and the power to annul statutory instruments (see page 33), vests by statute in both Houses of the Oireachtas.

Powers of Dáil Éireann

Dáil Éireann, because it is elected by popular franchise, has greater powers than Seanad Éireann. Dáil Éireann nominates the Taoiseach and approves other members of the Government. The Taoiseach, the Tánaiste and the Minister for Finance must be members of Dáil Éireann. The Government is responsible to Dáil Éireann alone though each Minister has the right to attend and to be heard in both Houses of the Oireachtas. A Taoiseach must resign on ceasing to retain the support of a majority of Dáil Éireann.

The Government must, in each financial year, prepare estimates of the receipts and expenditure of the State for presentation to Dáil Éireann for consideration (see page 36).

The assent of Dáil Éireann is necessary before the State may either declare or participate in any war. Every international agreement to which the State becomes a party must be laid before Dáil Éireann and every such agreement which is a charge on public funds must be approved by Dáil Éireann (see page 37). Dáil Éireann has superior constitutional powers in the legislative process (see page 26).

DÁIL ÉIREANN

House of Representatives

Dáil Éireann is the House of Representatives in our national parliament and is composed of members elected by popular franchise. The number of members is decided by statute law and depends on the size of the population. A revision of the number of members must be made at least every twelve years with due regard to changes in the population distribution. The High Court held, in *O'Malley v An Taoiseach* (1990), that this obligation is not discharged by revising the constituencies once in every twelve years; there is a constitutional obligation to revise the constituencies when a census discloses major changes in the distribution of population. The population is ascertained by the last completed census: *Article 26 and the Electoral (Amendment) Bill 1961*. The total number must be fixed at no less than one member for each 20,000 of the population and no more than one member for each 30,000 of the population. At present, there are 166 members of Dáil Éireann (*Electoral (Amendment) Act 1995*).

Uniformity of Representation

The Constitution provides that as far as is practicable there must be uniformity of representation. It should take the same number of votes to elect each Dáil Éireann member; a system of weighted voting is prohibited as undemocratic.

The *Electoral (Amendment) Act 1959* provided substantial disparities between different parts of the country by giving to fewer people in western areas more deputies and giving fewer deputies to more people in eastern urban areas. This was done because it was more difficult to represent large sparsely populated areas than it was to represent densely populated urban areas. This statute was challenged in *O'Donovan v Attorney General* (1961) on the ground that the ratio of members to the population was not, as far as was practicable, the same throughout the country. In declaring this statute invalid the High Court held it caused grave inequalities of parliamentary representation.

Constituencies

The country is divided into constituencies and each must elect at least three members of Dáil Éireann. This revision of constituencies is carried out by the independent Constituency Commission, established under the *Electoral Act 1997*, and composed of a judge of the Supreme or High Court, the Ombudsman, the Secretary of the Department of the Environment, the Clerk of Dáil Éireann and the Clerk of Seanad Éireann. The Commission reports to the Ceann Comhairle of Dáil Éireann. It is then a matter for the Oireacthas whether to accept the recommendations and enact them into law.

Eligibility for Election

Citizens who have reached the age of twenty-one years are eligible for election to Dáil Éireann, unless disqualified by the Constitution or by statute law. The Constitution prohibits the President, the Comptroller and Auditor General, a member of Seanad Éireann and judges from Dáil Éireann membership. This complies with the doctrine of the separation of powers.

The *Electoral Act 1992* disqualifies certain persons from election to either House of the Oireachtas. These include: persons who are not citizens of Ireland; persons who have not reached the age of twenty-one years; a member of the Commission, or a judge; an advocate general, or a registrar of the Court of Justice, or a member of the Court of Auditors of the European Community; members of the Defence Forces and Garda Síochána on full pay; civil servants; persons of unsound mind; persons sentenced to at least six months' imprisonment within the State; and undischarged bankrupts. Other statutes disqualify members of the boards of certain bodies which are appointed by the executive.

Right to Vote

Citizens who have reached the age of eighteen years and are entered on the electoral register have the right to vote in Dáil Éireann elections. The extension of this franchise to non-citizens was approved in a referendum in 1984, and the *Electoral (Amendment) Act 1985* conferred the Dáil Éireann franchise on British citizens resident in the State. Similar voting rights may be extended to citizens of member states of the European Union provided reciprocal voting rights are extended to Irish citizens. Local authorities must compile a register of electors annually. A voter may exercise only one vote at a Dáil Éireann election.

Secret Ballot

The Constitution declares that voting must be by secret ballot. What constitutes a secret ballot was discussed in *McMahon v Attorney General* (1972) where the Supreme Court held that any procedure which violated the right to electoral secrecy — in that case the practice of writing the voter's number on the ballot paper counterfoil — infringed this constitutional guarantee.

Register of Political Parties

To contest a Dáil Éireann election it is not essential to belong to a political party. A candidate who is a member of a registered political party may add the name of that party to the ballot paper: *Electoral Act 1963*. This statute established a formal register of political parties. Parties then represented in Dáil Éireann were automatically registered. Other political parties will be registered if they are genuine and are organised to contest Dáil Éireann or local elections: *Loftus v Attorney General* (1979).

Proportional Representation

Members of Dáil Éireann are elected on the system of proportional representation by means of the single transferable vote. This method allows the voter to give some measure of support to all the candidates by marking the ballot paper in the order of preference for the candidates.

Election Process

When the President dissolves Dáil Éireann the proclamation states the date the new Dáil Éireann must meet. A general election must be held within thirty days of the dissolution. The incoming Dáil Éireann must meet within thirty days of the polling date which is fixed by the Minister for the Environment.

Once Dáil Éireann is dissolved the Clerk of Dáil Éireann, a civil servant, issues writs to the returning officer in each constituency directing the holding of an election for the full number of members to serve for that constituency.

The Constitution permits statute law to allow the Chairman of Dáil Éireann, the Ceann Comhairle, to be automatically re-elected without having to take part in the election. Returning officers are responsible for organising the election. When the counting of votes is completed the returning officer endorses the names of those elected for that constituency on the writ and returns it to the Clerk of Dáil Éireann. The newly elected members are notified to attend Dáil Éireann which assembles on the date declared by the President.

Term of Office

A candidate on election becomes a member of Dáil Éireann. On signing the roll the member takes a seat and remains a member until the next dissolution or unless the member dies, resigns or is disqualified. The Constitution states that the same Dáil Éireann cannot continue for more than seven years or such shorter period which may be provided by law. The *Electoral Act 1963* sets a maximum period of five years.

SEANAD ÉIREANN

Senate

The second House of the Oireachtas is a Senate, Seanad Éireann. It consists of a static sixty members. Membership can be acquired in three ways.

Eleven citizens may, with their prior consent, be appointed by the Taoiseach who is appointed on the reassembly of Dáil Éireann after a general election.

A further six members are elected by university graduates who have reached the age of eighteen years and are Irish citizens, though candidates need not be graduates. At present Dublin University and the National University of Ireland have three seats each. In 1979 the Constitution was amended to allow redistribution by law of these six seats among the existing universities and other institutes of higher education. No law has been enacted in this regard despite the establishment of two new universities and other institutions of higher education.

The remaining forty-three seats are elected from five panels of candidates linked, at least nominally, to certain interests or services. Five are elected from the cultural and educational panel; eleven from the agricultural panel; eleven from the labour panel; nine from the industrial and commercial panel; and seven from the administrative panel.

To be nominated for election to the panels, a person must be twenty-one years of age, a citizen, and be proposed by either four members of the

Oireachtas or a registered nominating body. These nominating bodies are connected with the interests and services of the panel to which they nominate candidates. A general election for Seanad Éireann panels must be held within ninety days of the dissolution of Dáil Éireann.

Unlike the Dáil Éireann electorate, which consists of the adult citizenry and others permitted by law to vote, the electorate for the Seanad Éireann panels is very restricted. Only members of the new Dáil Éireann, the outgoing Seanad Éireann and the elected members of county councils and borough corporations are entitled to vote in this election, which is by secret postal ballot, on the system of proportional representation by means of the single transferable vote.

Term of Office

The first meeting of the new Seanad Éireann takes place on a date fixed by the President on the advice of the Taoiseach. A member holds office until the day before the polling day for the panels for the next Seanad Éireann. Seanad Éireann is not dissolved when the President dissolves Dáil Éireann.

THE OIREACHTAS AND INTERNATIONAL CONFLICT

Time of War

The Constitution provides that the assent of Dáil Éireann is necessary before the State either declares or participates in any war. However, the Government may, in case of actual invasion, take the necessary steps for the preservation of the State. Should Dáil Éireann not be sitting, it must be summoned to meet at the earliest practicable date.

State of National Emergency

Time of war includes a time when there is taking place an armed conflict in which the State is not a participant but in respect of which each of the Houses of the Oireachtas shall have resolved that arising out of such armed conflict a national emergency exists affecting the vital interests of the State.

On 2 September 1939 the Houses of the Oireachtas resolved that arising out of the conflict in Europe a state of national emergency existed. Despite pacification in Europe after 1945, this national emergency was not revoked until 1 September 1976. On that date the Houses of the Oireachtas resolved that 'arising out of the armed conflict now taking place in Northern Ireland a national emergency exists affecting the vital interests of the State'. These resolutions were revoked in 1994.

No article of the Constitution can be invoked to invalidate any law which is enacted for the express purpose of securing the public safety and the preservation of the State in time of war, armed rebellion or national emergency. As a consequence, a statute enacted under this constitutional provision is withdrawn from judicial review and constitutional rights may be restricted or suspended as long as that statute remains in force.

The necessity for such drastic powers was explained in *The State (Walsh) v Lennon* (1942) by Gavan Duffy J. when he said: 'In time of war or armed rebellion the apprehension of judicial intervention may at some delicate moment hamper the legislature or the executive authority when Government needs all possible strength and freedom to steer the ship of State through the crisis, consequently the Constitution has placed in the hands of the Oireachtas, as law-giver, special authority to suspend judicial control over the other organs of government during any such emergency.'

THE OIREACHTAS AND LEGISLATION

Meaning of Legislation

Legislation is the laying down of legal rules by a competent authority. Such rules are laid down for the future and without reference to any actual dispute. Legislation is found in enacted law and is the product of a body constituted for the purpose of making laws. That body, under the Constitution, is the Oireachtas. Enacted laws are also called statutes.

Superior Legislation

Legislation may be superior or subordinate. Superior legislation is law enacted by the legislature. These are known as Acts of the Oireachtas. A proposal submitted for the purpose of being passed into law is known as a Bill and, depending on its length and complexity, may be divided into parts, sections and subsections, and have a number of schedules.

The purpose of a Bill may vary. It may introduce topics into the law which have not been previously legislated. For example, the *Hire-Purchase Act 1946* was the first occasion that a law was enacted which regulated this commercial practice (see page 361). A Bill may amend existing laws. The *Hire-Purchase (Amendment) Act 1960* altered the previous statute. A Bill may propose, inter alia, to repeal existing statutes. The *Companies Act 1963* repealed a number of statutes then in force. A Bill may consolidate the law on a particular subject by incorporating a number of statutes into one. For example, the *Social Welfare (Consolidation) Act 1980* collected a diverse number of existing statutes into one. Lastly, a Bill may codify the law by attempting to incorporate both statutory and common law rules into a single statute. This is not a common legislative practice: the *Sale of Goods Act 1893* is such an example.

Legislation as a Source of Law

Subject to the Constitution and the laws of the European Union, legislation is our most important source of law. For historical reasons we have had different superior legislators over the past centuries. Enacted legislation continues to form part of our law until repealed or found to be inconsistent with the Constitution. First, there are the statutes of the old Irish Parliament prior to 1800, though these are few in number; second, there are the statutes of the English Parliament from 1719 to 1782; third, there are the statutes of the United Kingdom Parliament from 1800 to 1922; fourth, there are the statutes of the Oireachtas of Saorstát Éireann; and last, there are the enactments of the Oireachtas established under the 1937 Constitution.

The Constitution and Legislation

While law-making is the central role of the Oireachtas the Constitution restricts the enactment of certain laws. For example, the prohibition on enacting any law which is repugnant to the Constitution is the major limitation placed on the legislative role of the Oireachtas. Apart from such constitutional restrictions the Oireachtas has complete discretion in the law-making field.

Judicial Review of Legislation on Constitutional Grounds

The Constitution grants to the High Court and, on appeal, the Supreme Court, the power to declare statutes unconstitutional. When deciding whether a statute offends the Constitution the courts adopt the approach that a law passed by the Oireachtas, the elected representatives of the people, is presumed to be constitutional unless and until the contrary is clearly established. This presumption of constitutionality does not extend to statutes enacted before the Constitution was adopted. Where the statute can be given both a constitutional and an unconstitutional construction the courts favour a constitutional interpretation. The Constitution must be read as a whole. Applying such a global approach, all its provisions are to be given due weight and effect. The true purpose and range of the Constitution would not be achieved if it were treated as no more than the sum of its parts.

Once the courts adjudicate that parts of a statute are unconstitutional, that part of the law is null and void. A subsequent statute cannot negative a decision in this regard. Only the People in a referendum can negative such a decision by amending the Constitution. The Supreme Court, in *Article 26 and the Electoral (Amendment) Bill 1983*, held that a proposal to confer voting rights on non-citizens was unconstitutional. Such a proposal was carried when put later to the People in a referendum.

It was decided by the Supreme Court in *Cahill v Sutton (1980)* that a challenge to a statute was confined to a person whose interest had been adversely affected, or stood in real or imminent danger of being adversely affected, by the operation of that statute.

The Courts and Legislation

The judges over the years have formulated certain guidelines to assist themselves in interpreting statutes. These canons of construction are mere guidelines rather than rigid rules of law.

The literal rule expounds the traditional view that the judges accept the letter of the statute as the exclusive and conclusive evidence of the mind of the legislators by giving the words of the statute their usual and ordinary meaning. In *Inspector of Taxes v Kiernan* (1982) the question arose for taxation purposes whether a person who kept pigs was 'a dealer in cattle'. Since the expression was first used in an 1842 statute, it was argued that it should be given its meaning from that era, which would have included pigs. The Supreme Court held that cattle meant the bovine kind and could not include pigs. 'When', explained Henchy J., 'the word which requires to be given its natural and ordinary meaning is a simple word which has a widespread and unambiguous currency, the judge construing it should draw primarily on his own experience of its use. Dictionaries or other literary sources should be looked at only when alternative meanings, regional usages or other obliquities are shown to cast doubt on the singularity of its ordinary meaning, or where there are grounds for suggesting that the meaning of the word has changed since the statute in question was passed.' Technical words are given technical meanings. The High Court, in *Burke v Aer Lingus plc* (1997), held that the words 'embarking' and 'disembarking' related to a particular activity, namely air travel, had a quasi-technical significance, and therefore could not be strictly interpreted in accordance with their ordinary meaning and popular usage, as suggested in *Inspector of Taxes v Kiernan*.

The golden rule is resorted to where the literal interpretation of the statute would lead to such an absurdity as to make it self-evident that the legislature could not have meant what it appeared to say. The judges then read into the statute saving clauses so as to preserve the previous principles of law.

A different approach is taken with the mischief rule. This requires the judge to look at the law which existed before the statute was passed to examine the mischief, or defect, which the statute was intended to remedy, or cure. The statute should then be construed in such a way as to suppress the mischief and advance the remedy. The *Family Home Protection Act 1976* provides that one spouse cannot, without the prior consent in writing of the other spouse, convey the family home to another. In *Nestor v Murphy* (1979) both spouses agreed in writing to sell off the family home and later tried to avoid the transaction on the ground that the consent of the non-owning spouse had not been obtained in writing in advance. The Supreme Court held that such an interpretation of the statute would have negatived its effect. The mischief which the statute sought to remedy was the disposition of the family home without the knowledge or consent of the other spouse.

The judges use the *ejusdem generis* rule (of the same kind or nature) to restrict the meaning of subsequent general words to things or matters of the same kind, or genus, as the preceding particular words. In *Dillon v Minister for Posts and Telegraphs* (1981) election material was not accepted for free posting because it contained the suggestion that politicians were dishonest. The regulations prohibited the posting of indecent, obscene or grossly offensive character. 'That assemblage of words', explained Henchy J. in the Supreme Court, 'gives limited and special meaning to the expression grossly offensive character ... applying the maxim *noscitur a sociis*, which means that a word or expression is known from its companions, the expression ... must be held to be infected in this context with something akin to the taint of indecency or obscenity.'

Special statutes are not affected by subsequent general statutes unless the earlier statute is inconsistent with the latter one, or unless there is some express reference to the earlier statute. This rule is contained in the maxim *generalia specialibus non derogant:* the general does not derogate from the special. Thus, the Supreme Court, in *Hutch v Governor of Wheatfield Prison* (1992), held that a general statute, which provided that a person convicted summarily of an indictable offence could suffer a sentence of twelve months, had not indirectly or impliedly altered, repealed, amended or derogated from an earlier special statute, which provided that a young person convicted of an indictable offence tried summarily could only suffer a sentence of three months.

There is a presumption, in the absence of a clear and unequivocal intention of the Oireachtas to the contrary, that a statute applies prospectively and not retrospectively. The High Court, in *Dublin Heating Co. Ltd v Hefferon* (1992), decided that liability for reckless trading created by the *Companies (Amendment) Act 1990* could not be applied to events which occurred before the statute was enacted.

THE LEGISLATIVE PROCESS

Central Role of the Oireachtas

The making of law is the major function of the Oireachtas which may include amending or repealing existing laws. Each of the constituents of the Oireachtas, the President, Dáil Éireann and Seanad Éireann, play an active role in this process. However, the Constitution grants to Dáil Éireann greater prerogatives in the law-making process. While Seanad Éireann may reject or delay proposed Bills, it cannot completely obstruct Dáil Éireann. Similar comments apply to the President's role in this process.

Applying procedural criteria, proposed measures can be divided into four categories: ordinary Bills, Bills to amend the Constitution, taxation Bills and abridged-time Bills.

Ordinary Bills

An ordinary Bill passed by Dáil Éireann is sent to Seanad Éireann. Seanad Éireann has ninety days, or any longer period agreed to by both Houses of the Oireachtas, known as the stated period, to consider ordinary legislation. Should the Bill pass without amendment within the stated period, it proceeds to the President on the next stage of the process. Should the Bill be amended it returns to Dáil Éireann for its further consideration. Where Seanad Éireann rejects the Bill completely or returns it to Dáil Éireann with amendments which are unacceptable to that House, the Bill lapses. Such a Bill will not lapse where Dáil Éireann passes a resolution, within 180 days after the stated period, declaring that the Bill is deemed to have passed both Houses of the Oireachtas. Seanad Éireann can only delay legislation and cannot prevent its enactment, if that is the will of Dáil Éireann.

Where Seanad Éireann rejects a Bill which is later deemed to have passed both Houses of the Oireachtas by a resolution of Dáil Éireann, Seanad Éireann may exercise a constitutional option. A majority of Seanad Éireann, together with at least one-third of Dáil Éireann, may petition the President not to sign such a Bill on the ground that it contains proposals of such national importance that the views of the People ought to be ascertained. Should the President, after consulting with the Council of State, accept the petition, the Bill must either be approved by the People in a referendum or by a resolution of a new Dáil Éireann within eighteen months. This procedure has never been resorted to.

Seanad Éireann may initiate an ordinary Bill, though in such cases the stated period does not apply. When passed it goes to Dáil Éireann and, if amended, it is treated as a Bill which has been initiated in Dáil Éireann and the procedure, already explained, is followed.

Bills to Amend the Constitution

A proposal to amend the Constitution must be initiated in Dáil Éireann. A Bill containing such a proposal must not contain any other proposal. Its progress through the Houses of the Oireachtas is identical to that for an ordinary Bill, except that such a Bill, instead of proceeding to the President, must be submitted to the People in a referendum for decision. The Supreme Court decided, in *Finn v Attorney General* (1983), that the courts have no jurisdiction to review the constitutionality of a Bill, whatever its nature. An attempt to injunct such a Bill from being put before the People, when it had already passed both Houses of the Oireachtas, failed. The Supreme Court decided, in *McKenna v An Taoiseach* (1996), that the use by the Government of public funds in a campaign designed to influence the voters was unconstitutional. A Referendum Commission has been established by the *Referendum Act 1998* (see page 7).

A proposal for the amendment of the Constitution which is submitted to the People is held to have been approved where a majority of the votes cast at such referendum are cast in favour of its enactment. The President, on being satisfied that the provisions of the Constitution in this regard have been complied with, signs and promulgates the Bill as a law.

Taxation Bills

A Money Bill contains taxation provisions, or the imposition of charges for the payment of public debt, or the appropriation of public money, or the raising or guaranteeing of public loans. The Ceann Comhairle of Dáil Éireann certifies a Bill to be a Money Bill. A Money Bill must be initiated in Dáil Éireann and, once passed, it goes to Seanad Éireann for consideration only. Seanad Éireann may, within twenty-one days, make recommendations to Dáil Éireann regarding its contents, which may be accepted or rejected. Seanad Éireann cannot reject or amend such Bills.

The sole response of Seanad Éireann to a Money Bill is to challenge the certificate of the Ceann Comhairle. A resolution, passed at a sitting of Seanad Éireann attended by at least thirty members, requests the President to refer this question to a Committee of Privileges which is composed of an equal number of members from each House of the Oireachtas and chaired by a Supreme Court judge. Should the President, after consultation with the Council of State, accede to the request, the President appoints the Committee's membership. If the Committee is equally divided the chairman exercises a casting vote and the decision is final. This certificate of the Ceann Comhairle has never been challenged.

Should the President refuse Seanad Éireann's request, or should the Committee of Privileges fail to report within twenty-one days after the date on which the Bill was first sent to Seanad Éireann, the certificate of the Ceann Comhairle stands.

Abridged-time Bills

The period of time in which Seanad Éireann has to consider proposed legislation coming from Dáil Éireann may be abridged by Dáil Éireann, at the request of the Taoiseach, with the concurrence of the President, after consultation with the Council of State. The Bill must, in the opinion of the Government, be urgently and immediately necessary for the preservation of public peace and security, or by reason of a domestic or international emergency. A Bill to amend the Constitution is excluded. But such a Bill, when enacted as law, remains in force for only ninety days unless both Houses of the Oireachtas by resolutions extend this period.

This method of legislating has never been used and this process must not be confused with legislation enacted under a time of war or state of emergency (see page 22). All these statutes to date have been enacted as ordinary Bills. Of course, in the future, laws under the emergency may be enacted as abridged-time Bills.

Legislation and the President

The Taoiseach presents to the President for signature and promulgation into law all Bills passed, or deemed to have been passed, by both Houses of the Oireachtas. As a general rule the President does not sign a Bill earlier than the fifth day and later than the seventh day after a Bill has been presented. At the request of the Government, with the concurrence of Seanad Éireann, the President may sign a Bill earlier than the fifth day. Every abridged-time Bill must be signed on the day of presentation.

A Bill to amend the Constitution, after it has passed or, deemed to have passed both Houses of the Oireachtas, is referred to the People in a referendum. If passed by a majority of the voters it is signed forthwith by the President. Such a Bill lapses if rejected by a majority of the voters.

A Bill becomes law from the day it is signed by the President unless a contrary intention appears from the Bill. This date is printed in the statute after the introduction. Some statutes enacted and signed into law may not become operational until some future date. For example, the *Criminal Justice Act 1993*, signed by the President on 3 April 1993, came into operation one month after the date of its passing. The *Extradition (European Convention on the Suppression of Terrorism) Act 1987*, signed by the President on 21 January 1987, was not to come into operation until 1 December 1987.

A common method of bringing enacted legislation into operation is by the exercise of some executive act. For example, the *Criminal Justice Act 1984* was signed on 6 December 1984 with some sections brought into operation from 1 March 1985 by a statutory instrument signed by the Minister for Justice.

Referral of Bills to the Supreme Court

Under Article 26 of the Constitution the President, after consultation with the Council of State, may refer an ordinary Bill to the Supreme Court for a decision as to whether all or any of its provisions are repugnant to the

Constitution. This discretionary power must be exercised within seven days, and the Bill is not signed, pending the court's decision. The Supreme Court, consisting of at least five judges, must consider the Bill or the sections referred to it. Argument, on behalf of the Attorney General, who generally supports the Bill, and by counsel assigned by the court who generally argues against the Bill, are heard. The decision of the majority of the judges is the decision of the court and no assenting or dissenting opinion may be disclosed. The decision must be given within sixty days in open court.

Where the Supreme Court decides the Bill, or any part of it, is repugnant to the Constitution, the President must decline to sign it, and the Bill lapses. Should the Supreme Court find no constitutional objection the President must sign it as soon as possible after the court's decision is pronounced.

The President cannot refer a Money Bill or a Bill to amend the Constitution, or an abridged-time Bill, to the Supreme Court under Article 26 for a decision as to its constitutionality.

A consequence of the Supreme Court ruling that a Bill referred by the President is constitutional, is that its constitutional validity can never again be questioned. A badge of constitutionality attaches for all time.

Exercise of Discretion to Refer Bills

This power to refer Bills to the Supreme Court has been exercised by Presidents on twelve occasions:

1. *Article 26 and Offences Against the State (Amendment) Bill 1940*: The Supreme Court advised the President that internment without trial was constitutional. The High Court, in *The State (Burke) v Lennon* (1940), had held internment to be unconstitutional. This statute remains part of our law and cannot be challenged as to its constitutionality again (see *In re Ó Láighléis*, page 38).
2. *Article 26 and the School Attendance Bill 1942*: The Supreme Court found the Bill unconstitutional because the State might require a higher standard of elementary education from parents educating their children in ways other than by attending state schools (see page 292).
3. *Article 26 and the Electoral (Amendment) Bill 1961*: The Supreme Court advised the President that the revision of the constituencies, having regard to the ratio of members of Dáil Éireann to the population, was evenly distributed throughout the country. The High Court, in *O'Donovan v Attorney General* (1961) (see page 19), had decided that an earlier statute in this regard was unconstitutional. This statute has since been repealed.
4. *Article 26 and Criminal Law (Jurisdiction) Bill 1975*: The Supreme Court advised the President that the arrest and trial of suspects within the State for certain offences committed in Northern Ireland and elsewhere was constitutional. This statute continues in force.

5. *Article 26 and Emergency Powers Bill 1976*: The Supreme Court advised that the President had power to refer a Bill enacted pursuant to a state of emergency under Article 28 of the Constitution, though once it was established that the procedural requirements had been fulfilled the Constitution could not be invoked to invalidate such a Bill (see page 22).
6. *Article 26 and Housing (Private Rented Dwellings Bill) 1981*: The Supreme Court advised the President that the Bill which deprived landlords of substantial portions of their proper rents was an unjust attack on property rights and unconstitutional. The Bill was enacted as a consequence of the decision in *Blake v Attorney General* (1981) where rent restriction legislation was declared unconstitutional.
7. *Article 26 and the Electoral (Amendment) Bill 1983*: The Supreme Court advised the President that an attempt to confer voting rights in Dáil Éireann elections on non-citizens was unconstitutional. A referendum was held in 1984 which amended the Constitution in this regard, and the *Electoral (Amendment) Act 1985* extended Dáil Éireann franchise to British citizens resident in this country (see page 20).
8. *Article 26 and Adoption Bill (No. 2) Bill 1987*: The President was advised by the Supreme Court that the adoption of legitimate children in certain circumstances was constitutional.
9. *Article 26 and the Matrimonial Home Bill 1993*: The Supreme Court advised the President that the automatic ownership as joint tenants of the matrimonial home by spouses enforced on all married couples by the Bill was a breach of the constitutionally protected rights of the family.
10. *Article 26 and the Regulation of Information (Services Outside the State for the Termination of Pregnancies) Bill 1995*: The Supreme Court advised the President that the Bill, which applied to information required by a woman for the purpose of availing herself of services provided outside the State for the termination of pregnancy, was not repugnant to the Constitution.
11. *Article 26 and the Employment Equality Bill 1996*: The Supreme Court advised the President that the Bill which was to provide for greater equality in the workplace was repugnant to the Constitution because, inter alia, while making laudable provision for access to employment by disabled citizens, to transfer the cost of solving one of society's problem to employers was an undue hardship, and that to render an employer, who neither knows nor approves of an employee's misbehaviour, vicariously liable to severe criminal sanctions was unjust, irrational and inappropriate.
12. *Article 26 and the Equal Status Bill 1996*: The Supreme Court advised the President that the Bill, which contained similar provisions as those in the Employment Equality Bill, was repugnant to the Constitution for broadly the same reasons.

SUBORDINATE LEGISLATION

Definition and Source

The Constitution declares that the power of making laws for the State is vested solely in the Oireachtas. Subordinate legislation, or delegated legislation, is law laid down by a body or a person to whom the superior legislature has delegated by statute the power to make such laws. While subordinate legislation is enacted in a different manner to superior legislation, it is essential to note that both possess the same quality as law.

Subordinate legislation is a relatively recent source of law and has become necessary because of the complex structure of present-day government and society. It is impractical to have every law, many of a trivial or parochial nature, enacted by the usual parliamentary procedures. To facilitate good government the Oireachtas has devolved limited legislative powers to various bodies and persons.

Unconstitutional Delegation of Legislative Powers

The Supreme Court explained, in *Cityview Press Ltd v An Comhairle Oiliúna* (1980), the constitutional limitations on the delegation of legislative powers. O'Higgins CJ. said: 'The test is whether that which is challenged as an unauthorised delegation of parliamentary power is more than a mere giving effect to principles and policies which are contained in the statute itself. If it be, then it is not authorised: for such would constitute a purported exercise of legislative power by an authority which is not permitted to do so under the Constitution. On the other hand, if it be within the permitted limits — if the law is laid down in the statute and details only are filled in or completed by the ... subordinate body — there is no unauthorised delegation of legislative power.' Applying that test, in *O'Neill v Minister for Agriculture* (1997), the Supreme Court ruled that it was inconceivable that the legislature would have contemplated or authorised the creation of a licensing scheme by the executive which so manifestly prevented citizens from working in an industry for which they were qualified and prevented potential customers from availing of such services.

Categories of Subordinate Legislation

1. The first category, executive subordinate legislation, permits the Government as a collective authority to perform a legislative function. For example, the Government by order activates Part V of the *Offences Against the State Act 1939* which establishes the Special Criminal Court and, again by order, brings its operation to an end. *The Misuse of Drugs Act 1977*, as amended, proscribes the possession of approximately 250 drugs. The Government may by order make additions to this number.

2. The second category, statutory orders, instruments or regulations, are made by Ministers empowered under numerous statutes. For example, under the *Road Traffic Act 1961* the Minister for the Environment can make statutory instruments covering a wide variety of road traffic matters. Statutory instruments are collected together annually and each is given a distinctive number for reference. Thus S.I. No. 275 of 1994 is the *European Communities (Single-Members Private Limited Companies) Regulations 1994* (see page 405).
3. The third category, municipal subordinate legislation, are commonly contained in bye-laws. A bye-law is an ordinance affecting the public, or some portion of the public, imposed by some authority clothed with statutory powers, ordering something to be done or not to be done and accompanied by some sanction or penalty for its non-observance. According to Walsh J. in *The State (Harrington) v Wallace* (1988): 'A bye-law within its own sphere is something which carries an authority akin to a statute.' Local authorities, in particular, are endowed by various statutes with the limited power of enacting bye-laws which are restricted in application to the area for which the local authority has responsibility. This power to make bye-laws is conferred on others. The Commissioners of Public Works may make bye-laws for the care, management, maintenance, control and regulation of the use of canals: *Canals Act 1986*. The Commissioner of the Garda Síochána is empowered to make bye-laws in relation to minor traffic control: *Road Traffic Act 1961*.
4. The fourth category of subordinate legislation, known as autonomous subordinate legislation, entrusts limited legislative powers into private hands by statute. For example, wide control is given to registered companies under the *Companies Act 1963*, as amended. The Incorporated Law Society, the professional body for solicitors, is given power by the *Solicitors Act 1954*, as amended, to make regulations governing the conduct of its members. The Medical Council, under the *Medical Practitioners Act 1978*, as amended, has similar powers over members of the medical profession. Control of Subordinate Legislation by the Oireachtas in the relevant statute delegating the legislative power may, but not must, provide some method of control over the making of subordinate legislation. In general, statutory instruments must be placed before the Houses of the Oireachtas and become effective if not annulled by a resolution of either House. For example, Dáil Éireann may at any time annul the order of the Government which caused internment without trial to be brought into force under the *Offences Against the State (Amendment) Act 1940*. Bye-laws when drafted must be submitted to the Minister for the Environment.

Judicial Control of Subordinate Legislation

The courts will not compel the appropriate body to make subordinate legislation. The *Civil Liability Act 1961*, section 60, provides that a road authority shall be liable for damage caused as a result of their failure to maintain adequately a public road. The section was to come into operation on such day as may be fixed by government order. No order was made and an injured party sought, in *The State (Sheehan) v Government of Ireland* (1987), to compel the making of such an order. This was refused by the Supreme Court because the Oireachtas, by the manner in which it had couched the language of the section, in particular by its choice of the word 'may', and by vesting the discretion in the Government and not a Minister, showed that the discretion to bring the section into operation was not limited in any way as to time or otherwise.

The courts have always cast a wary eye on delegated legislation. In *Burke v Minister for Labour* (1979) a body charged with fixing the minimum wages of hotel industry employees refused to consider proposals made by the employees in the hotel industry. The orders made were not required to be laid before the Houses of the Oireachtas. The Supreme Court held the orders invalid because the Committee had failed to satisfy the requirements of basic fairness.The general principle is that a power must be exercised by the authority in which it has been vested by the legislature. The High Court, in *Lyons v Kilkenny Corporation* (1987), ruled that where a power to make bye-laws is conferred by statute on a local authority, that power cannot be delegated to an officer of a local authority. The courts will declare subordinate legislation to be invalid where it is unreasonable, which means arbitrary, unjust or impartial. The courts do so on the ground that the Oireachtas intends the delegated power to be exercised reasonably. The Supreme Court, in *Cassidy v Minister for Industry and Commerce* (1978), declared a maximum prices order, which controlled the price of intoxicating liquor in the urban district of Dundalk, invalid as unreasonable. It was oppressive and unfair to apply the same maximum prices in both public bars and lounge bars.

The third ground on which subordinate legislation may be attacked is that it is *ultra vires*, that is, beyond the powers of the person or body exercising the power. Subordinate legislation must be within the powers of those exercising it. This was decided in *Cooke v Walsh* (1984). The *Health Act 1970* obliged health boards to provide certain medical services, including hospitalisation, free for persons with limited means. The Act permitted the making available of any such service only to a particular class of eligible persons. The Minister for Health, by statutory instrument, excluded eligible persons who received treatment for injuries received in road accidents to which they were entitled to compensation. The Supreme Court declared the statutory instrument *ultra vires* on the ground that the exclusion of such persons was not authorised or contemplated by the Act, and was an attempt by the Minister to amend the statute by delegated legislation instead of by appropriate superior legislation.

Chapter 4
THE GOVERNMENT

Executive Power

This chapter concentrates on the executive power of government under the doctrine of the separation of powers. This is the branch of government entrusted with carrying the laws into effect. The executive power includes the framing of policy, a matter on which the Constitution is silent.

The Government

The Constitution declares that the executive power of the State shall be exercised by and on the authority of the Government, or as it is often referred to, though not in the Constitution, the Cabinet. The Government, one of the three institutions of government vested with constitutional powers, does not possess unlimited powers. The Government cannot act in contravention of the Constitution (see *Crotty v An Taoiseach* later) or in contravention of the laws.

The Government consists of between seven and fifteen members, nominated by the Taoiseach, approved by Dáil Éireann and appointed by the President. Members of the Government must be members of either House of the Oireachtas, though a maximum of two members of Seanad Éireann may be members of the Government. The Taoiseach, the Tánaiste and the Minister for Finance must be members of Dáil Éireann. A member of the Government resigns by placing a resignation in the hands of the Taoiseach for submission to the President. The Taoiseach may, for reasons which seem sufficient, request a member of the Government to resign, and should that member refuse, the appointment is terminated by the President.

The head of the Government (the Prime Minister) is called the Taoiseach and is appointed by the President on the nomination of Dáil Éireann. The Taoiseach must be a member of Dáil Éireann and, together with other constitutional duties, must keep the President generally informed on domestic and international policy. The Taoiseach must resign on ceasing to retain the support of the majority of Dáil Éireann, though the Taoiseach and the Government continue in office until their successors are appointed.

The Taoiseach nominates a member of the Government, also a member of Dáil Éireann, to be Tánaiste (deputy Prime Minister). The Tánaiste acts as head of the Government on the Taoiseach's absence, incapacity or death. The

Supreme Court ruled, in *Riordan v An Tánaiste* (1998), that there was nothing unconstitutional in the absence from the State of both the Taoiseach and Tánaiste at the same time.

All members of the Government have the right to attend and be heard in both Houses of the Oireachtas.

Responsibility to Dáil Éireann

The Constitution provides that the Government is responsible to Dáil Éireann. The Taoiseach, and the Government, must resign on ceasing to command the support of the majority of Dáil Éireann. though they remain in office until their successors are appointed.

Collective Responsibility

The Government meets and acts as a collective authority and is collectively responsible for all Departments of State. The Supreme Court ruled, in *Attorney General v Tribunal of Inquiry into the Beef Industry* (1992), that discussions at Government meetings were confidential. Following a constitutional amendment, the discussions at Government meetings may be disclosed where the High Court rules that it is necessary for (a) a proper administration of justice, or (b) following an application made by a tribunal, which has been established under the authority of the Houses of the Oireachtas, to inquire into a matter of public importance.

Executive Privilege

At common law there was a principle which held that the executive organ of government could, by its own judgment, withhold relevant evidence from the courts during judicial proceedings. This claim to privilege was made on the ground that production of the material would be contrary to public policy and detrimental to the public interest and public service. This rule has been severely restricted by the Supreme Court in *Murphy v Dublin Corporation* (1972) (see page 12). The enactment of the *Freedom of Information Act 1997* makes available for public inspection current files on executive policy though some records are exempted from disclosure, such matters relating to law enforcement and public safety, security, defence and international relations.

Financial Affairs of the State

One of the executive duties of the Government is to manage the financial affairs of the State. In each financial year the Government must prepare estimates of the receipts and estimates of the expenditure of the State and present them to Dáil Éireann for consideration.

The Constitution declares that all State revenues from whatever source arising must, subject to such exceptions as may be provided by law, form one fund. This is known as the Central Fund. Dáil Éireann must not pass any vote or resolution, and no law may be enacted, for the appropriation of revenue unless the purpose of the appropriation has been recommended by a message from the Government signed by the Taoiseach.

When the estimates have been debated and agreed to, a Bill is introduced to appropriate from the Central Fund the total sum mentioned in the schedule to the Bill, which is considered necessary for the effective running of the State. Being a Money Bill, Seanad Éireann has only twenty-one days to consider it (see page 28), and the President cannot refer it to the Supreme Court (see page 29), though it may be challenged as to its constitutionality after its enactment.

There are three paramount features in the management of State finances. The executive initiates action, the legislature supervises these actions, and finally there is inspection and audit by an independent official. The Constitution creates the office of the Comptroller and Auditor General. Appointed by the President on the nomination of Dáil Éireann, the holder of that office cannot be a member of the Oireachtas and cannot hold another position of emolument. Removal from office, for stated misbehaviour, requires a resolution of both Houses of the Oireachtas. The President, on receipt of such resolutions from the Taoiseach, removes the Comptroller and Auditor General from office.

The Comptroller and Auditor General has two tasks. First, no money must be permitted to leave the Central Fund without statutory authority. Secondly, an audit of income and expenditure must be made annually with a report to Dáil Éireann.

International Affairs of the State

The executive power of the State with regard to external relations is exercised by the Government. The Supreme Court decided, in *Crotty v An Taoiseach* (1987), that the exercise of this power was subject to judicial review. The Government was injuncted from ratifying the Single European Act, a Treaty, on the ground that the State's right to conduct its external relations was part of what was inalienable and indefeasible in what the Constitution described as a sovereign, independent, democratic state. An attempt to make a binding commitment to alienate to other states the conduct of foreign relations, which the Treaty purported to do, was inconsistent with the Government's duty to conduct those relations. Following that decision, an amendment to the Constitution was approved by the People in a referendum which permitted the State to ratify the Single European Act (see page 76).

The courts will not interfere with the policy of the executive which falls short of constitutional transgression: *Boland v An Taoiseach* (1974).

International agreements to which the State becomes a party must be laid before Dáil Éireann and the State cannot be bound by any such agreement involving a charge on public funds unless its terms have been approved by Dáil Éireann. A treaty of extradition between Ireland and the United States of America was signed. It was laid before both Houses of the Oireachtas but was not approved by Dáil Éireann. The treaty contained the provision that each state was to bear certain expenses arising out of extradition requests. The Supreme Court, in *The State (Gilliland) v Governor of Mountjoy Prison* (1986), held that since the treaty involved a charge on public funds, it was invalid in that it had not been approved by Dáil Éireann. The treaty was subsequently approved by Dáil Éireann.

An international agreement cannot become part of the domestic law of the State save as may be determined by the Oireachtas. Legislation has enacted many international agreements into statute law. An individual cannot avail of the benefits contained in an international agreement to which the State is a party unless it has been enacted into domestic law. That was decided by the Supreme Court in *In re Ó Láighléis* (1960) where a person interned without trial argued that internment offended the European Convention for the Protection of Human Rights and Fundamental Freedoms, which Ireland signed in Rome on 4 November 1950, and which came into force on 3 September 1953 (see page 62). According to Davitt P.: 'Where there is an irreconcilable conflict between a domestic statute and… the provisions of an international agreement, the courts administering the domestic law must give effect to the statute. If this principle were not to be observed it would follow that the executive government, by means of an international agreement, might … be able to exercise powers of legislation contrary to the letter and spirit of the Constitution.'

In that case internment without trial could not be challenged on constitutional grounds because the statute had been held to be constitutional when the President sought the advice of the Supreme Court: *Article 26 and the Offences Against the State (Amendment) Bill 1940* (see page 30).

Chapter 5

THE ADMINISTRATION OF JUSTICE

Judicial power

Under the Constitution the judicial function is the third organ of government power and consists of the interpretation of the Constitution and the law, and its application by rule or discretion to disputes which arise between the State and the individual, and between individual and individual. Justice is to be administered in courts established by statute law by judges appointed in the manner prescribed in the Constitution. The judges in exercising the judicial functions under the Constitution jealously uphold the constitutional doctrine of the separation of powers, and guard against intrusion by either the legislature or the executive (see page 12).

Public Justice

Justice must not only be done but must be seen to be done. 'Publicity', explained Ó Dálaigh CJ. in *Beamish & Crawford Ltd v Crowley* (1969), 'deserved or otherwise, is inseparable from the administration of justice.'

This duty to administer public justice is not an absolute one. The Constitution allows exceptions and various statutes implement this provision. Some such statutes are mandatory. The *Criminal Procedure Act 1967*, section 17 states that no person shall publish any information as to any preliminary examination other than the fact that such examination had been held in relation to a named person, and of the decision, except the publication of such information as the court permits at the request of the accused person. Other statutes grant a discretion to the trial court. The *Companies Act 1963*, section 205, provides that where a court is hearing an action, which involves the disclosure of information seriously prejudicial to the legitimate interest of the company the court may order that the hearing or any part of it shall be in private. The Supreme Court, in *In re R. Ltd* (1989), refused to permit the total hearing in private of a case where it was alleged that the publication of some matters would be prejudicial to the company. The court held that part of the case might be heard in private. In any event the decision of the court must be given in public. The High Court held, in *Roe v Blood Transfusion Service Board* (1996), that the public disclosure of the identity of the parties to civil litigation was essential if justice was to be administered in public and that the court had no jurisdiction to allow a party to prosecute civil proceedings using a fictitious name.

The Judiciary

Judges of the ordinary courts are appointed by the President on the advice of the Government. A judge cannot be a member of the Oireachtas or hold any other position of emolument, and on appointment makes a constitutional declaration to 'duly and faithfully and to the best of his knowledge and power execute the office without fear or favour, affection or ill-will towards any man, and that he will uphold the Constitution and the laws'. Should this declaration not be made within ten days of entering office, a judge is considered to have vacated that office. Matters relating to the number of judges, terms of appointment, remuneration, age of retirement and pensions, are to be regulated by statute. The effect of the non-observance of a regulatory statute was considered in two cases. The High Court, in *The State (Walshe) v Murphy* (1981), quashed a criminal conviction on the ground that the judge making it had not been validly appointed in that he had not the qualifications required by statute. Where a judge remained in office after the statutory date of retirement had passed was considered in *Shelly v Mahon* (1990), where a criminal conviction was challenged. A statute was enacted which retrospectively permitted the extension of the age of retirement of that judge and provided that everything done by him should be deemed always to have been valid except where it conflicted with a constitutional right of any person. The Supreme Court held that since there was no trial before a court properly constituted and presided over by a judge whose appointment was valid under the Constitution, which was a constitutional right, the conviction must be quashed.

Judicial Independence

The judges are independent of the legislature and the executive in the exercise of their judicial functions. Without this independence a judge could not impartially decide the issue in any particular case. One judge has said: 'To decide justly between citizens, or to preserve impartially the delicate balance, in a modern democracy, between the legitimate needs of the State and the inherent rights of the individual, is a task that is rendered easier and more likely of fulfilment by the existence of a judiciary free in the exercise of its functions from control or influence not only by the executive or the legislature but also by any citizen or group of citizens.'

The first way the Constitution guarantees independence to the judiciary is by granting security of office. A judge can only be removed from office for stated misbehaviour or incapacity by resolutions passed by both Houses of the Oireachtas. The President, on being notified of such resolutions by the

Taoiseach, removes that particular judge from office. Since the enactment of the Constitution no judge has been removed from office.

The second protection given to the judiciary by the Constitution is that their remuneration cannot be reduced while in office. In *O'Byrne v Minister for Finance* (1959) a widow of a judge claimed that income tax paid by her late husband was an unconstitutional reduction of his salary. The Supreme Court rejected this claim. Maguire CJ. said: 'To require a judge to pay taxes on his income on the same basis as other citizens and thus to contribute to the expenses of government cannot be said to be an attack upon his independence.' The Supreme Court held, in *McMenamin v Ireland* (1997), that the obligation not to reduce remuneration while in office, included pensions payable on retirement.

The common law developed two further protections for the judiciary. The first is the law of contempt. Civil contempt consists of disobedience to the judgments, orders or other processes of the superior courts. Criminal contempt consists of acts tending to obstruct the due process of justice. It includes contempt in the face of the court, consisting of words or actions in a court that interfere with the course of justice. A physical attack on a judge, juror, lawyer or witness, or the use of threatening language is contempt. This was the allegation in *The State (DPP) v Walsh* (1981) where, after a conviction for capital murder, a newspaper published an item drafted by the defendant which referred to the Special Criminal Court as a 'sentencing tribunal'. The Supreme Court found this statement calculated to undermine the reputation of the Special Criminal Court as a source of justice.

The second protection granted by the common law is that judges enjoy immunity from action when performing their judicial functions. In *Macaulay & Co. Ltd v Wyse-Power* (1943) an action against a judge for slander for remarks made during legal proceedings about the plaintiff was dismissed because, as Maguire J. in the High Court explained: '... it was better that an individual should suffer than the course of justice be hindered and fettered by apprehensions on the part of the judge that his own words might be made the subject of the action'. The High Court ruled, in *Deighan v Ireland* (1995), that an action did not lie against a judge who erroneously imprisoned a person for contempt of court.

THE SYSTEM OF COURTS

Superior and Inferior Courts

There must be, according to the Constitution, a Supreme Court and a High Court. These courts are known as superior courts. Other courts, known as inferior courts, of a limited and local nature, may be created by statute.

The *Courts (Establishment and Constitution) Act 1961* formally established the hierarchical system of courts envisaged by the Constitution. These courts are collectively known as the ordinary courts, each detailed below, as distinct from special courts which are considered later in this chapter under 'The Trial of Offences'.

The District Court

This is the lowest court in the system though it handles an enormous number of cases. While there is a single District Court for the convenient exercise of its business, the country is divided into over 200 District Court areas. There is a President of the District Court, and a number of District judges. Barristers and solicitors of ten years' experience can be appointed. District judges retire at sixty-five years though this may be extended to seventy years.

The Circuit Court

This is the next court in the system. It consists of a President of the Circuit Court, who is *ex officio* a judge of the High Court, and a number of ordinary judges. Though there is a single Circuit Court the country is divided into eight circuits, and the judge assigned to each circuit travels to different towns within that circuit a number of times each year. There are, because of the volume of business, permanent Circuit Courts sitting in Dublin and Cork. Barristers of ten years' experience can be appointed judges of the Circuit Court and such judges retire at the age of seventy years.

The High Court

The High Court exercises jurisdiction over the whole of the country. Generally it sits in Dublin though it visits other centres to hear cases. It consists of a President, who is *ex officio* a judge of the Supreme Court and a member of the Council of State, and eighteen judges. Barristers of twelve years' standing, and judges of the Circuit Court of four years' standing, can be appointed to the High Court, and judges retire at seventy years of age.

Generally a High Court judge, when hearing a case, sits alone, except in jury cases which are discussed later in this chapter. But in cases of importance three judges may sit, in a divisional court, at the direction of the President of the High Court. In such cases, each judge may give a separate judgment and the decision of the court is by majority. When trying criminal cases the High Court is known as the Central Criminal Court.

The Court of Criminal Appeal

This court sits to hear certain criminal appeals. It consists of one judge of the Supreme Court and two judges of the High Court. The decision of the court is by majority and only one judgment is given. When hearing appeals from courts martial, this court is known as the Courts Martial Appeal Court.

The Supreme Court

The Supreme Court stands at the apex of our judicial system. It consists of the Chief Justice, who is head of the judiciary, President of the Supreme Court, an *ex officio* member of the Council of State and a member of the Presidential Commission; and five ordinary judges. The President of the High Court is *ex officio* a judge of the Supreme Court. Other judges of the High Court by invitation sit as Supreme Court judges though not in constitutional cases. Barristers of twelve years' standing, judges of the High Court, and judges of the Circuit Court of four years' standing may be appointed to the Supreme Court. The retirement age is seventy years.

In constitutional cases five judges sit, whereas in legal cases three judges form a quorum. Except in certain constitutional cases each judge, in keeping with judicial tradition, may deliver a separate judgment and the decision of the court is that of the majority.

JURISDICTIONS OF THE COURTS

Definition of Jurisdiction

Jurisdiction means the authority or power of a court. Not every court has similar or equal jurisdictions. Jurisdiction is of three kinds. A court has original jurisdiction where the case can be completely heard before it. Where a court hears appeals from a lower court it exercises appellate jurisdiction. Where a court is consulted by a lower court on points of law it has consultative jurisdiction.

For the sake of clarity, jurisdiction will be divided into criminal jurisdiction and civil jurisdiction. All courts, with minor exceptions, exercise both types of jurisdiction. Apart from the fact that civil jurisdiction has a different purpose than criminal jurisdiction, the procedures of each are different.

Civil Jurisdiction of the Courts

The District Court is possessed of original jurisdiction in civil matters in that damages of up to £5,000 can be awarded in contract and civil wrong cases. It can order ejectment where the annual rent does not exceed the like amount. It grants liquor and dance hall licences. The decision of the District judge, who sits alone when hearing the case, can be appealed to the Circuit Court, and the District Court can consult with the High Court on points of law. The District Court exercises appellate jurisdiction from certain quasi-judicial decisions.

For example, the *Street and House to House Collections Act 1962* confers a right of appeal to the District Court from a refusal of a chief superintendent to grant a permit.

The original jurisdiction of the Circuit Court is limited to £30,000. An appeal lies from the decision of the Circuit Court judge, who sits alone when hearing the case, to the High Court, and the Circuit Court may consult the Supreme Court on points of law. An unsuccessful party in a District Court case may appeal to the Circuit Court which rehears the case and substitutes its own decision. Decisions of some administrative tribunals, such as the Employment Appeals Tribunal, may be appealed to the Circuit Court: *Unfair Dismissals Act 1977*. On appeals in general it must be noted that a decision may only be appealed once and the decision of the Appeal Court is final, though there are exceptions to this rule.

The High Court can award unlimited damages. Its original jurisdiction is wide and covers matters such as civil wrongs, succession, trusts, wards of court and the winding up of companies. In some cases, defamation, for example, a jury decides the extent of the defendant's liability and the amount of damages to be awarded. The High Court exercises its appellate jurisdiction by hearing appeals from the Circuit Court and such other appeals as provided by law. For example, the High Court hears appeals from decisions of the Controller of Patents: *Patents Act 1964*.

The High Court exercises its consultative jurisdiction by hearing a Case Stated from the District Court. A District judge may, during or at the end of a case, be requested by either party to obtain the opinion of the High Court on a point of law which has arisen. This point of law, and the facts of the case, are set out in writing and transmitted to the High Court. At that hearing the parties are represented and, having decided the issue, it is returned to the District Court which must accordingly act on it. Apart from the importance for the particular case, the point of law so decided is a precedent for all future similar cases; the doctrine of precedent is considered on page 58.

An important portion of the original jurisdiction of the High Court extends to the question as to whether any statute is invalid or inconsistent having regard to the provision of the Constitution. Another important jurisdiction permits the High Court to test the validity of a person's detention by the process of an application under Article 40.4.2° of the Constitution (see page 69).

The Supreme Court has no original jurisdiction in civil matters. It hears appeals from the High Court in cases where the validity of a law has been challenged as to its constitutionality. It hears all appeals from the High Court in legal cases unless prohibited by statute law. The Supreme Court ruled, in *In re Morelli* (1968), that it had appellate jurisdiction to hear an appeal regarding costs in a probate matter because no clear statutory provision prohibited such appeal. Where there is clear statutory prohibition, as in certain patents cases, the Supreme Court ruled, in *Beechams Group Ltd v Bristol Myers Co.* (1983), that it must refuse to exercise its appellate jurisdiction.

The Supreme Court has a number of consultative jurisdictions. The President may consult (and has done so twelve times) the Supreme Court as to the constitutionality of certain Bills presented for signature (see page 29). The High Court and the Circuit Court may consult the Supreme Court by way of Case Stated.

Supervisory Jurisdiction of the High Court

The High Court possesses considerable supervisory jurisdiction over inferior courts, administrative bodies and persons. This jurisdiction is exercised by way of judicial review. Relief by way of judicial review is discretionary and may be refused in instances of delay in bringing the proceedings or where other remedies are available. An order of *certiorari* is used to check a body or person who has exceeded their legal powers. For example, in *The State (Gleeson) v Minister for Defence* (1976), a private soldier had his discharge from the army quashed by *certiorari* because he was not afforded fair procedures before his dismissal.

An order of prohibition prevents a body or person from exercising a power it does not legally possess. In *The State (Williams) v Kelleher* (1983) an order of prohibition made against a District judge prevented the continuance of a preliminary investigation of an indictable offence because the proper documents had not been served on the defendant before the investigation. An order of *mandamus* compels a body or person to perform a legally imposed duty. For example, in *The State (King) v Minister for Justice* (1984) a number of solicitors in Waterford were granted an order of *mandamus* to compel the Minister to exercise statutory powers to direct the Commissioners of Public Works to put the Waterford courthouse into proper repair.

Article 40 of the Constitution confers on the High Court jurisdiction to inquire into the detention of a person (see page 69).The High Court has considerable jurisdiction in the granting of an injunction to compel or prohibit the performance of some act (see page 228).

Criminal Jurisdiction

In criminal cases the District Court hears summary offences. In such cases the defendant is not entitled to a trial by jury, either because the offence is minor (see page 129) or because the defendant has waived the right to a jury trial, which is possible in certain cases. In summary cases the maximum punishment which can be imposed on conviction is six months' imprisonment and/or a fine. Examples are common assault and driving a motor vehicle without insurance.

An indictable offence, one on which a defendant is of right entitled to a jury trial, can be heard in the District Court where the governing statute permits, the defendant consents and the permission of the Director of Public Prosecutions has been obtained. In such cases the maximum sentence on conviction is twelve months and/or a fine. Examples are serious assaults and stealing.

Where a defendant elects for jury trial, or in serious cases such as murder where there must be a jury trial, the District Court conducts a preliminary investigation. The District Court must be satisfied that there is sufficient evidence to return the defendant for trial by jury to a higher court. Where the District Court is not satisfied the defendant is discharged. The Supreme Court decided, in *Costello v DPP* (1984), that a statutory power exercisable by the Director of Public Prosecutions to return a person for jury trial after a discharge by the District Court was unconstitutional.

The Circuit Court, which consists of a judge and jury in criminal trials, hears indictable offences sent to it by the District Court. Such cases include serious assaults and stealing. The Circuit Court judge may impose on a convicted person whatever punishment is permissible by statute or common law. A defendant sent for trial may plead guilty, thus avoiding the necessity for a trial. The Circuit Court exercises its appellate jurisdiction by hearing the appeals of those convicted in the District Court. The appeal may be against the conviction and/or the sentence. Where the appeal is against conviction the case is completely reheard, with the Circuit Court reaching its own conclusion. Where the appeal is solely against the sentence the Circuit Court can leave the punishment unaltered, decrease it or increase it, but only to the maximum which the District Court could impose. Only the convicted person is permitted to appeal; the State has no right to appeal an acquittal or the insufficiency of the penalty.

The Central Criminal Court, the High Court exercising its criminal jurisdiction, tries serious crimes such as murder, attempted murder, conspiracy to murder and serious sexual offences. Cases are heard by a High Court judge and a jury.

The Court of Criminal Appeal hears appeals from the Central Criminal Court, the Circuit Criminal Court and the Special Criminal Court. The appeal is not a rehearing of the case but is based on the transcript of the evidence given at the trial and is usually confined to points of law, or that the verdict was against the weight of the evidence. Few convictions are quashed on the latter ground. Where the verdict is appealed the court may affirm it, or may quash it and in some such cases order a retrial. On the question of the severity nt, the court may refuse to alter it, reduce it or increase it within m allowed by law. The *Criminal Procedure Act 1993* provides that where a person has been convicted on indictment and alleges that a newly discovered fact shows that there has been a miscarriage of justice in relation to the conviction, or that the sentence imposed is excessive, an application may be made to the Court of Criminal Appeal for an order quashing the conviction or reviewing the sentence.

The Supreme Court has little criminal jurisdiction. It can only hear appeals from the Court of Criminal Appeal provided that court or the Director of Public Prosecutions certified that the case involved a point of law of public importance. When the *Courts and Court Officers Act 1995* is fully operational, the Court of Criminal Appeal will stand abolished and its jurisdiction will vest in the Supreme Court, which can then hear a range of criminal appeals.

THE TRIAL OF OFFENCES

Due Course of Law

Because a criminal conviction has serious consequences, such as imprisonment and the loss of the individual's good name, the Constitution provides that no person should be tried on any criminal charge except in due course of law. This means there must be basic fairness of procedures. The courts have formulated procedures which must be observed during criminal trials. Many of these protections are reflected in the rules of evidence, considered later.

Many of the protections afforded to those on trial are constitutionally based. Some are worthy of note. In advance of the trial the accused must be furnished with the evidence to be given by the prosecution. During the trial the accused must be allowed to cross-examine witnesses by counsel or solicitor, where retained. An accused must be allowed to give evidence and to call witnesses. And lastly, the accused must be permitted to address the court.

The Supreme Court decided, in *The State (Healy) v Donoghue* (1976), that where an accused faces a serious charge and because of poor education or immaturity requires the assistance of a qualified lawyer in the preparation and conduct of the defence, the State must, where the accused is without means, provide legal aid from public funds. The accused must be informed of this right to free legal representation.

The Supreme Court, in *The State (O'Connell) v Fawsitt* (1986), held that an accused is entitled to have criminal offences tried with reasonable expedition having regard to the circumstances of the case. *The State (McGlinchey) v Governor of Portlaoise Prison* (1982) decided that an accused should have all criminal charges outstanding disposed of at the same time. The Supreme Court, in *Z. v Director of Public Prosecutions* (1994), decided that an accused seeking to prohibit a trial on the ground that circumstances had arisen which would render it unfair, such as pre-trial publicity, must establish there was a real risk that a fair trial could not be obtained.

Bail

Bail is the setting at liberty of an accused person upon that person or others becoming sureties, or guarantors, for the appearance of the accused at the trial. The accused is bailed into the custody of the sureties who must ensure the attendance of the accused at the trial, or be liable to the State for the sums secured in the event of a non-appearance. Bail was developed because detention in custody pending trial can be a great hardship on an accused and the prospect of acquittal may be reduced because of an inadequately prepared defence. The presumption of innocence is a strong rule of constitutional and legal importance.

The fundamental test in deciding whether to grant bail is the probability of the accused evading justice. The High Court, in *The People (AG) v O'Callaghan* (1966), refused bail because the accused, if released, might interfere with witnesses. The Supreme Court rejected this reason and granted bail. The failure to grant bail was, according to Walsh J., 'a form of preventive justice which has no place in our legal system'. The Supreme Court decided in, *The People (AG) v Gilliland* (1986), that the test for granting bail in extradition proceedings was the same as that in criminal cases, and in *DPP v Ryan* (1988), refused to depart from the principle laid down in *O'Callaghan's* case. As a result of a constitutional referendum, the *Bail Act 1997*, when it is brought into operation, provides that a court may refuse bail to a person charged with a serious offence, where the court is reasonably satisfied that such refusal is considered necessary to prevent the commission of a further serious offence by that person. Bail, when granted, may be subject to conditions.

Summary Trial

Minor offences may be tried in courts of summary jurisdiction, which is trial without a jury. Summary trials take place in the District Court. Reference should be made to the criminal jurisdiction of the District Court (page 45) and to minor offences (page 129).

Trial by Jury

Except in summary trials, or trials in special courts, or military courts, no person must be tried without a jury. A jury consists of twelve lay persons drawn at random from the population at large. At common law a jury's verdict had to be unanimous though the *Criminal Justice Act 1984* permits a majority verdict of ten jurors to two. This departure from the common law rule did not offend the Constitution: *O'Callaghan v Attorney General* (1993).

In a jury trial the function of the judge is to decide questions of law and direct the jury accordingly to ensure the rules of evidence and fair procedures are observed, and on conviction to impose punishment. The function of the jury is to decide on the guilt or innocence of the accused.

The composition of a jury was considered by the Supreme Court in *de Búrca v Attorney General* (1976) where the challenged law confined jury service to those with real property of a certain rateable valuation. The statute was unconstitutional because, as Henchy J. explained: 'The jury must be drawn from a pool broadly representative of the community.' The *Juries Act 1976* provides that jury panels must be drawn from citizens aged between eighteen and seventy years who are entered on the Dáil Éireann electoral register. Certain categories of persons are ineligible, excused or disqualified.

Trial by jury in criminal matters is part of the jurisdiction of the Circuit Criminal Court and the Central Criminal Court, which is the High Court exercising its criminal jurisdiction.

Trial by Military Court

The next method of trial permitted by the Constitution is that by military court. Military courts are of two kinds. Military tribunals may exercise criminal jurisdiction during a time of war or armed rebellion or may be established by statute to deal with extraordinary situations. Members of the Defence Forces on active service may be tried by court martial: *Defence Act 1954*. An appeal lies to the Courts-Martial Appeal Court.

Special Courts

Special courts may be established by statute when it is considered that the ordinary courts are inadequate to secure the effective administration of justice and the preservation of public peace and order. Part V of *the Offences Against the State Act 1939* is the relevant law which is activated, and deactivated, by government order. The Houses of the Oireachtas have no role in this regard. The present Special Criminal Court was established in 1972.

The constitutional provisions relating to judges of the ordinary courts do not apply to members of the Special Criminal Court. Members of that court must be a judge of the High Court, Circuit Court or a District judge; or a barrister or solicitor of seven years' standing; or be an army officer above the rank of commandant. Members are appointed, and removed, at the will of the Government. The Supreme Court held, in *Eccles v Ireland* (1985) that while a Special Criminal Court did not attract the constitutionally expressed guarantees of judicial independence, it did possess, derived from the Constitution, a guarantee of independence in the carrying out of its functions. This court can try a great variety of offences from capital murder to simple assault. A Special Criminal Court consists of three members and the decision is that of the majority. An appeal lies to the Court of Criminal Appeal.

Trial for Contempt of Court

Apart from the four methods of trial enumerated in the Constitution, the courts assume the power to punish any act which plainly tends to create a disregard for the authority of the courts. Contempt *in facie curiae*: in the face of the court, is punished by the court before which the offence is committed. The Supreme Court decided, in *Keegan v de Búrca* (1973), that where imprisonment is imposed it must be for a definite period. The Supreme Court ruled, in *The State (DPP) v Walsh* (1981) (see page 41), that the contempt of scandalising a court is generally triable by jury.

Prosecution of Offences

All indictable offences, other than those prosecuted in the District Court, must be prosecuted in the name of the People at the suit of the Attorney General or some other person authorised in accordance with law. The office of the *Director of Public Prosecutions* was established in 1974 and, though a civil servant, the Director is independent in the exercise of that office.

The complainant in summary proceedings, known as a common informer, has complete control over the case and is independent of the Director of Public Prosecutions. The Supreme Court ruled, in *The State (Ennis) v Farrell* (1960), that a common informer could initiate, and manage, a complaint of an indictable offence during its summary stages, but that once the defendant was returned for trial by the jury the prosecution must be taken over by the Director of Public Prosecutions.

THE LAW OF EVIDENCE

Rules of Procedure and Evidence

To achieve a fair administration of justice, the common law developed rules of procedure and evidence which have been supplemented by the Constitution and by statute. Each court has its distinctive rules of procedure. Since the rules of evidence are the creation of the common law or by statute, they are open to challenge on constitutional grounds.

The law of evidence is concerned with what, and how, facts may be proved in a court. Only relevant evidence is admitted, though there are situations where relevant evidence is inadmissible. For example, unconstitutionally obtained evidence may be excluded though it is relevant (see page 55).

Trial Procedures

Prior to a civil trial, pleadings are exchanged between the parties which set out detailed facts to be relied on by each party: surprise is an element rarely found in court proceedings. Plaintiff's counsel opens the case by giving a brief account of the issues. The plaintiff and witnesses are examined on oath and may be cross-examined by defendant's counsel. When the plaintiff's case has closed, counsel for the defendant opens the defendant's case and calls the defendant and witnesses to give evidence on oath. These may be cross-examined by plaintiff's counsel. Counsel then makes closing speeches. Where the defendant has given evidence, defendant's counsel makes the first speech and plaintiff's counsel is last. Where the defendant has not given evidence, defendant's counsel has the last word. Where there is a jury, as in some High Court cases, the trial judge explains the relevant law and reviews the evidence before the jury retire to reach a verdict. In civil cases the jury decide both the issue and the amount of damages. Where there is no jury, the judge may give an immediate decision or may reserve that decision, until a written judgment is prepared and given at a later date.

In a criminal trial by jury the prosecution must serve a book of evidence on the accused which contains statements of the evidence and a list of the exhibits which may be produced at the trial. Where the accused is raising a defence of alibi, notice must be given to the prosecution. The procedures are similar to that in civil cases, already explained, except where the verdict is guilty the judge and not the jury imposes the punishment. At common law a jury's verdict has to be unanimous, though the *Criminal Justice Act 1984* permits a majority verdict of ten jurors to two.

Burden and Standard of Proof

In civil actions the burden of proof is on the plaintiff on the facts pleaded and not admitted by the defendant. At a criminal trial it is borne by the prosecution on every issue except that of insanity, and issues in which the burden of proof is cast on the accused by statute law. Where the accused's fitness to plead is raised, or insanity is the defence, the burden of proof is on the accused. The Supreme Court, in *Abbey Films Ltd v Attorney General* (1981), saw nothing unconstitutional in a statute imposing on an accused the onus to establish a limited and specific matter in criminal cases.

In civil cases the standard of proof is the balance of probabilities. In criminal cases the standard is proof beyond reasonable doubt. The High Court ruled, in *O'Leary v Attorney General* (1991), that every person accused in every criminal trial had a constitutionally protected right to the presumption of innocence. The party with the burden of proof will be successful when, at the end of the evidence, the court considers that the required standard of proof has been reached. Proof on the balance of probability is the standard where the accused bears the burden of proof. In proceedings to establish paternity, which relates to a child whose parents are not married, the matter is decided on the balance of probabilities: *Status of Children Act 1987.*

Judicial Notice

Evidence need not be given of facts of which the court will take judicial notice. Notorious facts, such as the fact that there are seven days in a week, need not be formally proved in evidence. Trials would be prolonged and tiresome where such facts needed formal proof.

A judge takes judicial notice of the law. Witnesses on the subject are not heard, though the judge must hear experts where foreign law is in issue. Judicial notice is taken of the contents of statutes without formal notice of their due passage through the Oireachtas, though it may be open to a party to formally prove that a statute had not been enacted in accordance with the Constitution.

Presumptions

A presumption is an assumption which is made by the law until evidence to the contrary is adduced. The law acknowledges a number of presumptions. The first is that everything is presumed to have been done lawfully until some evidence to the contrary is proved. This presumption of legality is expressed in the maxim *omnia praesumuntur rite esse acta.* It is useful for it saves the time and expense of calling witnesses to prove facts. For example, on a charge of assaulting a garda formal proof of appointment is not necessary unless questioned by the defendant. The Supreme Court, in *Clark v Early* (1980), refused to apply the maxim where a document produced after the death of a person alleged to be his will, but which did not satisfy the statutory formalities on the ground that there was no evidence of the deceased's intention to enter into the formality of making a will.

The *Status of Children Act 1987* provides that any presumption of law as to the legitimacy or illegitimacy of any person is abrogated. Where a woman gives birth to a child during a subsisting marriage to which she is a party or within the period of ten months after the termination by death or otherwise of a marriage to which she is a party, then the husband of the marriage shall be presumed to be the child's father unless the contrary is proved on the balance of probabilities. Where a married woman, who is living apart from her husband, under a decree of divorce *a mensa et thoro* or a deed of separation, gives birth to a child more than ten months after the decree was granted or the deed was executed, her husband is not presumed to be the child's father unless the contrary is proved on the balance of probabilities. Where the birth of a child is registered, the name of the person entered as the father on the register shall be presumed to be the child's father unless the contrary is proved on the balance of probabilities.

Where there is evidence of a ceremony of marriage, the validity of the marriage is presumed until the contrary is proven. Where a man and woman are proved to have lived together as man and wife, the law presumes, unless the contrary is clearly proved, that they lived together in consequence of a valid ceremony of marriage.

Where there is no acceptable affirmative evidence that a person was alive at some time during a continuous period of seven years or more, then where it is proved first, that there are persons who would be likely to have heard of that person over that period, secondly, that those persons have not heard of that person, and thirdly, that all due inquiries have been made appropriate to the circumstances, that person will be presumed to have died at some time within that period. The High Court held, in *In re Lavelle* (1940), that death should be presumed where a man, twenty-six years of age when he emigrated, had not been heard of for twenty-nine years.

Testimony

All sane persons not subject to constitutional or diplomatic immunity are competent and compellable to give evidence. In general, an accused person is an incompetent witness for the prosecution but competent to give evidence on his or her own behalf, and competent though not compellable to give evidence for a co-accused. As a general rule, the accused's spouse is an incompetent witness for the prosecution. The *Criminal Evidence Act 1992* provides that a spouse is a compellable witness for the prosecution only in respect of cases of physical violence or sexual offences against the other spouse, or the children of the spouse or of the accused, or against any person who was at the material time under seventeen years of age. The spouse of an accused is a competent but not a compellable witness for the accused.

The general rule is that all evidence must be made on oath, though an affirmation may be made where the witness holds no religious belief. The *Criminal Evidence Act 1992* provides that the evidence of a person under fourteen years of age may be received otherwise than on oath or affirmation if the court is satisfied that the child is capable of giving an intelligible account of events which are relevant to the proceedings.

Privilege

Some witnesses may decline to answer certain questions and cannot be punished for such refusal. This is called privilege. A witness is not bound to answer any question where the answer, in the opinion of the court, would tend to incriminate that witness. There are statutory exceptions to this rule, such as the *Companies Act 1963*, section 245, though any answer given cannot be used in other civil or criminal proceedings except perjury in respect of any such answer. The High Court decided, in *In re Aluminium Fabricators Ltd* (1984), that the examination under the section formed part of winding up proceedings, and that answers given in the course of such examination could be used in proceedings brought against directors for fraudulent trading and misfeasance (see page 427).

Communications between spouses are privileged. The High Court decided, in *E.R. v J.R.* (1981), that the privilege belonged to the spouses, and not to a minister of religion acting as a marriage counsellor and called as a witness in a matrimonial action between the spouses. The privilege could be waived by the mutual consent of the spouses.

Communications passing between a client and legal advisers may not generally be given in evidence without the consent of the client. Legal professional privilege extends beyond communications between clients and legal advisers during or relating to an actual or expected litigation. It extends to communications for the purpose of obtaining legal advice, though the Supreme Court ruled, in *Smurfit Paribas Bank Ltd v AAB Export Finance Ltd* (1990), that this privilege did not extend to communications for the purpose of obtaining legal assistance other than legal advice. The Supreme Court ruled, in *Murphy v Kirwan* (1994), that the privilege was not available in cases where there is an allegation against the person claiming the privilege which contains a clear element of moral turpitude, fraud, criminal conduct or conduct constituting a direct interference with the administration of justice, such as a false malicious bringing of a legal action.

State secrets are privileged from disclosure, though the scope of this privilege has been eroded by the Supreme Court *in Murphy v Dublin Corporation* (1972) (see page 12). The High Court, in *Cully v Northern Bank Finance Corporation Ltd* (1984), upheld a claim by a Central Bank employee that to give evidence would be in breach of an oath of secrecy given when entering employment. The High Court held, in *DPP v Holly* (1984), that a blanket claim of privilege by a garda in relation to a written report could not be maintained. Had specific grounds been advanced by the garda, the court trying the case would have examined the report to ascertain whether the claim to privilege could be maintained in the public interest.

Journalists have no immunity from being compelled in legal proceedings to disclose information which comes their way in the course of their professional duties. This was the rule stated by the Court of Criminal Appeal in *In re Kevin O'Kelly* (1973) where a journalist who had refused to give evidence of a conversation with an accused person was held in contempt of court.

Corroboration

The general rule in both civil and criminal cases alike is that a court may act on the testimony of one witness. Corroboration, however, is required before there can be a conviction for perjury and for certain sexual assaults. Corroboration is confirmatory evidence and may consist of the evidence of a second witness, or the conduct of the person against whom it is required, or a statement made by that person. Whatever its nature, it must implicate that person in a material way.

Hearsay

The rule against hearsay provides that assertions of persons, other than the witness who is testifying, and the assertions in documents produced to the court when no witness is testifying, are inadmissible as evidence of the truth of that which is asserted. There are exceptions to this rule; the major one concerns confessions in criminal cases.

Confessions

A confession of guilt, whether verbal or written, is only admissible where it is not made in breach of constitutional rights, or in consequence of an unlawful threat, or inducement of a temporal nature made or held out by a person in authority.

Unconstitutionally Obtained Evidence

The Supreme Court laid down the rule in *The People (AG) v O'Brien* (1965), per Walsh J.: 'Evidence obtained… as a result of a deliberate conscious breach of the constitutional rights of an accused person should, save in … excusable circumstances … be absolutely inadmissible.' In that case the court ruled that the breach of constitutional rights which had occurred by searching the accused's home without a properly completed search warrant, where stolen property was found, was not deliberate and conscious but mere inadvertence.

The Court of Criminal Appeal, in *The People (DPP) v Madden* (1977), refused to admit a confession which had been taken at a time when the accused was in unlawful custody in that he had been detained longer than was permissible under the *Offences Against the State Act* 1939. This rule applies in civil cases. In *C. v C.* (1981) the parties to a marriage entered into a separation agreement. One of the terms prohibited the wife from visiting the husband's home. While the husband was on holidays, the wife entered his home and removed letters and photographs which she tendered as evidence in maintenance proceedings. The High Court ruled that these items were inadmissible because they had been obtained in flagrant violation of the husband's constitutional right to the inviolability of his home. Evidence obtained in a drugs raid on a dwelling was inadmissible in *The People (DPP) v Kenny* (1990) because of a defect in the search warrant.

In these cases the interest of the individual prevailed over the public interest. But in *The People (DPP) v Shaw* (1982) there was a real dilemma in that the accused had been kept in custody longer than was legally permitted because gardaí believed that the victim of the crime was still alive. The Supreme Court accepted that an extraordinary excusing circumstance existed, which justified an illegal detention and the admitted confessions made during that detention.

Illegally Obtained Evidence

Where evidence is obtained in breach of a legal, as distinct from a constitutional right, the courts have discretion whether to admit or to exclude such evidence. In *DPP v McMahon* (1987) members of the Gardaí in plain clothes entered licensed premises to ascertain whether breaches of the gaming laws were being committed. A search warrant was necessary, which had not been obtained, and the question arose whether the observations of the gardaí could be admitted in evidence. The Supreme Court ruled that the gardaí were trespassers, that the public portion of the licensed premises, not being a dwelling, was not constitutionally protected and the trial court had the discretion to admit or exclude the evidence.

In *Minister for Justice v Wang Zhu Jie* (1991) gardaí entered premises in the course of routine inquiries. The question arose whether they could give evidence of breaches of the law which they observed. The High Court decided that in the circumstances the gardaí were not trespassers because property owners impliedly consent to gardaí entering to make inquiries in the enforcement of the law. Where the owner objected to the entry, or objected to their continued presence, the gardaí became trespassers.

PERSONNEL OF THE LAW

Attorney General

The Constitution creates the office of Attorney General who is the legal adviser to the Government in matters of law and legal opinion. Appointed by the President, on the nomination of the Taoiseach, the Attorney General is not a member of the Government. The Attorney General retires from office when the Taoiseach resigns, and like other members of the Government, continues in office until a new Taoiseach is appointed. While Attorneys General have all been lawyers, this is not a constitutional requirement. The Attorney General defends constitutional actions and may, in some cases, endeavour to vindicate constitutional rights. Additional responsibilities may be conferred by law. For example, the Attorney General has a function in extradition matters, and enforces charitable trusts.

Director of Public Prosecutions

The office of the Director of Public Prosecutions was established by statute in 1974. Most serious crimes must be prosecuted in the name of the People at the instance of the Director of Public Prosecutions who, though a civil servant, is independent in the exercise of these functions.

Legal Profession

The Bar is the senior branch of the legal profession. Barristers specialise in court advocacy and the giving of legal opinion. To enter the profession a person must be either a university graduate or have passed examinations set by the King's Inns, the professional body for barristers. The student must dine a number of times at the Inns and is then 'called to the Bar' in the Supreme Court by the Chief Justice. After some years as a junior counsel the barrister may take silk and become a senior counsel by applying to the Government.

To become a solicitor a person must be a university graduate, or a law clerk of seven years' experience, pass examinations set by the Law Society of Ireland, the professional body for solicitors, and become apprenticed for a period of time to an experienced solicitor. The scope of the solicitor's work is wide: the drafting of wills, conveyancing, the preparation for counsel of cases which are to be heard in the higher courts, and the appearance in minor court cases.

Quasi-judicial Offices

A Commissioner for Oaths is appointed by the Chief Justice and is usually, though not always, a solicitor. The major function of a Commissioner for Oaths is the verifying of affidavits, which are statements in writing and on oath, and other legal documents.

The office of Peace Commissioner was created by statute in 1924. Appointments are made by the Minister for Justice. A Peace Commissioner may perform certain functions. The power to remand persons charged with criminal offences on bail or in custody was, in *O'Mahony v Melia* (1989), held unconstitutional by the High Court as an impermissible interference in the judicial domain in that a Peace Commissioner was neither a court nor a judge. The issue of a search warrant prior to the commencement of a prosecution was upheld by the High Court in *Ryan v O'Callaghan* (1987) because it was part of the criminal investigation process and was executive rather than judicial in nature.

THE DOCTRINE OF PRECEDENT

Origins and Meaning

The vast body of common law was not created by legislation but was developed through the centuries by the judges applying the customary law to new situations. In this way consistency and uniformity were achieved. Precedent is probably the most outstanding feature of the common law. In simple terms it means the application of a principle of law as laid down by a higher court on a previous occasion in a case similar to that before the court. This is known as the doctrine of *stare decisis.*

Ratio Decidendi and Obiter Dictum

The entire decision of the higher court is not binding: only that part of the decision, known as the *ratio decidendi*, the grounds of the decision, is binding. The remainder of the decision, the *obiter dictum*, are comments and do not constitute binding precedent.

Types of Precedent

An authoritative precedent is one which an inferior court must follow whether it approves of it or not. A persuasive precedent is one which a court is under no obligation to follow. It may, at its discretion, adopt or ignore the precedent.

Where a precedent is followed it is said to be applied. A precedent is overruled by an act of superior jurisdiction and such a decision is formally deprived of all authority. It is void and a new principle is substituted. Two courts of equal authority, for example two judges of the High Court, have not the power to bind or overrule each other. The position was explained in *Irish Trust Bank Ltd v Central Bank of Ireland* (1976) by Parke J. when he said: 'A court may depart from a decision of a court of equal jurisdiction if it appears that such a decision was given in a case in which either insufficient authority was cited or incorrect submissions advanced or in which the nature and wording of the judgment itself reveals that the judge disregarded or misunderstood an important element in the case or the arguments submitted to him or the authority cited or in some other way departed from the proper standard to be adopted in judicial determination.' One judge may distinguish the latter case from the former by holding the facts in each case to be different, thus allowing a different legal principle to be formulated. One judge may refuse to follow the decision of the other and the law remains uncertain until the Supreme Court, or the Oireachtas, decides between the conflicting decisions. But this problem rarely arises in practice though it has occurred. For example, in *The State (McCaud) v Governor of Mountjoy Prison* (1985) the High Court, per Egan J., decided a particular problem one way, whereas the

High Court, per Barrington J., in *The State (Gilliland) v Governor of Mountjoy Prison* (1986) decided the opposite (see page 38). The Supreme Court, by upholding the view of Barrington J., deprived Egan J.'s decision of authority.

Precedent in Our Legal System

Though not recognised in the Constitution, the doctrine of precedent is strongly adhered to in our courts. 'The laws which we have taken over', said Kingsmill Moore J. in the Supreme Court, in the *Attorney General v Ryans Car Hire Ltd* (1965), 'is based on the following of precedent and there can be no question of abandoning the principle of following precedent as the normal, indeed almost universal procedure.' While judicial precedent is a very valuable source of law it can be, and often is, overruled by legislation, though not in constitutional cases.

The Doctrine of Precedent in Practice

The standing of a decision laid down by a court depends to a great extent on the status of the court giving it. The higher the court the more universally followed the decision will be.

The decisions of the Supreme Court bind all lower courts. Because it is the highest court it cannot be bound by decisions of any other court. The Supreme Court, and other courts, occasionally adopt as persuasive precedent the decisions of the American Supreme Court, the English House of Lords and the Australian courts. But an Irish court is not bound by any decision of a foreign court. Murnaghan J. in *In re Tilson, infants* (1951) said: 'The archaic law of England rapidly disintegrating under modern conditions need not be a guide for the fundamental principles of a modern state. It is not a proper method of construing a new Constitution of a modern state to make an approach in the light of legal survivals of an earlier law.'

The Court of Criminal Appeal in criminal cases binds the Central Criminal Court, the Special Criminal Court, the Circuit Court and the District Court. Of course, its decisions are not binding on the Supreme Court. The Court of Criminal Appeal in *The People (AG) v Moore* (1964) declared its freedom to depart from its earlier decisions.

The High Court is bound by the Supreme Court. In *McDonnell v Byrne Engineering Ltd* (1978) the Supreme Court ordered a retrial of a civil action because the High Court judge had disregarded a previous decision of the Supreme Court and indicated that he intended to do so in similar future cases. The High Court binds the Circuit Court and District Court. The decisions of the Circuit Court are usually followed by the District Court though the latter is not bound to do so. And the decisions of the District Court, as the lowest court in our system, are not binding on any other court.

The Supreme Court and its Previous Decisions

The Supreme Court is not bound by its own previous decisions. This principle was declared by that court in *The State (Quinn) v Ryan* (1965), when it was decided that it was not bound by its own previous decisions in constitutional cases. 'This is not to say, however', said Walsh J. 'that the court would depart from an earlier decision for any but the most compelling reasons. The advantages of *stare decisis* are many and obvious so long as it is remembered that it is a policy and not a binding, unalterable rule.' In that case the court refused to follow a 1952 decision of its own. The Supreme Court, in the *Attorney General v Ryans Car Hire Ltd* (1965), applied this new rule in legal cases.

Since these landmark decisions, the Supreme Court has on numerous occasions refused to follow its own previous decisions. For example, in *Lynch v Burke* (1995), a trusts case (see page 232), the Supreme Court overuled its own previous decision in *Owens v Greene* (1932). On the other hand, in *Ryan v Director of Public Prosecutions* (1989) the court refused to depart from its decision in *The People (AG) v O'Callaghan* (1966) (see page 48).

Law Reporting

Since the decisions of the superior courts bind inferior courts there must be some system of court reporting. Since 1922 judicial decisions of Irish courts are to be found in four sets of reports, though for financial reasons not all decisions have been reported. It is now common to find references and extracts in textbooks of unreported judgments. These unreported judgments are circulated by the judges and are retained by law libraries, universities and other institutions of learning.

The Irish Reports are published in parts during the year and are bound into one volume. These are cited: [1935] IR 325. Thus the particular case is to be found in the 1935 volume of the *Irish Reports* at page 325. The *Irish Law Times Reports* were published with the *Irish Law Times* and *Solicitor's Journal* by the Incorporated Law Society. These are cited: 108 ILTR 97. Thus, the case of *In re Kevin O'Kelly* is found in volume 108 (1973) of the *Irish Law Times Reports* at page 97. These reports ceased in the 1970s, though the *Irish Law Times* continues as a legal magazine under different management.

The *Irish Jurist Reports* were published together with the Irish Jurist, an academic legal journal. These are cited: [1939] Ir.Jur.Rep. 82. This refers to the 1939 volume of the *Irish Jurist Reports* at page 82. These reports ceased publication in 1965, though the *Irish Jurist* continues to be published. In 1981 the *Irish Law Reports Monthly* first appeared. These are cited: [1981] ILRM 324. Thus on page 324 of the 1981 volume of the *Irish Law Reports Monthly,* the case of *Somjee v Minister for Justice*, is to be found.

TRIBUNALS

Exercise of Limited Judicial Powers

All legal disputes are not settled in courts by judges. The Constitution permits the exercise of limited functions and powers of a judicial nature by persons or bodies who are neither courts nor judges. Criminal matters must be disposed of by courts and judges. The administration of justice in this regard is only permitted where the function or power is of a limited nature. This restriction has no application where the court decides that a tribunal is exercising administrative rather than judicial powers. In *McDonald v Bord na gCon* (1965) the Supreme Court ruled that the banning of a person from a greyhound track was an administrative rather than a judicial decision.

Where it is a judicial matter only limited powers may be exercised. The Supreme Court ruled, in *In re O'Farrell* (1960), that the striking off of a solicitor from the roll of solicitors by the Law Society was not a limited power. Statute has transferred this function to the High Court. The High Court held, in *M. v The Medical Council* (1984), that the powers to advise, admonish or censure a doctor were limited powers of a judicial nature. The power to strike a doctor off the medical register was reserved to the High Court.

Control by the Courts of Administrative Tribunals

While the courts cannot review the evidence before a tribunal or substitute its verdict, the courts do exercise considerable control over how tribunals perform their functions. The courts insist that the tribunal should reach a conclusion on some evidence; the conclusion must be *bona fide* and the tribunal must observe fair procedures.

Scope and Types of Tribunals

The range and scope of functions carried out by tribunals, and their composition, are varied. Tribunals may consist of one person or a number of persons. They may hear oral evidence or may act on written submissions. Where oral evidence is heard the rules of evidence may be ignored and procedures familiar to courts may be departed from. Some tribunals may be established to inquire into a particular matter: the Tribunal of Inquiry into the Beef Industry, with a sole member, was to report to Dáil Éireann.

Other tribunals may adjudicate on rights. It is impossible to list all the tribunals which operate under a variety of statutes in this regard so some examples must suffice. Under the *Unfair Dismissals Act 1977*, as amended, the Employment Appeals Tribunal, a three-person body, hears cases from persons who allege unfair dismissal from their employment (see page 455).

An Bord Pleanála hears planning appeals against either the granting or refusing of a planning application (see page 267).

EUROPEAN CONVENTION ON HUMAN RIGHTS

Ireland and European Convention on Human Rights

Following the ending of World War II serious efforts were made to establish institutions in Europe which would co-operate on various matters to avoid a repetition of two devastating wars during the previous short period of forty years. The European Economic Community, now the European Union, is the most singularly successful institution (see Chapter 7, page 76). Another such institution, the Council of Europe, drafted a document on human rights, known as the *European Convention for the Protection of Human Rights and Fundamental Freedoms*. The Convention established a commission and a court and provided a mechanism to hear complaints by individuals against governments, who had signed the Convention, for alleged breaches of its provisions.

The Government of Ireland signed the Convention in Rome on 4 November 1950, ratified it in 1953 and recognised the competence of the Commission to receive petitions and recognised the jurisdiction of the court. The Convention came into force on 3 September 1953.

This Convention is not part of statute law; its provisions cannot be enforced and a breach cannot be remedied in our courts. An attempt to show that measures taken under a statute were contrary to the Convention failed in *In re Ó Láighléis* (1960) because, explained Maguire CJ. in the Supreme Court, 'the Oireachtas had not determined that the Convention of Human Rights . . . is to be part of the domestic law of the State' (see page 38).

A person who claims that some law or some administrative action is in breach of the Convention must first exhaust domestic remedies before initiating a claim. Should the complaint be upheld before the Commission or the Court, the State must amend the law or cease the administrative practice. One state may lodge a complaint against another state or an individual may lodge an application against his or her own state. The sole sanction against a state which fails to honour its obligations under the Convention is expulsion from the Council of Europe.

Ireland as a Party under the Convention

A case alleging breach of the Convention is initiated before the Commission. If deemed admissible an effort must be made to find a friendly resolution. Failing such agreement, the case proceeds on the merits before the Commission, and after a decision is given may be referred to the Court. Ireland has been a party before the European Court of Human Rights on a number of occasions. While internment without trial was held to have breached the Convention in *Lawless v Ireland* (1961), (Ó *Láighléis* of the previous paragraph) the Court held that the Government had derogated from its terms, which it could do in times of national emergency. The Convention was breached in *Airey v Ireland* (1979) because of the State's failure to provide legal aid in matrimonial matters. Legal aid is now available in matrimonial matters. The absence of divorce was held, in *Johnston v Ireland* (1987), not to breach the Convention, though the absence of succession rights for illegitimate persons was a breach of the right to respect family life. The *Status of Children Act 1987* provides illegitimate children with succession rights.

The criminalisation of certain sexual activities was held, in *Norris v Ireland* (1989), to have breached the guarantee of privacy. The *Criminal Law (Sexual Offences) Act 1993* repealed the offending laws (see page 147). Following the decision of the European Court of Human Rights in *Keegan v Ireland* (1994) that the unmarried father's exclusion from the adoption process breached the right to respect for family life, the *Adoption Act 1998* was enacted which confers consultation rights on the unmarried father in the adoption process (see page 287).

The only occasion on which one state successfully proved that another state breached the Convention was in *Ireland v United Kingdom* (1978) when the European Court of Human Rights held that inhuman and degrading treatment had been inflicted on some persons arrested for the purpose of being interned without trial in Northern Ireland.

Chapter 6

FUNDAMENTAL RIGHTS

Constitutional Rights

The Constitution declares that the individual is possessed of certain fundamental rights. In the last forty years it is these provisions of the Constitution which have produced a great welter of fertile litigation. Individuals have repeatedly sought the assistance of the courts in the protection of these rights and the courts have responded by declaring that these rights are real and paramount. The courts have held that these constitutional rights cannot be negatived by the State or by any other body or person.

Source of Constitutional Rights

For many years the view was held that the fundamental rights declared in the Constitution were not created by the Constitution because if they were, then by amendment, these rights could be negatived. According to Walsh J., in *McGee v Attorney General* (1974), 'the Constitution confirms . . . their existence and gives them protection. The individual has natural and human rights over which the State has no authority.' This traditional view, that the natural law was the fundamental law of the State and as such antecedent and superior to all positive law, including the Constitution, was rejected by the Supreme Court in *Art. 26 and the Regulation of Information (Services Outside the State for Termination of Pregnancies) Bill 1995.* Instead, that court took the view, according to Hamilton CJ., that 'the courts in interpreting the Constitution and in ascertaining and declaring what are the personal rights which are guaranteed by the Constitution and in determining, where necessary, the rights which are superior and antecedent to positive law or which are imprescriptible or inalienable, must . . . interpret them in accordance with their ideas of prudence, justice and charity.'

All Constitutional Rights Not Expressed

The question has arisen as to whether the fundamental rights expressed by the Constitution are the only fundamental rights of which the individual is possessed. For example, the right to marry is obviously a natural or human right though not expressed in the Constitution. According to Kenny J. in *Ryan v Attorney General* (1965) 'there are many personal rights of the citizens which follow from the Christian and democratic nature of the State which are not mentioned' in the Constitution.

Who then should declare these implied constitutional rights? Kenny J. in *Ryan's* case said: 'In modern times this would seem to be a function of the legislature rather than of the judicial power but it was done by the courts in the formative period of the common law and there is no reason why they should not do it now.'

Constitutional Rights cannot be Absolute

Common sense dictates that an individual cannot be possessed of an absolute constitutional right. If such were the case then other individuals would have no rights. Again according to Kenny J. in *Ryan's* case: 'None of the personal rights of the citizen are unlimited; their existence may be regulated by the Oireachtas when the common good requires this.' There are legal limitations on the exercise of all constitutional rights. The majority of the cases on constitutional rights are concerned with whether the restrictions are justified on the ground of the common good.

Constitutional Rights and Constitutional Duties

The existence of a constitutional right in one person implies a corresponding duty on the State and others to respect that right. 'Liberty to exercise a right, it seems to me', said Ó Dálaigh CJ. in *Educational Co. of Ireland v Fitzpatrick* (1961), '*prima facie* implies a correlative duty on others to abstain from interfering with the exercise of such right.'

Constitutional Rights can be Surrendered

Every individual waives, abandons or surrenders constitutional rights regularly and on a temporary basis. For example, a person going to work waives personal liberty, freedom of association and freedom of expression in return for the benefits which employment brings. To take the more serious step of a permanent surrender of a constitutional right, the view seems to be that this can be done provided the individual has clear knowledge of what is being done and understands the consequences of that action.

A Hierarchy of Constitutional Rights

Each constitutional right has the same status and value. It is impossible to elevate one right above the others or to subjugate any one right to the other rights. Accepting this principle, a difficulty arises where the exercise of constitutional rights by different individuals collides. The advancement of one right by one individual may be to the detriment of a different right of another individual. This dilemma is illustrated in *The People (DPP) v Shaw*

(1982) where the constitutional right to life of one individual clashed with the constitutional right to personal liberty of another. In the Supreme Court, Griffin J. explained: 'Where such a conflict arises, a choice must be made and it is the duty of the State to protect what is the more important right, even at the expense of another important, but less important, right. The State must therefore weigh each right for the purpose of evaluating the merits of each, and strike a balance between them, and having done so take such steps as are necessary to protect the more important right.'

In *Attorney General v X* (1992) the right to life of the unborn child clashed with the equal right to life of the mother, which was threatened by suicide. The Supreme Court decided that the right to life of the mother took precedence over the right to life of the unborn child. Obviously each case must be judged on its merits, and it cannot follow that, as a general rule, any particular right will take precedence over other rights.

The Availability of Constitutional Rights

Some fundamental rights are declared to attach to citizens while others attach to persons. The availability of these rights to non-citizens has been canvassed in some cases and ignored in others. The courts in *The State (Nicolaou) v An Bord Uchtála* (1966), a case on adoption, and *Somjee v Minister for Justice* (1981), a case on citizenship, refused to decide the issue. On the other hand, in *The State (McFadden) v Governor of Mountjoy Prison* (1981) the High Court held that a non-citizen was entitled to avail of the right to fair procedures in extradition matters, and in *The State (Trimbole) v Governor of Mountjoy Prison* (1985) the Supreme Court afforded a non-citizen the constitutional protections relating to personal liberty. The High Court, in *Northampton County Council v A.B.F.* (1982), afforded a non-citizen the constitutional right relating to the family. The courts have decided that constitutional rights which are conferred on citizens are not available to recognised legal entities such as companies, local authorities and statutory bodies.

Remedies for Breach of Constitutional Rights

Should an individual feel aggrieved by the operation of a particular law, a declaration may be sought in the High Court to have it declared unconstitutional. The consequence of a successful challenge is that the law is null and void and cannot be enforced against any individual. For example, following the successful challenge in *McGee v Attorney General* (1974) the impugned law could not be used to prevent the plaintiff and other married persons having access to artificial contraception.

An individual may be released from detention because the law is unconstitutional: in *The State (Sheerin) v Kennedy* (1966) a prisoner was released after the law, under which he was imprisoned, was declared unconstitutional (see page 130). The same result may occur where the State has not observed some constitutional procedure: in *The State (Gilliland) v Governor of Mountjoy Prison* (1986) an extradition order was quashed because the constitutional requirement to have the extradition treaty approved by Dáil Éireann was not observed (see page 38).

An aggrieved individual may complain, by way of application to the High Court under Article 40 of the Constitution, that his or her detention is not in accordance with law: in *The State (Trimbole) v Governor of Mountjoy Prison* (1985) the provisions of section 30 of the *Offences Against the State Act 1939* were used as an excuse to detain an individual pending extradition proceedings, and the courts ordered his release. The subsequent extradition order, valid in itself, could not retrieve the situation because it was tainted with the original illegality.

PERSONAL RIGHTS

Equality Before the Law

The Constitution declares that all citizens shall, as human persons be held equal before the law. But the State may, in its laws, have regard to the differences of capacity, physical and moral, and of social function between citizens. This guarantee cannot mean that all laws must apply to all citizens regardless of age, ability, capacity or status. It means that the laws must not invidiously discriminate, which is defined as unjust, unreasonable or arbitrary, between citizens. An individual, by reason of his or her human attributes or ethnic or racial, social or religious background, is not to be treated as the inferior or superior of other individuals in society. There have been many cases in which this guarantee was pleaded, but two such cases will illustrate the courts' response. In *O'G. v Attorney General* (1985) a provision which prohibited a widower, in certain circumstances, from adopting a child already in his custody, fell foul of this guarantee. The High Court held that widowers as a class were no less competent than widows to provide for the material needs of children, and their exclusion as a class must have been based on a belief that a woman, by virtue of her sex, had an innate capacity for parenthood which was denied to a man and the lack of which rendered a man unsuitable as an adopter.

The Supreme Court decided, in *McKinley v Minister for Defence* (1992), that a common law rule which allowed a husband to sue a wrongdoer for the loss of the consortium of his wife because of injuries caused to her and did not extend a similar right of action to a wife was discriminatory. The court ruled that the right of action should be available to both spouses.

Apart from the area of employment, where discrimination is outlawed on the ground of sex, there are no laws which prohibit discrimination on the grounds of sex, religion, race, creed, colour, age or sexual orientation.

Right to Life of the Unborn

Because the sanctity of human life is recognised in all civilised societies, based on the nature of man, the express right to life is one of the fundamental rights recognised and protected by the Constitution.

The express right to life of the unborn was inserted into the Constitution by an amendment in 1983. The equal right to life of the mother is also acknowledged. Which right prevails when the two conflict was considered in *Attorney General v X* (1992). The Supreme Court ruled that the right to life of the mother, a fourteen-year-old girl who was suicidal, prevailed over her unborn child's right to life.

Two amendments were added to the Constitution in 1992. The first provides that the guarantees granted to the unborn of the right to life and the mother's right to life shall not limit freedom to travel between this State and another state. The second provides that these rights shall not limit freedom to obtain or make available in this State, subject to such conditions as may be laid down by law, information relating to services lawfully available in another state. The *Regulation of Information (Services outside the State for Termination of Pregnancies) Act 1995* is the relevant law which the Supreme Court advised the President was constitutional: *Article 26 and the Regulation of Information (Services outside the State for the Termination of Pregnancies) Bill 1995.*

Right to Die

As the process of dying is part, and an ultimate inevitable consequence of life, the right to life necessarily implies the right to have nature take its course and to die a natural death. This right did not include the right to have life terminated or death accelerated and was confined to the natural process of dying. The Supreme Court decided, in *In re a Ward of Court* (1995), that life was not to be artificially maintained by the provision of nourishment by abnormal artificial means which had no curative effect and which was intended merely to prolong life, unless the individual concerned so wished.

Right to Bodily Integrity

This right to bodily integrity was first expounded in *Ryan v Attorney General* (1965), though on the evidence presented in that case it was held that the fluoridation of the public water supply was not an interference with that right. This right was acknowledged to be possessed by prisoners and was extended in *The State (Richardson) v Governor of Mountjoy Prison* (1980) to include the right of those in custody not to have their health endangered.

Freedom to Travel

The right to travel outside the State was established in *The State (K.M.) v Minister for Foreign Affairs* (1979) where a statute which prevented an illegitimate child under the age of one year from travelling outside the State with anyone except the mother was held unconstitutional. This principle was applied in *Lennon v Ganley* (1981) where an injunction to prevent the Irish rugby team from travelling to South Africa was refused.

Personal Liberty

The Constitution guarantees that no citizen is to be deprived of liberty save in accordance with law. Various statutes, and the common law, permit the arrest and detention of the individual in certain circumstances. Some of these powers are examined on page 166 when looking at trespass to the person. Should the law grant a power of arrest which is abused, various remedies are available to the wronged party. The Supreme Court ruled in *The State (Trimbole) v Governor of Mountjoy Prison* (1985) that a wronged party is entitled, as far as possible, to be put in the position he or she was in before the wrongful act. In that case the wronged party was set at liberty.

An Order under Article 40 of the Constitution

Habeas corpus, the most celebrated remedy for the violation of personal liberty developed by the common law, is enshrined in Article 40 of the Constitution. The High Court shall, on a complaint being made to it by or on behalf of any person that he/she is unlawfully detained, order the person in whose custody he/she is to produce that person before the court and to certify in writing the grounds of detention. The High Court must, once the person is produced and on giving the detainer an opportunity to justify the detention, order the release of the person detained unless satisfied that such detention is in accordance with law.

The Supreme Court decided, in *The State (Rogers) v Galvin* (1983), that the High Court cannot make an order for release without affording the detainer an opportunity to be heard. The Supreme Court ruled, in *The State (Trimbole) v Governor of Mountjoy Prison* (1985) (see page 67), that once the High Court ordered the release of a detained person, a stay could not be put on that order pending an appeal to the Supreme Court. Where the appeal was successful, and the High Court had wrongfully released a person, the Supreme Court could order a rearrest.

This process may be directed against any person or institution. It has been used to question a child's detention in a children's home; to determine the legality of detention by the gardaí; to test detention by the prison authorities; to test detention in a mental hospital; and applied for by one parent against the other where the custody of a child was in issue.

The Constitution declares that this process cannot be invoked to prohibit, control or interfere with any act of the Defence Forces during the existence of a state of war or armed rebellion (see page 22).

Freedom of Expression

The Constitution guarantees to the citizen the right to express freely their convictions and opinions. Because the education of public opinion is a matter affecting the common good, the State may endeavour that the organs of public opinion, while preserving their rightful liberty of expression including the criticism of government policy, are not to be used to undermine public order or public morality or the authority of the State.

In the *Attorney General for England and Wales v Brandon Book Publishers Ltd* (1987), it was argued that the publication of the memoirs of a deceased member of the British Intelligence Service would be a breach of confidentiality which existed between employer and employee. The High Court ruled that since no question of public order or morality or the authority of this State being undermined arose, there was no authority in the court to prevent publication.

The defence of the integrity of the State is an integral part of government. The Supreme Court, in *The State (Lynch) v Cooney* (1982), upheld the decision to refrain RTÉ by an order under the Broadcasting Authority Act 1960, as amended, from transmitting election broadcasts by Sinn Féin candidates in a general election. The ban was justified on the ground that other members of the organisation had been convicted of serious offences and others had said certain things on previous occasions. 'It follows', said O'Higgins CJ., 'that the use of such organs of opinion for the purpose of securing or advocating support for organisations which seek by violence to overthrow the State or its institutions is a use which is prohibited by the Constitution.'

There are many curtailments by law on freedom of expression. The *Broadcasting Authority Act 1961*, as amended, permits the prohibition of broadcasts of matter which would be likely to promote, or incite to crime, or would tend to undermine the authority of the State. The *Offences Against the State Act 1939* makes it unlawful to set up in type, print, publish, send through the post, distribute, sell or offer for sale any document which contains anything incriminating, treasonable or seditious (see page 140). The *Offences Against the State (Amendment) Act 1972* makes it an offence to publish an oral or written statement which constitutes an interference with the course of justice. It is a contempt of court to publish any matter which is *sub-judice*: under judicial consideration. The communication of official information is a crime (see page 140).

To preserve public order, it is an offence to use insulting or threatening words which amount to a breach of the peace. According to the *Prohibition of Incitement to Hatred Act 1989*, it is an offence to use words, written or visual images or sounds so as to stir up hatred against persons on account of their race, colour, nationality, religion, ethnic or national origins, membership of the travelling community or sexual orientation.

To preserve public morality, blasphemy (see page 140) and obscenity (see page 141) are crimes. Censorship of publications is governed by the *Censorship of Publications Acts 1923–1967*. The censorship of films was established by the *Censorship of Films Acts 1923–1992. The Video Recordings Act 1989* regulates the sale, hire and supply of video recordings.

Right to Communicate

The right to express convictions and opinions freely contains, by implication, the complementary right of having those views communicated to, and received by, other individuals. This right was upheld in *Attorney General v Paperlink Ltd* (1984) where the High Court ruled that since the act of communication was the exercise of such a basic human faculty, a right to communicate must inhere in an individual by virtue of human personality and must be guaranteed by the Constitution. The High Court, in *Carrigaline Community Television Broadcasting Co. Ltd v Minister for Transport* (1997), decided that both private citizens and the media are constitutionally protected, in expressing freely, not merely their own opinions, but also the opinions of others.

Freedom of Assembly

The Constitution guarantees to the citizen the right to assemble peaceably and without arms. The exercise of this right is subject to public order and morality.

The law prevents or controls meetings which are calculated to cause a riot or breach of the peace. A meeting on private property without the consent of the owner is a trespass. It is a public nuisance to obstruct the highway with a meeting, though a parade or procession is not unlawful. The offence of 'watching and besetting' is committed when premises are picketed, though picketing in furtherance of a trade dispute is permitted: *Industrial Relations Act 1990* (see page 470).

It is an offence under the *Offences Against the State Act 1939* to hold a meeting or procession in any public place within one-half mile of the Oireachtas, where either House is sitting, which has been prohibited by a garda not below the rank of chief superintendent and a garda calls on those taking part to disperse. It is an offence to picket a court.

Freedom of Association

The Constitution guarantees to the citizen, subject to public order and morality, the right to form associations and unions. The types of organisations which may be formed are unlimited. These may be for a sporting, social, charitable, commercial and political purpose.

Except in the area of employment law, it is for the members of an organisation to decide on their fellow members. There is no law which prohibits discrimination on the ground of sex, class, colour and creed.

As regards the freedom to form associations and trade unions much more is said on the topic on page 468. As with other rights, law may curtail the scope of this guarantee. For example, associations formed for treasonable, anti-constitutional or illegal purposes cannot claim this freedom of association.

Religious Liberty

The Constitution declares that the State acknowledges that the homage of public worship is due to Almighty God: it will hold his Name in reverence and will respect and honour religion. Freedom to practise religion, and freedom of conscience are, subject to public order and morality, guaranteed to every citizen.

The State guarantees not to endow any particular religion and not to impose any discrimination on the ground of religious belief. The Supreme Court, in *Quinn's Supermarket Ltd v Attorney General* (1972), declared unconstitutional a statutory instrument which controlled the opening hours of meat shops because it discriminated in favour of kosher meat shops, used by the Jewish community, and against those shops which serviced the rest of the community. In *Mulloy v Minister for Education* (1975) a scheme which gave salary credits to lay teachers who served abroad and denied the plaintiff, a teacher and a Catholic priest who had served abroad, was declared unconstitutional.

Legislation providing aid for schools must not discriminate between schools under the management of different denominations, nor should such legislation affect prejudicially the right of any child to attend a school receiving public money without attending religious instruction at that school.

The property of a religious denomination shall not be diverted save for necessary works of public utility and only on payment of compensation.

Family Rights

The Constitution guarantees family rights with regard to marriage, and education. These are discussed in Part Eight, under Family Law (see page 272).

Property Rights

The Constitution declares that man has the natural right, which is superior to positive law, to the private ownership of property. In recognition of this right, the State guarantees to pass no law to abolish this right, or the general right to transfer, bequeath and inherit property. But the State also recognises that the exercise of the right to private property may, in civil society, be regulated by the principles of social justice and, accordingly their exercise may be delimited when the common good so requires. The State shall, in particular, by its laws protect as best it may from unjust attack and, in the case of injustice done, vindicate the property rights of every citizen.

The courts have decided that where any property right is abolished or restricted the absence of compensation will make the law invalid where it constitutes an unjust attack on property rights. The courts have ruled that where any right is abolished or restricted, the absence of compensation will make the law invalid where it constitutes an unjust attack on property rights.

There are many legal restrictions on the exercise of contractual rights. The Supreme Court, in *Blake v Attorney General* (1981), held unconstitutional laws which restricted recovery of premises and prohibited rent increases as an unjust attack on the property rights of landlords.

The law may place restrictions on the use to which property may be put. The High Court ruled, in *Central Dublin Development Association v Attorney General* (1975), that town and regional planning was an attempt to reconcile the exercise of property rights with the demands of the common good. The Supreme Court held, in *O'Callaghan v Commissioners of Public Works* (1985), that restrictions placed on a landowner on whose land a national monument stood were for the common good.

Laws may provide for the compulsory acquisition of property. A statute which permitted the creation of a burden on land by the erection of electricity pylons was held unconstitutional by the Supreme Court in *ESB v Gormley* (1985) because compensation was not paid. In *Dreher v Irish Land Commission* (1984) the payment in land bonds rather than money for land compulsorily acquired was held constitutional.

Laws provide an intricate system of taxation. The Supreme Court found, in *Brennan v Attorney General* (1984), that the valuation system on which agricultural rates was assessed was unconstitutional because it lacked uniformity and could not be revised. The Supreme Court decided, in *Madigan v Attorney General* (1986), that the residential property tax was constitutional in that it only extended to more expensive dwellings and was only payable by those with a stated minimum income.

Right to Earn a Livelihood

The unspecified constitutional right to earn a livelihood was first acknowledged in *Murtagh Properties Ltd v Cleary* (1972) where a demand, backed by the threat of a picket, was made that women should not be employed as bar-workers solely because they were women. The High Court held this threat breached the women's constitutional right. A statute which creates a business monopoly in favour of one party effectively prevents others from providing a similar service. Such a statute which granted a monopoly to An Post to carry letters was, in *Attorney General v Paperlink Ltd* (1984), held to be constitutional.

Statute may render certain activities criminal, of which gaming is one. It was claimed, in *Cafolla v Attorney General* (1985), that the restriction placed on the monetary limits as to the stake and prize money from gaming machines, valid when the law was enacted, had by inflation infringed the right to earn a livelihood. The Supreme Court rejected this claim because the common good required strict control on the facilities for gaming. Where a party voluntarily contracts for employment it is not a breach of this right where the employer refuses to allow the employee to abandon the contract. This was decided by the High Court in *Egan v Minister for Defence* (1988) where an army officer was not allowed to retire early and thus claim a gratuity and pension, though he could resign at any time.

The restrictions placed on casual trading in public places was considered to be constitutional in *Hand v Dublin Corporation* (1991). The Supreme Court ruled, in *Lovett v Gogan* (1995), that the holder of a licence was entitled to an injunction to prevent non-licensed persons from carrying passengers on the same route because it breached the constitutional right to earn a livelihood.

Inviolability of Dwelling

The Constitution declares that the dwelling of the citizen is inviolable and shall not be forcibly entered save in accordance with law. In *Director of Public Prosecutions v Gaffney* (1988) the gardaí entered a dwelling without a warrant, other legal authority or invitation to make an arrest. The Supreme Court ruled that the arrest effected on foot of that unlawful and unconstitutional entry was illegal. In *The People (DPP) v Kenny* (1990) the Supreme Court ruled that evidence obtained in a drugs raid on a dwelling was inadmissible at the trial because the search warrant was defective (see page 56).

Right to Fair Procedures

One of the implied rights developed by the courts is that of fair procedures. This means that courts, and all other bodies or persons making decisions which affect the individual, must act fairly. The common law developed the rules of natural justice which the courts have used as the corner-stone in developing the right to fair procedures.

The first rule of natural justice is *nemo judex in sua causa*: never be a judge in one's own cause. The party making the decision should be without bias or without the appearance of bias. Where it was alleged that a student had committed plagiarism, which was denied, the High Court held, in *Flanagan v University College Dublin* (1989), that the complainant, the Registrar of the College should not have deliberated with the Committee of Discipline which had been established to decide the issue.

The second natural justice rule is *audi alteram partem*: hear both sides. A party affected by a decision must be given an adequate opportunity to present a case. To adequately do so, that party must be informed of the matter and must be afforded an opportunity to comment on the material put forward by the other side. The hearing need not be oral. In *The State (Ingle) v O'Brien* (1975) the revocation of a taxi driver's small-vehicle licence was declared invalid because no notice of the intention to revoke the licence was given and the taxi driver had no opportunity to oppose the revocation. This rule has been invoked to protect office holders from being pre-emptively dismissed from office. In *Garvey v Ireland* (1979) the Commissioner of the Garda Síochána had his removal from office by the Government declared invalid because he was not given any opportunity to make representations before his removal. See also *The State (Gleeson) v Minister for Defence* on page 45.

Chapter 7
THE EUROPEAN UNION

Background to the Union

Following the devastation of two major wars and the colonial decline of European states, the notion that European nations could cordially live together finally dawned. The Treaty of Paris, signed in 1951, established the first inter-European community: the European Coal and Steel Community. While this merely dealt with two commodities, it was the impetus needed to attempt a more ambitious and grand scheme of European economic co-operation. These efforts culminated in the Treaty of Rome, signed in 1957 by France, Germany, Italy, Belgium, the Netherlands and Luxembourg.

Ireland became a member of the European Economic Community on 1 January 1973, following a referendum which was held on 10 May 1972 to amend the Constitution to allow for membership. The United Kingdom and Denmark joined at the same time. The European Union (EU) was further extended by the membership of Greece in 1981, of Spain and Portugal in 1986, and by Finland, Sweden and Austria in 1995, bringing the total membership to fifteen. Other European countries will join over the coming years.

The Constitution was further amended to allow Ireland to ratify: (a) the *Single European Act* (1987); and (b) the Treaty on European Union, commonly known as the Maastricht Treaty (1992); and, (c) the Amsterdam Treaty (1998), which made limited, but important, amendments to the existing treaties.

Aims of the European Community Treaty

The EU is founded on the general principles of liberty, democracy, human rights and fundamental freedoms and the rule of law. More specifically, the EU 'shall have as its task, by establishing a common market and an economic and monetary union and by implementing the common policies or activities . . . to promote throughout the Union a harmonious and balanced development of economic activities, sustainable and non-inflationary growth respecting the environment, a high degree of convergence of economic performance, a high level of employment and of social protection, the raising of the standard of living and quality of life, and economic and social cohesion and solidarity among member states.'

INSTITUTIONS OF THE EUROPEAN UNION

The European Parliament

The European Parliament, is directly elected every five years by the people of the EU, and exercises the powers conferred upon it by the treaties. The Parliament must hold an annual session, and may meet in extraordinary session at the request of a majority of its members or at the request of the Council or the Commission.

The Parliament shall participate in the process leading up to the adoption of EU acts by exercising its powers under the procedures laid down and by giving its assent or delivering advisory opinions. The Parliament may question the Commission, debate in open session the annual report of the Commission and force the Commission to resign. The Parliament may pass resolutions on matters it considers appropriate, though these have no legal standing. As noted below the Council must consult the Parliament on particular issues.

While the Parliament is elected by popular franchise, there is no uniformity of representation. Ireland elects fifteen members to the Parliament: Munster, five; Dublin, four; Leinster, three; and Connacht/Ulster, three.

The Council of Ministers

The Council is the real power in the EU despite additional powers being conferred on the Parliament. To ensure that the objectives set out in the treaties are attained, the Council must ensure co-ordination of general economic policies of the member states, have power to take decisions, and confer on the Commission, in the acts which the Council adopts, powers for the implementation of the rules which the Council lays down. The Council may reserve the right, in specific cases, to exercise directly by implementing powers itself. The procedures used must be consonant with principles and rules laid down in advance by the Council, acting unanimously on a proposal from the Commission and after obtaining the opinion of the Parliament.

The Council consists of a representative of each member state at ministerial level, authorised to commit the government of that member state. The Council is presided over by a President, an office which rotates around the member states every six months. Decisions must be unanimous in some instances and by qualified majority in others.

The European Commission

To ensure the proper functioning and development of the EU, the Commission must ensure that the provisions of the treaties and the measures taken by the institutions pursuant thereto are applied, formulate recommendations or deliver opinions on matters dealt with in the treaties, if it expressly so provides or if the Commission considers it necessary, have its own power of decision and participate in the shaping of measures taken by the Council and by the European Parliament in the manner provided for in the treaties, and exercise the powers conferred on it by the Council for the implementation of the rules laid down by the Council. In doing so it may instigate proceedings before the Court of Justice for a decision as to whether its provisions have been breached. Another significant power is the exclusive right of initiative concerning EU legislation.

The Commission consists of twenty members nominated by the governments of the member states. The large countries all nominate two Commissioners each and the other countries, like Ireland, nominate one. It is independent. Commissioners serve for five years which is renewable. There is a President. The President and the other members of the Commission thus nominated are subject as a body to a vote of approval by the Parliament. The Commission acts by a majority of its members.

The European Court of Justice

The Court of Justice has the task of interpreting the treaties and the laws governing the EU. The court has been active in three main areas. The Commission, or a member state, may claim in proceedings that another member state has not observed the treaties. The court exercises control over the other institutions of the Union at the request of a member state or an individual. Courts and tribunals of the member states may seek the court's view by way of preliminary ruling on the interpretation of the Treaty. Irish courts have done so on many occasions.

The court consists of fifteen judges with at least one from each member state. It issues a single judgment. The court is not bound by the rule of *stare decisis* or precedent as Irish courts are (see page 58). Judges serve for four years. The court is assisted by Advocates General whose duty it is, acting with complete impartiality and independence, to make, in open court, reasoned submissions on cases brought before the Court of Justice, in order to assist it in the performance of its task. An Advocate General does not participate in the deliberations of the court.

A Court of First Instance is attached to the Court of Justice with jurisdiction to hear and determine at first instance, subject to a right of appeal to the Court of Justice on points of law only in certain classes of action.

The European Court of Justice should not be confused with the European Court of Human Rights, which is a different and distinct institution (page 62).

The Court of Auditors

The Court of Auditors carries out the audit by examining the accounts of all revenue and expenditure of the EU. The Court of Auditors must provide the Parliament and the Council with a statement of assurance as to the reliability of the accounts and the legality and regularity of the underlying transactions.

Members are completely independent in the performance of their duties. They must neither seek nor take instructions from any government or from any other body.

SOURCES OF EUROPEAN UNION LAW

Primary Source

The primary source of EU law is the treaties. While there are other sources of law, this primary source is paramount in every respect. In instances of conflict the treaties prevail.

Secondary Source

In order to carry out their task and in accordance with the provisions of the treaties, the Parliament acting jointly with the Council and the Commission shall make regulations and issue directives, take decisions, make recommendations or deliver opinions (Articles 189–92). These secondary sources of law cannot conflict with the treaties and where any measure does it is null and void. There are different sources of secondary laws.

A regulation has general application and is binding in its entirety and directly applicable in all member states. The regulation is the true method by which the institutions of the EU legislate. Regulations are applicable in member states without any further action by a national body. A regulation must be published in the Official Journal of the Community and enters into force on the date specified therein.

A directive is binding as to the result to be achieved upon each member state, but it leaves to the national authority the choice of form and methods. In Ireland some legislative acts, such as an Act of the Oireachtas or a statutory instrument, are required to implement directives.

A decision is binding in its entirety upon those to whom it is addressed. A decision is addressed to a limited and defined group of persons. A recommendation or an opinion has no binding force.

Judgments of the Court of Justice

Unlike Irish courts which apply the common law doctrine of precedent (see page 58) the Court of Justice follows the civil law system whereby one court does not bind other courts and a court is not bound to follow its own previous decisions. While the Court of Justice is not bound by its own previous decisions the judgments of that court form a corpus of EU law of major significance. Apart from the actual decision in each individual case, the court pronounces on matters of general importance to the institutions of the Union.

INTEGRATION OF EUROPEAN UNION LAW INTO IRISH LAW

Constitutional Amendment

Over the years Ireland signed many international agreements. On each such occasion was it necessary to amend the Constitution? If not, why was it necessary to amend the Constitution to facilitate membership of the European Union? The reason was that the Community is possessed of law-making institutions. The Constitution provides that the Oireachtas is the sole legislature for the State. Consequently, to allow the measures effected by the EU to have the force of law in the State it was imperative to amend the Constitution, which has occurred on three occasions. Membership has resulted in the surrender of sovereignty in a number of respects, including legislative sovereignty, to institutions not established by the Constitution. Part of Article 29.4.3° of the Constitution reads: 'No provision of this Constitution invalidates laws enacted, acts done or measures adopted by the State necessitated by the obligations of membership of the European Union or of the Communities, or prevents laws enacted, acts done or measures adopted by the European Union or by the Communities or institutions thereof, or by bodies competent under the Treaties establishing the Communities, from having the force of law in the State.'

The amendment of the Constitution did three things. First, it enabled the State to join the EU, and its predecessors. Second, it protects from constitutional challenge acts necessitated by membership of the EU. Third, the provisions of the Constitution cannot prevent the laws of the EU from having the force of law in the State.

Statute Law

The *European Communities Act 1972*, as amended, provides that the treaties governing the EU and the existing and future Acts adopted by the institution of the Union shall be binding on the State and shall be part of the domestic law thereof under the conditions laid down in those treaties.

Many Acts of the Oireachtas have been enacted, and hundreds of statutory instruments have been made because of our membership of the EU.

In the Judicial Domain
Irish courts must implement principles, rules and regulations of the Union. A party in legal proceedings can raise EU law to displace an Irish legal rule to the contrary. Where a question of EU law is raised in an Irish court, the matter may be referred for an authoritative opinion to the Court of Justice. All our courts which exercise civil jurisdictions have referred questions to the Court of Justice for advice.

FOUNDATIONS OF THE EUROPEAN UNION

Citizenship of the Union (Article 8)
Every person holding the nationality of a member state shall be a citizen of the Union. Citizens of the Union shall enjoy the rights conferred by the Treaty and shall be subject to the duties imposed thereby. Citizens of the Union may vote in elections for members of the Parliament and have the right to petition the Parliament.

Free Movement of Goods (Articles 9–37)
The Union is based on a customs union which is to cover all trade in goods and shall involve the prohibition between member states of customs duties on imports and exports and of all charges having equivalent effect, and the adoption of a common customs tariff in their relations with third countries. Member states must refrain from introducing between themselves any new customs duty on imports or exports or any charges having equivalent effect, and from increasing those which they already apply in trade with each other. Quantitative restrictions on imports and all measures having equivalent effect shall be prohibited between member states.

Agriculture (Articles 38–47)
The operation and development of the common market for agricultural products is to be accompanied by the establishment of a common agricultural policy (CAP) among the member states.

Free Movement of Persons (Articles 48–51)
The free movement of workers is to be secured within the EU. This right entails, subject to limitations justified on grounds of public policy, public security or public health, the right to accept offers of employment actually made, to move freely within the Union for this purpose, to stay in a member state for the purpose of employment, and to remain in the member state after having been employed in that state.

Right of Establishment (Articles 52–8)

Freedom of establishment includes the right to take up and pursue activities as self-employed persons and to set up and manage undertakings, firms and companies.

Free Movement of Services (Articles 59–66)

Restrictions on the freedom to provide services within the EU are to be progressively abolished. Services include activities of (a) an industrial character; (b) a commercial character; (c) craftsmen; and (d) the professions.

Free Movement of Capital (Articles 67–73)

Member states are to progressively abolish between themselves all restrictions on the movement of capital belonging to persons resident in member states.

POLICY OF THE EUROPEAN UNION

Rules on Competition (Articles 85–94)

The following are prohibited as incompatible with the common market: all agreements between undertakings, decisions by associations of undertakings and concerted practices which may affect trade between member states and which have as their object or effect the prevention, restriction or distortion of competition within the common market. Any abuse by one or more undertakings of a dominant position within the common market or in a substantial part of it is prohibited as incompatible with the common market in so far as it may affect trade between member states.

Tax Provisions (Articles 95–102)

A member state cannot impose, directly or indirectly, on the products of other member states any internal taxation of any kind in excess of that imposed directly or indirectly on similar domestic products. Furthermore, a member state cannot impose on products of other member states any internal taxation of such a nature as to afford indirect protection to other products.

Economic and Monetary Policy (Articles 102a–116)

Member states must conduct their economic policies with a view to contributing to the achievement of the objectives of the EU. The member states and the EU shall act in accordance with the principle of an open market economy with free competition and favouring an efficient allocation of resources. To achieve the free movement of goods, labour and capital, it is necessary to harmonise the diverse national laws which operate in each member state. The aim is to remove distortions which hinder the achievement of the objectives of the EU rather than the total unification of the laws of member states.

Social Provisions (Articles 117–28)

Member states agree on the need to promote improved working conditions and an improved standard of living for workers so as to make possible their harmonisation while the improvement is maintained. The Commission has the task of promoting close co-operation between member states in the social field, particularly in matters relating to: (a) employment; (b) labour law and working conditions; (c) basic and advanced vocational training; (d) social security; (e) prevention of occupational accidents and disease; (f) occupational hygiene; and (g) the right of association, and collective bargaining between employers and workers. Member states must ensure the application of the principle that men and women receive equal pay for equal work.

Part Two
THE LAW OF CONTRACT

Chapter 8

FORMATION OF CONTRACT

Nature of a Contract

A contract is an agreement giving rise to obligations enforced or recognised by law. A contract exists when legally capable persons have reached agreement, or where the law considers them to have reached agreement. A valid contract attaches rights and obligations to each party. The law of contract, substantially judge-made law, concerns itself with all contracts. Not alone does it apply to contracts worth considerable sums of money, but the same rules govern simple contracts, such as the purchase of a newspaper, having a haircut or taking a bus journey.

The agreement of the parties is the feature which distinguishes a contract from other legal obligations. While in theory the parties are free to contract in whatever way they please, it is only to be expected in reality that the law, both statute law and common law, will regulate this area of law with rules which govern either the substance or the form of particular contracts. For example, the common law attempts to protect young persons from onerous contracts, and contracts contrary to the common good are illegal. Statute law has regulated certain contracts, particularly in the area of consumer protection such as the sale of goods, with the Oireachtas laying down major rules which impinge on freedom of contract and the non-observance of which has serious consequences for one of the contracting parties.

Form of a Contract

There is a widespread misconception that a contract is invalid and unenforceable unless all or some part of it is in writing. It is commonplace to hear expressions such as, 'ah well, since I didn't sign anything I'm not bound'. Unless a special form is required by statute law (some of which are discussed later on page 93), a contract may be in any form whatsoever. The parties to the contract dictate both the form and the contents. Thus a contract may be in writing; or it may be verbal; or it may be by inference from the conduct of the parties; or it may be by some combination of these three forms. For example, the hire-purchase of a television will be in writing, the purchase of a bunch of flowers will be verbal, and a contract will be inferred where a motorist serves himself or herself petrol in a self-service garage.

The more valuable the contract the greater the likelihood that it will be reduced into writing. But common sense dictates that commercial life would grind to a halt should every contract, even of the simplest nature, be reduced into writing. It cannot be stressed too often that a verbal contract is as binding as a written one, and that the principles of contract law are similarly applicable.

Essentials of a Contract

For a contract to be valid, and therefore binding on the parties, it must be possessed of three essential ingredients. They are: (i) an agreement; (ii) an intention to be contractually bound; and (iii) consideration. Whether all or any of these ingredients are present is a question of fact to be deduced from the circumstances in each particular case. To assist in this inquiry, in instances of disputes between the parties, the courts have developed certain well-settled rules.

AGREEMENT

Parties must be Ad Idem

The first essential of a valid contract is an agreement between the parties. Should a dispute arise, it becomes necessary to discover whether an agreement had been reached, and what were its terms. This is achieved by a close examination of the negotiations surrounding the transaction. The court seeks to ascertain whether the parties were *ad idem*: agreed on the essential point. In *J.L. Smallman & Co. Ltd v O'Moore* (1959) a buyer, when sued for the price of goods supplied, resisted the claim on the ground that the goods had been supplied to a company and not to him personally. The High Court held that the parties were not *ad idem* in that the seller thought it was supplying goods to a partnership, whereas the buyer had contracted on behalf of a company. To assist in resolving this question as to whether agreement was reached, the court will subdivide the inquiry into whether there was both an offer and an acceptance.

Existence of an Offer

An offer exists where the party making the offer undertakes to be contractually bound, should a proper acceptance be made by the party to whom the offer is made. To constitute an effective offer, the terms must be unconditional, clear and certain. In *Russell & Laird Ltd v Hoban* (1922) a sale note, subject to confirmation, was given when goods were ordered. Later, when the buyer sent a contract note confirming the sale note, but with variations, the seller cancelled the order. It was held that the offer was merely conditional and had not been accepted by the seller. It was held in *Boyers & Co. v Duke* (1905) that a mere quotation is not an offer, but it was decided by the High Court, in *Dooley v T.L. Egan & Co. Ltd* (1938), that a quotation coupled with the words 'subject to immediate acceptance' did constitute a valid offer.

An offer may be made to an individual, or to a specific group, as in *Billings v Arnott & Co.* (1946) where an offer was made by the company to its employees, or to the world at large as in *Kennedy v London Express Newspapers Ltd* (1931) where the offer was made to the readers of a newspaper.

An Invitation to Treat

An offer must be distinguished from a mere 'invitation to treat', which has been defined as a first step in negotiations which may, or may not, be a prelude to a firm offer being made by one of the parties. A sign outside a farm which reads 'Tomatoes for Sale', or a sign outside a garage which reads 'Open for Petrol' are invitations to treat and do not constitute offers.

The display of items in a shop window, with or without a price attached, is an invitation to treat. A prospective buyer cannot compel the sale of the goods because an offer has not been made. The display is a possible prelude to a sale, but negotiations must first take place. A notice attached to an article displayed in a shop window, with a cash price and a weekly sum, was not, according to the High Court, in the *Minister for Industry and Commerce v Pim Bros* (1966), an offer for sale, but an invitation to treat for the sale of the goods with an indication that credit facilities were available. Similarly, the display of goods on the shelves of a supermarket is merely an invitation to treat. The customer makes an offer to buy when the goods are carried to the cash-desk, which the assistant may accept or reject. Where the goods are incorrectly priced, the customer cannot insist on the sale of the goods at that, or indeed, any price.

Communication of Offer

An offer is invalid unless and until it is communicated. This communication may take any form. It may be verbal, in writing, or be implied from conduct. Many offers will be made verbally, in shops, markets and auctions. Others will be in writing, for example, those on the outside of boxes which invite the public to answer questions, fill out a slogan, include a sum of money in return for some gift offered. Or the offer may be implied from conduct, as when the purchaser is allowed to operate a pump which supplies petrol in a self-service garage.

The party making the offer may qualify it in some way and until that condition is fulfilled there can be no agreement. That was decided by the

Supreme Court in *Kelly v Irish Nursery & Landscape Co. Ltd* (1983) where the seller of property stated that no agreement enforceable at law was to be created until the exchange of contracts, a condition accepted by the buyer. An action to enforce the agreement failed on the ground that no exchange of contracts had taken place.

Acceptance

An acceptance exists when the party to whom the offer is made unqualifiedly accepts it. The acceptance must correspond exactly with the terms of that offer. It was decided, in *Central Meat Products Ltd v Carney* (1944), that 'an acceptance in principle' did not constitute a valid acceptance. Nor is the mere acknowledgement of an offer an acceptance. The making of a counter-offer is a rejection of the original offer which cannot subsequently be accepted.

In most instances of everyday contracts there is little difficulty in deciding whether an offer has been accepted. The handing of an item by the shop assistant to the customer, or the marking up of the price of the item on the cash register constitute acceptance. But where the parties carry on lengthy negotiations, it may be difficult to decide exactly whether an offer was made, and when it was accepted. The court must look at any correspondence, and the surrounding circumstances, and decide whether on a true construction the parties agreed to the same terms. This type of situation is illustrated by the case of *Pernod Ricard & Comrie plc v FII Fyffes plc* (1988) where the courts were called on to resolve a dispute which arose following intense negotiations, regarding the purchase of very valuable shares, conducted by a large number of persons over three days. The courts had to examine the negotiations in detail and, on the facts, held that an offer had been made by the defendant which had been accepted by the plaintiff.

Subject to Contract

In some contracts, particularly those relating to the sale of land or premises, one party, or both parties, may wish to stay their hand while such matters as finance, planning permission, disposal of existing property, or the investigation of the seller's title to the property are resolved. In such instances the parties may use the expression 'subject to contract'. In the Supreme Court in *Boyle v Lee* (1992), according to O'Flaherty J.: 'The expression "subject to contract" or "subject to a formal contract being drawn up" or the like is *prima facie* a strong declaration that a concluded agreement does not exist. I would hold that there must be cogent evidence of a contrary intention before such a phrase is put to one side. I would equate it to "existence of contract denied".'

Communication of Acceptance

An acceptance must, as a general rule, be communicated to the party making the offer by the party accepting the offer. An acceptance is effective from the moment it is communicated. Two exceptions to this general rule apply.

The first exception is where the proper means of communicating acceptance is by post. In such cases, the acceptance is effective from the moment the letter is properly posted. The Supreme Court ruled, in *Kelly v Cruise Catering Ltd* (1994), that a contract of employment was completed when the employee living in Dublin posted the contract, which had been sent to him by post, to the employer situated in Norway. Where instantaneous communications are used, such as the telephone, telex or fax, the contract is made when the acceptance is received.

The second exception to this rule exists where the offer includes a term which provides that the performance of some act by the party to whom the offer is made will constitute a complete acceptance. These are known as unilateral contracts. Examples are an offer promising a reward on the return of a lost dog, or where goods will be sent, subject to availability, on the completion of a form to be returned together with the appropriate amount to the party making the offer. The publishers of an English newspaper which circulated in Ireland, in *Kennedy v London Express Newspapers Ltd* (1931), offered a free accident insurance scheme for the benefit of its registered readers, who were those registered with a newsagent, or were postal subscribers. A reader had registered with a newsagent and when she was killed in an accident her husband claimed under the policy. The Supreme Court held that a valid contract existed from the moment of registration and the publisher was bound by its terms.

In unilateral contracts the offer can normally be accepted by the performance of the required act. There is no necessity to give notice of acceptance to the party making the offer. The method of acceptance may be chosen by the party making the offer, such as by telephone or by letter. Should a particular method of acceptance be prescribed, an acceptance by another method is invalid.

Termination of Offer

An offer remains open until terminated by any one of four possible methods. First, an offer may be accepted. Second, an offer may be withdrawn at any time prior to its acceptance. But once a valid acceptance is made, the party making the offer is bound by a completed contract, and the offer cannot subsequently be withdrawn. In *Billings v Arnott & Co.* (1946) employers posted a notice offering employees who joined the Defence Forces during World War Two one-half of their salary while in military service. When an employee stated that he intended to avail of this offer, he was informed he could not do so because another employee from the same department had already done so and he could not be spared. Despite this the employee joined the army and, when the war was over, sued his employers, who were held liable by the High Court because the offer could not be validly withdrawn once it had been accepted. To be effective, actual notice of revocation must reach the party to whom the offer was made. Should the revocation be communicated by post, it takes effect from the moment of receipt and not from the time of posting.

Third, an offer may lapse in certain circumstances and thus become incapable of acceptance. An offer may lapse with the passage of time. This occurs where an acceptance is not made within the time period prescribed by the party making the offer. Where no specified time limit is prescribed, an offer lapses when a reasonable time has passed. What is a reasonable time is a matter of fact in each case. For example, in *Kelly v Park Hall School Ltd* (1979) no closing date was agreed in a sale of land. After various exchanges between the parties the seller wrote to the buyer that unless the contract was returned duly executed within seven days, the offer would be deemed to have been withdrawn. This letter did not reach the buyer until the seven-day period had expired. The seller repudiated the contract and an action for specific performance was successful. The Supreme Court ruled that while it was an implied term that the written contract would be signed without delay, by their delay in sending out the contract the seller waived that term to the extent that they could have insisted only on reasonable compliance with the requirement of promptitude. It would be inequitable to allow the seller to insist on compliance within an arbitrarily imposed and unreasonably short period for signing and returning the formal contract.

Fourth, an offer terminates when rejected by the party to whom the offer is made. A rejected offer cannot subsequently be accepted. Rejection is ineffective unless actually communicated to the party making the offer. An attempt to accept an offer on new terms, not contained in the offer, is a rejection accompanied by a counter-offer.

Inclusion of Additional Terms

Once agreement is reached between the parties, it is not permissible for one to unilaterally introduce additional terms, unless such a right is reserved in the contract. Thus in *Ryle v Minister for Agriculture* (1963), after the parties had entered into a contract, the defendant sought to alter the term as to payment. The Circuit Court held that once a binding contract had been created, its terms could not be unilaterally altered by the defendant. But the introduction of an additional term may be accepted by the other party.

INTENTION TO BE CONTRACTUALLY BOUND

Intention to be Legally Bound

The intention to be contractually bound is the second essential ingredient of a valid contract. It follows that where this intention to be legally bound is absent there is no enforceable contract. For example, the promise to give a friend a lift to a football match is hardly meant to be a binding contract. On the other hand, the giving of a lift to a workmate on a regular basis, where the workmate is contributing towards the travelling expenses, is probably a binding contract.

When seeking the presence of this intention to be contractually bound, the courts tend to distinguish between commercial contracts and social contracts, though the use of the word 'contract' in this context is confusing. The former are more likely to be enforced, whereas the latter may not.

Social Contracts

Because parties to a social arrangement rarely intend to be legally bound, the courts make that assumption, though it may be rebutted by evidence to the contrary. In *Mackey v Jones* (1959) an uncle verbally promised his nephew, then fourteen years old, that if he came to live and assist on the farm, the farm would be willed to him. On the uncle's death the farm was left to another relative. The Circuit Court held that there was no binding agreement, only a statement of intention, though the nephew recovered two years' wages. In *Rogers v Smith* (1970) a mother promised her son that the cost of supporting her would be recoverable from her estate on her death. The Supreme Court refused to hold that a binding contract existed. The son, in his evidence, said that he would have supported his mother without her promise.

Commercial Contracts

Where parties in business agree, it is presumed they intend to be legally bound. Of course, this presumption may be rebutted by evidence to the contrary.

CONSIDERATION

Meaning of Consideration

To be successful in an action in contract, it must be proven that one party gave, or promised to give, some advantage to the other party in return for the latter's promise. This advantage moving from one party to the other party is known in law as consideration and is the third essential ingredient of a valid contract. Consideration was once judicially defined as 'either some right, interest, profit or benefit accruing to one party, or some forbearance, detriment, loss or responsibility given, suffered or undertaken by the other party'. It is a complete defence in legal proceedings to prove that no consideration was given. The law does not recognise a bare promise. It is a bare promise to promise a car to another as a gift. Should the promise go unfulfilled it cannot be enforced. But should the car be promised in return for £50, that is consideration and the contract is enforceable. The High Court ruled, in *Aga Khan v Firestone* (1992), that a signed document giving a party the right of first refusal with regard to a stud farm was a voluntary and unenforceable promise in that it was not supported by consideration.

Consideration is not necessary in a deed under seal. A deed takes effect when it is signed, sealed and delivered. The requirement that a deed be sealed is now laxly interpreted. At one time it was necessary to affix a personal seal; now a small red circle, on which one's thumb print is impressed, is sufficient.

Rules Relating to Consideration

The courts have developed a number of rules governing consideration. These were formulated in cases where the question as to the presence of consideration arose. Consideration must be real or sufficient in that some value, however trivial, must be given. Once a contract is freely entered into, the court will not assess the relative value of the contributions made by each party. Should a person choose to sell a new car which cost £12,000 for ten pence, the court will not intervene unless there has been fraud, duress, misrepresentation or some other element which vitiates the contract (see Chapter 9). While consideration must be real, it need not, in the eyes of the law, be adequate. The request to forbear from bringing legal proceedings is sufficient consideration. This was decided by the High Court in *Commodity Broking Co. Ltd v Meehan* (1985), though in that case the action failed because it could not be proved that the defendant requested the forbearance of the legal proceedings.

Consideration must move from the promisee. This means that a party can only enforce a promise if that party has provided the consideration. An action on the promise will fail should the consideration have moved from a third party. In *McCoubray v Thomson* (1868) a father transferred land to his son in consideration of which the son undertook to pay his sister a sum of money. When the son failed to pay, and was sued by his sister, the action was dismissed because no consideration moved from the sister to support her brother's promise. Consideration must not be past. Should one party have performed some service prior to the other making the promise, that service cannot support the promise. Should I arrive home to find my windows cleaned, and when the window cleaner calls later I agree to pay, and then change my mind, the window cleaner cannot succeed in an action because the consideration is past.

Consideration must not be illegal. For example, should illicit drugs be promised as consideration, it is illegal (see page 112).

Accord and Satisfaction

Should one party agree to waive, or abandon, contractual rights against the other party, such waiver must be supported by consideration, otherwise it is not binding and the party who has waived any right can later seek to enforce the contract in accordance with its original terms. In *Drogheda Corporation v Fairtlough* (1858) premises were let for ninety-nine years at £11 per annum. Some years later the rent was reduced to £5 per annum. Twelve years later the Corporation sued for the arrears of rent calculated at the original rent. The action succeeded because the payment of a lesser sum under a verbal agreement, rather than by deed, could not be deemed satisfaction of the larger sum unless some advantage, however small, was given.

Where a waiver is supported by consideration, what in reality happens is that a new contract is substituted for the old one. This process is known as 'discharge by accord and satisfaction': the accord being the agreed waiver and the satisfaction being the new consideration.

Equitable Estoppel

The common law rule, explained in the previous paragraph, that a creditor is not bound by a promise to accept part payment of a debt in full satisfaction, is inconvenient and unfair. Equity (see page 222) mitigated this rule by providing that where parties have contracted and afterwards enter upon a course of negotiations which has the effect of leading one of the parties to suppose that the strict legal rights arising under the contract will not be enforced, then the party who otherwise might have these rights will not be allowed to enforce them where it would be inequitable, having regard to the dealings which have taken place between the parties. This is known as equitable estoppel, or promissory estoppel, or, in more recent times, legitimate expectation.

A husband, in *Cullen v Cullen* (1962), promised some land to his wife, knowing that their son was going to build on it, with her blessing. The High Court later estopped the husband from asserting title to the land on which the son had built a house. In *Kenny v Kelly* (1988) a student was accepted and paid a deposit for a place on a course in University College Dublin which was later deferred for one year. The following year she was not offered a place and the college denied that a deferral had been granted. The High Court ruled that the promise to delay the enforcement of legal rights is of the essence of the doctrine of promissory estoppel and that the college was estopped from asserting that the student was not entitled to a place on the course. A father, in

Smyth v Halpin (1997), suggested to his son that he build an extension to the family home on the basis that the house would belong to him after both his parents were deceased. Having built the extension the son discovered on his father's death that the house had been willed to his mother for her life and then to one of his sisters. The High Court ruled that ownership in the house be transferred to the son because 'it was difficult to conceive that the [son] would ever have adopted his father's suggestion in relation to the extension to the house if it was not understood that he was to become the ultimate owner of the entire house'.

FORM OF A CONTRACT

No Particular Form Required by Law

Earlier in this chapter it was explained that, as a general rule, no particular form is necessary in the making of a contract. A contract may be in writing, verbal, or implied from conduct. The form of the contract is a matter to be decided by the parties, though in some instances a written contract, or some written terms, may be insisted upon by one party. For example, one party may incorporate an exemption clause into the contract (see page 97).

Special Forms Required by Law

In a limited number of cases statute law requires a particular form to be used. This provides better evidence of the terms and can later prevent disputes or assist in their resolution. It may also prevent the stronger party to a contract from taking advantage of the weaker party.

Some contracts, such as those unsupported by consideration, or the promise of a gift, must be by deed, a written document which, to be effective, must be signed, sealed and delivered. All contracts may be deeds but in practice few are, though a major exception are those involving the sale of land or premises.

Some contracts must, under the appropriate statute, be in writing. Examples are bills of exchange, assignments of copyright, transfers of company shares, and hire-purchase agreements.

Certain contracts need to be evidenced in writing. The *Statute of Frauds (Ireland) 1695*, section 2, states: 'No action shall be brought . . . to charge the defendant upon any special promise to answer for the debt, default, or miscarriage of another person . . . or upon any contract or sale of lands . . . or upon any agreement that is not to be performed within the space of one year from the making thereof unless the agreement upon which such action shall be brought, or some memorandum or note thereof, shall be in writing, and signed by the party to be charged ... or some other person ... by him lawfully authorised.'

The memorandum or note need not be prepared for the purpose of satisfying this statutory requirement of written evidence. Letters written by the parties, or their solicitors, or estate agents, setting out the terms of the agreement have been held to constitute a memorandum, though the writer did not intend the documents to be such. Where no single document fully records the transaction, it may be possible to produce a sufficient memorandum by taking together two or more documents. The memorandum must contain the names of both parties to the contract or describe them in such a way as to make it possible to identify them. The property must be identified together with the price to be paid. Should these material terms be stated then the contract will be enforceable, unless it can be shown that the parties intended additional terms to be essential.

The memorandum must be signed by the person to be charged, or an agent. This requirement is liberally interpreted: initials will suffice, as will a rubber stamp or an illiterate's mark. The Supreme Court, in *Casey v Irish Intercontinental Bank* (1979), held that where a solicitor had instructed the typing of a letter setting out the material terms on headed notepaper, he was adopting the heading as his signature where the letter had not been personally signed.

A contract within the *Statute of Frauds* which is not properly evidenced in writing is unenforceable. The statute often caused hardship, particularly where an oral contract had been wholly or partly performed. Equity, therefore, developed the doctrine of part performance, under which a party who had partly performed the contract could enforce it, even though there was no written evidence of its terms. Equity would refuse to allow the statute to be used as 'an engine of fraud'.

TERMS OF A CONTRACT

Meaning of Terms

The contents of a contract are its terms. These determine the limits to which the parties are bound. It is the terms of a contract which define the rights and obligations of the parties. The terms of a contract may be either express or implied. In most contracts some terms will be actually agreed upon, while other terms will be implied. For example, on the purchase of a newspaper, the price and the fact that a particular newspaper is desired, are express terms. Implied would be the terms that it is today's newspaper and that all the pages are filled with readable print or photographs. It is unusual for all the terms of a contract to be expressed. Attempts are often made, by reducing the terms into writing, to do so. Whether this succeeds will depend on the actual circumstances of each case.

Express Terms

Material statements made by the parties during negotiations leading to the conclusion of a contract are divided into two. First, there are statements which the parties intend to be binding. Second, there are statements, called mere representations, which help to induce the making of the contract but are not intended by the parties to form part of the contract. For example, the enticement with words such as 'it's the best buy in town' or 'you won't get a better bargain anywhere' are mere representation.

Construction of Express Terms

The meaning to be given to the terms in a contract depends on the words used. Where the contract is in writing, there is a general rule that the courts will not look beyond the writing, but there are many exceptions to this rule. Where a contract is made verbally, the ascertainment of its terms is a question of fact.

To construe the express terms of a contract, whether written or verbal, the courts have formulated rules of construction. Words are presumed to have their ordinary meaning while legal terms are given a technical meaning. Should a term admit to both a legal and illegal meaning, the legal meaning is preferred in an attempt to give the contract meaning. Where the terms are irreconcilable the intention of the parties prevails.

Use of Parol Evidence

In general, verbal or parol evidence cannot be admitted to add to, vary or contradict a written document. There are obvious reasons for holding that once parties reduce an agreement to writing, they should be bound by the writing alone. But the rigid application of this rule in every case would lead to injustice. Consequently, extrinsic evidence may be admitted to assist the court in reaching a just conclusion.

Parol evidence may be admitted to explain the subject matter of the contract, as in *Chambers v Kelly* (1873), where confusion arose over the expression 'all the oaks' in a contract for the sale of timber. Evidence was admitted which proved that the parties had designated part of the land as an oak plantation and that oak trees on other parts of the land were not included. Oral evidence may be admitted where the written document is not the entire contract, as in *Clayton Love v B & I Steampacket Co.* (1970) (discussed on page 100), where the High Court admitted parol evidence of telephone conversations which could be added to the written terms to form one contract.

Contra Proferentem Rule

Where a written contract is used, one party may have insisted that the other party accept the terms — known as standard term contracts — or do without the contract. In such instances the idea that parties negotiate on equal terms is a myth. One party, the one in the stronger economic position, will exclusively dictate the terms of the contract. The weaker party may attempt to contract elsewhere, but will be met with similar terms. Examples of such situations are the widespread use of exemption clauses, retention of title clauses, and contracts of insurance. In such cases freedom of contract has been curtailed.

To redress this perceived imbalance, the courts developed the *contra proferentem* rule. Terms in such contracts are construed against the party who insisted on their inclusion. Where a term in the contract is so ambiguous as to admit of two possible constructions, the court will favour the interpretation advanced by the party who did not draw up the term. Judge Clark in *Western Potato Co-Operative Ltd v Durnan* (1985) explained: 'In so far as any part of the clause proves to be in conflict with or contradictory of the obligations imposed on the defendant, or proves to be ambiguous in its application to the facts of the case, then, under the rules of construction, it is to be construed against the plaintiff, *contra proferentem*, the contract having been prepared on behalf of the plaintiff as a standard form in use by them . . . and couched generally in terms protective of the plaintiff.'

Implied Terms

As already noted, the parties to a contract may expressly state every term of the contract. More usually, the parties will simply agree to the basic purpose of the contract and a few obvious terms, and leave the detailed terms to be implied. In cases of dispute, the courts will, independently of statutory requirement (see next section), imply terms in two situations. First, a term not expressly agreed upon by the parties may be inferred on the basis of the presumed intention of the parties. The courts do nothing more than the parties would have done had they alerted their minds to the matter. The court repairs what is called an intrinsic failure of expression for the purpose of giving business efficacy to the contract. Second, a term may be implied as a matter of law, independently of the intention of the parties, and derived from the nature of the contract. The Supreme Court, in *Sweeney v Duggan* (1997), per Murphy J., explained that to imply a term 'it must be not merely reasonable but also necessary . . . it cannot be implied if it is inconsistent with the express wording of the contract and furthermore it may be difficult to infer a term where it cannot be formulated with reasonable precision.' In that case the court refused to imply a term which obliged an employer to procure insurance to cover injury to employees, or to warn employees of the absence of such insurance.

The High Court, in *Dundalk Shopping Centre Ltd v Roof Spray Ltd* (1979), held that it was an implied term that the defendant would use reasonable care and skill when installing a roof which later proved to be defective. The Supreme Court, in *Tradex (Ireland) Ltd v Irish Grain Board Ltd* (1984), refused to imply a term that letters of credit had to be opened by the plaintiff prior to the first delivery of goods, because such a term was unnecessary to give business efficacy to the contract in view of the fact that the parties had agreed a specific date for the maturing of the letters of credit. The High Court ruled in *Aga Khan v Firestone* (1992) that it would be illogical to imply a term which would have the effect of defeating the contract.

The courts have also held that some terms must be implied in order to protect constitutional rights, which take precedence over contractual rights which are mere legal rights. For example, in *Educational Co. of Ireland v Fitzpatrick* (1961) (discussed on page 468), the Supreme Court held that employees who, when first employed were not required to belong to a trade union, had the constitutional right to dissociate and could not subsequently be compelled to join a trade union. The Supreme Court, in *Glover v BLN Ltd* (1973) (discussed on page 453), decided that an office holder under contract could not be dismissed without being accorded the right to fair procedures. This constitutional right is discussed on page 74.

Terms Implied by Law

Various statutes, and statutory instruments, have curtailed freedom of contract in that, irrespective of the wishes of the parties, terms will be implied into particular contracts, generally to grant protections to the perceived weaker party to the contract. By virtue of the *Sale of Goods Acts 1893–1980* and the *European Communitites (Unfair Terms in Consumer Contracts) Regulations 1995*, (discussed on page 334) and the *Consumer Credit Act 1995* (discussed on page 361), many terms are implied into these commercial contracts. The *Minimum Notice and Terms of Employment Act 1973* and the *Holiday (Employees) Act 1973* imply terms for the protection of employees in employment contracts (see page 74).

EXEMPTION CLAUSES

Nature of Exemption Clause

An exemption clause is a contractual stipulation which totally excludes, or partly diminishes, the liability of one party either in contract or in tort. A party wishing to rely on such a clause must show that it was incorporated into the contract, and it covered the loss or damage suffered.

Incorporation into the Contract

The first rule with regard to exemption clauses is that, in order to be effective, they must be incorporated into the contract either by signature or by notice.

It is a rule of law that a person who signs a contractual document is bound by the terms whether read or not. This rule applies to those who cannot read, and to a party who does not understand the language in the document. In *Knox v Great Northern Railway* (1896) the plaintiff's horse was seriously injured when boxed by the defendant's porter. The plaintiff's groom then signed a contract for the horse's carriage, subject to conditions, one of which read 'that at the reduced rate the company carry at owner's risk'. It was held that boxing the horse was necessarily and immediately connected with the carriage as to form one transaction. The fact that the contract was signed after the injury was immaterial.

An applicant for a loan, in *O'Connor v First National Building Society* (1991), signed a form containing the words 'No responsibility can be accepted by the society for the condition of the property'. The High Court held that this clause absolved the building society from any liability in respect of the poor condition of the premises which were subsequently purchased by the applicant having been inspected by the building society (see also page 195).

Should the exemption clause be printed on a document which is exchanged, or posted up in the place where the contract is made, it will only be incorporated into the contract where reasonable notice of its existence is given to the party adversely affected by it. The party relying on the clause is not obliged to actually bring it to the notice of the other party. Whether such reasonable notice is given depends on three factors.

The first factor is the nature of the document on which the clause is printed. Where the document is not intended to have contractual force but is more in the nature of a receipt, the exemption clause is not incorporated into the contract. For example, a cinema ticket is in the nature of a receipt because its purpose is to show that the admission price has been paid. But where the document is intended to have a contractual effect, for example, to retrieve goods, the exemption clause is incorporated when the receipt is exchanged. In *Miley v McKechnie Ltd* (1949) a garment was left to be cleaned and a receipt was given which read on its face, 'All orders accepted without guarantee', and directed attention to conditions printed on the back. The garment was damaged and an action was dismissed on the ground that the receipt containing the conditions was sufficient to exempt liability. The *Sale of Goods and Supply of Services Act 1980* requires a limiting clause to be specifically brought to the attention of the consumer.

The second factor is the degree of notice. The party relying on the exemption clause need not prove that the notice was actually brought to the attention of the other party. All that must be shown is that reasonable steps were taken to do so. In *Early v Great Southern Railway* (1940) an excursion ticket was purchased which, on its face, referred the passenger to special conditions which could be inspected in the company's timetable. The Supreme Court dismissed a claim by an injured passenger despite the fact that a timetable was not available at the station where the passenger purchased the ticket. It was held that the company had acted reasonably: had the passenger asked for the timetable and been refused, the action might have succeeded. In *Henigan v Ballybunion Picture House Ltd* (1944) an overcoat was deposited in the cloakroom, for which there was no charge and in which there was no attendant. Several notices were displayed which read: 'The management will not accept responsibility for loss or damage to property of patrons left in this hall.' The overcoat was stolen and an action was dismissed because the notices were displayed in a reasonably conspicuous manner.

Where the exemption clause is contained in documents passing between the parties, all the surrounding circumstances must be examined to ascertain whether it was incorporated into the contract. In *Sugar Distributors Ltd v Monaghan Cash & Carry Ltd* (1982) the exemption clause, a retention of title clause, was printed on the front of invoices which had passed between the parties in the course of business for a period of fifteen months. The buyer's managing director never read the small print on invoices and even had he, it would not have made any difference. The clauses, three in number, were not intimidatory in complexity. The High Court held that the seller had given reasonable notice. In *Tokn Grass Products Ltd v Sexton & Co. Ltd* (1983) the contract was contained in four typewritten sheets. At the bottom of each were the words: 'Terms and conditions of sale overleaf'. On the reverse side thirteen clauses were printed, some of which exempted liability for faulty goods supplied. The High Court held this method of exclusion effective because the letter accompanying the contract warned the purchaser to study it carefully. But in *Western Meats Ltd v National Ice & Cold Storage Ltd* (1982) the exemption clause was ineffective. The trade conditions provided that all goods were stored at the owner's risk. There was no evidence that these conditions were brought to the plaintiff's attention, only evidence that these conditions were printed on all letters and forms after the parties had contracted. The High Court held that a business, offering a specialist service but accepting no responsibility for it, must bring home clearly to the party dealing with it, that it accepted no such responsibility.

The third factor is the time of notice. An exemption clause is only incorporated into a contract where notice is given either before or at the time of contracting. A hotel could not rely on a notice in the bedrooms because the contract was made at the reception, unless the patron examined the room before agreeing to book it. Likewise, the owner of a car park, where admission was gained by ticket from a machine, would be unable to rely on an exemption clause which drivers only saw after entering the car park.

Effectiveness of Exemption Clauses

Given that an exemption clause has been incorporated into the contract, the next question which may arise is, is it effective to exempt the party relying on it from liability? For example, in *Leonard v Great Northern Railway Co.* (1912) a claim for the loss of goods missing when the consignment reached its destination was dismissed because the claim was not made within the required three days. In that case the exemption clause was effective; but in *Alexander v Irish National Stud Ltd* (1977) it was not. A horse which had been sent to the stud was killed due to the stud's negligence. The conditions stated that the stud was not responsible in the event of an accident occurring to any horse. The High Court ruled that an ordinary sensible customer would understand the words to extend to inevitable risks and not to injuries caused by negligence. The clause was inapplicable. On the other hand, in *Regan v Irish Automobile Club Ltd* (1990) a marshal at a motor race signed a form which agreed to absolve all persons having connection with the race meeting from liability arising out of accidents howsoever caused, resulting in damage or personal injury. The High Court held that the use of the word 'accident' would not include negligent accidents, but the qualification by the words 'howsoever caused' was wide enough to embrace negligent accidents. In addition, the use of the word 'liability' presupposed some form of wrong. A claim for personal injuries caused by negligence was dismissed.

Should one party to a contract, who supplies something essentially different from that which was contracted for, avail of the protection granted by the exemption clause? The answer is no, the reason being that a fundamental breach of contract has been committed. Each contract contains a central, or main, clause, and a breach of that clause which strikes at the root of the contract is a fundamental breach.

This problem was considered in the leading case of *Clayton Love v B & I Steampacket Co.* (1970) where the parties contracted to transport a cargo by sea at a particular temperature which was not maintained, and the cargo perished. The shipper relied on a clause which exempted it from liability for any damage or loss. The Supreme Court held that a fundamental breach had been committed because the customer received something radically different from the service it had contracted for, and that an exemption clause could only avail a party when the contract was being carried out, and not when it was being deviated from.

Modification by Statute

Statute may regulate the use of exemption clauses. The *Sale of Goods and Supply of Services Act 1980* prohibits in some instances and curtails in others the use of exemption clauses (page 340). Another statute, the *Hotel Proprietors Act 1963*, regulates the use of exemption clauses in contracts within its ambit.

CONTRACTUAL CAPACITY

General Rule as to Capacity to Contract

The general principle is that all persons have full contractual capacity to enter into binding contracts. Since the law prohibits certain types of contracts, it also imposes a number of exceptions to this general rule.

CONTRACTUAL CAPACITY OF MINORS

Definition of Minority

By virtue of the *Age of Majority Act 1985*, a minor, for the purposes of contract law, is a person under the age of eighteen years who is not, or has never been, married. The law governing minors' contracts is founded on two principles. The law, on the one hand, protects minors from inexperience, and on the other, tries not to cause unnecessary hardship on adults who deal with them. Contracts with minors can be divided into three types: (i) binding; (ii) voidable and (iii) void.

Contracts Binding on Minors

Common sense indicates that minors enter into all kinds of contracts regularly. Where minors contract for goods or services and pay for these at the time, few legal difficulties arise for the adult dealing with the minor. The minor has the identical rights which an adult possesses. However, problems arise where goods or services are obtained by a minor on credit. In such circumstances the law provides that a minor is only bound by a contract for necessaries, which are defined as goods necessary to support life and extend to articles which maintain the particular minor in the state, station and degree of comfort to which the minor is accustomed. Consequently, the minor is not bound for contracts of mere luxury, or ornament. The test in each case is what is reasonable for that particular minor. An action for the price of a horse which had been obtained on credit, in *Skrine v Gordon* (1875), was dismissed because, said the judge: 'We all know that hunting is a good sport and a manly exercise but still that only shows it is a sport, and luxuries or amusement are quite distinct from necessaries.' A minor is not liable for necessaries if adequately supplied already, though the seller may be unaware of this. The *Sale of Goods Act 1893* provides that where necessaries are sold and supplied to a minor, only a reasonable price need be paid. As a result of these rules minors are very rarely, if ever, sold goods or services on credit.

A minor is bound by contracts of employment, apprenticeship, training, education, and advancement. At present a minor under the age of fifteen years cannot engage in full-time employment. A contract of apprenticeship is an agreement on the minor's part to serve for a definite period, and on the employer's part to teach the apprentice a trade or calling. In *Sister Dolores v Minister for Social Welfare* (1962) it was held that young girls training to be children's nurses were not employed but were in a similar relationship which exists in any educational establishment between management and students. For these contracts to be binding on the minor they must not, on the whole, be harsh and oppressive. Long working hours, poor wages, insufficient or inadequate training, or the appropriation of large commissions from a minor's earnings would be harsh and oppressive.

Minors and Voidable Contracts

A minor may avoid certain contracts. This means that the contract is binding on both parties until the minor, either before reaching majority or within a reasonable time thereafter, repudiates it. The adult party cannot repudiate such a contract: the option lies exclusively with the minor. This rule applies to a contract of continuing obligation. In *Blake v Concannon* (1871) a minor, who had leased some land and repudiated on coming of age, was held liable for rent up to the date of repudiation. The plaintiff, in *Stapleton v Prudential Assurance Co.* (1928), effected a life assurance policy while a minor and continued to pay premiums until she was thirty years of age. An action to recover the premiums failed because she had not repudiated the contract within a reasonable time after reaching her majority.

A minor can repudiate a contract which is not beneficial. In *Keay v Great Southern Railway* (1941) a minor of twelve years held a season train ticket which enabled her to travel to and from school. It was issued at a reduced rate on the special condition which absolved the company for liability for negligence. When the minor was injured, the High Court held that the contract could be repudiated because by depriving her of common law rights it could not be said to be for her benefit. In *Harnedy v National Greyhound Racing Association* (1944) the High Court ruled that a contract, which contained a clause excluding a minor greyhound owner from suing in respect of injuries to the dog, was not beneficial and could be repudiated.

Minors and Void Contracts

Certain contracts entered into by minors are absolutely void. These contracts are a nullity and can be neither confirmed by the minor nor enforced against the minor. The *Infants Relief Act 1874* declares that all contracts entered into by a minor for the repayment of money lent, or to be lent, or for goods supplied, other than a contract for necessaries, are absolutely void. It should be noted that this statute refers to contracts against the minor and it follows that the minor may be able to enforce such contracts against the adult party. The *Betting and Loans (Infants) Act 1892* makes void any promise by a person after reaching majority to repay a loan contracted during minority.

OTHER CATEGORIES

Lunatics and drunkards can avoid contractual liability provided the other party is aware of that condition at the time of contracting. In *Hassard v Smith* (1872) a person of unsound mind leased property and, when later he sought to repudiate the transaction on that ground, the court ruled that provided the contract was fair and *bona fide* it could only be set aside had the other party known of the incapacity at the time the lease was executed. Such a voidable contract may be ratified during a lucid, or sober, period and thus becomes completely valid. The *Sale of Goods Act 1893* provides that lunatics and drunkards must only pay a reasonable price for necessaries.

The doctrine of sovereign immunity, which holds that sovereign states and their rulers are immune from action in the courts of this State, is a generally recognised principle of international law. The Supreme Court decided, in *Government of Canada v Employment Appeals Tribunal* (1992), that an action by a former employee of the Canadian Embassy for unfair dismissal must be dismissed on the ground of sovereign immunity. But this immunity can be waived and should a diplomat initiate an action in contract, that diplomat may be sued by way of counter-claim.

Under the common law it was a principle that the State could not be sued for the wrongs, including those in contract, of its servants. Since the Supreme Court decision in *Byrne v Ireland* (1972), where it was held that the State was liable in tort for the negligent acts of its servants, it follows that the State may be liable in contract.

Proper Law of the Contract

The parties to a contract, as a matter of general principle, are entitled to nominate which law is to be the proper law of the contract. Should they fail to do so, the courts must determine the issue. Generally, contracts made in

Ireland are governed by Irish law. Should the parties expressly state that Irish law is the proper law of the contract, Irish courts will entertain actions on the contract irrespective of where the contract was made and whether the parties have any real connection with this country. This was decided by the Supreme Court in *Kutchera v Buckingham International Holdings Ltd* (1988) where Canadian parties entered into a contract in Canada and expressly provided that the proper law of the contract should be that of Ireland. The *Contractual Obligations (Applicable Law) Act 1991*, which incorporates the *European Convention on the Law Applicable to Contractual Obligations* into domestic law, contains the law in this regard.

Chapter 9
INVALID CONTRACTS

Meaning of Invalidity

A contract containing the three essentials may be neutralised where it contains some element which invalidates it. In the previous chapter it was explained that the law invalidates some contracts of minors, contracts otherwise valid and enforceable. In this chapter we examine circumstances in which the law may generally invalidate a contract. There are numerous grounds and the consequences differ according to the ground invoked. For example, a contract may be void for mistake, or it may be voidable when induced by duress or misrepresentation, or it may be unenforceable because some statutory formality has been neglected, or it may be illegal because it offends the common law or the provisions of a statute.

MISTAKE

Operative Mistake

In general a mistake made by one or both parties to a contract has no effect on its validity. But a contract may be void where the parties contract under a fundamental mistake of fact. This rule only applies to a mistake of fact of such a nature that it destroys the basis of the agreement. This is known as operative mistake. An operative mistake may be common, mutual, or unilateral.

Common Mistake

A mistake is common where the parties labour under the same misunderstanding. Both are mistaken about the same thing. For example, a common mistake occurs where the parties agree to insure the life of a third party who, unknown to both, is dead.

Mutual Mistake

There is mutual mistake where the parties negotiate at cross-purposes. In this instance each party makes a different mistake. The owners of a derelict building, in *Monaghan County Council v Vaughan* (1948), wanted it demolished and removed. They published an ambiguous advertisement and accepted a tender from a builder who believed he was to be paid a sum for doing the work. The owners intended they should be paid for the concession of giving the debris. When the work was done the builder claimed the money. The High Court, holding there was mutual mistake, rectified (see page 128) the contract in favour of the owners. In *Clayton Love v B & I Steampacket Co.* (1970) (see page 100) one party contracted for the fish consignment to be carried as a delicate refrigerated cargo, whereas the other contracted on the basis that the goods would be carried at atmospheric temperature. The seller, in *Irish Life Assurance Co. Ltd v Dublin Land Securities* (1989) (see page 128), owned a portfolio of ground rents which it was anxious to sell and also owned land subject to compulsory purchase order which it did not intend to sell. Due to an oversight this land was included in the contract for sale signed by both parties. When this was discovered, the seller sought to exclude the land but the purchaser refused. The purchaser sought rectification. The Supreme Court refused to rectify the contract because the seller could not show what the continuing intention of the parties to the agreement was.

Unilateral Mistake

Where one party is mistaken, and the other party knows of this, there is unilateral mistake: one party is attempting to take advantage of the other's mistake. In *Gun v McCarthy* (1884) a lease was executed at a rent lower than the landlord intended, and of which unilateral mistake the tenant was aware. The court granted rescission (see page 127) rather than rectification because it should be left to the parties to decide whether they wished to enter a fresh contract. Premises, in *Nolan v Graves* (1946), were sold at public auction to the purchaser at, she contended, the price of £4,550. The seller maintained the price was £5,550 and refused to complete the sale at the lower price. The High Court held there was unilateral mistake of which the purchaser had endeavoured to take advantage.

Mistake as to the Nature of a Document

It is a rule of law that a party is bound by a contract which is signed, whether read or not, or whether it was understood or not. But a party who signs a document under a fundamental mistake as to its nature may be able to avoid it. That party may plead *non est factum*: it is not my deed. For example, in the *Bank of Ireland v McManamy* (1916) a document purporting to be a guarantee was signed in blank in the honest belief that it was a document of a wholly different nature, i.e. an order for goods. In the absence of negligence the court held that the guarantee was not binding.

Mistake of Law

A mistake of law may, in certain circumstances, enable the party at a loss to recover. The rule that a party cannot be excused from performing a duty by saying that he or she did not know the law: *ignorantia juris neminem excusat*, is not the same as saying that every person is presumed to know the law. Money paid under a mistake of law by itself, and without more, cannot be recovered. But where there is something more in addition to a mistake of law, such as behaviour by the party who demanded the other party's conduct which shows that of the two, that party is primarily responsible for the mistake, there may be a remedy. A sum of money was overpaid in redeeming an annuity on a cottage in *Rogers v Louth County Council* (1981). The Supreme Court permitted the recovery of the excess money, holding that the payment had not been made voluntarily and that the council, who computed the sum, were primarily responsible for the mistake.

MISREPRESENTATION

Caveat Emptor

As a general principle a party to a contract is not under a duty to disclose all, or any, known facts regarding the subject matter to the other party. Parties may protect their own interests. The rule is *caveat emptor*: let the buyer beware. Silence on the part of the seller is golden. There are exceptions to this rule. For example, insurance contracts require disclosure (see page 367).Where one party makes a positive false statement which deceives the other, this is a misrepresentation and may render the contract voidable at the option of the party misled. It may also be misrepresentation to suppress material facts.

Meaning of Misrepresentation

A misrepresentation is a false statement of a material fact made by one party which induces another to contract. For a statement to be effective as a misrepresentation it must have been relied on by the party complaining. Mere representations, or statements of opinion, cannot amount to misrepresentation. 'The best bargain in the world' or 'I don't think you'll find a better bargain elsewhere' are statements which are not meant to be legally binding. In the High Court, in *Donnellan v Dungoyne Ltd* (1995), where tenants were being sought for a new shopping centre, O'Hanlon J. noted that the 'press releases which were published from time to time, the very colourful and informative brochures prepared for the preview, and the encouraging remarks attributed to the developer, were all of a character which were well within the bounds of what was permissible in the important task of attempting to "sell" the centre to potential tenants.'

The parties, in *Smith v Lynn* (1954), interested in buying the same house, inspected the premises which, according to the advertisement, 'was in excellent structural and decorative repair'. After the purchase, finding the premises full of woodworm, the buyer re-advertised the premises using the original advertisement and, when the defendant asked why he was reselling, said it was for personal reasons. The defendant purchased, and on discovering the property's true condition, refused to complete the sale. An order for specific performance was granted on the ground that the advertisement was a trader's puff and not a misrepresentation. The misrepresentation must be relied on. Thus, in *Donnellan v Dungoyne Ltd* (1995), the High Court held that the plaintiff would have entered into a tenancy agreement for a shop lease in a shopping centre even if the developer had not given a firm commitment that all or nearly all of the other units had been let, though had he had a more accurate picture of the true situation he would have held out for greater concessions on the rent.

Innocent Misrepresentation

Where a party makes a misrepresentation believing it to be true, that party commits innocent misrepresentation. The seller, in the *Smelter Corporation of Ireland v O'Driscoll* (1977), was always reluctant to dispose of her land and finally did so on being told by a buyer's agent that should she refuse to sell, the local authority would compulsorily acquire the land. The agent believed what he said, but the statement was untrue. The Supreme Court refused to order specific performance of the contract. During an inspection of the seller's property, in *Gahan v Boland* (1984), the buyer inquired as to whether a projected motorway would affect the property. The seller gave an assurance that it would not, and this led the buyer to agree to purchase. In fact the projected motorway was planned to pass through the property, a fact not discovered until after the agreement was made. The Supreme Court ordered rescission of the contract.

Fraudulent Misrepresentation

An untrue statement made knowingly, or without belief in its truth, or made carelessly without regard to whether it is true or false, amounts to fraudulent misrepresentation. The seller of a house, in *Carbin v Somerville* (1933), who claimed it was damp free and the roof was in good condition, was guilty of fraudulent misrepresentation because he knew both statements to be false. The Supreme Court held the buyer was entitled to rescind the contract. In *Sargent v Irish Multiwheel Ltd* (1955) a garage, knowing it was untrue, advertised a truck for sale as English assembled. This was fraud and the court awarded damages. The seller of a fishery, in *Fenton v Schofield* (1966), claimed that in the previous four years an average of 300 fish had been caught and that a large sum of money had been spent renovating the property. Both untrue statements were made knowingly and damages were awarded to the buyer. The seller of land, in *Doran v Delaney* (1996), who produced a map to the buyer which showed access to a public road and failed to disclose that the access was over a piece of land owned by a next door neighbour, was held by the High Court to have committed fraudulent misrepresentation. Where a fiduciary relationship (see later) exists between the parties, the suppression of material facts may amount to fraudulent misrepresentation. A company, in *Aaron's Reefs Ltd v Twiss* (1895), brought an action to enforce payment on shares which had been allotted to the defendant, who claimed that the company's prospectus was a fraudulent document which had induced him to purchase the shares. The court ruled that the prospectus was a fraudulent document in that it concealed material facts and the repudiation of the contract by the defendant was fatal to the claim. The tort of fraud, discussed on page 222, should be referred to at this point.

DURESS AND UNDUE INFLUENCE

Duress

A contract can be avoided where it is made under duress, which is defined as actual or threatened violence to, or the imprisonment of, the party coerced, or a spouse or family. A serious threat to damage property amounts to duress. The High Court decided, in *Headfort v Brockett* (1966), that a threat to take legal action to assert legal rights did not constitute duress.

Contracts and Fiduciary Relationships

The law makes the presumption that undue influence has been exerted in contracts of a fiduciary nature. A fiduciary relationship exists where there is trust and confidence between the parties. In those circumstances the law insists that no undue advantage is gained by one party over the other. The law insists that the weaker party exercises a free will in the course of the transaction.

When eighteen years old the plaintiff, in *White v Meade* (1840), entered a convent first as a lodger and later as a postulant. When she came of age she assigned her property to the convent without advice from relatives, friends or a professional adviser. When she left the convent she was allowed to set aside the transfer on the ground that it had been executed under undue influence. In *King v Anderson* (1874) an agent who managed property bought it from his principal who, fifteen years later, sought to set aside the transaction. It was held that where an agent deals with a principal which confers a benefit on the agent, the agent is under a duty to ensure that the principal has competent and independent advice. This was not proved so the transaction was set aside. Delay did not defeat the action. A daughter who had just reached her majority while living with her mother, in *McMackin v Hibernian Bank* (1905), signed a guarantee to secure her mother's debts. The bank was aware of the circumstances. It was held that the transaction could be set aside because the law recognised that a young person, living with or under the influence of a parent, is likely to remain for some time under parental dominion after reaching majority. The Supreme Court ruled, in *Bank of Novia Scotia v Hogan* (1997), where a wife created a mortgage on property she owned in favour of the bank to secure her husband's indebtedness to the bank, that the relationship between the bank and the wife did not give rise to a presumption of undue influence because there had been no opportunity to exercise any such undue influence over her.

Rebutting Undue Influence

Where the presumption of undue influence exists the onus of proving that no impropriety took place is on the party seeking to uphold the transaction. A gift to the Catholic Church was upheld, in *Kirwan v Cullen* (1854), where it was proved that the beneficiary had ceased to be the donor's confessor two years before the gift was made.

Rebutting this presumption is generally done by showing there was a full disclosure of all material facts: that the consideration was adequate; and that the weaker party was independently advised. In *Provincial Bank of Ireland v McKeever* (1941) a mortgage of property by the beneficiaries under a will, when they became of age, to the bank to secure an overdraft incurred by the trustees in the management of the property, was upheld. The High Court decided that the presumption of undue influence was rebutted because the nature of the transaction was understood by the beneficiaries resulting in a free exercise by them of independent wills. A young man who suffered from an alcohol problem, in *Smyth v Smyth* (1978), was not allowed to set aside a sale to his uncle of property willed by another uncle, because his uncle had not influenced his decision to sell and a fair price had been paid.

UNCONSCIONABLE BARGAIN

Nature of Unconscionable Bargain

The law will grant relief against unconscionable bargains in cases where one party is in a position to exploit a particular weakness of the other. The burden of justifying such a transaction is on the party seeking to uphold it. While the case law shows that the courts have come to the aid of aged, poor and illiterate persons there is no reason to suppose that it might not assist others. The principle of law in this regard was set out by Sullivan MR. in *Slator v Nolan* (1876): 'If two persons — no matter whether a confidential relation exists between them or not — stand in such a relation to each other that one can take an undue advantage of the other, whether by reason of distress or recklessness or wildness or want of care and where the facts show that one party has taken undue advantage of the other . . . a transaction resting upon such unconscionable dealing will not be allowed to stand.' In that case a destitute young man was able to set aside a sale of his inheritance to a relative because advantage had been taken of his recklessness. In *Grealish v Murphy* (1946) a sixty-year-old farmer, living alone and mentally deficient, gave his farm, after consulting his solicitor, to the defendant, a thirty-two year old haulier and unrelated to the plaintiff. The High Court held the settlement to be improvident. The independent advice was suspect because the solicitor was unaware of all the material facts and of the full extent of the plaintiff's mental deficiency.

But in *Kelly v Morrisroe* (1919) an elderly woman was offered the market value for her property, coupled with the right of residence, rent free, during her lifetime. The woman consulted her former employer who advised her and accompanied her to the solicitor's office where the deed was read and explained to her. After her death her estate unsuccessfully sought to have the transaction set aside. The court held that the woman had all the advice and protection necessary. In *McCormack v Bennett* (1973) an elderly father, independently advised, in consideration of the affection he bore his daughter, transferred all his property to her. On his death other members of the family sought to have the transaction set aside. The High Court ruled that while the transaction was *prima facie* improvident in that it made no provision for the deceased or his wife, it was evident that it had been made in consequence of the free exercise of the father's will.

Unenforceable Contracts

Certain contracts cannot be enforced by the courts unless the party seeking to do so can prove that the proper statutory formalities, as to writing for example, have been observed. We have already, in the previous chapter (page 93), considered the necessity for writing under the *Statute of Frauds (Ireland) 1695*. The necessity for observing the formalities in hire-purchase contracts is considered on page 361.

ILLEGAL CONTRACTS

Contract for Illegal Purposes

A contract for an illegal purpose, or for a purpose which offends the common good, is void. The courts are reluctant to declare a contract illegal and only do so where it clearly offends the Constitution, or where a statute clearly prohibits such a transaction, or where a well-established common law principle forbids it.

The court hearing the case will itself take cognisance of the illegality, as in *McIllvenna v Ferris* (1955), where the High Court held that it could not ignore the illegality, which had not been pleaded by the parties. The onus of proving illegality lies on the party asserting it.

Contracts which Offend the Constitution

A contract which offends the provisions of the Constitution will not be enforced. The High Court ruled, in *Ennis v Butterly* (1997), that an agreement by persons to cohabit was incapable of being enforced as a matter of public policy as that would have given such arrangements a status similar to that of marriage.

Contracts Illegal by Statute

Many contracts are forbidden by statute and the following are a mere sample. Certain contracts of insurance which do not disclose an insurable interest are illegal: *Insurance Act 1936*. A contract which permits an increase in the interest rate in default of payment is illegal: *Moneylenders Act 1936*. The *Gaming and Lotteries Act 1956* provides that contracts of gaming or wagering are void. No company, association or partnership of more than twenty persons can be formed for the purpose of carrying on any business, other than bankers, solicitors and accountants, unless it is registered as a company: *Companies Act 1963*, as amended.

Any agreement in a contract relating to the sale, lease or letting of property which makes the purchaser, lessee or tenant liable to pay the fees or expenses of an auctioneer or house agent in respect of that transaction is void: *Auctioneers and House Agents Act 1973*. The *Family Home Protection Act 1976* provides that the conveyance of the family home without the prior written consent of the other spouse, is void. The *Protection of Young Persons (Employment) Act 1996* prohibits the employment of persons under the age of fourteen years.

A contract which infringes the provisions of a statute is illegal. A claim for expenses incurred in training a greyhound was resisted, in *O'Shaughnessy v Lyons* (1957), because it included a sum for transportation. The Circuit Court ruled that the transportation of goods for reward without a licence was illegal, being contrary to statute, and that part of the claim was dismissed.

Contracts Illegal at Common Law

The common law will not enforce wagering agreements. In *Anthony v Shea* (1952) money lent which, to the lender's knowledge was to be used by the borrower for gaming, could not be recovered. A contract tending to impede the administration of justice is illegal. A promise by an accused person to indemnify a bailsman is illegal, though in *Rand v Flynn* (1948) the bailsman was allowed to recover expenses from the accused incurred while endeavouring to secure his attendance in court. In *Nolan v Shiels* (1926) a cheque was given as payment to prevent a prosecution for indecent assault. When the cheque was dishonoured, an action failed to recover the money, because the consideration was illegal.

An agreement to defraud the Revenue is illegal. The High Court, in *Starling Securities Ltd v Woods* (1977), refused to order the specific performance of a contract for the sale of property where a reduced sum was stated in the contract with the purpose of reducing liability for stamp duty. In *Whitecross Potatoes (International) Ltd v Coyle* (1978) a defence was made that the transaction was illegal as being for smuggling purposes. On the evidence the defence was dismissed. The High Court acknowledged that had the intention of the parties been at the time of its formation that it was to be performed by a smuggling operation, the contract would have been unenforceable.

A contract which interferes with a public servant in the execution of his/her duty is void. In the *Lord Mayor of Dublin v Hayes* (1876) the defendant, on being appointed to a public office, agreed to pay over to the Corporation, fees he was entitled to collect in return for a fixed salary. He was sued when he refused to honour this pledge. The case was dismissed because to uphold it might tend to encourage corrupt practices among public officials.

The courts will not enforce a contract which involves the performance of an illegal act in a foreign country as in *Stanhope v Hospitals Trust Ltd* (1936), where the High Court refused to award compensation for losses incurred in a foreign country where the sale of lottery tickets was illegal. A contract tainted with sexual immorality is void in that *ex turpi non oritur actio*: from an evil cause no action arises.

The courts will not make an order which has the effect of compelling a party to act illegally. This was decided in *Namlooze Venootschap De Faam v Dorset Manufacturing Co. Ltd* (1949) where it was contrary to a statutory instrument to export foreign currency without permission. The defendant received permission, but by the time a dispute over the quality of the goods was resolved, the time limit on the permission had expired. The High Court held that while the contract was legal it would be contrary to the common good to grant relief because it would compel the performance of an act prohibited by law.

The courts will not enforce an agreement savouring of champerty, which is the assistance of another to recover property in any action on condition of sharing it when recovered. The Supreme Court, in *Fraser v Buckle* (1996), held void a contract to assist beneficiaries to recover property from the estate of a distant relative who had died in the USA on condition that a third share of the property recovered would be paid to the plaintiff.

COMPETITION LAW

Law Favours Competition in Business

As will be noted later in the chapter the common law, by applying restraint of trade principles, attempted in a limited way to prevent and outlaw anti-competition practices. The *Restrictive Practices Acts 1972–1987* introduced some statutory control over anti-competitive practices in the Irish business world but the supervisory mechanism was cumbersome. Having regard to the importance which the European Union places on competition, a more comprehensive system of control against anti-competitive practices has been introduced by the *Competition Act 1991*, as amended.

The objectives of the *Competition Act 1991* are to prohibit anti-competitive agreements and practices and to prohibit the abuse of a dominant position, a regime which is supervised by the Competition Authority.

Rules of Competition

(1) *Anti-competitive agreements, decisions and concerted practices*: All agreement between undertakings, decisions by associations of undertakings and concerted practices which have as their object or effect the prevention, restriction or distortion of competition in trade in any goods or services are prohibited and void. An undertaking is defined as 'a person being an individual or a body corporate or an unincorporated body of persons engaged for gain in the production, supply or distribution of goods or the provision of a service'. The Supreme Court ruled, in *Deane v Voluntary Health Insurance Board* (1992), that 'gain' was not limited to pecuniary gain or profit, and that 'for gain' connoted an activity carried on, or a service supplied, in return for a charge or payment and that accordingly the defendant, a statutory non-profit making organisation, was an undertaking.

While the purpose of the statute is to prohibit anti-competitive practices, the Act acknowledges that such practices are a necessary part of business. Consequently, the Competitive Authority may issue licences with regard to anti-competitive agreements, which, in essence, grants exemptions from the effects of the Act. In other words, an admittedly anti-competitive agreement, which would otherwise be void, is valid and enforceable.

However, before a licence may be granted, an agreement: (a) must contribute to improving the production or distribution of goods or services or to promote technical or economic progress; (b) must allow consumers a fair share of the benefits; (c) must not impose terms which are not indispensable for the attainment of the objectives of the agreement; and, (d) must not afford the undertaking the possibility of eliminating competition in respect of a substantial part of the products or services in question. Thus, a whole range of agreements, such as agreements to fix purchase or selling prices, or exclusive dealing contracts, will continue to be part of business practice provided they are licensed. A licence is granted for a specified period, which may be extended, and may contain conditions. Once issued, a licence may be amended or revoked in certain circumstances.

The Competition Authority may grant a certificate which states that an agreement, decision or concerted practice has no anti-agreement features.

(2) *Abuse of dominant position*: Any abuse by one or more undertakings of a dominant position is prohibited. While the statute does not define abuse it gives some examples of abusive practices, such as imposing unfair purchase or selling prices, imposing unfair trading conditions, applying dissimilar conditions to equivalent transactions with other trading parties thereby placing them at a competitive disadvantage. Dominance means a position of economic strength enjoyed by an undertaking which enables it to prevent effective competition being maintained on the relevant market by affording it the power to behave to an appreciable extent independently of its competitors, its customers and ultimately of the consumers.

The High Court ruled, in *Masterfoods Ltd v HB Ice Cream Ltd* (1993), that HB, with a market share of not less than 70 per cent for nearly a quarter century, and having regard to the small number of competitors and their relatively low market shares, was dominant in the market for impulse-buy ice creams, though it had not abused that position when it insisted that only its products be stored in freezer cabinets which it supplied to retailers. The High Court ruled, in *Donovan v ESB* (1992), that the defendant was then in a dominant position in the market for the supply of electrical contracting services.

Licences and certificates cannot be granted in relation to abuses of a dominant position.

Right of Action

Any person who is aggrieved in consequence of any agreement, decision or concerted practice or abuse of a dominant position shall have a right of action for relief against any undertaking which has been a party to this agreement. There are a number of reliefs which the court may grant: (a) an injunction; (b) a declaration that the agreement is void; (c) damages; and (d) exemplary damages.

Any undertaking or association of undertakings concerned, or any other person aggrieved by a licence or a certificate of the Competition Authority may appeal to the High Court and on the hearing of such appeal the court may confirm, amend or revoke the licence or may cancel or refuse to cancel the certificate.

Competition Authority

The Competition Authority consists of a chairman and not less than two and not more than four other members, each of whom is appointed by the Minister for Trade and Employment. Its main tasks are to: (a) grant licences; (b) grant certificates; (c) carry out such studies and analyses as are requested by the Minister; and, (d) to carry out an investigation into a possible abuse of a dominant position if requested by the Minister.

CONTRACTS IN RESTRAINT OF TRADE

Nature of Such Contracts

A contract in restraint of trade restricts a party from freely exercising a trade, profession or calling. Long before statutory regulation, outlined above, the common law regarded such contracts, though these are strictly clauses in a contract, as *prima facie* void because of their anti-competitive nature. Despite the intervention of statutory regulation the common law rules continue to be relevant because not all contracts, it seems, are captured by the *Competition Act 1991*, as amended. Thus, contracts of employment, the rules of voluntary bodies and contracts for the sale of a business may contain restraint of trade clauses. Another such category, exclusive dealing contracts, are now clearly subject to statutory regulation.

A contract in restraint of trade cannot be enforced unless (a) it is reasonable as between the parties; and (b) it is consistent with the interests of the public good. The onus of upholding the restriction as reasonable and necessary lies on the party seeking its enforcement.

Employment Contracts

The freedom of an employee to carry on an activity which adversely affects a former employer may be circumscribed by agreement. On the one hand, the employer has an interest in protecting the business, and on the other hand, the former employee has the right to earn a livelihood in a chosen field. The courts must strike a balance between these conflicting interests and, consequently, will only enforce such restriction provided it is reasonable. What is reasonable in each case is a matter of fact.

The restriction may be on a range of activities, or have some geographical application, or may apply for some time period, or, and this is the common practice, may be a combination of these restrictions. The courts may, in the appropriate case, sever the unreasonable part and enforce the remainder.

An exclusive ladies' hairdresser, in *Oates v Romano* (1950), employed an assistant who had agreed on entering employment that, should he leave, he would not carry on 'a like business' within a radius of one mile of the premises, which was situated in the centre of Dublin city, for a period of three years. The Circuit Court held that since this restriction precluded the assistant from the hairdressing business, it was unnecessarily wide for the hairdresser's proper protection and was void. An injunction was obtained, in *Arclex Optical Ltd v McMurray* (1958), pending a full hearing of the case, against a salesman who had agreed in writing when entering employment that for a period of five years he would not engage in any of the businesses carried on by his employers after leaving that employment, restraining him from canvassing existing customers.

The restriction on the period of time within which the prohibited activity cannot be performed must be reasonable. A chemist, in *ECI European Chemical Industries Ltd v Bell* (1981), in possession of the employer's manufacturing and testing techniques, production processes and trade secrets, had agreed in writing on taking up employment not to work for a competitor for a period of two years after leaving his employment. He was prevented by a High Court injunction from taking up employment with a competitor when he terminated his employment. The geographical area to be protected must be reasonable. A teacher in a business academy in Belfast, in *Skerry v Moles* (1908), agreed in writing when entering employment, not to carry on a similar business in Dublin, Belfast or Cork during a three-year period after leaving this employment. On leaving, he established a similar business in Belfast. It was held that the restraint relating to Belfast was reasonable but not the ones relating to Dublin and Cork. The restriction relating to time was held to be reasonable. The court severed the void parts and enforced the remainder. The total clause was held void in *Mulligan v Corr* (1925) where a solicitor employed an apprentice on condition that on qualifying he would not practise within thirty miles of two named towns and twenty miles of another. The Supreme Court held that the geographical area was too large and went far beyond what was reasonably required for the protection of the employer. The court examined the possibility of severing the reasonable portions, but on the evidence held it could not be done.

A clause in restraint of trade may not be invoked where an employee has been dismissed unfairly or without due cause. In such a case the protection, even where reasonable, will be lost. In *Coleborne v Kearns* (1912) a motorcycle sales assistant agreed in writing that if he 'left' his employment 'for any cause whatsoever' he would not, for a period of seven years, start a similar business within fifteen miles of the town in which his employer's premises was situated. He was dismissed for no good reason and immediately started his own motorcycle business in a nearby town. It was held that leave did not mean dismissal, because dismissal for an innocent purpose would have left him without redress against oppressive terms.

Restraints in Rules of Voluntary Associations

The rules of a voluntary association to which a person belongs may attempt to restrict the employment, career or trade activities of its members. To be enforceable the restriction must be reasonable. The relationship between a trade union and its members is based on contract and consequently the restraint of trade doctrine applies. In *Langan v Cork Operative Bakers Trade Union* (1938) a trade union gave financial assistance to members who wished to emigrate, subject to the proviso that a member who returned was not to work as a baker in that locality. The High Court held that a baker was entitled to repudiate the agreement on making restitution, because the agreement was an unreasonable restraint of trade. The rules of the governing association of a sport which interferes with the livelihood prospects of those participating must be reasonable. In *Macken v O'Reilly* (1978) a world famous showjumper complained that the rules of the body which governed the sport, which obliged competitors representing Ireland to ride only Irish bred horses, constituted an unreasonable restraint of trade. The Supreme Court held the restraint reasonable because the wider public interest of promoting the Irish horse required this. The showjumper could carry on his profession freely, except that should he choose to ride non-Irish bred horses he could not represent his country.

Restraints on the Sale of a Business

The purchaser of a business can restrict the seller from engaging in similar enterprises in the future. The need to impose such a restriction is accepted by the courts because the proprietary interest in the goodwill of the business may be worthy of protection. Such restrictions will not be enforced where they are deemed to be wider than are reasonably necessary for that protection. In *John Orr Ltd v Orr* (1987) the seller of a business, who continued to work for the company, agreed not to compete or solicit in markets or trades similar to those of the company he sold, or the parent company which bought the business, for a one-year period after termination of employment. After resigning, the seller immediately established a company in England trading in similar goods. The High Court held that the restraints relating to the company he sold were reasonable, but those relating to the parent company were not, and severed the unreasonable portions, which were void, and enforced the remainder. In *RGDATA Ltd v Tara Publishing Co.Ltd* (1995), an association of independent retailers sold two publications designated as their 'official publications' and agreed not to engage or become involved in the publication of any publication within the State for a period of twenty years. The High Court decided that, while it was reasonable to include restrictions which precluded the association indefinitely from publishing a comparable magazine under the same title, it was unreasonable to preclude it indefinitely from engaging in the business of publishing magazines generally. Thus, the offending parts of the agreement were severed and the association was then free to publish or assist in the publication of magazines or other publications if, but only if, the magazines or publications were not described, represented or held out to be the association's official publications.

Chapter 10

DISCHARGE OF CONTRACTS

Meaning of Discharge

Every valid contractual obligation gives rise to a corresponding contractual right. Where the obligation of one party is fully discharged, the corresponding right of the other party is extinguished. When all obligations and rights are extinguished, the contract is discharged. A contract may be discharged in a number of ways.

Discharge by Performance

A contractual obligation is discharged by a complete performance. The performance must be exactly in accordance with the terms. A party is entitled to the benefit of a complete performance in accordance with the undertaking of the other. When that occurs, the contract is entire and whether that is so is a matter of construction in each case. In *Coughlan v Moloney* (1905) a builder agreed to build a house by a certain date. The work was left incomplete. The owner had another builder finish it, and the original builder sued for the work done. The claim was dismissed.

Substantial Performance

The requirement that the contract be completely and exactly performed may, in many cases, be unjust. One party may get a benefit without being bound to pay and the other party is penalised. To correct this imbalance the courts have developed the doctrine of substantial performance. Where there is substantial performance, which means a performance as complete as a reasonable person could expect, the contract may be discharged. This compromise of substantial performance is only available where the parties genuinely dispute whether the completed terms meet the contract standard. The High Court held, in *Kincora Builders Ltd v Cronin* (1973), that a builder who had knowingly refused to insulate an attic, could not avail of substantial performance in that there had been an abandonment of the contract.

Partial Performance

Where one party is unable, or unwilling, to make more than a partial performance, the general principle of law is that there is no discharge of contract. There are exceptions to this rule. For example, where the contract is divisible, the completion of each part acts as a complete performance of that part. Where performance is by instalment, it is possible to recover payment for each completed instalment unless the intention of the parties is to treat the contract as a unified one.

Where performance is prevented by one party, the other party can sue for the work done. Where a partial performance is acceptable to the parties, the contract is discharged.

Tender of Discharge

When one party unsuccessfully attempts to perform, this is known as tender. Where the tender consists of an attempt to perform the contract, such as the provision of a service or the delivery of goods, the refusal to accept usually discharges the contract.

A tender of payment relieves that party from making further tenders, but it does not discharge the liability to pay. The payment of a lesser sum of money is not usually a discharge of the greater sum owed. Payment by cheque is only a conditional payment until it is paid or dishonoured.

Where there are several debts outstanding between the parties, it is sometimes vital to ascertain which payments have discharged which debts. In the absence of express agreement the courts apply a number of rules. The debtor can appropriate any payment to any debt. Where the debtor fails to indicate which debt is to be discharged the creditor can apply the payment in any way. Where neither party appoints a particular debt the court assumes that the first payment discharges the earliest debt incurred.

Discharge by Agreement

Discharge by agreement is the application of the common-sense rule that a contract may be terminated in the same way it was created. In an executory contract, that is, one wholly unperformed by either party, a simple waiver discharges the contract. Consideration is the exchange of promises not to enforce the contract. In an executed contract, that is, one wholly or partly performed by one party, to be effective, a discharge must be supported by consideration, or by deed.

Discharge may occur by the parties making a subsequent contract about the same subject-matter. The High Court decided, in *Headfort v Brockett* (1966), that prior to a breach, a contract may be rescinded by a subsequent agreement, the terms of which are so inconsistent with the terms of the first that both cannot stand together and this applies where the second agreement is not performed.

Discharge by Notice

Discharge by notice is the third method of terminating a contract. Many contracts are for a single transaction while others are of a continuing nature. Invariably such contracts expressly provide for their termination by a stated period of notice, or on the occurrence of particular events. Where the parties fail to cover the matter, the courts have decided that contracts can be terminated by reasonable notice. In *Fluid Power Technology Co. Ltd v Sperry Ltd* (1985) the parties made two contracts, the first to terminate on six months' notice by either party setting out fully in writing the reasons for such termination. No provision in this regard was made for the second contract. The High Court ruled that six months, rather than nine months, was reasonable notice to terminate the second contract. The court also held that there was an obligation to exercise the termination power in a *bona fide* manner, which had been done. Where the parties have expressly provided the circumstances in which the contract may be terminated, the courts will not imply further terms. In *Grehan v North Eastern Health Board* (1989) an attempt failed to terminate an agreement by giving three months' notice because the agreement had exhaustively set out the circumstances in which the contract could be terminated, which did not contain a term for termination by notice. The High Court rejected the suggestion that a notice term was required to give the contract efficacy and, accordingly, the term that the contract could be terminated by reasonable notice would not be implied (see page 96 for implied terms).

Discharge by Operation of Law

The fourth method by which contract may be discharged is by operation of law. This means that some principle of law intervenes to discharge the contract. For example, the law discharges a contract where it merges into a higher obligation. Thus a written agreement swallows a verbal one made on the same terms and between the same parties. And contracts for personal service are automatically discharged by the death of the party performing the service. Probably the most important example of the law operating to discharge a contract is the provisions of the *Statute of Limitations 1957*, as amended. Actions for breach of contract must be commenced within a certain time, otherwise the right of action becomes statute-barred, and the party suffering the breach is permanently debarred from a remedy. Simple contracts become barred after six years, whereas special contracts, such as those for the recovery of land, are barred after twelve years. These time periods run from the time of the breach, or from the date of a written acknowledgement of liability, or the part payment of the statute-barred debt. Reference should be made to page 161, where this topic is enlarged upon when discussing tortious liability.

Discharge by Frustration

The fifth method of discharging a contract is by frustration. Where a contract from the outset is impossible to perform, it is void. But occasionally a contract, possible to perform when made, becomes impossible to complete because of some intervening act not caused by either party. To meet this eventuality the courts have developed the doctrine of frustration. Under this rule the courts imply a term which gives effect to the unexpressed but presumed intention of the parties that the contract should be terminated in those circumstances. According to O'Flaherty J., in the Supreme Court in *Bates v Model Bakery Ltd* (1993): 'Frustration occurs whenever the law recognises that without default of either party, a contractual obligation has become incapable of being performed because of some intervening illegality, or because the circumstances in which performance is called for would render it as something different from that which was undertaken by the contract.'

A contract is frustrated where its performance would involve a breach of the law. In *O'Crowley v Minister for Finance* (1934) a judge was appointed for life to courts established by the first Dáil Éireann, courts which were later abolished by statute. The High Court held that since the office had been abolished by statute, the plaintiff could no longer act in it and was no longer entitled to payment because any existing contract had been discharged by impossibility of performance. The Circuit Court held, in *Kearney v Saorstát & Continental Shipping Co. Ltd* (1943), that the sinking of a vessel through no fault of the employer, on which an employee served, frustrated the contract of employment. The High Court decided, in *Flynn v Great Northern Railway* (1955), that an employment contract was terminated where the employee's permanent incapacity was such as to frustrate the business object of the contract.

The doctrine cannot be invoked where the event which makes performance of the contract impossible was caused by the negligence of one of the parties. In *Herman v Owners of SS Vicia* (1942) a ship put into Dublin on the way to Britain to await travel warrants to ensure safe access to British ports because of wartime conditions. These warrants were refused and the owners of the ship pleaded frustration of the employment contracts of the seamen when they claimed damages to cover repatriation expenses. The defence failed in the High Court because the failure to obtain the documentation was due to the owners' negligence. Nor can the doctrine be pleaded where the event should have been anticipated, as in *McGuill v Aer Lingus Teo.* (1983), where one party was aware of the threat or possibility of a strike but, anxious to obtain the business, undertook the risk of contracting without safeguarding its position.

A contract cannot be discharged by frustration where a term expressly covers the event which is alleged to constitute frustration. The Supreme Court held, in *Browne v Mulligan* (1977), that for the doctrine to apply, the event on which reliance is placed must not have been anticipated by the parties. In that case the employment contract dealt with the possible termination in the event of insufficiency of funds by a hospital in which the plaintiff was employed. The Supreme Court ruled, in *Neville & Sons Ltd v Guardian Builders Ltd* (1995), that an intervening event which rendered the contract more onerous to perform, was not one which significantly changed the nature of the defendant's obligation under the contract and the defence of frustration failed.

Discharge by Breach

The fifth method of discharge is by breach of the contract. This occurs where one party fails to perform contractual obligations, or where that party repudiates the contract either expressly or impliedly without justification. A contract is not discharged unless the other party elects to treat the breach as a repudiation. Every breach cannot be treated as a repudiation: it depends on the nature of the term breached.

One party to a contract may, before the time fixed for performance, indicate that the terms of the contract will not be observed. Such conduct is known as anticipatory breach. The striking feature of this rule is that acceptance of the breach entitles the other party to claim damages before the time fixed for performance has passed. In *Leeson v North British Oil & Candle Co.* (1874) the seller, in a contract to supply paraffin over a winter season, said in January that due to a strike they could not guarantee supplies for a period of two months. The buyer refused to take orders from his own customers. In an action for loss of profits it was argued that the buyer's refusal to accept orders was precipitous and that he should have ordered from the seller on the off-chance that supplies would be available. The court held that the seller's statement of their inability to perform the contract was a breach on which the buyer could successfully sue.

A breach of contract sufficiently serious to entitle one party to repudiate the contract is known as a fundamental breach. For example, in *Robb v James* (1881) the buyer of goods at an auction was to collect and pay for them within twenty-four hours. When he failed to do so, the seller resold the goods, and an action by the buyer failed because it was essential to the contract that the goods be collected and paid for. A claim for breach of contract was successful in *Dundalk Shopping Centre Ltd v Roof Spray Ltd* (1979) where the High Court held that the effective waterproofing of a roof within a reasonable time was a fundamental term of the contract.

A fundamental term is often referred to as a condition. A warranty, defined as a term collateral to the main purpose of the contract, does not entitle the wronged party to repudiate the contract. Conditions and warranties are considered when discussing the sale of goods in Chapter 35, page 334.

Chapter 11
REMEDIES IN CONTRACT LAW

Damages

An award of damages following a breach of contract is designed to compensate the wronged party. A party in breach is not liable to compensate for total loss resulting from the breach. The leading case, that of *Hadley v Baxendale* (1854), decided in England but applied in Irish courts since, laid down the rule that the damages should be such as may fairly and reasonably be considered, either arising naturally according to the usual course of things for such breach of contract itself, or such as may reasonably be supposed to have been in the contemplation of both parties at the time the contract was made, as the probable result of the breach.

In *McGrath v Kiely* (1965) a surgeon was requested in the preparation of an accident claim to present a report on a patient's injuries. He failed to mention a particular injury and the patient received less damages than was usual. An action against the surgeon in the High Court succeeded. Henchy J. explained: 'If, when giving the report, he had considered the consequence of the omission of any reference to a substantial item of personal injuries, he must have realised as a reasonable man that the plaintiff was liable in consequence to suffer damage as she suffered.'

Damages for breach of contract are intended to compensate the wronged party. They attempt to place that party in the same position, so far as money can do, as if the contract had been completed. But the wronged party must minimise the loss suffered as far as can reasonably be done.

Where the amount of compensation is to be decided by the court, the damages are known as unliquidated damages. Nominal damages are a token award made where there has been a contractual breach, but little actual loss. Damages are substantial where they place the wronged party in the position he or she would have been, had the contract been properly performed, as in *McGrath v Kiely*, where the court awarded a sum which the original court would have added, had the full extent of the injuries been known. Exemplary damages are a sum awarded by the court which is greater than the actual pecuniary loss suffered. Such awards have been made against landlords who evict tenants without adhering to the proper legal procedures.

The courts may award damages for inconvenience or loss of enjoyment when these are within the presumed contemplation of the parties. In *Johnson v Longleat Properties Ltd* (1976) the High Court awarded damages for inconvenience where the party had to move out of a house, constructed by a builder, while remedial work was carried out.

Liquidated Damages

When contracting parties make a genuine pre-assessment of the loss that might result from any particular breach and agree accordingly, this sum, known as liquidated damages, becomes payable in the event of a breach. This sum fixed, and nothing more, can be recovered. In *Toomey v Murphy* (1897) the parties agreed that if the construction of a house was not completed by a fixed date the builder would pay 'a penalty as liquidated damages' at the rate of £5.00 per week. The plaintiff sued for thirty-two weeks and was successful.

On the other hand, courts are reluctant to allow a party, under such a provision, to recover a sum which is obviously and considerably greater than the loss. For this purpose the courts have drawn a distinction between penalty clauses, which are invalid, and liquidated damages clauses, which will generally be upheld. A clause is penal where it is designed to deter a party from breaking the contract. In *Schiesser International (Ireland) Ltd v Gallagher* (1971) an employment contract provided that, should the employee resign within three years of returning to Ireland from Germany, where he travelled and was trained at the employer's expense, he should repay these. When the employee left two years after returning, the Circuit Court held that the clause was in the nature of a penalty in that the sum to be repaid was the same whether the employee resigned one day after his return or he left one day short of the three years. The court only awarded a sum for actual loss proved.

Quantum Meruit

Where a party sues to recover an unliquidated sum for services actually rendered, that party is said to claim a *quantum meruit*, which means as much as is deserved. Such an action is based on the promise, express or implied, to pay for the service. The distinction between a *quantum meruit* and a claim for damages is that the former is a claim for reasonable remuneration, whereas the latter is a claim for compensation. Where a party was appointed engineer and town surveyor subject to ministerial sanction, in *O'Connell v Listowel UDC* (1957), it was held, when the sanction was refused, that reasonable remuneration on a *quantum meruit* must be paid for the six months' service rendered.

Specific Performance

The court may, by an order of specific performance, enforce the due performance of the contract. But not all contracts may be enforced in this way. For example, the High Court refused, in *Duggan v Allied Irish Building Society* (1976), to grant specific performance of a contract to advance money. Nor will contracts for personal services be specifically enforced.

Specific performance is a discretionary remedy. It will not be granted against a party, the victim of innocent misrepresentation: see *Smelter Corporation of Ireland v O'Driscoll* (page 108). Generally, this remedy will not be granted where damages are an adequate remedy and, conversely, damages may be awarded where the court deems it inappropriate to grant specific performance. This occurred in *Duggan's* case. Specific performance may not be awarded in hardship cases, or may be awarded, as in *O'Brien v Kearney* (1995), with a reduction in the purchase price of the property.

Injunction

An injunction is a court order directing a party to do, or to refrain from doing, a specific act. The courts may restrain a party by injunction from committing a breach of contract. Injunctions are granted in cases in which monetary compensation is an inadequate remedy. This occurred in *Fruid Power Technology Co. Ltd v Sperry Ltd* (1985) (page 122) where one party purported to terminate the contract pre-emptorily without the required notice, in order to contract with a third party. The High Court granted an injunction because compensation would be an inadequate remedy in that the damage done to the business would be irreparable.

This remedy is a common feature in disputes concerning contracts in restraint of trade (page 116) and breach of constitutional rights (page 66).

Rescission

The right to rescind is one in which a party to a transaction sometimes has to set that transaction aside and be restored to his or her former position. The purpose of rescission is to release the parties from the contract. A party rescinding a contract must be restored to the position prior to the contract. Therefore, property must be returned, possession given up and accounts taken of profits or deterioration. Damages are not recoverable, because the purpose of this remedy is to place the party recovering in the position he or she would have been in, had the contract been performed.

Rescission may be claimed in cases of mistake: see *Gun v McCarthy* (page 106). But the High Court decided in *Ferguson v Merchant Banking Ltd* (1993) that rescission would not be granted where the mistake by one of the parties is neither shared nor contributed to by the other party, who is unaware that the contract does not give effect to the intention of that party. Rescission may be granted in cases of fraudulent misrepresentation: see *Carbin v Somerville* (page 109); undue influence: see *White v Meade* (page 108); and unconscionable bargain: see *Grealish v Murphy* (page 111).

Rectification

Where parties to a contract agree on terms and that agreement is reduced into written form, which either does not contain those agreed verbal terms or contains different terms to those agreed, the court may rectify the written document to conform to the terms verbally agreed. The court is concerned with defects in the recording of the contract and not in its making.

The Supreme Court, in *Irish Life Assurance Co. Ltd v Dublin Land Securities* (1989) (page 106), ruled that to grant rectification of a contract, the party seeking it must establish a common continuing intention in relation to a particular provision of the contract agreed between the parties up to the point of execution of the formal contract. That party must establish by convincing proof that the instrument does not reflect the common intention of the parties, especially where long negotiations have taken place, during which both had legal advice. The party seeking relief must show what the common intention of the parties was. The High Court held, in *Lac Minerals Ltd v Chevron Mineral Corporation of Ireland* (1995), that while privity of contract was not an essential precondition to a claim for rectification, there must be some nexus between the person claiming rectification and the document in respect of which rectification was sought. In that case the plaintiff could not seek rectification because it was not a party to the agreement and did not derive any interest under it.

A mistake made by both parties, or merely known to one, is a ground for rectification: see *Monaghan County Council v Vaughan* (page 105).

Part Three
CRIMINAL LAW

Chapter 12

CRIMINAL LIABILITY

Purpose of the Criminal Law

The purpose of the criminal law is to forbid conduct that unjustifiably inflicts or threatens substantial harm to the individual or to the public interest. The preservation of public peace and order is achieved by giving fair warning of the nature of the offensive conduct and by imposing punishment which reflects an emphatic rejection by the community of both the crime and the offender. The courts not alone seek to do justice by imposing the punishment deserved, but also strive to punish equally offenders who possess an equal degree of guilt. The purpose of sanctions is to punish past wrongdoing and to deter repetitions. Reform of the offender through rehabilitation is a secondary consideration, though much modern penal legislation is directed towards that end.

Definition of a Crime

A crime is defined as a wrongful act which directly and seriously threatens the security or well-being of society, and which is unsafe to be redressed by the mere compensation of the injured party. It is a wrongful act against the community with punishment imposed by the courts and enforced by the executive.

THE CLASSIFICATION OF CRIME

Constitutional Division of Crimes

The Constitution distinguishes between minor and other offences for the purposes of trial. A minor offence is not defined by the Constitution, so it falls to the courts to supply a definition. The Supreme Court, in *Melling v Ó Mathghamhna* (1962), laid down the following criteria for determining this question: (i) how the law stood when the statute was passed; (ii) the severity of the penalty; (iii) the moral quality of the act; and (iv) its relation to common law offences. 'Punishment', according to Lavery J., 'is the most important consideration.' By and large the subsequent cases have been decided on the issue of punishment. There are three broad types of cases:

(i) those where imprisonment is a possible punishment; (ii) those where the sole penalty is the imposition of a fine; and (iii) those where the loss of a licence follows conviction.

The Supreme Court, in *Conroy v Attorney General* (1965), decided that an offence which carried six months' imprisonment and/or a fine of £100 was a minor offence. But in *The State (Sheerin) v Kennedy* (1966) the Supreme Court held that an offence which merited a two-year sentence in a borstal institution was a non-minor offence. The Supreme Court held, in *In re Haughey* (1971), that an offence which carried an unlimited prison sentence was considered to be non-minor. These cases suggest that where imprisonment is less than six months, the offence is minor and where it is two years or more, it is non-minor. Further cases may decide where precisely the line can be drawn.

Offences may be punished by fine rather than imprisonment. What are the limits in this respect? The High Court held, in *Cullen v Attorney General* (1979), that the imposition of an unlimited fine in lieu of damages for negligent driving created a non-minor offence. The punishment for illegal fishing is the forfeiture of gear and catch which, in *Kostan v Ireland* (1978), was valued in the region of £100,000. The High Court held the offence to be non-minor. The Supreme Court, in *The State (Rollinson) v Kelly* (1984), held that the imposition of a £500 fine rendered the offence a minor one. From these cases it can be seen that the line can be drawn somewhere between £500 and £100,000.

A third sanction which may be imposed is the loss of a licence. In *Conroy v Attorney General* (1965), mentioned earlier, together with imprisonment and/or a fine there was a mandatory disqualification from driving for a stated period. The Supreme Court held the disqualification was not in the nature of a punishment, but was the withdrawal of a statutory right and this could not be considered when deciding whether the offence was minor or non-minor. The High Court decided, in *The State (Pheasantry Ltd) v Donnelly* (1982), that the loss of a wine licence on conviction for a third time under the licensing laws was considered too remote in character to be taken into account when deciding whether the offence was minor or non-minor.

The consequence of deciding this crucial question as to whether an offence is minor or non-minor was considered on page 48 when examining the various methods of trials.

Statutory Division

The common law divided crimes into felonies and misdemeanours. The *Criminal Law Act 1997* abolished this distinction and in its place provided for arrestable offences, which are defined as offences for which a person of full capacity may be punished by imprisonment for a term of five years or by a more severe penalty. Therefore, arrestable offences are the most obvious serious offences such as murder, rape and kidnapping.

Procedural Division

This division divides crimes according to their method of trial. Minor offences, known as summary offences, are tried in the District Court without a jury. Non-minor offences, known as indictable offences, are tried by a jury in the Circuit Court or Central Criminal Court or in the non-jury Special Criminal Court. The trial of offences is discussed fully on page 47. From this procedural division it can be seen why the classification of crimes into minor and non-minor offences is so important: it dictates the method of trial.

INGREDIENTS OF A CRIME

Actus Reus and Mens Rea

To secure a conviction for a felony or misdemeanour, it must be proved beyond a reasonable doubt that the accused committed a guilty act, the *actus reus*, with guilty intent, the *mens rea.*

The *actus reus* consists of some act or some omission forbidden by law. The conduct of the accused must come within the forbidden action. The *actus* must be directly attributable to the accused and not to another person, unless the accused incited that other person or they shared a common purpose. The *actus* must be done voluntarily.

The *mens rea* means a blameworthy state of mind. What the law regards as blameworthy varies from offence to offence. It may be intentional conduct, as in murder or rape, where the consequences are foreseen and desired; or it may be reckless or grossly negligent, as in manslaughter, where the consequences are foreseen but not necessarily desired; or it may be negligent, as in dangerous driving, where the consequences are not foreseen in circumstances where the law requires foresight.

Motive

Motive is not an ingredient in the legal definition of a crime. Motive may assist in the solution of a crime, but it is not an essential proof in a trial. An act is none the less criminal where it is motiveless and a good motive does not excuse a crime.

Strict Liability

Until the middle of the last century it was the common law judges who exclusively created new offences as the necessity arose. When statute intervened, the difficulty arose as to whether *mens rea* was an ingredient of statutory crimes. The courts inclined to regard solely the words of the statutes without importing the element of *mens rea*, because what was being created in language of great exactitude was a host of minor offences carrying relatively light penalties. A strict interpretation of the wording of these statutes excluded *mens rea.*

But courts are only inclined to impose strict liability where the penalty is trivial. In more serious crimes created by statute the courts do not impose strict liability because they argue that the legislature would not encroach on individual rights without expressly and clearly saying so. As one judge explained: 'The Oireachtas may make acts crimes although the accused was not aware that he was committing an offence. But, to effect this, clear language must be used. In the absence of such an indication, the general rule is that the guilty mind or criminal intent must be established in relation to each ingredient of the offence.'

CRIMINAL CAPACITY

Minority

In criminal law a minor's liability depends on age. It is a principle of law that a minor under seven years cannot commit a crime. Such a minor is *doli incapax*. The law considers that since the minor cannot distinguish right from wrong, not having reached the age of reason, the minor cannot form the guilty intention (the *mens rea*) to commit a crime.

Every minor between the ages of seven and fourteen years is presumed to be *doli incapax*. This presumption may be rebutted by proving mischievous disposition. This incapacity was discussed in malicious damages cases. The High Court held, in *Cashman v Cork County Council* (1950), where some boys under the age of fourteen set fire to a motorcycle in a shed, that the act was wanton and deliberate. Two boys aged nine and ten years, in *Goodbody v Waterford Corporation* (1953), were playing on a lorry when one boy lit a match and goods were burned. The High Court held it was a thoughtless and irresponsible act done on the spur of the moment. Minors become fully capable of criminal behaviour on reaching their fourteenth birthday.

DEFENCES TO CRIMES

Insanity

Insanity exempts from criminal responsibility a person who commits an act which otherwise would be criminal. The *M'Naghten Rules* (1843) are the recognised authoritative statement on legal insanity. These rules were formulated in reply to a number of questions submitted to the judges following the acquittal of Daniel M'Naghten, on the ground of insanity, of the murder of Sir Robert Peel's secretary.

The rules are three in number. First, every person is presumed to be sane and to possess a sufficient degree of reason until the contrary is proved. Second, to establish a defence of insanity, it must be clearly proved that, at the time of committing the act, the accused was labouring under such a defect of reason from disease of the mind as not to know the nature and quality of the act being done, or, where it was known, that the accused did not know he was doing wrong. Third, if the person was conscious that the act was one that ought not to be done, and if that act was at the time contrary to the law, it is punishable. The Court of Criminal Appeal, in *Attorney General v O'Shea* (1931), held that mental abnormality did not amount to legal insanity. The same court, in *Attorney General v O'Brien* (1936), decided the M'Naghten Rules were not the sole test of insanity because those rules were confined to persons with insane delusions. This view was restated by the Supreme Court in *Doyle v Wicklow County Council* (1971). In that case a youth burned down a slaughterhouse because he considered the killing of animals as senseless and unnecessary. He knew his act was wrong, contrary to law and forbidden by society, but believed he should not be punished because of a distorted judgment and emotional disturbance. The Supreme Court ruled in *The People (DPP) v O'Mahony* (1985) that the defence of diminished responsibility did not form part of Irish law.

Where such a defence is raised, the onus of proof rests on the accused and it must be established to the satisfaction of the court on the balance of probabilities. A verdict of guilty but insane is a verdict of acquittal. The Supreme Court ruled, in *DPP v Gallagher* (1991), that the role of the court when such a verdict was made was to order that person's detention until the Government decided the issue of continued detention or release. That person may apply to the Government for release on the grounds that he was not suffering from any mental disorder warranting his continued detention in the public and private interest. The Government must inquire into all the relevant circumstances and must apply fair procedures in its consideration.

Drunkenness

The common law regarded drunkenness as aggravating guilt. It did not afford an excuse for the commission of a crime because, unlike insanity, it was induced voluntarily. Drunkenness continues to offer no defence unless it produces temporary insanity or it negatives the specific intention required for the crime charged.

Far from being a defence, drunkenness may be an ingredient which assists in proving the commission of an offence. In *The People (AG) v Regan* (1975) the Court of Criminal Appeal held the fact that the accused had consumed a significant quantity of alcohol before the commission of events on which the charge was based, was relevant and admissible on a charge of dangerous driving.

Duress

It is a defence to prove that the offence was committed while under the coercion of another. This defence is rarely successful because the courts regard it with suspicion.

In *Attorney General v Whelan* (1934) the scope of the defence of duress *per minas* was stated. On a charge of receiving stolen money, the accused claimed he did so under threats of personal violence. The Court of Criminal Appeal, per Murnaghan J. explained: 'It seems to us that threats of immediate death or serious personal violence so great as to overbear the ordinary power of human resistance should be accepted as a justification for acts which would otherwise be criminal . . . where the excuse of duress is applicable it must . . . be clearly shown that the overpowering of the will was operative at the time the crime was actually committed and, if there was reasonable opportunity for the will to reassert itself, no justification can be found in antecedent threats.' The court noted that duress, no matter how great, was no defence to murder and the Court of Criminal Appeal so held in *The People (DPP) v Murray* (1977) where a wife pleaded that she had killed in the presence of, and under the will of her husband.

Self-defence

The common law rules relating to self-defence have been replaced by statutory rules contained in the *Non-Fatal Offences Against the Person Act 1997* which provides that the use of reasonable force is permissible to protect any person from injury, assault or detention caused by a criminal act or to prevent crime or a breach of the peace (see page 167). The use of reasonable force to protect property is also permissible.

Diplomatic and Other Immunities

In accordance with the principles of international law, foreign diplomats and their families are immune from prosecution for criminal offences which are committed within the State. These principles are incorporated into the *Diplomatic Relations and Immunities Act 1967*. The members of the Oireachtas cannot be arrested while going to, in, and coming from the Houses of the Oireachtas, though they may be arrested elsewhere. This immunity is excluded in cases of treason, felony and breach of the peace though, of course, they may be arrested elsewhere. There is complete immunity from criminal prosecution and civil action for utterances made within the Oireachtas by its members.

Those taking part in judicial proceedings are immune from prosecution for things said in the course of those proceedings provided what is said is relevant to the proceedings in progress (see Judicial Immunity on page 41).

CRIMINAL PARTICIPATION

Degrees of Participation

Often there is only a single participant in a crime. Where there are more than one, all may possess an equal degree of guilt or, depending on the actual circumstances, some may attract a greater or lesser amount of guilt than others. There are three possible degrees of participation in a criminal offence.

Principal Offender

The principal in the first degree is the person who commits the *actus reus* with the necessary *mens rea*, or who instigates an innocent agent to perform the *actus reus*. The agent, having no blameworthy intention, incurs no criminal liability.

Aider and Abettor

The common law provided that the principal in the second degree was one who rendered aid, assistance or encouragement at the time the crime was actually committed. The principal offender and the abettor must be acting in a common purpose. In *The People (AG) v Ryan* (1966) the accused was one of a gang who attacked an unarmed group after a dance which resulted in the death of one. The inflicter of the injuries was convicted of murder and the accused of manslaughter. The Court of Criminal Appeal held that the accused's presence in the group of attackers, where knowingly to lend the assailant support in his enterprise, was sufficient for conviction.

Accessories

The *Criminal Law Act 1997* provides that any person who aids, abets, counsels or procures the commission of an indictable offence shall be tried and punished as a principal offender. The common law considered such a person to be an accessory before the fact. To be convicted, that person must know the particular deed contemplated before its performance, and assent or approval must have encouraged the principal offender. In *The People (DPP) v Madden* (1977) one of the accused who stole a car used in a murder in which he did not participate, though he knew that something was going to be done to the victim, was properly convicted of murder as an accessory before the fact.

A person who, with knowledge that a crime has been committed, shelters or conceals the offender in such a way as to enable that person to evade justice, is an accessory after the fact. Some active assistance, however slight, with the intention to assist the offender is necessary. Passive activity, such as abstaining from arresting the offender, is not enough.

PRELIMINARY CRIMES

Inchoate Crimes

Preliminary, or inchoate crimes, are underdeveloped crimes in which the *mens rea* of the intended crime is present, whereas any act done is only a step towards the execution of the full crime. In every crime some brief or prolonged active conduct by the offender must precede the ultimate end. This preparatory activity consists in a single step, or a series of steps, taken in furtherance of the desired end. Any of these steps may amount to one, or more, of the inchoate crimes which are independent and complete crimes.

Attempt to Commit a Crime

'An attempt', according to Haugh J. in *The People (AG) v Thornton* (1952), 'consists of an act done by the accused with a specific intent to commit a particular crime; that it must go beyond mere preparation, and must be a direct movement towards the commission after the preparations have been made; that some such act is required, and if it only remotely leads to the commission of the offence and is not immediately connected therewith, it cannot be considered as an attempt to commit an offence.' In that case a conviction for unlawfully attempting to procure a poison, knowing it was intended to be used in a miscarriage, was quashed because the evidence only showed that the accused asked a doctor about that particular drug. The mere desire to commit a crime was not sufficient to constitute an attempt.

The accused, in *Attorney General v Richmond* (1935), broke into a loft, laid a trail of wood-shavings, and placed a bottle of paraffin and a wick in position. The Court of Criminal Appeal upheld a conviction for attempted arson. Mere words are insufficient to constitute an attempt. A conviction of attempting to procure an act of gross indecency was quashed in *The People (AG) v England* (1947) by the Court of Criminal Appeal because, per Gavan Duffy P.: 'There are numberless ways in which a man may describe the attractive facility for crime to another in lucid terms without incurring a charge of attempting to turn the hearer into a criminal; everyone has come across instances both in literature and on the screen. And something more beyond description is reasonably required by the law for an attempt to procure the commission of a crime.'

The Court of Criminal Appeal decided, in *The People (AG) v Dermody* (page 146), that there cannot be convictions for the substantive offence and for an attempt to commit the same offence.

Conspiracy to Commit a Crime

A conspiracy is an agreement by two or more persons to commit an unlawful act, or an agreement to commit a lawful act by unlawful means. It is, as one judge said, 'the consensus of two minds'. It was held in *The People (AG) v Keane* (1975) that conspiracy to commit an offence should not be charged where the substantive offence can be laid.

It is not a conspiracy to combine, or agree, to do any act in furtherance of a trade dispute. This immunity from criminal liability is granted by the *Industrial Relations Act 1990* (page 474).

Incitement to Commit a Crime

It is an offence to incite another to commit an offence. This is so whether that other person accepts or rejects the incitement. The essential ingredient is the soliciting of another towards a criminal action. In *The People (AG) v Capaldi* (1949) the accused brought a girl to a doctor, and when she was found to be pregnant he asked the doctor to 'do something for her' and said 'there is ample money to meet your fees'. The Court of Criminal Appeal upheld a conviction for incitement to commit an abortion because, said Maguire CJ. : 'The jury must necessarily have taken the view that the accused was doing something essentially different from giving vent to a mere desire, and was in fact seriously and specifically seeking to employ the doctor to perform an illegal operation on a . . . female for reward.'

JURISDICTION OF THE COURTS

Jurisdiction as to Place

The jurisdiction of our courts over criminal activity extends, not alone over the land, islands and waters of the State, but to Irish-registered ships both on the high seas and within the territorial waters of another state. In *The People (AG) v Thomas* (1954) a trial for a manslaughter which occurred on a passenger ship between Liverpool and Dublin, while it was fifteen miles off the Welsh coast, was rightly conducted in Dublin. But any offence committed abroad on an Irish-registered aircraft is considered to have been committed where the offender is: *Air Navigation and Transport Act 1936*, as amended.The *Criminal Law (Jurisdiction) Act 1976* confers jurisdiction on the courts of this State to try persons for certain offences which are committed in Northern Ireland and Britain. The *Sexual Offences (Jurisdiction) Act 1996* provides that certain sexual offences against children committed outside the State by a citizen or a person ordinarily resident in the State may be tried in this State provided the act is an offence in the place where the act was committed and is an offence under Irish law.

Jurisdiction as to Time

As a general principle there is no time limitation on the prosecution of crimes. A person may face prosecution at any time for an offence, though for practical reasons, a prosecution is brought as soon as possible after the commission of the crime. Otherwise witnesses may die, become aged or ill, be untraceable, or merely forget the events in question. In *The State (O'Connell) v Fawsitt* (1986) the accused was returned for trial in 1982 and the case was adjourned periodically until 1985. The Supreme Court ruled that an accused was entitled to be tried with reasonable expedition and that in this case there had been excessive and inexcusable delay.

There are exceptions to this general rule. In cases of homicide the victim must die within a year and a day of the assault for a murder prosecution to follow. Prosecution for certain sexual offences must be commenced within a year. And almost all prosecutions for summary offences must be commenced within six months.

Chapter 13

OFFENCES AGAINST PUBLIC ORDER

OFFENCES AGAINST THE STATE

Treason

The most serious crime known to the criminal law is treason. It breaches that loyalty due to the State and constitutes an attack on its properly constituted organs of government. The *Treason Act 1939* defines the offence as the 'levying of war against the State, or assisting any State or person, or inciting or conspiring with any person to levy war against the State, or attempting by force of arms or other violent means to overthrow the organs of government established under the Constitution, or taking part or being concerned in or inciting or conspiring with any person to make or to be concerned in any such attempt.' Treason may be committed in or outside the State.

Usurpation of Government

The *Offences Against the State Act 1939* creates offences closely related to treason. The usurpation of the function of government may be committed in three ways. First, it may be committed by setting up, maintaining, or partaking in any body purporting to be a government, or legislature not authorised by the Constitution. Second, it consists of the establishing, maintaining or partaking in a court or tribunal not constitutionally based. Third, the setting up, maintaining or partaking in any army or police force not authorised by law is prohibited.

The offence of obstruction of government consists of preventing or obstructing or intimidating any arm of government, whether legislative, executive or judicial by force of arms or other violent means. In *The People (DPP) v Keogh* (1983) the accused, armed with a stout pole, aimed blows at a garda in the course of a riot. This was held by the Court of Criminal Appeal to amount to an attempt to prevent, by violent means, members of the Garda Síochána from performing their duties. A similar offence relates to obstructing the exercise of the President's duties.

Interference with the military or police force by violence with the intention to undermine public order or the authority of the State is an offence. To incite or encourage any civil servant to refuse, neglect or omit to perform any duty is prohibited. The promotion of secret societies within the army or Garda Síochána is an offence.

Unlawful Organisations
It is an offence to belong to an unlawful organisation which is one formed for treasonable, anti-constitutional, criminal, or illegal purposes. It is prohibited to administer an unlawful oath or to take an unlawful oath.

Official Secrets
It is an offence under the *Official Secrets Act 1963* to give or to get, or possess, or publish any information of a military nature, or any other matter which prejudices the safety of the State. It is an offence to communicate official information.

Sedition
Sedition consists of attempts at meetings or in speeches or by publication to disturb the tranquillity of the State, and the Constitution provides that it must be punished by law.

Public Order Offences
The *Criminal Justice (Public Order) Act 1994* creates a number of offences. Riot is where twelve or more persons are present together and use, or threaten to use, unlawful violence for a common purpose and where conduct, taken together, causes a person of reasonable firmness to fear for his/her, or another person's safety. The offence of violent disorder occurs where three or more persons assemble for a similar purpose, and the offence of affray is committed where two or more persons assemble for a similar purpose.

Force may be used in the suppression of riotous assembly. It is lawful to use reasonable force in the protection of life or property. Force is not reasonable where it is greater than the force necessary for the purpose, or disproportionate to the evil being prevented. In *Lynch v Fitzgerald* (1938) damages were awarded to the father of a youth killed by the gardaí when they fired on a riotous assembly where it was not as a last resort to protect lives or property.

OFFENCES AGAINST RELIGION

Blasphemy
Blasphemy, or blasphemous libel, consists of indecent and offensive attacks on Christianity, or the scriptures, or sacred persons or objects calculated to outrage the feelings of the community. The denial of Christian teaching is not

sufficient. In *Corway v Independent Newspapers Ltd* (1997), it was alleged that a cartoon which showed a stout comic figure of a priest in an old-fashioned surplice holding the host in one hand and a chalice in the other, and three government ministers in caricature each with a hand up indicating rejection of the host and chalice, with the words 'Hello, progress — bye-bye father' was a blasphemous libel. The High Court held that it was not clear that at first sight there was beyond argument a case to answer if the matter was tried, and that since it was an isolated cartoon in a national newspaper which had not made a practice of offending Christian or Catholic beliefs, the public interest would not be served by instituting such a prosecution. It is an offence to disturb public worship held in a church, churchyard or burial ground in a riotous, violent or indecent manner.

OFFENCES AGAINST PUBLIC MORALS

Bigamy

The *Offences Against the Person Act 1861* provides that any person who marries another during the lifetime of his or her spouse is guilty of bigamy. It is a defence to prove that the spouse had been continually absent for at least the previous seven years and was not known by the person marrying again to be alive within that time.

Public Indecency

A person who, at, or near, or in sight of any place which the public habitually pass, commits any indecent act, commits an offence. Indecency means any act which offends modesty, causes scandal or injures the morals of the community.

It is an offence to show for gain or reward an indecent or profane performance. In *Attorney General v Simpson* (1959) it was decided that there must be an intention to deprave or corrupt those viewing the performance (in that instance *The Rose Tattoo* by Tennessee Williams), whose minds were open to such immoral influences. The District Court held there was no such intention.

A public sale, or exposure for sale, or exposure to public view of any indecent book, picture or print is an offence. Soliciting for the purposes of prostitution in any public place, the organisation of prostitution, living on the earnings of prostitution, and the keeping of a brothel, are offences contrary to the *Criminal Law (Sexual Offences) Act 1993*.

OFFENCES AGAINST THE ADMINISTRATION OF JUSTICE

Perjury

The giving of false evidence on oath is perjury. The evidence in question may be given in a court or before other statutory tribunals at which evidence on oath may be heard. The perjured evidence must be material; it cannot be perjury where the evidence is extraneous or irrelevant. The statement must have been made with knowledge as to its falsity.

Contempt of Court

A contempt of court is anything which tends to create a disregard for the authority of the courts of justice. This may be an open insult or resistance to the judge who presides, or disobedience to court orders, or any words or actions tending to lower their authority (see pages 41 and 50).

Chapter 14

OFFENCES AGAINST THE PERSON

HOMICIDE

Nature of Homicide

The killing of a human is homicide. There are three categories of homicide. Justifiable homicide may occur in the following ways: the killing of a person who assaults or resists and who cannot be arrested otherwise; or the killing of a person, as a last resort, after all other means have failed, in the suppression of a riotous assembly, or in the prevention of an atrocious crime.

Excusable homicide is of two kinds. Misadventure is the unfortunate mischance arising out of a lawful act, such as the playing of a game. Self-defence excuses a homicide provided no more force than is necessary is used. Felonious homicides consists of murder, manslaughter and infanticide.

Murder

Murder is the unlawful killing with malice aforethought of a human being. A sane person over the age of reason may commit murder. For a prosecution to succeed, it must be proved that the victim was living at the time of the impugned action. It is not murder to kill a foetus in the womb, or a child in the process of being born. To constitute murder the child must have had an existence independent of the mother. But it may be abortion, which is considered later.

It is a common law rule that the victim must have died within a year and a day of the assault. Otherwise, it would be difficult to trace to the offender the cause of the victim's death after a longer interval. The actions of the offender must exclusively cause the victim's death. The Court of Criminal Appeal, in *The People (AG) v McGrath* (1960), rejected the contention that a *novus actus interveniens*, namely, the removal of the victim to hospital by car, was the cause of death. The court held that death was caused by a blow struck by the accused.

The *mens rea* of murder is traditionally called malice aforethought. To the lay person it denotes ill-will, or premeditation. To the law it means intention. The jury, when convicting for murder in *Attorney General v O'Shea* (1931), recorded a rider to their verdict 'unpremeditated crime committed during a period of mental abnormality'. The Court of Criminal Appeal refused to equate such a rider with an acquittal because premeditation is not an element of murder. Malice aforethought is present, according to the *Criminal Justice Act 1964* where 'the accused intended to kill or cause serious injury to some person whether the person is actually killed or not'.

Statutory Murder

According to the *Criminal Justice Act 1990* where a person (other than a child or young person) is convicted of (a) the murder of a member of the Garda Síochána acting in the course of duty; or (b) a prison officer acting in the course of duty; or (c) murder done while committing certain offences created by the *Offences Against the State Act 1939*; or (d) murder, committed within the State for a political motive, of a head of a foreign state or of a member of the government of, or a diplomatic officer of, a foreign state, the court shall in passing sentence specify as the minimum period of imprisonment to be served by that person a period of not less than forty years.

The *mens rea* required for statutory murder was laid down in *The People (DPP) v Murray* (1977) where fleeing bank robbers, who shot a plain clothes garda, had their convictions for capital murder quashed by the Supreme Court which held that there must be an intention to kill a garda, or recklessness, which means an advertence to the possibility that the person to be killed is a garda and then the taking of that risk.

Self-defence

At common law the use of force is lawful for the necessary defence of any person, rules which are now contained in the *Non-Fatal Offences Against the Person Act 1997* (see page 134, dealing with self-defence in general). But the justification is limited by the necessity of the occasion, and the use of unnecessary force is unlawful. The Court of Criminal Appeal, in *The People (AG) v Keatley* (1954), ordered a retrial where defence of another was pleaded to a charge of manslaughter. The accused struck a fatal blow in defence of his brother who had been attacked by the deceased. The self-defence plea may be rejected where excessive force is used. In *The People (AG) v O'Brien* (1969) the deceased kicked the accused, who kicked back, and a fight developed during which both fell to the footpath and punched each other. The deceased got on top of the accused who then used a knife he was carrying to kill the deceased. The Court of Criminal Appeal ruled that the verdict of manslaughter should stand. In *The People (AG) v Commane* (1975) a conviction for murder was upheld where the deceased attacked the accused, who then rendered the deceased immobile by a forceful blow with a blunt object and then strangled him.

The Supreme Court ruled, in *The People (AG) v Dwyer* (1972), that a murder charge should be reduced to manslaughter where a person was subjected to a violent attack and used more force than was necessary, but no more force than was honestly believed to be necessary in self-defence.

Manslaughter

Manslaughter is a diverse crime covering unlawful homicide which is not murder or infanticide. Manslaughter is divided into voluntary manslaughter and involuntary manslaughter.

In voluntary manslaughter the malice aforethought of murder may be present, but some circumstance mitigates the crime to manslaughter. The common law acknowledged provocation as the only voluntary manslaughter. Provocation is some act, or series of acts, done by the deceased to the accused, which would cause in any reasonable person, and actually caused in the accused, a sudden and temporary loss of self-control, which rendered the accused so subject to passion as to make him or her for the moment not the master of his or her own mind. This defence was accepted in *The People (DPP) v MacEoin* (1978) where the accused, in defending himself against an attack with a hammer by the deceased, lost control and killed the deceased. The Court of Criminal Appeal, per Kenny J. explained: 'When the defence of provocation is raised... the judge should rule on whether there is any evidence of provocation which, having regard to the accused's temperament, character and circumstances, might have caused him to lose control of himself at the time of the wrongful act and whether the provocation bears a reasonable relation to the amount of force used by the accused.' Where such evidence exists, the court must consider the defence.

Involuntary manslaughter includes all unlawful homicides without malice aforethought, though some mental element akin to unlawfulness is necessary and this elusive factor lies somewhere between *mens rea* and negligence. The rules in this regard were laid down in *The People (AG) v Dunleavy* (1948) by the Court of Criminal Appeal where the manslaughter arose from the driving of a car. Davitt J. said: 'There are different degrees of negligence, fraught with different legal consequences.' Ordinary negligence in the driving of a motor car does not render a person guilty of manslaughter. The higher degree of negligence necessary to prove dangerous driving is not necessarily sufficient either. To prove manslaughter the fatal negligence must be of a very high degree, such as to involve the risk or likelihood of substantial personal injuries to others.

Suicide

At common law it was a crime to take one's own life. This crime was called self-murder, or *felonia de se*. The *Criminal Law (Suicide) Act 1993* abolished the crime of suicide and created the new offence of aiding, abetting, counselling or procuring the suicide, or the attempted suicide, of another person.

Infanticide

This modern felony was created by the *Infanticide Act 1949*. Where a woman, by any wilful act or omission, causes the death of her child under the age of twelve months, but at the time the balance of her mind was disturbed by reason of her not having fully recovered from the effect of giving birth to the child then, notwithstanding that the circumstances would amount to murder but for the statute, she should be guilty of infanticide and be punished as if she was guilty of manslaughter.

SEXUAL OFFENCES

Rape

The *Criminal Law (Rape) (Amendment) Act 1990* defines rape as a sexual assault that includes penetration (however slight) of the anus or mouth by the penis, or penetration (however slight) of the vagina by any object held or manipulated by another person.

There must be an absence of consent. An absolute defence to a charge of rape is consent, which must be given freely. The failure or omission to offer resistance to the act does not of itself constitute consent.

Any rule of law by which a husband cannot be guilty of the rape of his wife was abolished by the *Criminal Law (Rape) (Amendment) Act 1990.*

The judge has a discretion, having regard to all the evidence given, whether the jury should be given a warning about the danger of convicting the accused on the uncorroborated evidence of the complainant. The victim's complaint, made shortly after the attack, may be given in evidence, not as to the truth of the attack but to establish her consistency of complaint. Under the *Criminal Law (Rape) Act 1981* no evidence may be adduced, without the leave of the judge, about any sexual experience, other than that to which the charge relates.

Unlawful Carnal Knowledge

The unlawful carnal knowledge, meaning intercourse, of a female under the age of seventeen years is an offence: *Criminal Law (Amendment) Act 1935.*

These offences are identical to rape in that intercourse is essential, but the element of consent is removed by statute because females under the age of seventeen are considered incapable of consenting to sexual intercourse.

It was decided in *Dermody's* case (page 137) that there cannot be a conviction for rape and a conviction for unlawful carnal knowledge in relation to the same incident.

Sexual Assaults

Aggravated sexual assault is a sexual assault which involves serious violence or the threat of serious violence or is such as to cause injury, humiliation or degradation of a grave nature to the person assaulted.

An indecent assault upon a female constitutes the offence of sexual assault. An assault is indecent where accompanied by circumstances of indecency. Consent is a defence unless the female is under the age of fifteen years. A woman may indecently assault another woman.

Any indecent touching of a male without his consent is a sexual assault. Consent is a defence unless the male is under the age of sixteen years. Should a woman allow a male under the age of sixteen years to have intercourse with her, she commits a sexual assault upon him.

Incest

A male person who has sexual intercourse with a female who is, to his knowledge, his mother, sister, daughter or granddaughter, is guilty of incest. A female over the age of sixteen who permits her father, brother, grandfather or son to have sexual intercourse with her, knowing him to be so related, is guilty of incest. These offences were created by the *Punishment of Incest Act 1908*. Consent is not a defence because the law considers sexual intercourse between closely related persons to be immoral.

Bestiality, Sodomy and Gross Indecency

The offence of bestiality is the penetration of an animal by a male, or of a female by an animal: *Offences Against the Person Act 1861*. Sodomy, or buggery, is the penetration per anus of a man or a woman. It is an offence where the male victim is under seventeen years of age: *Criminal Law (Sexual Offences) Act 1993*; and the female victim is under seventeen years of age: *Criminal Law (Rape) Act 1981*. Gross indecency is an act of a gross nature and purpose between male persons which falls short of buggery, and is only an offence where one party is under seventeen years of age: *Criminal Law (Sexual Offences) Act 1993*.

Abduction

It is an offence, under the *Non-Fatal Offences Against the Person Act 1997*, without lawful authority or reasonable excuse, to intentionally take or detain a child under the age of sixteen years so as to remove or keep the child from the person having lawful control of that child. In certain circumstances, a parent or guardian may commit this offence.

Abortion

An abortion is a miscarriage or the premature expulsion of the contents of the womb before the gestation term is completed. To procure an abortion by means of any poison, noxious substance, instrument, or any other thing is a crime: *Offences Against the Person Act 1861*. It is an offence for a woman to procure, or attempt to procure, an unlawful miscarriage, as it is for another person to procure it for her. However, there is one difference. In the case of the woman, it is essential that she is actually pregnant at the time, whereas in the case of any other person it is immaterial whether the woman was pregnant at the time. The accused, in *The People (AG) v Coleman* (1945), was convicted of the unlawful use of an instrument with intent to procure a miscarriage.

An unlawful abortion is not legally regarded as murder because the unborn, having no existence apart from the mother, is considered in law as having no existence at all. The unborn are acknowledged to be possessed of the constitutional right to life (see page 68).

FALSE IMPRISONMENTS

False Imprisonment Simpliciter

By virtue of the *Non-Fatal Offences Against the Person Act 1997*, a person commits the crime of false imprisonment who intentionally or recklessly takes or detains, or causes to be taken or detained, or otherwise restricts the personal liberty of another without that other's consent. A person acts without the consent of another if the person obtains the other's consent by force, or threat of force or by deception. False imprisonment is also a tort (see page 164).

Kidnapping

The most aggravated species of false imprisonment, known as kidnapping, is the stealing and carrying away, or secreting of a person, against that person's will. Consent is a defence where the person is over fourteen years of age. A conviction for kidnapping a fourteen-year-old boy was quashed by the Supreme Court, in *The People (AG) v Edge* (1943), where it was proved that he went to live with the accused voluntarily.

ASSAULT AND HARASSMENT

Assault

According to the *Non-Fatal Offences Against the Person Act 1997*, a person commits an assault who, without lawful excuse, intentionally and recklessly, directly or indirectly, applies force to, or causes an impact on the body of another, or causes another to believe on reasonable grounds that he or she is likely immediately to be subjected to any such force or impact, without the consent of the other. Force includes the application of heat, light, electric current, noise or any other form of energy and the application of matter in solid, liquid or gaseous form (see page 163 for assault as a tort).

Serious Assaults

The *Non-Fatal Offences Against the Person Act 1997* creates two serious assault offences. A person who intentionally or recklessly causes serious harm to another, which means injury which creates a substantial risk of death, or causes serious disfigurement, or substantial loss or impairment of the mobility of the body as a whole or of the function of any particular bodily member or organ, commits an offence.

And a person who assaults another, causing him or her harm, which includes harm to body or mind and pain and unconsciousness, is guilty of an offence.

Assaults on Garda Officers

It is an offence to assault, or resist, or wilfully obstruct a garda officer in the due execution of duty.

Harassment

According to the *Non-Fatal Offences Against the Person Act 1997*, it is an offence for a person, without lawful authority or reasonable excuse, by any means including the use of the telephone, to harass another by persistently following, watching, pestering, besetting or communicating with him or her. Harass means to act intentionally or recklessly towards the other person in such a way as to seriously interfere with his or her peace and privacy, or which causes alarm, distress or harm, and that a reasonable person would realise that these acts had the same effect.

Chapter 15

OFFENCES AGAINST PROPERTY

Larceny

Under the *Larceny Act 1916* a person commits larceny who, without the consent of the owner and without a claim of right made in good faith, takes and carries away anything capable of being stolen, with the intent at the time to permanently deprive the owner of it. Each ingredient must be present for the conduct to amount to stealing. The owner's consent must be full and free and not obtained by a trick, intimidation, threat or duress. The express owner includes a part owner, or the person having possession or control of the goods, or a person having special property in them. The taking must be done intentionally, without a mistake and with knowledge that the goods are the property of another.

A claim of right means an honest belief that the taker has the right to possess the property, despite the fact that this belief is erroneous or unreasonable. In *The People (AG) v Grey* (1944) the terms of employment allowed an employee free gas for domestic use. Because of the war gas was unavailable, so he used electrical equipment belonging to his employers. The Court of Criminal Appeal held that the employee should be acquitted if, when he took the equipment, he had an honest belief that he could do so, even though this belief was wrong in law or in fact. The same court held, in *The People (DPP) v O'Loughlin* (1979), that where a person was found in possession of machinery, he should have been allowed to adduce evidence as to his belief that he was entitled to take it because the owner allegedly owed him a sum of money.

To constitute stealing, there must be a taking which may be actual or constructive. An actual taking is the seizing of the goods acquisitively and not the mere touching or moving of them inquisitively. The complete abstraction of a purse from a lady's handbag, which was returned by the accused when the owner was alerted, was held by the Court of Criminal Appeal in *The People (AG) v Mill* (1955) to be a sufficient asportation to constitute larceny.

A constructive taking can be achieved in a number of ways. Larceny by a trick occurs where a person with the necessary intent obtains goods from the owner, by means of some trick, who does not intend to part with the entire right of property in them, but only with its possession. Larceny by finding is committed where goods are found which the finder reasonably believes can be returned to the owner, but instead, appropriates them to his or her own use. Larceny may be committed by a bailee, who is one lawfully in possession of another's property, such as on loan or for safekeeping. When the bailee converts the goods to his or her own use, a larceny has been committed. The intention of the bailee at the time the goods are received is irrelevant: the material time, that is, when the larceny is committed, is the moment the bailee forms the intention to keep the goods.

The *mens rea*, or specific intention of larceny, is the intention to permanently deprive the owner of the goods. Such intention must exist at the moment the goods are taken. For example, those who take cars merely for joy-riding cannot be convicted of larceny because the intention to permanently deprive the owner of the vehicles is absent. On the other hand, where the car is destroyed after it has been used for joy-riding, the culprits may be guilty of larceny. *The Road Traffic Act 1961* created the offence of taking a car without the consent of the owner. The intention of permanent deprivation is not an ingredient of this offence.

Robbery

Robbery is committed where a person steals, and immediately before or at the time of that act, uses force on the victim, or puts or seeks to put any person in fear that the victim may be subjected to force: *Criminal Law (Jurisdiction) Act 1976.*

The ingredients of larceny must be present together with some element of force or fear of force. The force need only be directed against some person, and not the owner of the property which it is intended to steal. For example, it is robbery where force is used against one spouse to force the other spouse to part with property. The form and degree of violence may vary and is not confined to personal violence.

Where the actual stealing fails, the offence amounts to assault with intent to rob. Actual violence is not necessary: the putting in fear that violence will be used, coupled with the intention to rob constitute this crime.

Burglary

The *Criminal Law (Jurisdiction) Act 1976* creates two distinct burglary crimes. Simple burglary is the entering of any building as a trespasser with the intention to steal, or to inflict grievous bodily harm, or to rape, or to do any unlawful damage. This crime is committed despite an inability to achieve the intended result.

Aggravated burglary is committed where, at the time of simple burglary, the offender is possessed of any firearm, imitation firearm, an explosive, or other offensive weapon.

It was decided, in *The People (AG) v O'Brien* (1969) (discussed on page 144 when examining self-defence), that a knife was properly described as an offensive and not a defensive weapon.

Handling Stolen Goods

According to the *Larceny Act 1990* a person handles stolen property if (otherwise than in the course of the stealing), knowing or believing them to be stolen property, he or she dishonestly receives the property or dishonestly undertakes or assists in its retention, removal, disposal or realisation by or for the benefit of another person, or arranges to do any of these things.

A handler of stolen goods may be convicted, though the thief evades justice. The same person cannot be convicted of larceny and the dishonest handling of the same goods.

Where the original receipt is innocent and *bona fide*, the subsequent discovery that the goods are stolen does not convert the innocent receiving into an offence. Nor does the continued possession of goods on discovering the true facts alter the position.

The goods stolen must be identifiable with goods found in the accused's possession. A prosecution failed in the *Attorney General v Conway* (1926) because bags of wheat found with the accused could not positively be said to belong to the alleged owner. The property must be received in the form in which it was stolen. In the *Attorney General v Farnan* (1933) a prosecution failed because the accused received currency notes whereas coins had been stolen.

Where goods are recovered and returned to the owner's possession, this recovery deprives the goods of the character of stolen property. This rule defeats measures taken by an owner to entrap a culprit after detecting that a theft has taken place.

The *mens rea* of dishonest handling of property may be proved in various ways. The possession of goods recently stolen may, in the absence of reasonable explanation, infer that the possessor either stole or received them knowing them to have been stolen. The possessor may have purchased the goods at below market price, or in unusual places, or at unusual times. The test to be applied in such cases was stated in *The People (AG) v Berber and Levey* (1944) by the Court of Criminal Appeal. Black J. said: 'To set up ordinary prudence as the test of guilty knowledge is to make imprudence a necessary badge of fraud, whereas a reasonable mind may often be satisfied that property was received under circumstances indicating a transaction that was casual or incautious, indiscreet or venturesome, or even rash, without being criminal.'

Criminal Damage

According to the *Criminal Damage Act 1991* it is a crime to damage, destroy, deface, dismantle, render irreparable or unfit for use, prevent or impair the operation of any property. Property is defined as anything of a tangible nature, including money, animals and computer data belonging to any person, or to a person having lawful custody or control of it, or having in it any proprietary right or interest, or legal charge over it. The statute creates three offences. First, the offence of damaging the property of another without lawful excuse. Second, the aggravated offence of damaging any property without lawful excuse with the intention to endanger the life of another. Third, damage to any property belonging to the accused or another with the intent to defraud.

Arson

Arson is the malicious burning of premises. To constitute arson there must be some actual burning, though the entire premises need not be consumed by fire. It is an offence to maliciously set fire to premises with the intention to injure any person inside. To maliciously set fire to premises with the intention to defraud is an offence. Where the premises belong to the accused, no intention to defraud is inferred from the actual burning. The intention to defraud is often proved, as in the *Attorney General v Kyle* (1933), by the fact that the premises were insured.

Forcible Entry

To forcibly enter the property of another, or State property, is an offence. It is a further offence to remain in forcible occupation of the same property. By virtue of the *Prohibition of Forcible Entry and Occupation Act 1971* it is a good defence to a charge to prove that the accused is the owner or *bona fide* claimant to the property. On a forcible entry charge, it is a good defence to prove that the use and enjoyment of the property were not interfered with, and the entrant left when requested by the owner or a garda in uniform.

Forgery

The making or altering of a document with the intention to defraud another person of some right or property is forgery. This common law definition has been complemented by the *Forgery Act 1913* which provides that the making of a false document to be used as genuine is forgery. The documents covered include wills and codicils, deeds and bonds, bank notes and valuable securities, documents of title to land and goods, and policies of insurance.

Embezzlement

An employee who fraudulently intercepts, and then converts, money or goods before they come into the legal possession of the employer is guilty of embezzlement. *The People (AG) v Warren* (1945) decided that a rates collector, appointed by a local authority, was not an employee and could not be convicted of embezzlement.

Fraudulent Conversion

A person who is entrusted with another's property and appropriates it, or the proceeds from it to his or her own use or benefit, or to the use or benefit of a third party, commits the offence of fraudulent conversion. According to Ó Dálaigh J., in the Court of Criminal Appeal in *The People (AG) v Singer* (1975): 'The fiduciary element is the essential basis of the offence, and the entrustment is a genuine entrustment in which the fiduciary ownership has been lawfully obtained but which, so to speak, subsequently goes wrong.'

A solicitor who received money as a deposit on a house purchase was, in *The People (AG) v Murphy* (1947), guilty of fraudulent conversion when he kept the money rather than paying it over to the seller. A solicitor who received a bank draft made payable to a named person in the course of the administration of an estate, and caused that person to endorse it and later lodged it to his own bank account was, in *The People (AG) v Cowan* (1957), convicted of this offence.

To be guilty it must be proved that the accused received the money on behalf of another. There was some doubt on this point in the case of *Attorney General v Lawless* (1930) where the officer of a county council kept monies which he was entitled to by statute but the right to which he had waived on being appointed to his office. A matron of a nursing home who received a lump sum when admitting a patient, a practice discontinued some years previously by the order of nuns who ran the nursing home, had a conviction quashed in *The People (AG) v Heald* (1953) because it was not established that the money had been received on behalf of the nuns.

False Pretences

A false pretence of fact whereby a person, knowing it to be false, obtains from another any goods, or money, or valuable security, for his or her own benefit, with the intention to cheat or defraud that other, commits the offence of false pretences. 'Intent to defraud', explained Walsh J. in *The People (AG) v Thompson* (1960) in the Court of Criminal Appeal, 'is an essential ingredient of the offence although there are many cases in which it may be inferred from the facts of the case. Generally speaking it may be said that where money is obtained by false pretences there is a *prima facie* case of an intent to defraud.' It was decided, in *The People (AG) v Finkel* (1951), that the sale of counterfeit USA dollars for cash was a false pretence.

Part Four
THE LAW OF TORTS

Chapter 16

NATURE OF TORTIOUS LIABILITY

Nature of Tort

The word tort, from the Norman French, means a wrong. In Irish law the word tort is used to describe wrongs committed by one person against another which are considered of such a nature to warrant the award of compensation to the wronged party, but not so serious as to amount to a crime attracting punishment by the State on behalf of the common good. The law of torts is concerned with civil liability as distinct from criminal liability. It is distinguished from contractual liability in that it arises from obligations imposed by law as distinct from liability arising from obligations agreed between the parties. Some conducts, such as trespass to the person, and libel, are both a crime and a tort.

In civil actions the aggrieved party is the plaintiff, while the offending party is the defendant. The choice of court in which to take the action depends on the extent of loss and damage: see Civil Jurisdictions on page 43. An action is commenced in the High Court by Summons; it is commenced in the Circuit Court by Civil Bill; and in the District Court it is commenced by Civil Process.

Definition of Tort

A tort is a civil wrong for which the normal remedy is an action for unliquidated damages. This definition does little to indicate the acts or omissions which may lead to an award of compensation. A study of the various torts indicates that the law protects the person, reputation and property of the individual. Unliquidated damages are damages assessed by the court, in contrast to liquidated damages assessed by the parties. A tort consists of the breaching of a duty fixed by law and not one fixed by the parties as in the law of contract.

Legal Injury and Damage

Actual loss is not essential for a cause of action to arise in tort. The early torts developed were considered absolute, and a breach of that right, whether there was any actual loss, was actionable *per se*. In such instances there is legal injury without actual harm, or *injuria sine damno*. Trespass and libel are torts actionable *per se*. But in torts developed in modern times, such as negligence, some actual loss must have occurred.

Not all actions which result in damage are actionable. To be actionable some right recognised and protected by law must be breached. Where harm results without the violation of a recognised legal right, or *damnum sine injuria*, the injured party is left without a legal remedy. Examples are a trader ruined by the legitimate competition of rivals, or a petrol station losing business where the local authority reroutes a road and diminishes traffic.

Intention and Motive

In general, the intention to do, or to refrain from doing, the tortious act is necessary before liability can attach. The intention to injure is not necessary: the intention to do the act which causes the injury is. For example, where one person uses defamatory words against another, the intention to utter the words must be proved though there may have been no intention to cause embarrassment, hurt or scandal. The uttering of defamatory words in sleep would not be actionable because the appropriate intention is absent.

In tort law a good motive does not excuse a wrongful act and malice does not make a lawful act unlawful. The reason a person commits a tort, in general, is irrelevant. For example, a pianist practising for an important concert, or a neighbour burning vegetation to eradicate rats may both be committing nuisances. In defamation, the presence of malice negatives the defences of qualified privilege and fair comment. While the general rule is that motive is irrelevant, it may have a bearing on the amount of damages recoverable after liability has been established. Damages may be increased or reduced depending on whether malice is proved.

Causation

To be successful in an action in tort, the wronged party must prove that the loss was caused by the wrongdoer's unlawful act. This is known as causation. Liability is only imposed where the chain of causation between the two parties is unbroken. This chain is broken by a *novus actus interveniens*, a new act intervening, which may be caused by a third party, or by the wronged party.

The courts are reluctant to exonerate a wrongdoer on this ground. In *Cunningham v McGrath Bros* (1964) the defendants, while doing some work on a shop front, left ladders unattended. These were causing an obstruction and were moved by an unknown person to another place. The ladders fell and injured the plaintiff. The Supreme Court rejected a plea of *novus actus interveniens* on the ground that the defendants, in creating the nuisance, should have anticipated as a reasonable and probable consequence that some person would attempt to abate the nuisance, and in so doing, create a danger.

The owners of a boat, in *Conole v Redbank Oyster Co.* (1976), knowing it was unseaworthy and unsafe, took some fifty children out in it, which sank with ten children drowned. A plea that the deaths were caused by the defective boat was rejected. The Supreme Court ruled that the sole cause was putting to sea in a boat which was known to be defective.

Remoteness of Damage

Where it is proved that a wrongdoer caused the damage, the next question for determination is: for what loss should the wrongdoer be responsible? A historical event will illustrate this dilemma. The Great Fire of Chicago in 1871 was reputed to have been started by a milkmaid who brought a lantern with her when milking a cow. The cow kicked the lantern which set fire to the hay. The fire spread to the barn, which burned the house together with the other houses in that street, and before the fire was extinguished, half of Chicago city had been burned. The law has applied two different rules to such a situation.

In earlier times the rule was that once it was shown that a tort had been committed, the wrongdoer was liable for all the loss which flowed directly from it. Thus all the damage caused by the fire in Chicago would have been the responsibility of the milkmaid or her employer. In recent times the courts have developed a more restrictive rule. Now the wrongdoer is only liable for foreseeable harm resulting from the action. This attitude was summarised in the Supreme Court in *Burke v John Paul Ltd* (1967) by Budd J. who said that: 'In determining liability for the consequences of a tortious act of negligence, the test is whether the damage is of such a kind as a reasonable man would have foreseen.' Applying this test to the Chicago fire, the reasonable person might have foreseen damage to the barn and house, but hardly to half the city.

Remedies for Tortious Behaviour

The remedies for tortious behaviour may be judicial or extra-judicial. Judicial remedies available from the courts are damages and injunctions. Injunctions are discussed on page 228.

The measure of damages is that amount of money which will compensate the wronged party for the loss caused. General damages compensate for the breach of the legal right, and special damages recoup actual out of pocket expenses. In actions for personal injuries, there are awards of both general and special damages.

Damages are nominal where there has been a mere technical breach of a legal right with no real loss being suffered. For example, a simple trespass without more would merit an award of nominal damages. An additional sum, known as exemplary damages, is awarded where the court disapproves strongly of the wrongdoer's conduct. For example, a landlord who commits trespass by evicting a tenant without observing the proper legal processes, may be penalised by an award of exemplary damages.

The task of assessing damages falls to the tribunal hearing the case. In most instances this is done by a judge, though in other cases it will be done by a jury of twelve lay persons. It was decided, in *McGrath v Bourne* (1876), that an appellate court may overturn a jury award where no reasonable proportion exists between the damages awarded and that which the appellate court would have awarded. The Supreme Court, in *Foley v Thermocement Products Ltd* (1954), restated this jurisdiction. The damages awarded by the lower court may be reduced as being excessive, or may be increased as being inadequate by the appeal court.

There are a number of extra-judicial remedies surviving from ancient times which a wronged party can avail of without resorting to the courts. For example, force is allowed in the defence of the person, goods and property. A nuisance may be abated, and distress damage feasant allows an occupier of land to detain animals which stray on the land until compensation has been paid by the animals' owner.

LIABILITY FOR TORTIOUS CONDUCT

General Rule as to Liability

The general principle which pertains in the law of tort is that every person who commits a tortious act is responsible for that act. While the actual wrongdoer is the primary responsible party, there are occasions when a different party may be sued. For example, an employer is vicariously liable for the torts committed by employees while acting in the course of their employment (see page 204). A number of categories require special mention with regard to tortious liability.

The State

Since the decision of the Supreme Court in *Byrne v Ireland* (1972) the State is vicariously liable for the tortious acts of its employees committed in the course of their employment. In that case the plaintiff was injured as she walked on a public footpath which had recently been repaired by workers from a department of State. The Supreme Court held that the common law rule whereby the Crown was immune from action for the wrongful acts of its servants did not survive the enactment of the Constitution. The argument that the State was the successor of the Crown and was possessed of the like immunities was emphatically rejected. And in *Ryan v Ireland* (1989) the

Supreme Court held that the State as an employer had failed to take reasonable care of one of its servants (see page 202).

Constitutional Immunities

The Constitution provides that the President is not answerable to either House of the Oireachtas, or to any court, for the exercise and performance of the powers and functions of that office, or for any act done or purported to be done in the exercise and performance of these powers and functions (see page 15). This immunity is confined to constitutional functions and does not extend to wrongs committed by the President in a personal capacity.

The members of each House of the Oireachtas are liable for their tortious acts in the same way as other individuals, except that they cannot be sued for utterances made in either House of the Oireachtas. This is known as absolute privilege (see pages 17 and 41).

Diplomatic Immunity

Foreign diplomats accredited to this country enjoy immunity from tortious liability by virtue of the *Diplomatic Relations and Immunities Act 1967*: see *Government of Canada v Employment Appeals Tribunal* (1992) on page 103. This immunity may be waived by the diplomat's government, or the diplomat may lose it by suing the other party. In such an action a counter-claim for damages may be made against the diplomat.

Trade Unions

A trade union may sue in tort but cannot be sued. The *Industrial Relations Act 1990* provides that an action against a trade union shall not be entertained by any court in respect of certain tortious actions. This immunity is restricted by the *Trade Union Act 1941* to unions possessed of a negotiation licence (see page 467 for trade unions).

Minors

Minors who have reached the age of discretion which is considered to be seven years of age are fully liable for their torts. This was decided by the High Court in *O'Brien v McNamee* (1953) where a seven-year-old child carried a lighted paper into a hay barn and caused a fire which resulted in damage. The child was held liable because malice, or the intention to cause loss, were not ingredients of trespass to land.

Parents are not liable for torts committed by their children. But where a party can prove that the child was acting as the parents' agent, or that parents allowed the child unreasonable opportunity of doing mischief, an action might be successful against the parents.

Death of a Wrongdoer

At common law the death of the wrongdoer extinguished the right of action. The maxim *actio personalis moritur cum personam*, a personal action dies with the person, applied. This rule was altered by the *Civil Liability Act 1961* which provides that all causes of action, except defamation, survive against the estate of the wrongdoer. Where proceedings were not commenced before the death of the wrongdoer, this must be done within two years of that event: *Statute of Limitations 1957*, as amended.

Concurrent Wrongdoers

Concurrent wrongdoers are two or more parties responsible to an injured party for the same loss. Where the actions of two or more parties cause independent items of damage, they are not concurrent wrongdoers. Concurrent wrongdoers are each liable for the entire loss caused, though each is entitled to recover fair contribution from the others. The plaintiff must be allowed an opportunity to recover full compensation. The matter, as far as is possible, should be litigated in the one action.

DEFENCES IN TORT

General Defences

There are a number of general defences which can be raised to answer most actions in tort. There are other special defences which can be raised in reply to particular torts and those are considered in the appropriate places in the chapters following.

Consent

Consent, or *volenti non fit injuria*, is a complete answer to many torts. To be effective, the consent must be full, free and unfettered. Mere knowledge of the risk, or *sciens*, is not sufficient. Consent may be express or implied. It is express where a barber cuts one's hair. It is implied where the user of the highway runs the risk of dangers from the reasonable use of the highway by others. Of course, should the consent be abused, the wronged party has a course of action.

Voluntary Assumption of Risk

A party who agrees to run the risk of injury from a specific source of danger, usually negligence, is said to have voluntarily assumed the risk. For example, a photographer taking close-up photographs in a showjumping arena, or a spectator at a cricket match accept certain types of risks arising from the activity being performed. This defence could hardly be raised should the roof of the arena or the stand in the cricket stadium fall down.

A passenger, in *Judge v Reape* (1968), having consumed alcohol, accepted a lift in a car from a driver who was drunk. A collision occurred and the passenger was injured. Ó Dálaigh CJ. in the Supreme Court explained: 'A person who knows or should know, that a driver is by reason of the consumption of alcohol not fit to drive, and who nevertheless goes as the driver's passenger, is not taking reasonable care for his safety and must therefore be found guilty of contributory negligence.'

Necessity

This defence consists of the deliberate commission of a tortious act to prevent some greater evil where there is no reasonable alternative. The pulling of a person, otherwise a trespass, who is drowning from the water, or the entering of premises, otherwise a trespass to land, to extinguish a fire which threatens life or property, are examples of this defence. In *Lynch v Fitzgerald* (1938) the plaintiff recovered damages for the death of his son killed by the gardaí when they opened fire because, while the gardaí could fire on an unlawful or riotous assembly, they could only do so where it was necessary as a last resort to preserve life.

Inevitable Accident

This is a defence where the consequences of an action are neither foreseen nor intended, and which could not have been avoided by any reasonable care exercised by the defendant. An act of God is a special form of inevitable accident. It occurs where damage is caused by the happening of natural causes, which a reasonable person could not have foreseen or guarded against. The High Court ruled, in *O'Brien v Parker* (1997), that automatism, which means a state of unconsciousness, was a valid defence but there must be a total destruction of voluntary control. Impaired, reduced or partial control was not sufficient.

Legal Authority

Whether a statute affords a defence for conduct otherwise tortious depends on the construction of that statute. In general, actions done in pursuance of an express statutory authority are immune from action unless performed negligently. Examples of legal authority as a defence are given under particular torts.

Limitation of Actions

The *Statute of Limitations 1957*, as amended, provides periods of time within which actions for tort must be taken. Where the action is not commenced within the appropriate time, it becomes statute-barred. It is an unanswerable defence to plead that the action was commenced outside the time allowed. In actions for personal injuries arising out of negligence, nuisance and slander, the period allowed is three years. The *Statute of Limitations (Amendment) Act 1991* provides that the three-year limit period runs from the date of accrual of the cause of action or from the date of knowledge. This is the date on which the plaintiff first had knowledge of certain facts, including the fact that the injury was attributable to the act or omission which it is alleged constituted negligence, nuisance or breach of duty.

In all other cases the period is six years. These periods are extended where the plaintiff is under a disability, such as lunacy or minority, when the tort was committed. The time in such instances begins to run when the disability ceases or from the date of knowledge.

Where the plaintiff issues proceedings within the proper time, the action may subsequently be dismissed for want of prosecution. In *Sheehan v Amond* (1982) the plaintiff, when a boy of ten years, issued proceedings in 1969 with regard to an accident which had occurred in 1966. Further legal documents were served in 1971, and the defence was served in 1972. In 1981 the defendant sought to have the action dismissed for want of prosecution, which the Supreme Court did.

Legal proceedings may be dismissed as an abuse of the legal process. This arose in *Cavern Systems Dublin Ltd v Clontarf Residents Association* (1984) where the defendants appealed a planning permission granted to the plaintiff. When the appeal, which had required extensive and costly preparation opened, it was revealed that the defendants had issued, but not served, legal proceedings challenging the planning permission. The plaintiff moved in the High Court to have the legal proceedings dismissed. The High Court held it was an abuse of the process of the court.

Chapter 17
TRESPASS

Nature of Trespass
Trespass is the oldest form of tortious liability which consists of the direct interference with the person, land or goods of another. Liability is strict: it is actionable *per se*. The defendant is liable once the right of the plaintiff has been infringed, though there was no actual loss. In such cases nominal damages are awarded, though where loss is proved adequate, compensation is given.

TRESPASS TO THE PERSON

Assault
Assault is the threat, or the attempt to apply force which puts another in reasonable apprehension that immediate violence will follow. The shaking of a fist at a near distance, with or without threatening words, or the pointing of a loaded gun from a reasonable distance, with or without threatening gestures or words, are assaults. Violent threats made during a telephone call, or threats made from the open window of a moving train, are not assaults. The essence of this tort is the apprehension of the use of immediate violence.Words cannot constitute an assault. Fawsitt J. in *Dullaghan v Hillen* (1957) explained: 'The commonplace but trite couplet, "sticks and stones may break your bones but words will never hurt you," and in which there is a definition of the law of assault, namely, that mere words, no matter how harsh, lying, insulting and provocative they may be, can never amount in law to assault.' But words which suggest the imminent use of force may constitute an assault.

Battery
Battery consists of the touching of another, either directly or indirectly, however slight, with either hostile intention or against that person's will. Striking with a fist or kicking are examples of direct battery. Throwing water over another, or removing a chair from under a person about to be seated, are examples of indirect battery. It is unnecessary to prove physical injury: the merest unauthorised contact is sufficient.

False Imprisonment

'False imprisonment', said Fawsitt J. in *Dullaghan v Hillen* (1957), 'is the unlawful and total restraint of the personal liberty of another whether by constraining him or compelling him to go to a particular place or confining him to a prison or police station or private place or by detaining him against his will in a public place. The essential element . . . is the unlawful detention of the person, or the unlawful restraint on his liberty. The fact that a person is not actually aware that he is being imprisoned does not amount to evidence that he is not imprisoned, it being possible for a person to be imprisoned in law without his being conscious of the fact and appreciating the position in which he is placed, laying hands upon the person of the party imprisoned not being essential. There may be effectual imprisonment without walls of any kind. The detainer must be such as to limit the party's freedom of motion in all directions. In effect, imprisonment is a total restraint of the liberty of the person. The tort is committed by mere detention without violence.' In *McAllister v Dunnes Stores Ltd* (1987) a cleaner at the defendant's premises, accused of stealing items of clothing, was arrested and searched. The High Court, in awarding damages for wrongful arrest and false imprisonment, held that the evidence had been deliberately fabricated. It is not false imprisonment to block a person's way, though it may be nuisance. There must be a total restraint on liberty; this was stressed in *Phillips v Great Northern Railway* (1903) where a train passenger was suspected of not having a proper ticket. On arrival in Dublin, while ordering a cab, she was told by a ticket collector not to move. She waited while the station master was brought. After further conversations the woman got into a cab and was driven away. Her action for false imprisonment failed because there was not 'a total restraint of the liberty of the person'. Overt surveillance by gardaí was held by the Supreme Court, in *Kane v Governor of Mountjoy Prison* (1988), not to be unlawful provided it was justified.Where a person consents to movement restrictions, false imprisonment occurs where there is a breach of that consent. An employer, in *Burns v Johnston* (1917), extended the working day by a half-hour which he was entitled to do. Most of the employees failed to give notice of leaving the employment. The factory gates were kept locked during working hours though a pass could be obtained from the gatekeeper. On the first day extended working hours came into operation, some employees demanded to be released at the former finishing time, which was refused. An action for false imprisonment failed.

DEFENCES TO TRESPASS TO THE PERSON

Consent

A person impliedly consents to ordinary social contact, such as being jostled in a bus queue, bumped against in a crowded place, having their hand shaken, or taking part in physical sports. Consent may be expressly given. Having a hair-cut, or a tooth extracted, or an ear pierced are common examples of express consents to an interference with the person. Where consent is pleaded, it must be shown that the terms of the consent had not been exceeded. Consenting to have a tooth extracted is not a permission to have all one's teeth extracted, the consent to an appendix removal does not extend to having a leg amputated, and taking part in a physical sport is not a consent to being assaulted. An example of consent negating a trespass is *Burns v Johnston*, cited earlier. Where consent is in issue, it must be shown to be genuine. Where it is obtained by fraud, duress or illegality the consent is negatived. An action for trespass failed in *Hegarty v Shine* (1878) where venereal disease had been communicated during sexual intercourse because the act had been voluntary and the consent was not negatived by a wilful concealment of the disease.

Self-defence

The defence of person or property is an answer to an action for trespass. The ambit of this defence was explained by Fawsitt J. in *Dullaghan v Hillen* (1957) thus: 'When one is wrongfully assaulted it is lawful to repel force by force, provided that no unnecessary violence is used. How much force and of what kind it is reasonable and proper to use, in the circumstances, is a question of fact. Resistance must "not exceed the bounds of mere defence and prevention" or . . . the force used in defence must be not more than commensurate with that which provoked it.' The owner of a shop in possession of a considerable sum of money, in *Ross v Curtis* (1989), fired a warning shot at a night intruder, part of a gang on a crime spree. The shot was aimed too low and injured the intruder who sued for damages. The High Court held that when the shot was fired, the owner feared he was in imminent personal danger, and that it was fired as a warning and he did not have reckless disregard for the safety of the intruder.

Justification by Law

The defence of lawful authority may be raised under different guises as a defence to trespass to the person. In *Humphries v O'Connor* (1867) the plaintiff went about the streets wearing an Orange emblem. A crowd followed and threatened her and she refused, when requested by a police officer, to remove the emblem. The officer removed it and an action for assault failed. The court held that the action was justified to prevent a breach of the peace.

The *Criminal Law Act 1997* contains the law on the powers of arrest. A person may arrest without warrant anyone who is, or whom he or she, with reasonable cause, suspects to be in the act of committing an arrestable offence. Where an arrestable offence has been committed, a person may arrest without warrant anyone who is, or whom he or she, with reasonable cause, suspects to be guilty of the offence. Where a garda, with reasonable cause, suspects that an arrestable offence has been committed, he or she may arrest without warrant anyone whom he or she, with reasonable cause, suspects to be guilty of the offence. An arrestable offence is one for which an adult person may be punished by imprisonment of five years or more, and includes an attempt to commit such offence. An arrest, other than by a garda, may only be effected by a person who, with reasonable cause, suspects that the person to be arrested would otherwise attempt to avoid, or is avoiding, arrest by the gardaí. A person who is arrested by a person other than a garda shall be transferred into the custody of the gardaí as soon as practicable.

In other instances the gardaí must have an arrest warrant, though a very large collection of statutes grant powers of arrest without warrant in addition to the powers granted under the *Criminal Law Act 1997*. As a rule, those statutory powers of arrest can only be exercised where reasonable suspicion exists that some offence under the particular statute has been, or is about to be, committed.

The common law does not permit detention without charge. O'Higgins CJ. in the Supreme Court in *The People (DPP) v Walsh* (1980) explained: 'An arrest and subsequent detention is only justified at common law if it is exercised for the purpose of which the right exists, which is the bringing of an arrested person to justice before a court.' In *Dunne v Clinton* (1930) two brothers suspected of having committed a serious crime went voluntarily to the garda station and were detained for over twenty-four hours before being charged. They successfully sued the gardaí for false imprisonment because they had not been brought to court as soon as was practicable.

In law there is no such concept as 'helping the police with their inquiries'. Either the person has been arrested or is in the garda station voluntarily. A detained person can question the legality of their detention in the High Court under Article 40 of the Constitution (see page 69).

Statute law provides exceptions to this common law rule. The *Offences Against the State Act 1939*, section 30, permits detention for up to forty-eight hours on suspicion of having committed a range of specified offences. The *Criminal Justice Act 1984*, section 4, permits detention for up to twelve hours of persons suspected of having committed an offence which carries a sentence of at least five years' imprisonment. The *Criminal Justice (Drug Trafficking) Act 1996* permits detention for up to seven days for a drug trafficking offence, though to be detained beyond forty-eight hours a court order must be obtained. We have seen on page 58 that confessions obtained while a person is illegally detained are not as a general rule admitted as evidence.

A person may be arrested for the purpose of extradition. The Supreme Court decided, in *The State (Quinn) v Ryan* (1965), that a statute which permitted the removal from this country of a person wanted for a crime in Britain without recourse to the courts was unconstitutional. The *Extradition Act 1965*, as amended, provides that a person wanted in another country must have a judicial hearing before an extradition order can be made. Extradition will not be ordered where it is likely that the constitutional rights of the individual will be infringed. The Supreme Court, in *Finucane v McMahon* (1990), refused extradition because there was a probable risk that the individual would be assaulted by prison staff if returned to Northern Ireland.

The offence must not be a political offence or an offence connected with a political offence. The *Extradition (European Convention on the Suppression of Terrorism) Act 1987* and the *Extradition (Amendment) Act 1992* provide that certain offences are not to be regarded as political.

The person effecting a lawful arrest may use reasonable force. But the use of excessive force is unlawful. In *Dullaghan v Hillen* (1952), quoted earlier, the Circuit Court held that customs officers used excessive force in effecting an arrest on a smuggling offence. In *Dowman v Ireland* (1986) a teenage boy accompanied by two children was arrested for stealing. When being put into a car by the gardaí he became concerned for the safety of the children who were being left behind and struggled and was injured. The High Court ruled that the gardaí were not acting in the course of their duty to effect an arrest or maintain one. The injury was caused when denying the boy the right to be concerned about the welfare of the young children.

TRESPASS TO LAND

Nature of Trespass to Land

Trespass to land is the direct and forcible interference with the land or premises of another. Entering, remaining on, or the removal of soil or vegetation from such land or premises is a trespass. 'All that is necessary to establish the tort of trespass is that the act should be voluntary', said Davitt J. in *O'Brien v McNamee* (1953). 'If a man is sitting on a wall and is pushed so that he falls into someone else's land and thereby commits trespass, his act is involuntary and he is not liable in tort; but if he is out shooting and thinks he has a right to be on the particular land, when in fact he has no such right, his act is voluntary, and he is liable for trespass even though he has no intention of trespassing.'

The maxim *cujus est solum, ejus est usque ad coelum et ad inferos*: to whom belongs the soil, his it is, even to heaven, and to the middle of the earth, applies in this regard. The owner of the soil owns all the land beneath it, unless it has been granted to another, for example, by way of a mining lease. The owner may claim in trespass against those who invade air space, though common sense must be used when considering this aspect of trespass.

Trespass to land is actionable *per se*. The owner is entitled to succeed in the absence of actual damage. The trespasser is punished for infringing the owner's right. Where actual loss is proved, substantial damages may be awarded.

The law of trespass protects the occupier rather than the owner, though in most instances the owner is the occupier. It was decided in *Brett v Mullarkey* (1873) that the bare possession of a church pew justified the occupier in defending by force that possession against the entry of another having no title to it. The occupier of premises may have a good action in trespass against the owner. For example, a landlord who enters the leased premises in breach of the agreement may be liable in trespass to the tenant.

Trespass ab Initio

A person who enters the land or premises of another under some legal right of entry, authority or licence given by law, and abuses that right in the slightest way becomes a trespasser *ab initio*. The entrant is liable for trespass from the moment of entry and not merely from the time the right was abused. The development of this rule illustrates how the law controls those given legal powers of entry from unlawfully interfering with the property rights of others by abusing these powers. There are many statutory powers of entry, some discussed later.

DEFENCES TO TRESPASS TO LAND

Consent

A licence is a consent which prevents the entry from being unlawful. A bare licence, which is one unsupported by consideration, can be withdrawn at any time. The occupier must allow the entrant a reasonable opportunity to leave before force to eject can be used. A shopper in a store or a visitor to a hospital have bare licences. But a licence coupled with an interest, which is one supported by consideration, can only be revoked in accordance with its terms. For example, a cinema patron of good behaviour has the right to remain on the premises until the performance paid for has finished.

Actions of Third Parties

The action of a third party exonerates the trespasser. The example of the man sitting on the wall who was pushed on to the land of another was made earlier. The owner of cattle, in *Moloney v Stephen* (1945), was not liable when they strayed on to a neighbour's land because a stranger left a gate open on a private right of way.

Justification by Law

A large collection of statutes grants a variety of public officials, and others, a right of entry on to land or premises. A few examples must suffice. Under the *Larceny Act 1916* the District Court may issue a warrant to permit the gardaí to search premises where reasonable suspicion exists that stolen goods are kept there. Under the *Consumer Credit Act 1995* an authorised person may enter premises at which hire-purchase and credit-sales business is carried on. The *Misuse of Drugs Act 1977*, as amended, gives extensive powers to the gardaí to search land and premises. The *Criminal Law Act 1997* permits the gardaí to enter, using reasonable force, and search premises, including a dwelling, to execute an arrest warrant. Also the gardaí may enter, using reasonable force, and search premises, including a dwelling, in order to effect an arrest for an arrestable offence, though with regard to dwellings special rules apply.

It has already been noted that where a person enters premises under a legal authority, and abuses such authority, that person becomes a trespasser *ab initio*. In *Brannigan v Dublin Corporation* (1926) a sanitary authority dumped rubbish and other noxious matter on the plaintiff's land. They could not rely on statutory authority. 'Assuming', said FitzGibbon J. in the Supreme Court, that the statute 'imposed a duty on the Corporation to cleanse the streets and to dispose of the refuse, it appears . . . impossible to contend successfully that an unauthorised trespass . . . upon private property for the purpose of dumping the refuse was the execution . . . of the duty imposed.'

Re-entry

The owner of property may re-enter it and expel a trespasser using reasonable force where necessary. An action for trespass to the person was dismissed in *Beattie v Mair* (1882), where the owner with 'force and strong hands' entered his own land and expelled the plaintiff who was in possession without any lawful title. But re-entry, like all forms of self-help permitted by law, is fraught with difficulties. For example, where the owner acquiesced for any time in the trespass, it is more advisable to proceed by way of ejectment proceedings.

Jus Tertii

Actual possession of the land or premises is sufficient to sustain an action for trespass against the trespasser. The occupier need only prove possession: it does not matter if that possession is wrongful against the true owner. The trespasser cannot set up the *jus tertii*, that is to say, the action cannot be defended by proving that the occupier's possession was wrongful against another.

Necessity

Necessity affords a good defence where, through an emergency, the land or premises of another are entered. The law would be at odds with reality if a person, having risked life and limb to enter a burning premises to attempt to rescue the occupants, or to quench the fire, should later be sued for trespass to land.

TRESPASS TO GOODS

Trespass to Goods

The tort of trespass to goods is the direct interference with the goods of another. Any application of force which amounts to a direct and physical disturbance is sufficient. The action must be wilful or negligent. It is a trespass to goods to strike the car of another, to beat another's cattle, or to deface the book of another. The defendant, in *ESB v Hastings & Co. Ltd* (1965), when resurfacing a road, opened a trench and allowed a mechanical shovel to damage a cable. The defendant was made aware by the plaintiffs of the presence of the cable in the general vicinity of its operation. The High Court awarded damages for trespass to goods.

Trespass to goods is actionable *per se*: an action may be sustained despite no actual loss being caused. The general rule is that the possessor of the goods at the time of the trespass may sue, though the possessor is not the owner of the goods.

Conversion

Conversion consists of dealing with the goods of another in a manner inconsistent with the ownership rights of that other. There are two essential ingredients. There must be a dealing with the goods and there must be an intention to deny the right of ownership. It differs from mere trespass in that it is committed in ways other than a direct interference. Stealing is the clearest example of conversion.

The corner-stone of this tort is title and not possession. To maintain an action the party must have either immediate possession or the title to the goods.

In some instances possession may have been lawfully acquired and its subsequent abuse amounts to conversion. For example, where goods are hired to another, the owner's rights are suspended and the hirer has the right to sue in respect of them. But should the hirer wrongfully dispose of them to a third party, the owner's right revives and the owner may sue the hirer and the third party. In *British Wagon Co. Ltd v Shortt* (1961) the plaintiff leased a bulldozer to the hirer who later sold it to the defendant. The High Court held that the defendant's refusal to return the machine amounted to a conversion. A watchmaker in Ennis, in *Morgan v Maurer & Son* (1964), sent a watch left for repairs to Dublin without the consent of the owner. When the watch was lost in the post, the owner successfully sued for conversion.

The objective of this tort is to protect the proprietary right of the owner to the use and possession of the goods. The owner is entitled to damages to compensate for any loss. In the *British Wagon Co. Ltd* case the court did not order the return of the machine. Instead, the owner was awarded the value of the machine, in addition to a sum which would have been earned had no deprivation taken place.

Detinue

This tort consists of the withholding of goods from one who is immediately entitled to their possession. It differs from mere trespass in that the element of detention is essential. Detinue is similar to conversion but differs in three ways. First, conversion consists of a denial of title, whereas a party who loses the goods may be liable in detinue; second, conversion consists of a single act of denial of ownership, whereas detinue is a continuing denial; and third, in detinue the return of the specific goods is central, whereas in conversion damages to compensate the owner for the loss are sufficient. Examples of detinue occur where the shoe repairer refuses to return the shoes, the garage owner refuses to return the car, or the picture restorer refuses to return a painting.

Detinue is proved by evidence that a demand for the return of the goods was made by the owner which is followed by a refusal by the detainer to deliver them up. In *Cullen, Allen & Co. v Barclay* (1881) a potato salesman was held not liable in detinue when, in breach of contract, he failed to return sacks which the owners had supplied to him to be filled with potatoes, because no demand for their return was made. This rule was also applied in *King v Walsh* (1932) where the defendant, having expressed an interest in purchasing a car, was allowed to take one from the plaintiff's premises with his consent. It was agreed that he would pay a deposit four days hence. The defendant took the car to Kerry and failed to pay the deposit. The plaintiff twice wrote letters which the defendant did not receive until his return to Dublin two weeks later. When proceedings were issued for the return of the car the claim failed because no demand had been made before proceedings had commenced.

There is no liability if the refusal to return the goods is reasonable. This was decided in *Poole v Burns* (1944) where an auctioneer retained a horse for five weeks after it came to her notice that it may have been stolen earlier from another party. The Circuit Court, in imposing liability, held that the delay in returning the horse almost five weeks after the gardaí had first investigated the complaint, was unreasonable. But Davitt J. explained: 'A bailee of property, who is in *bona fide* doubt as to the ownership thereof, is legally entitled to detain that property for a reasonable time in order to have enquiries made as to who is the proper owner.'

DEFENCES TO TRESPASS TO GOODS

Consent

The owner of goods may consent to interference with them by another. Where clothes are left to be cleaned, shoes to be repaired, a car left to be serviced, or shears left to be sharpened, the owner, by the nature of the transaction, is consenting to interference with them. Where the terms of the consent are exceeded, the owner may sue in trespass, though usually such claims are grounded in contract rather than tort.

Legal Justification

A collection of statutes gives a variety of persons the power to interfere with the goods of another. The gardaí may seize stolen goods, illegally held drugs, firearms and explosives. Certain officials can enter premises and seize documents or food samples. The county registrar or sheriff may, in lawful execution of a court order, enter premises and remove the occupants and their goods in ejectment proceedings. The same persons can enter and seize goods in order to satisfy a court judgment or in order to satisfy unpaid taxes.

Self-defence

Trespass to goods is justified where it is done in defence of the person or property. The killing of a dog engaged in a dangerous attack on a child, or sheep, would be justified. The destruction of a package, which gave a ticking sound, under the genuine belief that it contained a bomb would be justified. Where the goods of one person interfere with the enjoyment by another of property, a trespass against those goods may be justified. For example, where a car blocks a driveway it would not be a trespass to move it, provided some attempt was made to find the owner and the least interference with the car was made.

Jus Tertii

A person sued in trespass to goods cannot raise the defence that the goods belonged to another and not the plaintiff. A finder of goods could maintain a trespass action against a person who interfered with the goods, except the true owner. The law relating to finders is not absolutely clear, though some rules can, with some certainty, be stated. The finder of goods has a better title to them against every person except the true owner. The finder must take reasonable care of the goods and be prepared to return them to the owner, should the latter be ascertained. In *Quin v Coleman* (1898) a young girl found a purse which was later taken from her under false pretences. It was held that the police, who had taken possession of the purse when apprehending the offender, were obliged to return it to the girl after a reasonable time for establishing the true ownership had elapsed. This is usually taken to be a year and a day.

Where goods are found either attaching to, or under the surface of land, the landowner and not the finder is normally entitled to them. Where treasure trove, which consists of money, coin, gold, silver, plate or bullion, is found hidden in the earth or other private place and the owner is unknown, the items belong to the State on the ground, as was held in *Webb v Ireland* (1988), where the ownership of the Derrynaflan hoard was in dispute, that it was an attribute of State sovereignty.

Where the finder is under a duty to surrender the property to another, and where the true owner remains unknown, the goods belong to that party and not the finder. A garda found money on a public footpath, in *Crinion v Minister for Justice* (1959), and when the owner could not be found after a year and day, he sought its return. The Circuit Court held that where a servant or agent acting in the course of employment or agency, finds goods, these belong to his master, employer or principal.

Chapter 18
NUISANCE

Meaning of Nuisance

Nuisance in its legal sense is annoyance or harm. 'It has been said', explained O'Higgins CJ. in *Connolly v South of Ireland Asphalt Co.* (1977), 'that actionable nuisance is incapable of exact definition. The term nuisance contemplates an act or omission which amounts to an unreasonable interference with, disturbance of, or annoyance to another person in the exercise of his rights. If the right so interfered with belongs to the person as a member of the public, the act or omission is a public nuisance. If these rights relate to the ownership or occupation of land, or of some easement, profit, or other right enjoyed in connection with land, then the acts or omissions amount to a private nuisance.'

PUBLIC NUISANCE

Nature of Public Nuisance

Public nuisance is an annoyance which either affects the public at large or a section of it. It may consist of an act or omission which either obstructs the exercise of a right common to all, or inconveniences or endangers the public. It is primarily a crime because it affects the public. The offender may be prosecuted or the Attorney General may secure an injunction to prohibit its continuance.

A private individual can only sue in public nuisance where it is proved that the loss suffered was over and above that suffered by the public at large. In *Boyd v Great Northern Railway* (1895) a medical doctor, whose time had pecuniary value, obtained damages after being detained for twenty minutes at a level crossing while driving along a public highway. In *Smith v Wilson* (1903) an elderly farmer walked to market on a public road until it was obstructed by the removal of a bridge and the erection of a fence. As a result he was obliged to take a longer route and sometimes had to hire a car. He recovered damages.

Public nuisance is not actionable *per se*: to succeed, the plaintiff must prove loss which was reasonably foreseeable. 'The defendant created a danger on the highway', said Walsh J. in *Wall v Morrissey* (1969), 'which can amount to a public nuisance, but before the plaintiff can establish his right to damages he must satisfy the court that the injury which he suffered was a reasonably foreseeable event on the part of the defendant.'

It is common practice in an action to allege negligence together with nuisance.

PUBLIC NUISANCE ON THE HIGHWAY

The commonest forms of public nuisance are those committed on the public highway. The public highway extends from the boundary of private land or premises on one side across the road to other private lands or premises. In *McKenna v Lewis* (1945) it was argued that a ditch was not part of the public highway. 'There is', said Sullivan CJ. in the Supreme Court, 'no rule of law that such a ditch cannot be dedicated as part of the highway... and in the absence of any evidence to suggest that the fences as they now exist were not the fences bounding the road in question at the time of its dedication as a highway... the *prima facie* presumption would be that the highway extends from fence to fence and includes the ditch.'

Public nuisance can be committed by either obstructing or endangering the public highway. 'Speaking generally', explained Kingsmill Moore J. in *Cunningham v MacGrath Bros* (1964), 'any obstruction of the public highway is a public nuisance, prosecutable on indictment and a tort sounding in damages if any member of the public should suffer particular injury thereby.' In that case the leaving of a ladder for an unreasonable period on a public footpath was a public nuisance.

It is a public nuisance to endanger the highway for those using it. A sixty-year-old man recovered damages, in *Walsh v Morgan & Sons* (1939), when he was injured after colliding with a wooden sign placed on the footpath on a foggy evening in a normally lit street in Dublin. But the danger need not be placed on the highway. In *Stewart v Governors of St Patrick's Hospital* (1939) the occupiers of unfenced, vacant land adjoining the highway were liable for injuries received when the plaintiff tripped over a pipe which protruded on to the footpath. The owner of land which abutted the highway on which a tree grew was liable, in *Lynch v Dawson* (1946), to a motorist who was injured when branches became entangled in the lorry. The High Court held in *Gillick v O'Reilly* (1984) that animals, in that case cattle, could constitute a public nuisance on a busy road constructed for fast traffic.

Liability of Local Authority for the Highway

Local authorities are only liable for nuisances on the highway due to their misfeasance, which is the improper performance of some act already undertaken. *Molloy v Offaly County Council* (1951) held that a hole in the highway which was caused when other holes in the proximity were repaired was an obvious public nuisance for which the local authority was liable. But a local authority is not responsible for nonfeasance, which is the failure to act. A person injured as a result of nonfeasance of a local authority, however negligently, has no remedy. A pedestrian, in *Gallagher v Leitrim County Council* (1959), who fell into a hole in the footpath which was in a state of disrepair could not recover damages.

Section 60 of the *Civil Liability Act 1961* casts a statutory duty on local authorities to keep the public highway in a proper state of repair. This section can only be brought into effect by a Government order and to date this has not been done (see *The State (Sheehan) v Government of Ireland* (1987) (page 34). Despite the enactment of the *Roads Act 1996*, which imposes a duty and obligation to repair and maintain roads, it seems that the rule regarding misfeasance survives intact.

DEFENCES TO PUBLIC NUISANCE

Nuisance Existed before Public Dedication

It is settled law that where a lawful erection existed at the time the highway was dedicated to the public such dedication was accepted subject to any risk arising from the then existing state of things. This defence was successful in *Early v Moore* (1953) where a pedestrian was injured by a stone step and shoe scraper which were proved to have been in position before public dedication.

Knowledge of Danger

We have seen in *Stewart v Governor of St Patrick's Hospital* that occupiers of premises adjoining the highway are liable for artificial projections which injure those using the highway, and in *Lynch v Dawson* a landowner was liable for natural projections. What happens where the object causing the damage is detached from the land or premises? A landowner with trees on land which adjoins a highway or other land is bound to take such care as a reasonable and prudent landowner would take to guard against the danger of damage being done by one of them falling. In *Gillen v Fair* (1956) a branch of a tree growing on the defendant's land broke off in a storm and fell on a passing car, killing the driver and injuring the plaintiff. The tree was rotten though the defects were high up, not apparent to a casual glance, and were unknown to the landowner. The action failed on the ground that the landowner had not known, or could not have known, of the danger.

Act of Stranger

An occupier of premises adjoining the highway is not responsible for nuisances created on the highway by visitors to the premises. An action failed, in *McGowan v Masterson* (1953), where injuries resulted from paraffin spilled outside the defendant's premises by a visitor some time previously.

Temporary Interference

Where it is claimed that the obstruction of the highway amounts to a public nuisance, it may be possible to show that it was of a temporary nature. According to Walsh J. in *Wall v Morrissey* (1969): 'The temporary excavation of the highway is not of itself a public nuisance so long as it does not offend by exceeding, in either degree or duration, the temporary requirements of a person whose premises adjoin the highway. A public nuisance is constituted by exceeding this temporary requirement, or by failing to restore the position to the point where it does not operate as a withdrawal of part of the highway from the public, or by leaving the highway dangerous for members of the public using it.'

Necessity

The owner of property adjoining the highway may obstruct it to carry out essential repairs to the property. Kingsmill Moore J. explained the rule, in *Cunningham v MacGrath Bros* (1964), where it was held that ladders left for an unreasonable time on the highway caused a public nuisance. He said: 'The owner of property abutting on the highway may, for proper purposes connected with his property, cause such an obstruction, provided that neither in quantum nor duration does it extend beyond what is necessary; and this exception would extend to cover those doing the necessary work. Thus, although the ladders when in position obstructed the footpath, so long as their presence was necessary for chipping the plaster or fixing the bind they did not constitute a public nuisance; but as soon as the chipping was done and there was no need for the ladders to remain in position they did become a public nuisance and if anyone had been injured by them ...' that person could maintain an action for nuisance.

PRIVATE NUISANCE

Nature of Private Nuisance

A private nuisance is a substantial interference with the comfort of neighbouring occupiers according to ordinary sober common sense standards. Whether the action amounts to a nuisance is judged in terms of reasonable give and take between neighbours. An occupier cannot use the property in such a way as to impair the enjoyment in some substantial manner of another's property. The law is not concerned with 'trivial, fanciful or exaggerated inconvenience', per Henchy J. in *Mullin v Hynes* (1972). Generally, this substantial interference is proved by repetitive or continuous acts of nuisance. Private nuisance is not actionable *per se*. There must be proof of inconvenience or damage; personal injuries cannot be sued for in private nuisance. Personal discomfort is actionable provided it is substantial.

An occupier of property is under a general duty to neighbours to remove or reduce natural or man-made hazards which occur on the property. This duty is based on knowledge of the hazard, ability to foresee the consequences of not checking or removing it, and an ability to abate it.

The lawful occupier of the property is the party who can sue in private nuisance, even where that party is not the owner, because private nuisance offends against the enjoyment of property and those with an interest in the property but not in possession cannot suffer any inconvenience. Generally, the creator of the nuisance is responsible in law, whether or not that party is the owner of the property on which the private nuisance is committed. A landlord may be liable, in certain circumstances, for private nuisance created by a tenant. The landlord of premises, in *Goldfarb v Williams & Co. Ltd* (1945), having let them to a social and athletic club which operated dances and other social activities, was liable to a tenant living on an upper floor. The High Court held the landlord, aware of the construction and properties of the building, was responsible as having authorised the nuisance, which was inevitable where the premises were used as intended.

Instances of Private Nuisance

Thus, private nuisance takes a large variety of forms. Noise, heat, smoke, smell, dust, vibration, soil erosion, branches of trees, damage to foundations, fumes, sewage, dangerous leaves and blasting operations have all constituted private nuisance.

Horse racing on a Sunday in a residential locality, in *Dewar v City & Suburban Racecourse Co.* (1889), was stopped because it interfered with the ordinary comfort and enjoyment of neighbouring properties and with religious services in an adjacent church. In *New Imperial & Windsor Hotel Co. v Johnston* (1921) a limited injunction was granted against the owners of tea-rooms and restaurant, who used these premises opposite a hotel for dancing and other entertainment at night. A shop-owner in an old established residential area, in *O'Kane v Campbell* (1985), was prevented from opening the premises between 12 midnight and 6 A.M. in all seasons of the year. The High Court held that a night trader is responsible for the ordinary natural conduct of persons whom he attracts to the neighbourhood, where such conduct causes a nuisance to the property of others.

The owner of several houses which were let was, in *Wallace v McCartan* (1917), restrained from discharging sewage into a surface water sewer which had flowed on to another's land and polluted a stream from which cattle were watered. The letting of a dwelling as a tenement in a good residential area constituted a nuisance: *O'Connor v Byrne* (1945).

A swarm of bees, in *McStay v Morrissey* (1949), was not a private nuisance because they were not kept in unreasonable numbers or in an unreasonable part of the garden. In *Leech v Reilly* (1983) a neighbour who built a corrugated iron workshop, in which a joinery business was conducted along the line of the dividing wall, was liable to his next-door-neighbour for nuisance caused by noise, dust and flooding.

A factory which processed pharmaceutical products, which involved the storage, use and disposal of large quantities of toxic substances was situated, in *Hanrahan v Merck Sharp & Dohme (Ireland) Ltd* (1988), about a mile from a farm. The Supreme Court held that the farmer had established that he had not enjoyed the comfortable and healthy use of his land to the degree that would be expected by an ordinary person because offensive smells had led to his ill-health and toxic emissions were the most credible explanation for the ailments and abnormalities in his cattle.

Repeated spills of soil into the plaintiff's back-yard from a steep embankment on the defendant's land, was held, in *Daly v McMullan* (1997), to constitute a nuisance.

Nuisance by Barking Dogs

Where, on a complaint being made to the District Court by any person, it appears that a nuisance has been created as a result of excessive barking by a dog, the court may: (a) order the occupier of the premises in which the dog is kept to abate the nuisance by exercising due control over the dog; or (b) make an order limiting for a specified period the number of dogs to be kept by the occupier on the premises; or direct that the dog be delivered to a dog warden to be dealt with as if the dog was an unwanted dog: *Control of Dogs Act 1986*, section 25.

Threatened Nuisance

A threatened nuisance may be prevented by a *quia timet* injunction, that is, one restraining wrongful conduct that has not yet been committed but is merely apprehended. 'To sustain the injunction', said FitzGibbon LJ. in *Attorney General (Boswell) v Rathmines & Pembroke Joint Hospital Board* (1904), 'the law requires proof... of a well-founded apprehension of injury —

proof of actual and real danger — a strong probability, almost amounting to moral certainty... it will be an actionable nuisance.' An injunction sought to restrain the building of a smallpox hospital in an urban area was refused because there was a conflict of expert evidence on the suitability of the site and the risk of the spread of smallpox.

Local residents, in *Radford v Wexford Corporation* (1955), objected to the proposed building of a public toilet on the main street of the town on the grounds that it would depreciate the value of local properties; would cause loss to local traders; was not being erected on a suitable site; and would cause unemployed persons to gather to the annoyance of residents and the public. The High Court refused an injunction because a strong case of probability that the apprehended mischiefs would arise was not established, and there was no evidence to suggest that these were irreparable.

An injunction was granted in *Rabbette v Mayo County Council* (1984) to prevent blasting operations in a manner which caused a nuisance in the vicinity of building sites purchased for development purposes on which semi-detached houses had been built. On the other hand, an injunction was refused to residents, in *McGrane v Louth County Council* (1983), who objected to the proposed use of a site adjacent to their homes as a dump. 'I am prepared to accept, on the evidence', said O'Hanlon J. in the High Court, 'that dumps used by the county council in the past have been malodorous, unsightly and unhygienic, and what I have to assess ... is whether there is a real danger that such conditions will be produced again.' On this occasion the site was chosen after proper scientific appraisal, valuable farmland had been acquired for the site, and undertakings as to its management and the prevention of unauthorised dumping were given.

NUISANCE TO EASEMENTS

Nature of Easement

An easement is a right attached to a particular property which allows the occupier either to use the property of another in a particular manner, or to restrict the use by its occupier to a particular extent. Easements are more fully dealt with on page 257. An action for private nuisance lies for an interference with the enjoyment of an easement.

Instances of Nuisance to Easements

A property owner is entitled to the support of adjoining property, though in *Gately v Martin* (1900) the plaintiff was unsuccessful because he could not prove that the demolished building was of common origin with his own. The defendant, in *Callaghan v Callaghan* (1897), committed a nuisance by blocking two gullets into which a stream from his own land ran, thus diverting the water away from a neighbour's land.

It was held in *Abercromby v Fermoy Town Commissioners* (1900) that a landowner could not encroach on a strip of land along the bank of the River Blackwater and could not erect a barrier to its entrance because the public had acquired a right of way. The defendant, in *Smith v Wilson* (1903), was guilty of public nuisance by obstructing a public right of way, over which the plaintiff regularly travelled, by removing a bridge and erecting a fence. In *Geoghegan v Henry* (1922) a gate which was left unlocked was not an obstruction to a private right of way, though the constant leaving of the gate open was a nuisance.

Damages were awarded to owners of a premises, in *Scott v Goulding Properties Ltd* (1973), for an obstruction to ancient lights which occurred when a tall office building was erected nearby. But in *Leech v Reilly* (1983) the diminution of light, which resulted from the erection of a twenty-six foot high corrugated iron workshop in the next door garden was not considered substantial enough to constitute a nuisance.

The use of canoes on a river and lakes by an outdoor education centre was, in *Tennent v Clancy* (1987), prevented by injunction because it interfered with the fishing rights of the owner of the bed and soil of the river and lakes.

DEFENCES TO PRIVATE NUISANCE

Statutory Authority

Several statutes permit actions which amount to nuisance. Where legislation authorises conduct which may constitute a nuisance, the party charged with executing the statutory duty must not behave in a negligent manner. A local authority, in *Smith v Wexford County Council* (1953), charged with the statutory duty of keeping streams clear, deposited large quantities of earth and vegetable matter on pasture land. Some cattle ate the vegetable matter, which was poisonous, and died. The action was unsuccessful because the poisonous nature of the roots could not have been reasonably foreseen.

Consent

A party can consent to the creation or continuance of a nuisance. For example, to facilitate a neighbour building an extension, or altering a building, consent may be given either unqualifiedly or qualifiedly. A neighbour may consent to noise while a band practises. Where the activity committed extends beyond the consent given, an action for nuisance may be sustainable.

Prescription

Prescription or long continuance of the nuisance affords no defence in law. But with regard to certain nuisances, twenty years' continuance may convert the nuisance into an easement, and will be legally protected (see page 258).

Coming to the Nuisance

It is not a defence to claim that the party came to the nuisance. For example, where the buyer of a house complains about a nuisance to a neighbour who replies that the previous owner had no objection, he has not a sustainable defence. The purchaser of property is entitled to the protection which the law gives to established residents.

Particular Occupier

It is a good defence to show that the party complaining of the nuisance is extraordinarily sensitive to the activity in question. This is an application of the rule that nuisance is the interference with ordinary common sense standards.

ABATEMENT OF NUISANCE

Besides granting a party affected by a nuisance the ordinary remedies of damages and/or injunction, the law permits the exercise of a certain degree of self-help. It allows the aggrieved party to abate the nuisance, that is, to remove the cause of it without recourse to the courts.

Where a party resorts to self-help, recourse cannot be had to the ordinary remedies because action has removed the cause of complaint. Abatement is a remedy the law does not favour. Where a party is obstructed in the exercise of a common right, such as the use of the highway, that party may remove the obstruction. The same rule applies to private nuisance and the abator may enter another's property to do so. Usually a request must be made to the occupier to discontinue the nuisance and only when such a request is ignored or refused should the party annoyed abate the nuisance. Notice need not be given in a case of emergency, such as the flooding of premises. Finally, the right to abate a nuisance is a right to remove the cause of the nuisance and nothing more.

THE RULE IN *RYLANDS V FLETCHER*

Liability for the Unnatural use of Property

The legal principle, known as the Rule in *Rylands v Fletcher*, states that where 'a person for his own purposes brings on his lands and collects and keeps there anything likely to do mischief if it escapes, must keep it in at his peril and, if he does not do so, is *prima facie* answerable for all the damage which is the natural consequence of its escape.'

The facts of this well-known 1868 English case are these: the parties occupied adjoining properties, one worked a coal mine while the other had a mill. The mill-owner wished to obtain water power for the mill and constructed a reservoir in ignorance of the existence of a disused mine shaft under it. Water seeped into the mine causing considerable flooding.

This tort imposes strict liability for the escape of things likely to do mischief on escape. Some non-natural use of the property must be made which brings with it an increased danger to others. The bringing of substances, in small quantities and merely for the better enjoyment of the property, does not fall within the rule. Water, electricity, gas and central heating fuel necessary for domestic purposes cannot make the occupier liable. On the other hand, where the item is stored on premises for commercial purposes in large quantities, liability would be imposed.

Liability under this rule was imposed, in *Berkley v Flynn* (1982), where overflow from a farm slurry pit entered the underground water system causing pollution to a well from which water was drawn for domestic and farming purposes.

Defences to the Rule

This rule only applies where the offending substance is brought on to the property and stored there by the occupier. Thus, in *Healy v Bray UDC* (1962), liability was evaded where injuries were caused by a rock which was naturally on the land and which was dislodged and rolled down a hill, and in, *Daly v McMullan* (1997), where soil from a steep embankment spilled on to a neighbour's back-yard.

Liability does not lie where the damage is caused by the plaintiff's action or by an act of God. The action of a stranger is also outside the rule because the occupier has no control over such activity.

Where statutory powers are exercised, the rule is applicable unless negligence is proved. This was illustrated in *Broughton v Midland Great Western Railway* (1873) where the defendants, by statute, were empowered to make and maintain a canal. Prior to executing repairs, water was diverted into a drain specially designed for that purpose. Instead of flowing from this drain into a public sewer, the water flooded premises due to a blockage in the sewer. The absence of negligence led to a dismissal of the action.

LIABILITY FOR FIRE

The Common Law Rule

At common law liability for damage caused by fire which escaped from premises was strict. Liability was imposed whether the act which caused the fire was negligent or not. The law adopted this reasoning because fire was considered dangerous.

Modification of the Rule by Statute

This strict liability rule was considered unduly harsh at a time when open domestic fires were a necessity and most houses were built of wood. By a 1715 statute it was provided that no action could be maintained against a person 'in whose house, chamber or out-house' a fire was accidentally caused. The Supreme Court decided, in *Richardson v Athlone Woollen Mills* (1942), that a fire which accidentally started in a factory was not protected by the statute and the owners were liable for damage to adjoining premises. The following year the *Accidental Fires Act 1943* was passed which provides that no legal proceedings can be instituted by a person who has suffered damage by reason of a fire accidentally occurring on, or in, the building or land of another.

Fires which negligently begin, or which accidentally begin and are allowed negligently to spread, are not protected by the 1943 statute. In *McKenzie v O'Neill & Roe Ltd* (1977) accumulated papers were burned on a windy summer's day after a long dry spell. Although the fire seemed to be extinguished, it spread to adjoining premises and caused damage. The High Court found negligence proved in that adequate precautions had not ensured the fire was extinguished, nor were sparks prevented from being blown by the wind.

Chapter 19
NEGLIGENCE

Nature of Negligence
Negligence is the breach of a legal duty of care which results in loss to the party to whom the duty is owed. Three essential ingredients must be present before the tort of negligence arises. These are: (a) a legal duty of care; (b) a breach of that duty; and (c) loss from that breach.

Legal Duty of Care
In general there is no legal duty to avoid harming others though the courts in the last hundred years or so have recognised that a duty of care situation exists whenever a person should reasonably foresee that a course of conduct is likely to cause loss to another.

Negligence is the omission to do something which a reasonable person would do, or doing something which a reasonable person would not do. Whether or not a legal duty is owed in any particular circumstances is a question of law for the courts. New legal duties are given judicial recognition as the necessity arises.

The Neighbour Principle
The test applied by the courts in deciding whether a legal duty of care exists is the neighbour principle. This rule provides that reasonable care must be taken to avoid acts or omissions which can reasonably be foreseen as likely to injure a neighbour. A neighbour is a person so closely and directly affected by the act or omission that the performer ought reasonably to have that person in contemplation as being so affected when the performer directs his or her mind to the act or omission which is called into question.

Applying this neighbour principle, the law has recognised a number of well-established duty of care situations. Producers of goods, occupiers of premises, carriers of passengers and goods, employers, possessors of skills, highway users, and those who give advice owe a duty of reasonable care. Each of these categories is dealt with in detail later in this chapter.

Breach of Legal Duty
To establish negligence a party must prove that the wrongdoer committed a breach of a legal duty of care. The law does not impose a standard of absolute

care, except in respect of the manufacturer or producer of defective goods. Liability is not strict. The standard demanded is that of reasonable care. The question posed is whether a reasonably prudent person would have foreseen the danger to the injured party. There is a breach of the legal duty where the answer is yes. Where the answer is no, there is no liability imposed on the performer of the act which resulted in the loss.

Loss

To succeed in negligence it must be proved that personal physical injury or damage to property was caused by the breach of a legal duty of care. The courts may award damages for nervous shock. In *Mullally v Bus Éireann* (1992) a wife and mother suffered post-traumatic stress disorder after a bus crash in which her husband and three sons were seriously injured.

Contributory Negligence

In many instances which cause loss, one party will be completely faultless and the other party entirely at fault. What happens where both parties, by their negligence, contribute to the loss? The *Civil Liability Act 1961* provides that where a party suffers damage partly through his or her own fault and partly through the fault of another, that party may still recover compensation. The amount recoverable will be reduced by the contribution which that party's negligence bears to the total cause of the injury or damage.

It is common to find negligence apportioned. For example, in *O'Leary v O'Connell* (1968) a pedestrian's leg was broken after being struck by a motorcycle while crossing a road. Both parties were negligent for not keeping a proper look-out and fault was apportioned 85 per cent to the motorcyclist and 15 per cent to the pedestrian. A passenger in a car, in *Sinnott v Quinnsworth Ltd* (1984), injured when a car and bus collided, was held to be 15 per cent at fault for the failure to wear a safety belt.

Res Ipsa Loquitur

The onus of proving negligence, as in other torts, lies generally on the injured party. But in some cases the law presumes negligence because the wrongdoer has sole control of the cause of the incident and because the incident could not normally have happened without some element of carelessness. In such cases the rule *res ipsa loquitur*: the facts speak for themselves, is applied though the absence of negligence may be proved by the evidence.

The Supreme Court ruled, in *Lindsay v Mid-Western Health Board* (1993), that where a person entered hospital for a routine medical procedure and was subjected to an anaesthetic without any special features and there was a failure to return the patient to consciousness, the principle of *res ipsa loquitur* applied, though the defendants, by showing that they had exercised all reasonable care in carrying out the operation, had displaced the principle and so the plaintiff, in order to succeed, had to prove negligence. But, in *Collen Bros v Scaffolding Ltd* (1959), the burden of displacing a plea of *res ispa loquitur* was unsuccessful where collapsing scaffolding, which had been erected inside giant silos by the defendants, collapsed, injuring a workman who was thrown from a height of sixty feet to the ground.

Voluntary Assumption of Risk

A party who agrees to run the risk of injury from a specific source of danger, usually negligence, is said to have voluntarily assumed the risk. For example, a photographer taking close-up photographs in a show-jumping arena, or a spectator at a cricket match accept certain types of risks arising from the activity being performed. This defence could hardly be raised should the roof of the arena or the stand in the cricket stadium fall down.

A passenger, in *Judge v Reape* (1968), having consumed alcohol, accepted a lift in a car from a driver who was drunk. A collision occurred and the passenger was injured. Ó Dálaigh CJ. in the Supreme Court explained: 'A person who knows or should know, that a driver is by reason of the consumption of alcohol not fit to drive, and who nevertheless goes as the driver's passenger, is not taking reasonable care for his safety and must therefore be found guilty of contributory negligence.' The Supreme Court held, in *McCann v Brinks Allied Ltd* (1997), that by accepting a contract with a bank to transport consignments of cash the defendant agreed to carry out a hazardous activity, in respect of which it would be responsible for providing for the safety of its own employees.

PRODUCT LIABILITY

The Manufacturer of Goods

At common law a manufacturer of goods, who supplied them through intermediaries such as wholesalers and retailers without giving these an opportunity to examine the goods, was liable where, through negligence, the goods caused harm to the ultimate consumer. A tack found in bread was presumed, in *Denniston v McNamara* (1950), to have entered the bread before it left the bakery. But in *Butler v Johnston, Mooney & O'Brien* (1945), an action failed, where glass cut the eater's throat while consuming some bread, because the bakery proved that all reasonable precautions had been taken in its manufacture.

But statute has altered this aspect of the common law in a fundamental way. The *Liability for Defective Products Act 1991* holds the producers and manufacturers of goods strictly liable for the safety of their products. To succeed in a civil action an injured party will now only be required to prove (a) injury; and (b) that the injury was caused by a defect in the product. The statute imposes liability for damage caused wholly or partly by a defect in the product, irrespective of whether the producer or manufacturer is negligent or not.

The Controller of Goods

The controller of a dangerous object owes a high standard of care in preventing harm being caused by it. Such products include blades, guns and poisons. The more serious the danger the greater the obligation to avoid it. In *Sullivan v Creed* (1904) the owner of a loaded and cocked gun left it beside a fence where a fifteen-year-old boy found it and, not knowing it was loaded, pointed it playfully at a friend who was injured when it fired. In holding the owner liable, the court held that the measure of care owed was to be gauged by the measure of risk. In the case of a gun loaded and on full cock, the measure of care was at its maximum. But the exercise of reasonable care may exonerate a party. Thus, in *Cunningham v Blake* (1937) a gun was left in a study where, unknown to the owner, there was also ammunition. Despite a prohibition on his family entering this room his fourteen-year-old son went to the study, loaded the gun, and while playing a game fired it injuring a friend. It was held that having regard to the precautions taken the owner could not have reasonably foreseen what would happen.

The controller of small swing-boats at a carnival was liable, in *Keegan v Owens* (1953), to a person who, in attempting to stop one of them, injured his hand on a protruding nail. A telephone line, in *Fitzsimons v Bord Telecom Éireann* (1991), blown down in a severe storm, hooked itself to an overhead power line which crossed the telephone line at that point. The sizzling wire was blown about violently and started a number of small fires. A farmer, trying to extinguish these, touched the wire with a stick, was electrocuted and died instantly. The defendants had known some eighteen hours before the incident that the line was down and an emergency crew could have reached it within one hour of receiving that information. The High Court ruled that once the defendants were aware that the line was down, it constituted a danger that could behave in an unpredictable manner. They had an obligation to ensure that it was made safe and failure to do so rendered them liable for what happened.

This duty of care extends to a child trespasser who enters premises and steals dangerous items. Abattoir owners, in *Purtill v Athlone UDC* (1968), were liable to a fourteen-year-old boy who had frequently visited the premises with the knowledge of the owners' employees and stole some detonators which injured him. 'The detonators', said Walsh J. in the Supreme Court, 'were admittedly of a nature calling for care and ones which were known, or ought to have been known, to be capable of causing injury if wrongly used.'

The Supplier of Goods

The suppliers of goods for reward must take reasonable care that the goods are in reasonable condition. In *Cole v Webb Caravans Ltd* (1983) the High Court held that once a young girl, injured by a defective catch on a caravan door, proved that the caravan was supplied in a potentially dangerous condition, there was a case for the supplier to answer which could be done by adducing evidence that the thing had been obtained from a reputable source, or was subject to a reasonable inspection by the supplier which failed to show the defect, or that no inspection was carried out, but that the absence of inspection was reasonable in the circumstances.

A gratuitous lender of goods owes a duty of care to the borrower, where the goods are defective and cause injury or damage. This rule is illustrated by *Campbell v O'Donnell* (1967) where a householder suggested to a decorator, who had agreed to supply the equipment needed to decorate the house, that use might be made of a household ladder. The ladder was used to support a plank and when the ladder broke the decorator was injured. An action failed because there was no evidence that the householder had actual knowledge of the defect in the ladder, or that it was to be used in an unusual way, or that a reasonable examination of the ladder would have revealed the defect.

The Repairer of Goods

The duty to take reasonable care rests on the repairer of goods. A dealer in tractors and agricultural machinery, in *Hughes v J.J. Power Ltd* (1988), was liable for the faulty repairs to a combine harvester carried out by a mechanic. This duty may extend to a subsequent owner of goods. A garage, in *Power v Bedford Motor Co.* (1959), was liable to the widow of a subsequent owner of a car for negligent work carried out at the request of a former owner. The Supreme Court explained that the duty of care extended to persons doing work on an article which they foresee would be used by others without examination.

OCCUPIERS' LIABILITY

Liability of Occupiers

At common law the liability of the occupier depended on the status of the entrant who may have been (a) an invitee, (b) a licensee, or (c) a trespasser. The duties, liabilities and rights now provided in the *Occupiers' Liability Act 1995* are to have effect in the place of the duties, liabilities and rights which attached by the common law to occupiers of premises (which include land, water and any fixed or movable structures thereon and vessels, vehicles, trains, aircraft and other means of transport) in respect of dangers existing on their premises to entrants. An occupier, in relation to any premises, means a person exercising such control over the state of the premises that it is reasonable to impose on that person a duty towards an entrant in respect of a particular danger existing on those premises.

This Act divides entrants into (a) visitors, (b) recreational users, and (c) trespassers, and imposes a different duty on occupiers in respect of each class of entrant.

Duty Owed to Visitors

The Act defines a visitor as an entrant, other than a recreational user, who was present on the premises:

1. at the invitation or with the permission of the occupier or any member of the occupier's family who ordinarily resided on the premises, or
2. at the express invitation of the occupier or such family member, or
3. with the permission of the occupier or such family member for social reasons connected with the occupier or such family member, or
4. an entrant, other than a recreational user, present on the premises by virtue of an express or implied term in a contract, or
5. an entrant as of right

provided in each case that the entrant was so present for the purpose for which he or she was invited or permitted to be there, or for the purpose of the performance of the contract or for the purpose of the exercise of the right, and includes any such entrant whose presence on the premises became unlawful after entry and who was taking reasonable steps to leave.

An occupier of premises owes a duty of care, known as the common duty of care, towards a visitor. This common duty of care means a duty to take such care as was reasonable in all the circumstances (having regard to the care which a visitor may reasonably be expected to take for his or her own safety and, if the visitor was on the premises in the company of another person, the extent of the supervision and control the latter person may reasonably be expected to exercise over the visitor's activities) to ensure that a visitor does not suffer injury or damage by reason of any danger existing on the premises. The nature of this duty was explained, in *Mullen v Quinnsworth Ltd* (1991) (the facts of which are given later), in the Supreme Court by Griffin J.: '[The occupier] was not an insurer of [the entrant's] safety, but it owed her a duty to take reasonable care, in all the circumstances, to see that the premises were reasonably safe for her.'

The Act permits an occupier by express agreement or notice to extend this duty towards visitors. Equally, an occupier may by express agreement or notice restrict, modify or exclude this duty towards visitors, though this is not binding unless it is reasonable in all the circumstances. Where a notice is used the occupier must take reasonable steps to bring the notice to the attention of the visitor. Where injury or damage is caused to a visitor or property of a visitor by a danger of which the visitor is warned by the occupier or another person, that warning is not, without more, to be treated as absolving the occupier from liability unless, in all the circumstances, it was enough to enable the visitor, by having regard to the warning, to avoid the injury or damage caused.

While the following cases were all decided before the 1995 Act, they remain relevant as illustrations of how the courts are likely to apply the statute. A paying spectator at an agricultural show was injured, in *Coleman v Kelly* (1951), when a horse in a show-jumping event threw its rider and ran amuck in the crowd. It was held that the ground was not reasonably safe because it was normally used as a football ground and when converted for this event did not contain adequate safety features. An unforeseen event in *Callaghan v Killarney Race Co.* (1958), that of a horse in a race jumping the wing of a fence into a group standing nearby, excused the occupier from liability.

A shopper in a wholesale supermarket, in *Foley v Musgrave Cash & Carry* (1985), was injured when she tripped over a low-slung stationary trolley which projected marginally in an aisle. The Supreme Court ruled that the absence of a system for the removal of empty trolleys temporarily out of use from the premises used by customers amounted to negligence. A supermarket shopper, in *Mullen v Quinnsworth Ltd* (1991), was injured when she slipped on cooking oil spilled on the floor. The Supreme Court ruled that the part of the premises containing the display should have been designated a high-risk area for the purpose of the cleaning system, having regard to the inherent danger from oil spillages, the increased risk of spillage owing to the design of cooking oil bottles, and the unsuitable and unstable manner in which they had been stacked. The Supreme Court held, in *Duffy v Carnabane Holdings Ltd* (1996), that a patron at a disco, who slipped on the dance floor and injured his ankle could recover damages because, despite the system of warning patrons about taking glasses on to the dance floor, the availability of sufficient staff and the placing of mops and buckets at strategic places for cleaning up any spillages, there was evidence that for an appreciable length of time there were spillages and broken glass on the dance floor.

The child visitor may present a particular problem for the occupier because what may not be a danger to an adult may be a danger for a child. In *Bohane v Driscoll* (1929) a teacher of the senior class allowed the junior children into his room at lunch-time, to sit beside the fire when the weather was inclement. He removed the fireguard and a six-year-old was burned, and she recovered damages because the removal of the fireguard was a danger. A nine-year-old girl, in *Rooney v Connolly* (1986), went to her local church to light a candle at a shrine. The only vacant space for the candle was in the middle row. When she leaned over the first row of lit candles to insert her candle, the sleeve of her clothes caught fire and she was severely burned. The Supreme Court ruled that the candelabra was a danger and, having regard to the child's age, the occupier of the church was under a duty not to expose her to a danger of which he actually knew.

Duty Owed to Recreational Users

The Act defines a recreational user as an entrant who, with or without the occupier's permission or at the occupier's implied invitation, is present on the premises, without charge (other than a reasonable charge in respect of the cost of providing vehicle parking facilities) being imposed, for the purpose of engaging in a recreational activity, including an entrant admitted without charge to a national monument. A recreational activity is defined as any recreational activity conducted, whether alone or with others, in the open air, including any sporting activity, scientific research and nature study so conducted, exploring caves and visiting sites and buildings of historical, architectural, traditional, artistic, archaeological or scientific importance.

In respect of a danger on premises, an occupier owes a recreational user a duty (a) not to injure the person or damage his or her property intentionally, and (b) not to act with reckless disregard for the person or his property.

Duty Owed to Trespassers

The Act defines a trespasser as an entrant, other than a visitor or a recreational user. In respect of a danger existing on premises, an occupier owes a trespasser the same duty owed to a recreational user (see above). A trespasser openly taking a short-cut across a field, or a child coming into a garden to retrieve a ball, are owed this duty of care.

The child trespasser may pose a particular problem for an occupier. An eleven-year-old boy, in *McNamara v ESB* (1975), climbed into an electricity substation, came in contact with an uninsulated conductor which carried 10,000 volts, and was seriously injured. Since the substation was first built in 1929, with a flat roof added in 1956, the surrounding area had become built up with houses. At the time of the incident the barbed wire surrounding the substation was being repaired. The Supreme Court decided that liability should be determined by applying the following test. Having created and maintained a source of danger, could the defendant have reasonably foreseen that a child trespasser might attempt to enter the premises, and having done so, might be injured by reason of that danger, and whether reasonable steps were taken to avert injury? The court awarded damages. In the later case of *Keane v ESB* (1981) the Supreme Court, applying the test laid down in *McNamara's* case, held there was no liability where the trespasser, an eleven-year-old boy, climbed a six foot fence topped with three strands of barbed wire, and entered an electricity substation which was situated in an unfrequented field about a quarter-mile from a small country village. The occupier was aware, in *Crowley v Allied Irish Banks Ltd* (1987), that boys habitually trespassed on to the roof of the premises. When one of the boys fell from the roof and was injured, it was held that the occupier was negligent in failing to provide and maintain proper railings on the roof.

Where a person enters a premises for the purpose of committing a crime, or where present on the premises commits a crime, the Act provides that the occupier's sole duty is not to injure the trespasser or damage his or her property intentionally unless the court determines otherwise in the interests of justice. The Act does not affect the rules of law relating to self-defence, the defence of others or the defence of property (see page 134). We saw in *Ross v Curtis* (1989) (page 165) that reasonable force may be used to repel a thief, where the occupier feared he was in imminent personal danger.

LIABILITY OF CARRIERS

Nature of the Duty of Care

The duty of a carrier towards passengers and goods arises in tort and in contract. Reasonable care is the standard. Exemption clauses, considered on page 97, may attempt to exclude, or delimit, liability for negligence.

Maintenance of Vehicle

A bus passenger, in *Whelan v Gilbert* (1930), was injured following an accident caused by a flaw in the vehicle which was unknown to the owner. The court held that the care, human skill and foresight which would have avoided the accident were absent. Liability was imposed, in *Conole v Redbank Oyster Co.* (1976) (page 157), on a boat owner who, knowing it to be defective and unseaworthy, took fifty children out on a sea trip and when it sank, ten children were drowned.

Entering and Leaving of Vehicle

A passenger boarded a crowded tram, in *Paley v Dublin United Tramways* (1937), and while searching for a seat the start signal was given by another passenger. The tram moved, throwing the passenger to the floor. Damages were recovered because a passenger must be allowed reasonable time to reach safety before the vehicle moves. A passenger, in *Forsythe v Great Northern Railways* (1937), was informed before leaving on a journey from Dublin, that the first stop would be Donabate. In fact the train stopped at an earlier station and the passenger, believing he was at Donabate, attempted to alight but was injured when the train moved off. The railway company was liable, because the passenger was induced to alight at the first stop, and was negligent in allowing the train to start without seeing to passenger safety.

Operation of Vehicle

A passenger, in *Hannigan v Great Southern Railway* (1939), seated in a train carriage, got up to close the door as the train was about to depart. Unfortunately, at the same moment a porter, whom the passenger did not see and who did not see him, closed the door from the outside, catching the passenger's thumb in the door. It was held that the railway company had acted reasonably. A passenger, in *Glanfield v CIE* (1946), was seated with an infant on her knee in a train compartment alongside the door leading to the corridor. The ticket checker, who had an opportunity of seeing the position of the child's hand, slammed the door injuring the child. It was decided that the railway company was negligent.

PROFESSIONAL NEGLIGENCE

Nature of Duty of Care

A party who holds himself or herself out to the public as being possessed of a particular skill will be liable in negligence where there is a failure to take reasonable care in the exercise of that skill.

A solicitor, in *Wall v Hegarty* (1980), who improperly executed a will, was held by the High Court to owe a duty of care towards a legatee who lost a legacy when the will was declared invalid. A solicitor, in *Kelly v Crowley* (1985), acted for the purchaser of licensed premises, who intended to purchase an ordinary publican's licence but in fact purchased a hotel licence, and as a consequence had a renewal of the licence refused because the premises was not operating as a hotel. The High Court held the solicitor was negligent because he failed to establish the exact nature of the licence. In *Roche v Peilow* (1985) a search by a solicitor against a company, in the company's office which was building a house for sale, would have revealed that the land on which the house was built was mortgaged. After the house was built, the mortgagee refused to release the certificate of title until the mortgage was discharged. The purchaser was put to additional expense and sued his solicitor. The Supreme Court ruled that a solicitor was not acting reasonably where he automatically and mindlessly followed a general practice, when, by taking thought, he would have realised that the practice was fraught with peril for the client and was readily avoidable. The High Court ruled, in *O'Connor v First National Building Society* (1991), that while there was no absolute rule of law that a solicitor must always advise a purchaser that an independent inspection of the property by a suitably qualified person ought to be obtained, it was an established practice that such a duty *prima facie* arose, and it was for a solicitor who contended that no such duty arose in any particular case to show circumstances which negatived the existence of that duty. In that case the solicitor did not advise an inspection because he wrongly assumed the purchaser was a builder, though he admitted that had he known the true position, he would have advised an independent survey. The High Court ruled, in *Doran v Delaney* (1996), that where a client was intending to build a house on land which he was about to purchase, it was the duty of his solicitor to ensure that there was proper access to the site for that purpose.

A general medical practitioner, in *Boyle v Martin* (1932), wrongly diagnosed that a patient was suffering from dyspepsia, whereas his complaint was an appendicitis, from which he died. An action for negligence failed because there was no evidence of lack of skill in that the standard of skill required from a general practitioner was not of the same high degree expected from a specialist. In *Daniels v Heskin* (1954) a needle broke while a doctor was inserting stitches and, on his failure to find the broken part, he left it inside the patient, where it remained for six weeks. There was no evidence that the breaking of the needle was caused by negligence, or that the completion of the stitching and the deferring of its removal was unreasonable. An anaesthetist, in *O'Donovan v Cork County Council* (1967), did not administer a relaxant drug when, during an appendicitis operation, the patient suffered convulsions. An action for negligence following the patient's death was successful because convulsions, though rare, were foreseeable, and the departure from the general practice of administering a relaxant drug was negligent. The absence of evidence that the procedure adopted was a general and accepted procedure was *prima facie* evidence of negligence.

A general medical practitioner, in *Reeves v Carthy* (1984), failed to examine the patient and injected an unsuitable drug at the time when he was suffering from peritonitis. Another general practitioner injected the patient with an inappropriate drug and failed to recognise that the patient was critically ill. The failure to diagnose and treat the abdominal perforation promptly was negligence by both doctors, and the subsequent occurrence of a stroke in the patient was a foreseeable consequence of that negligence. In the process of giving birth to twins, in *Dunne v National Maternity Hospital* (1989), one baby suffered irreversible brain damage and the other died. The practice was to identify one foetal heart only. The Supreme Court ruled that despite the existence of a general and approved practice of monitoring two foetal hearts in such circumstances the doctor was not negligent, unless no doctor would have deviated from that practice if he was taking ordinary care, and that the practice had such inherent defects as would have been obvious on due consideration by the doctor. An eight-year-old girl, in *Lindsay v Mid-Western Health Board* (1993), operated on for an acute appendicitis, never regained consciousness after the operation and suffered irreversible brain damage. The case was dismissed because it was proved that there was no negligence in the anaesthetic procedure. The maxim *res ipsa loquitur*, which applied in this case (page 186), was rebutted by the evidence.

Those responsible for providing nursing care must exercise reasonable care. The owner of a nursing home was, in *Mooney v Terret* (1939), held liable to a patient for a burn obtained when a nurse negligently administered an anaesthetic. An epileptic patient taken off medication when admitted to hospital was owed a duty of care, in *Kelly v Board of Governors of St Laurence's Hospital* (1989), where he was permitted to go to the toilet during the night unattended and was injured when he jumped from an open window.

Accountants, in *Leech v Stokes* (1937), were not negligent in failing to prepare a balance sheet which would have disclosed discrepancies caused by a dishonest clerk, because they were not requested to do so. In *Golden Vale Co-operative Creameries Ltd v Barrett* (1987) accountants were engaged to provide information which would assist a client to decide whether to participate in a rescue operation to keep another company in business. The High Court held that where the client was anxious to press ahead, the accountants should have exercised a restraining influence and couched their report, which was more encouraging than was warranted by the trading and financial state of the company, in terms which could be justified objectively in every respect. Failure to do so was negligence.

A hotelier, in *Flanagan v Griffith* (1985), engaged an architect to prepare a structural report on premises he was acquiring. After purchase a flat roof gave trouble and it was claimed that, at the material time, it was structurally defective and that a stain on the ceiling under it should have raised a doubt as to its condition. The primary method of inspecting a flat roof was to examine the ceiling under it. This the architect did. Carefully testing the stain with a moisture meter and being satisfied that it was totally dry, the architect reached the conclusion that it was the insignificant residue of some previous problem, which had been resolved. The High Court dismissed the action.

Insurance brokers who advised an insured not to make a disclosure of a previous claim were, in *Chariot Inns Ltd v Assicurazioni Generali SPA* (1981) (page 368), negligent when the insurance company avoided the policy after a fire occurred in the premises. In *Western Meats Ltd v National Ice & Cold Storage Co. Ltd* (1982) (page 99) damages for negligence were awarded against cold storage merchants for meat delivered into refrigeration which was destroyed due to being stored at the incorrect temperature. Where a party is specifically engaged to safeguard the property of another it was held, in *Johnson & Johnson (Ireland) Ltd v C.P. Security Ltd* (1985), that there was a duty of care to protect it.

It was held in *Colgan v Connolly Construction Co. Ltd* (1980) that a subsequent owner of a house, not having purchased it from the builder, should recover damages from the builder for defects due to negligent workmanship when the house was being built originally. In *Hughes v J.J. Power Ltd* (1988) (page 189) a mechanic negligently repaired a combine harvester: the test applied was the standard of the ordinary skilled operative exercising and professing to have that special skill.

LIABILITY OF HIGHWAY USERS

Nature of Duty

Every highway user must take reasonable care not to cause injury or damage to other highway users. The standard of care is that of reasonable care. This duty of care extends to all users of the highway, including pedestrians.

Liability for Animals

When animals are brought on to the highway, the owner or controller must take reasonable care to ensure that injury or damage is not caused by them. A motorist at night, in *Furlong v Curran* (1959), on turning a right-hand corner came upon nine cows spread across the road which were in the charge of a drover who walked behind them, and behind the drover came a car with headlamps on, driven by the owner of the cows. It was held that the owner was negligent in putting so many cows on the road at night without sufficient lighting and in not bringing them to the correct side of the highway when approaching the corner.

At common law the ordinary duty of care did not extend to animals straying on to a highway. The *Animals Act 1985* enacts that so many of the rules of the common law relating to liability for negligence as excluded or restricted the duty which a person might owe to others, to take such care as was reasonable to see that damage was not caused by animals straying on to a highway, were abolished. There is now a duty to take care that damage is not caused by straying animals. A pet lamb, in *Dunphy v Bryan* (1963), which was customarily fed in the farmyard, escaped on to the highway and collided with a car. The owner of the car could not recover damages for loss because there was no absence of reasonable care. In *O'Reilly v Lavelle* (1990) eight to ten animals strayed on to the highway with one calf being killed when it collided with a car, which was badly damaged. The other animals ran up a lane which divided the cattle owner's land. In these circumstances the onus of proof shifted to the owner to show that the fencing was not defective in that cattle had escaped from and returned to the field on that occasion. The onus was not discharged and the car owner recovered damages.

Liability for Motor Vehicles

The negligent use of the motor vehicle is the cause of considerable litigation in our courts. Whether there is a breach of the duty to take reasonable care will depend on all the circumstances, such as the time, place, weather, the light, the highway, speed, manner of driving, other traffic, and state and condition of the driver.

While most road accidents involve injury and damage to other users of the highway, the duty of care extends to passengers in the motor vehicle which causes the incident. A front seat passenger was injured, in *Kingston v Kingston* (1968), after jumping from the car on being told by the driver, as the car was going down a steep hill, that the brakes had failed. Despite the driver bringing the car to a halt without injury to the other passengers, the Supreme Court held that the trial court could have decided that the driver was not negligent, just as there was evidence on which it could have arrived at a contrary verdict.

A heavier responsibility is placed on drivers when children show themselves to be present. The driver of a large van, in *Brennan v Savage Smyth & Co. Ltd* (1982), attempted to reverse in a car park where he had seen two children. One, a seven-year-old boy, jumped on to the bumper, jumped off again, and was walking behind the reversing van intending to remount the bumper when he was crushed between the van and a lamppost. The Supreme Court held that the driver should have ensured that the children were out of danger and should not have reversed without the assistance of a helper, which was the normal procedure. The court apportioned blame, 75 per cent to the driver and 25 per cent to the child. The Supreme Court held, in *Moore v Fullerton* (1991), that a driver of a lorry who had slowed to thirteen m.p.h. could not be found guilty of negligence. His failure to avoid a collision with a nine-year-old boy who ran out from behind a passing lorry would be to impose an artificially high and unreasonable standard of care.

But liability is not limited to the driving of motor vehicles. Liability extends to their use and control while on the highway. The driver, in *Curley v Mannion* (1965), parked his car on the correct side of the roadway and allowed his daughter to leave and re-enter the car by the rear off-side door. Seeing a lorry approach, she did not close it properly but merely pulled it to. After the lorry had passed, she opened the door again intending to close it properly, but hit a passing cyclist. The Supreme Court held that a person in charge of a motor vehicle must take precautions for the safety of others, which includes the duty to take reasonable care to prevent conduct on the part of passengers which is negligent.

How a person, not driving a motor vehicle though exercising control over it, may be liable is illustrated in *Cahill v Kenneally* (1955). A driver parked a bus in a street allowing two passengers to enter. There was easy access to the driver's cabin and the vehicle was started by the turning of a knob. One passenger, when the driver departed, entered the cabin, started the bus, drove it and crashed into a car. It was held that the bus driver was negligent in allowing the passengers to wait in an unattended vehicle. In *Dockery v O'Brien* (1975) the owner parked an unlocked car in a public place, leaving the key in the ignition switch. An intoxicated person, without the permission of the owner, entered and drove the car causing damage to another car, which was lawfully parked. The owner was liable because it was reasonably foreseeable that some unauthorised person would take the car and cause damage.

LIABILITY FOR NEGLIGENT MISSTATEMENTS

Nature of Duty

It is a principle of law that an action lies for negligent false statements. For liability to attach there must be a pre-existing relationship between the parties such as to justify one party relying on the statements of the other. The party making the statement is under a duty to take reasonable care to ensure that the information or advice given is accurate.

A company director, acting in a personal capacity, in *Securities Trust Ltd v Hugh Moore & Alexander Ltd* (1964), purchased shares in the defendant company and requested a copy of the memorandum and articles of association. On the faith of their contents the plaintiff company purchased shares in the defendant company. The printed articles contained an error, the company was wound up and the plaintiff company sued for negligent misstatement. The High Court dismissed the action because there was no special relationship between the two companies. The plaintiff company had relied on information supplied by its director. There was, of course, a special relationship between the director and the defendant company. Had he personally purchased further shares on foot of the information supplied, he would have been entitled to recover his loss.

In *Bank of Ireland v Smith* (1966) it was argued that an auctioneer, acting for the seller of property, should anticipate that any statement made about the property will be relied on by a purchaser and therefore a duty of care is owed to that purchaser, and an action should lie where the statement is incorrect and made carelessly. In that case the auctioneer published an advertisement which incorrectly stated a material fact. The High Court held that a special relationship must exist between the parties; the auctioneer did not owe a duty of care to the world at large. The absence of a special relationship between the parties proved to be fatal yet again in *Stafford v Keane, Mahony, Smith* (1980) where a client engaged auctioneers to find a property to be used as a residence, which would be a sound investment and be available for resale at a profit. The auctioneers introduced the client to a boarding school property on the market. The client claimed that the auctioneers stated that the premises could be converted cheaply to a residence and would make a handsome profit when resold. The auctioneer denied making any such representations. At the last moment the client's brother purchased the premises, which proved to be a poor investment. The actual purchaser sued the auctioneers for negligent misstatement. Finding on the facts that there had been no negligent misstatement, the High Court dismissed the claim, though the judge pointed out that had there been, the eventual purchaser could not have recovered because there was no special relationship between him and the auctioneers. Such a relationship did exist between the purchaser's brother and the auctioneers.

A special relationship may be created between an auctioneer acting for the seller and a prospective purchaser. In *McAnarney v Hanrahan* (1994) a purchaser arrived late at an auction and was told by the auctioneer that there had been a bid for the premises, but that the property had been withdrawn. The auctioneer said there had been negotiations with the landlord concerning the freehold which could be purchased for £3,000 because the lease had only five years to run. On the basis of these representations, both false, the premises were purchased. The freehold was eventually purchased for £30,000. The High Court ruled that the expressed assumption of responsibility for giving an opinion about the purchase of the freehold created a special relationship between the auctioneer and the purchaser. The court held there was negligent misstatement and awarded compensation.

A group of companies in financial difficulties, in *McSweeney v Bourke* (1980), engaged a bank to advise in respect of a possible take-over bid. The bid came to nothing but a number of alternatives, including the injection of capital by the two majority shareholders, were considered. The injection of capital made little difference and the group went into receivership. The shareholders sued the bank for damages for negligent advice. The action failed because the special relationship existed between the bank and the group of companies, and not between the shareholders and the bank. On the evidence, the High Court held that there was no negligence by the bank.

LIABILITY OF PUBLIC AUTHORITIES

Nature of Duty

Public authorities owe a duty to take reasonable care when exercising statutory powers. This duty was first recognised in *Siney v Dublin Corporation* (1980) where the Supreme Court ruled that a local authority, under a statutory duty to provide housing, were under a duty of care to a tenant to ensure that the premises was fit for human habitation at the date of the letting, which it was not. In *Ward v McMaster* (1989) a county council commissioned a report from an auctioneer in relation to a house when an application was made for a home loan under a statutory scheme. The report was seriously inaccurate. When the house proved to be uninhabitable the purchaser sued the county council. The Supreme Court held that a special relationship existed between the purchaser and the county council, which imposed on the council a duty of care towards the purchaser to ensure by a proper valuation and inspection that the house would be good security for any loan advanced. The county council ought reasonably to have foreseen that the purchaser would not incur the further expense of having a structural survey done, but would rely on that undertaken by the council.

Where a local authority granted permission for the retention of premises the Supreme Court ruled, in *Sunderland v McGreavey* (1990), that the local authority as planning authority did not owe a duty of care to the purchaser of premises, which became uninhabitable as a result of flooding from defective drainage, because no relationship of proximity existed between the parties which at law stood to be protected. The planning law imposed on planning authorities a duty towards the public at large and those laws did not include a purpose of protecting individual persons.

Where there has been a delegation by statute to a designated person of a power to make decisions affecting others, unless the statute provides otherwise, an action for damages by a person adversely affected by an *ultra vires* decision does not lie against the decision-maker, unless he or she acted negligently, or with malice, or in the knowledge that the decision was in excess of the authorised power. This was decided by the Supreme Court in *Pine Valley Developments Ltd v Minister for the Environment* (1987) where planning permission granted by the Minister was later found to be *ultra vires*. In reaching that decision the Minister had acted *bona fide* on advice given by the department's senior legal adviser.

EMPLOYER'S LIABILITY

Nature of Duty

An employer owes a duty of care towards his or her employees. This is the ordinary duty to take reasonable care applied to the particular relationship of employer and employee. The standard of care is that of a prudent employer who would not expose an employee to unnecessary risks. The duty may vary with the employee's age, knowledge and experience. This duty to take reasonable care of employees rests on the State. In *Ryan v Ireland* (1989) the Supreme Court ruled that this duty extended to a serving soldier, even in operations involving armed conflict or hostilities.

The scope of this duty is generally divided into four categories, though these overlap to some extent.

Duty to Provide Competent Staff

There is a duty on an employer to employ competent fellow employees for each employee. Before liability arises, it must be shown that the employer knew, or ought to have known, of the incompetence of the employee causing the injury. Previous acts of incompetence would prove this. This duty extends to the employee's general behaviour. An employee, in *Hough v Irish Base Metals Ltd* (1967), was injured when jumping away from a gas fire which had been placed near him for 'a bit of devilment' by another employee, an act often done in the repair shop. The Supreme Court refused to hold the employer liable on the grounds that the act was regarded by all present as a bit of fun, that it was over in an instant, that the practice had not been reported to anyone in authority, and that it was not easily detectable even with supervision. But in *Kennedy v Taltech Engineering Co. Ltd* (1989) liability was imposed where a supervisor used his authority to play an innocent prank. The employee, having finished work, was putting on his coat when he was called over by a supervisor who was talking to another employee carrying a metal plate with sharp edges. When the supervisor attempted to take a bag from the employee's pocket, the employee by way of reflex action, immediately grabbed the bag while it was in mid air. This had the effect of suddenly releasing the employee's hand which swung back hitting the metal plate and he was injured. The High Court regarded the entire incident as a single event because it was unreal to differentiate between the legitimate instruction the employee was obliged to obey and what transpired later.

A serving soldier acting in a defensive role with the United Nations, injured whilst on guard duty was, in *Ryan v Ireland* (1989), owed a duty by his commanding officer to take such precautions as were reasonable and practical, having regard to the functions which, as a member of the guard, the soldier was obliged to perform.

Duty to Provide Safe Place of Work

The employer must provide and maintain a reasonably safe place of work for the benefit of employees. An employee, in *Kielthy v Ascon Ltd* (1970), was killed when he fell from a wall, nine inches wide and three-and-a-half feet high, which had become a recognised route to and from the building site office. It was not the only, or safest, route available. The employer was liable because the Supreme Court held the duty was not to see that some modes of access offered were safe, but that all were safe.

Duty to Provide Proper Equipment

The employer has a duty to take reasonable care to provide and maintain proper equipment so as not to subject employees using it to unnecessary risks. A carpenter, in *Deegan v Langan* (1966), lost the sight of an eye after using a steel masonry nail which disintegrated when it was struck with a hammer. The employer was liable because he knew those nails were dangerous. An employer, in *Burke v John Paul & Co. Ltd* (1967), supplied a machine for cutting steel bars which, though safe for its purpose, had blunt blades. Liability was imposed because its operation increased the physical pressure on the employee which led to damage to his health. An employer, in *Brady v Backmann Instruments (Galway) Inc.* (1986), was not responsible to an employee who contracted a form of dermatitis by inhaling chemical fumes at his work-place. The Supreme Court ruled that while the disease was contracted at work, the result was so unique and improbable as not to be one which the employer could reasonably have foreseen.

It was claimed that protective clothing supplied, in *English v Anglo Irish Meat Co. Ltd* (1988), including a glove of chain mail to above wrist level and a plastic guard which extended up the arm to within a few inches of the elbow, was not adequate to protect an employee engaged in the boning of meat carcasses with a razor sharp blade. The High Court held that gauntlets which extended above the elbow were available and in use in the trade, and had these been provided it would have prevented the employee's injury to his arm just above the upper rim of the plastic guard. The Supreme Court, in *Kennedy v Hughes Dairies Ltd* (1989), held that it was unreasonable on the employer's part not to provide appropriate protective gloves and gauntlets to employees whose work involved the carrying of crates of empty bottles, some broken and consequently jagged, in an area where any employee might trip over or on another broken bottle or otherwise, causing injury to the most vulnerable but most easily protected part of the body, the hands and lower arms.

An employer may be liable for defective equipment left on the premises by a third party and used by an employee. In *Keenan v Bergin and Bishop* (1971) the carrier was held to be 80 per cent at fault in leaving a defective articulated trailer on the premises of the employer, who was found to be 20 per cent at fault because of a failure to inspect the vehicle which injured an employee.

Duty to Provide Safe System of Work

An employer must devise for employees a system of working which is reasonably safe. In *Flynn v Irish Sugar Manufacturing Co.* (1928) the employer was liable where an unseaworthy raft was provided to convey employees across a river in the course of their work. In *Bradley v CIE* (1976) the non-provision of a steel cage around a ladder which the employee had to mount to service signal lamps was not negligent because within the previous ten years there had been no reported accident on any of the other 1,000 steel ladders owned and used by the employer.

An employer is not relieved of this duty by forbidding an employee to perform certain tasks, or by an order not to perform the task in a particular manner, or where the employee is possessed of sufficient skill which allows the employee to recognise an obvious danger. This is illustrated by *O'Hanlon v ESB* (1969) where a skilled electrician needed particular equipment to carry out a particular task. On his failure to obtain this, he could have refused to continue the task or could have disconnected the power supply. Instead, he continued the task which he knew to be dangerous and in a manner forbidden by his employer. He was injured and his employer was liable because the risk of injury to the employee, in the absence of appropriate equipment, was reasonably foreseeable despite the employee's skill.

VICARIOUS LIABILITY

Nature of Duty

Where a party either expressly or impliedly authorises another to commit an act which injures or damages another, that party may in law be held responsible. That party may be liable to the same extent as if that party had actually committed the tort. The rule is *qui facit per alium, facit per se*: he who does something through another, does it through himself. Liability thus arising is called vicarious liability because it arises indirectly. It arises most commonly in the relationship between employers and employees, partners and co-partners, companies and agents.

The Control Test

In deciding whether one party is to be liable for the torts of another, the law does not look to the relationship *per se* between the parties. While generally an employer is responsible for the tortious acts of employees, it does not follow that the employer is responsible for all such torts. In deciding whether liability arises, the test applied by the courts is control. In *Moynihan v Moynihan* (1975) a two-year-old child was seriously burned when she pulled a pot of tea over herself in her grandmother's house. The child had been invited with her parents to a meal during which the child's aunt made tea and left the pot under a brightly coloured tea-cosy on the table. The child was left alone in the room. The Supreme Court held that the grandmother, as the householder and as the person in control of the hospitality being provided in her home, was vicariously liable for the negligence of her daughter in performing a gratuitous service in the course of providing such hospitality. 'On the evidence . . .', said Walsh J., 'the necessary element of control was vested in the grandmother and the daughter was in the *de facto* service of her mother for the purpose of the act in which she was alleged to be negligent.'

Employer's Liability for the Torts of Employee

Generally, an employer is vicariously liable for the torts of an employee committed in the course of employment. *Hughes v J.J. Power Ltd* (1988) (page 189) showed that an employer was liable for negligent repairs carried out by an employee. *Johnson & Johnson (Ireland) Ltd v C.P. Security Ltd* (1985) is an authority for the rule that where the employer contracts with another party, the employer is responsible for the criminal acts of an employee which causes loss to the other party. In that case a security officer in the defendant's employment was convicted of stealing goods from the premises he was employed to protect. The State, as an employer, is responsible for the negligent acts of its servants: see *Byrne v Ireland* (page 158).

Employer Not Responsible for Torts of Independent Contractor

An employer is not responsible for torts committed by an independent contractor employed. The distinction between an employee and an independent contractor is crucial. Who is an employee? An employee is engaged under a contract of service as an integral part of the business and is under the control of the employer in what he or she must do and how, when and where the employee must do it. On the other hand, an independent contractor is free to select the method of work, to provide personal plant and equipment, and to perform the work when the time is convenient. An independent contractor is under a contract for services to the employer.

This distinction between a contract of service and a contract for service is illustrated in *Walshe v Baileboro Co-operative* (1939) where a person was engaged to collect cans of milk from farmers, carry them to the creamery and return to the farmers the empty cans. A horse and cart was used and on one occasion, while the horse was left unattended, it injured the plaintiff. The High Court held that the person so engaged was an employee and not an independent contractor. 'He was', said Johnston J., 'under the control of the co-operative as to the doing of that work on a fixed road and at a time each day. It was the daily toil of an ordinary man and in no sense could he be said to be his own master.' An employee, in *Lynch v Palgrave Murphy Ltd* (1964), while stacking heavy bales of paper had his thumb crushed by the prong of a forklift truck. The forklift and its driver were hired by the employer who was entitled to give the driver directions where the truck was to be driven, the nature of the load to be carried and the place where the load was to be deposited, though the driver was employed, paid and liable to dismissal by the owner of the forklift, and its operation was a matter for the driver. A claim by the employee against his employer failed. The Supreme Court held that the employer had not sufficient control over the forklift driver at the material time.

The Course of Employment

Even where the person who is negligent is an employee, liability will not attach to the employer unless the employee is acting within the course of employment. Should the employer prove that the employee was on a frolic of his own, the employer is not responsible and the injured party must seek compensation from the employee personally.

A butcher and meat salesman, in *Duffy v Orr* (1941), was employed to accompany his employer on delivery rounds. On one occasion, unknown to his employer, he took the delivery van and injured the plaintiff. It was held that the employee was acting outside the course of employment. In *Doyle v Fleming's Coal Mine Ltd* (1953) a lorry driver stopped at a wood to inquire directions. As a result the plaintiff joined the lorry and, after making a delivery, the parties spent considerable time in a licensed premises. On the way back to the wood the lorry was involved in an accident. It was held that the employee was acting outside the course of employment.

The driver of a taxi, in *Quilligan v Long* (1953), at the end of his employer's business and without his authority, took the taxi home and parked it outside his house, leaving it unlocked, with the key in the ignition, from where it was stolen. It was held that the employee was not acting within the course of employment. The manager of a licensed premises, in *Reilly v Ryan* (1991), grabbed a customer and interposed him between himself and an intruder who had burst into the premises armed with a knife demanding money from the till. The customer was stabbed and an action against the employer failed. The High Court ruled that while an employee had authority to defend his employer's property and himself, the assault of the customer and his imposition between the manager and the robber was so excessive as to place it outside the course of employment.

In *Hough v Irish Base Metals Ltd* (1967) (page 202) an employer was not responsible for injuries caused to an employee by 'a bit of devilment' caused by a fellow employee. But in *Kennedy v Taltech Engineering Co. Ltd* (1989) (page 202) an employer was responsible for injuries to an employee caused by a prank played by a supervisor.

Liability for Driving of Motor Vehicles

In a number of cases the question arises whether the owner of a motor vehicle is liable for the negligent acts of the driver. In obvious cases such as the employer and employee relationship, the answer is yes, subject to what has been said earlier concerning the course of employment. Where such a relationship is absent, the answer depends on control. It was decided in *Hassett v Skehan* (1939) that where a motor vehicle was driven by a person other than its owner, the onus of disproving agency rested on the owner. A car owner, in *Mulligan v Daly* (1937), asked a friend to drive it to a garage for some repairs. When the friend reached the garage, the garage owner asked the friend to drive another person elsewhere. The friend did and was involved in a collision. It was held that the owner was not liable because the friend was then acting outside the scope of the agency. The seller of a defective car, in *Kett v Shannon* (1987), loaned another car to the buyer while it was being repaired. When the buyer returned that car, the seller was not present but an employee gave the buyer another car because the repairs to the original car had not been completed. The buyer using the car caused injury to a pedestrian who sued the seller for the negligence of the buyer in the driving of the car. The Supreme Court held that the employee had no authority to lend the car and that therefore the seller was not liable for the buyer's negligent driving.

Chapter 20

DEFAMATION

Nature of Defamation

The Constitution provides that the State shall by its laws protect as best it may from unjust attack and, in the case of injustice done, vindicate the good name of every citizen. The law of defamation is part fulfilment by the State of that duty. Defamation is the publication of a false statement which discredits another by lowering the estimation in which that person stands in the opinion of right-minded members of the community, or tends to hold that person up to hatred, ridicule, or contempt, or causes that person to be shunned or avoided by right-thinking members of society.

Publication of Defamatory Matter

Publication is the making known of the defamatory matter to some person other than the person of whom it is made. A maker, distributor, disseminator of a statement, publishes that statement. Publication solely to the party defamed is not sufficient. For example, where two persons engage in conversation in a private place, one cannot defame the other because there is no publication to a third party. Likewise, where a sealed letter is posted which contains defamatory matter, there can be no defamation in law because there is no publication. Where the receiver shows it to others, there is no publication in law because there was no publication by the wrongdoer.

Publication may take various forms. It could be contained in a letter: *Hynes-O'Sullivan v O'Driscoll* (1989); an enforcement notice: *Kennedy v Hearne* (1988); an article in a magazine: *Quigley v Creation Ltd* (1971); a photograph in a national newspaper: *Berry v Irish Times Ltd* (1973); by a notice in a horse-racing calendar: *Green v Blake* (1948); by a verbal accusation in a public street: *Coleman v Kearns Ltd* (1946); or words spoken at a meeting: *McCarthy v Morrissey* (1939).

Where a party is not named in the publication, the test which decides whether the words used refer to him or her is whether the words are such as would reasonably lead persons acquainted with that party to believe he or she is the person referred to. The Supreme Court so decided in *Duffy v News Group Newspapers Ltd* (1993) where a story recounted a surveillance operation where British Army soldiers spent a week hidden in the attic of a

GAA club in Crossmaglen and recorded details of terrorist plots planned just feet away. The plaintiff was chairman of the club, though he was not mentioned by name in the story.

Kinds of Defamation

There are two kinds of defamation, namely libel and slander. Libel is the communication of defamatory matter in a permanent and visible form, such as writing, printing, film, or in statue form. The *Defamation Act 1961* provides that broadcasting words by wireless telegraphy is considered a permanent form. Libel is actionable *per se*, that is, without proof of actual damage suffered. Libel is also a criminal wrong. Criminal libel consists of a defamatory attack on a person which tends to, or is likely to, cause a breach of the peace. A prosecution for criminal libel can only be commenced with leave of a High Court judge. An allegation that the plaintiff's recently deceased husband had engaged in criminal activity of a subversive nature in his early life, in *Hilliard v Penfield Enterprises Ltd* (1990), did not require prosecution because the defamation of the widow and daughter was not so serious as to warrant the invocation of the criminal law. It is not possible to libel the dead.

Slander is the speaking of defamatory words. The *Defamation Act 1961* provides that 'words' include visual images, gestures and other methods of signifying meaning. Slander is not a crime and is only actionable on proof of special damage, which means some real or actual loss, such as the loss of friendship or the loss of a contractual or other tangible business advantage.

There are four exceptions to the rule that special damage must be proved in slander cases. First, words which impute unchastity, or adultery, in any female. Second, words calculated to disparage a person in any office, profession, trade, calling, or business. A trade union official, in *McMullan v Mulhall* (1929), said to an employer, 'McMullan is not a member of a union and you sack him today. You can't employ him.' The Supreme Court ruled that these words did not touch the plaintiff in his vocation or calling. A doctor said of a solicitor, in *Bennett v Quane* (1948), that 'He brought an action in the Circuit Court instead of the District Court to get more costs for himself.' These words were held to have touched the solicitor in his profession. Third, in some particular actions for slander of title to property or goods it is unnecessary to prove special damage. Fourth, an imputation of past or current criminal conduct is actionable without special damage.

Examples of Defamatory Words

To succeed in defamation, the words complained of must tend to lower the reputation of the person they are written or spoken of in the eyes of right-thinking members of the community. Some examples of decided cases will illustrate the type of words, and the circumstances in which they were made, which may amount to defamation.

A series of reports in a newspaper which said that the plaintiff was 'a grabber', that he got a farm by 'grabbing', and referred to him as 'the Ennistymon grabber' were, in *McInerney v Clareman Printing & Publishing Co.* (1903), defamatory. In *Corcoran v W & R Jacob* (1945) the words, 'It was a piece of copper, ten or twelve inches long that Corcoran had', were defamatory when spoken by a security guard at the employer's premises because they meant that the employee had stolen his employer's property. A letter of the Turf Club, the controlling body for horse-racing, which requested the placing of the plaintiff's name on the defaulter's list was, in *Reilly v Gill* (1946), defamatory. In *Bennett v Quane* (1948) words, quoted earlier, which suggested that a solicitor had brought a case in a higher court merely to secure extra legal fees, were defamatory. Words published in a magazine which suggested that an actor had left Ireland to work abroad solely for the love of money, were defamatory in *Quigley v Creation Ltd* (1971). In *Berry v Irish Times Ltd* (1973) a photograph of a placard carried by protesters with the words 'Peter Berry Twentieth Century Felon Settor', was not defamatory because to assist in bringing to justice a fellow countryman in another country, who broke the law of that country, would not lower that person in the eyes of right-thinking members of the community. An allegation that a member of Dáil Éireann assaulted a journalist in public and on a public occasion was, in *Barrett v Independent Newspapers Ltd* (1986), considered defamatory. An allegation that a solicitor was a tax defaulter and a cheat and had no reputation was defamatory in *Kennedy v Hearne* (1988).

Innuendo

As a general rule the material words must be defamatory in their ordinary meaning. Where they are not, an injured party may yet succeed if innuendo is proved. This rule provides that words which are innocent when given their ordinary meaning may be defamatory when accorded a special meaning. For example, to suggest that a person was a 'Fagin', which would be taken to mean a thief or a handler of stolen goods, because of the well-known character in Dickens, is an innuendo.

The suggestion in a newspaper, in *Campbell v Irish Press Ltd* (1955), that the snooker table during an exhibition at which a world champion played 'told lies', meaning that it was uneven, was an innuendo and defamatory. In *Fullam v Associated Newspapers Ltd* (1956) a newspaper report that a successful and well-known professional soccer player never used his right foot except for balancing on, was an innuendo because it implied that he was not a competent player.

The words wrongfully written by a bank on a cheque presented for payment, 'Refer to drawer — Present again' and 'Return to drawer' were not an innuendo in *Pyke v Hibernian Bank* (1950), though in *Grealy v Bank of Nova Scotia* (1975) it was conceded by the bank that the words 'Refer to drawer' were defamatory.

Remedies in Defamation

Damages are the standard remedy in defamation. These are compensatory in that the injured party is entitled to redress for the damage to reputation. It was decided, in *Barrett v Independent Newspapers Ltd* (1986), that damages can also be awarded for anxiety, distress and injury to feelings arising from the publication. In certain circumstances, aggravated damages may be awarded. Allegations made in open court that a practising solicitor was a cheat and had no reputation, in *Kennedy v Hearne* (1988), merited aggravated damages.

An injunction may be granted to prevent either the publication, or further publication, of defamatory material. The Supreme Court ruled, in *Sinclair v St John Gogarty* (1937), that an interlocutory injunction to restrain the publication of a libel pending the hearing of the action should only be exercised in the clearest case where the court would find that the matter complained of was libellous. In that case an injunction was granted to prevent the publication of the novel *As I was Going Down Sackville Street* because it contained clear defamatory material.

DEFENCES IN DEFAMATION

Consent

A person may consent to the publication of defamatory material. A classic example is the revelation of matters, defamatory in nature, to a journalist in an interview, which are later published. The consent must be to the actual publication. The mere submission to a set of rules, as in *Green v Blake* (1948), did not constitute a consent to the publication by the stewards of the Turf Club of a defamatory decision following the investigation of a complaint against the owner of a horse which had run in a race.

Absolute Privilege

The defence of absolute privilege may defeat a claim for defamation. Absolute privilege extends to occasions in which complete freedom of expression is considered of such paramount importance that actions for defamation cannot be brought, no matter how outrageous or untrue the statement made, or however malicious the maker's motive.

The Constitution provides two absolute privileges for Oireachtas members. All official reports and publications of the Oireachtas, and utterances made in either House of the Oireachtas, wherever published, are privileged.

The common law provides the defence of judicial privilege which covers a wide range of pleadings, evidence and other statements made in the course of legal proceedings by judges, lawyers and witnesses. A judge, in *Macauley & Co. Ltd v Wyse Power* (1943), was sued for slander for remarks made during a case, which seriously assailed the reputation of the company. In dismissing the action, the High Court reasoned it was better that an individual should suffer than that the course of justice be hindered and fettered by apprehension on the part of judges that their words might be made the subject-matter of an action. But, of course, where this privilege is abused, liability might attach.

Qualified Privilege

In some circumstances a qualified privilege may apply which protects the maker of a defamatory statement. A qualified privilege occurs when a person makes a communication under some duty, or with an interest, to a person who is under some corresponding duty, or interest, to receive it. For example, a person reporting another to the gardaí on suspicion of being about to commit a crime is covered by qualified privilege. Likewise, a neighbour reporting a child's constant crying and screaming to the local authority. In each instance the complainant is under a duty, not necessarily a legal duty, to report the matter, and the receiver is under a duty to receive it. This privilege is lost where the report is made to someone not under a duty to receive it.

A solicitor, in *McKeogh v O'Brien Moran* (1927), in the course of defending a client, a nurse, to her employers, against allegations made by a doctor, was held not to be protected by qualified privilege because extraneous allegations of a defamatory nature were made against the doctor. A member of Dáil Éireann and of a local authority, in *McCarthy v Morrissey* (1939), asserted that a report, made by a doctor to the local health board on the cleanliness of certain children in the area, was not true. In an action for slander the defence of qualified privilege was successful, because per Hanna J.: 'Anything affecting the people whom he [the defendant] represented was a matter in which he was entitled, and in fact, bound, to take an interest.' In *Kirkwood Hackett v Tierney* (1952) the President of University College, Dublin, who made an allegation to a student, in the presence of the College Secretary, in respect of a money draft alleged to have been paid wrongly to the student, was protected by privilege because he was under a duty to investigate the matter.

Malice and Qualified Privilege

An occasion *prima facie* protected by qualified privilege may lose that protection where the allegation is motivated by malice. Malice is a wrong or improper motive existing in the mind of the maker of the allegation at the time of publication which actuates that publication. A party acting rashly, or improvidently, or stupidly is protected provided that party acts in good faith.

The question of malice was central in *Coleman v Kearns Ltd* (1946) where an employee, suspecting a customer of stealing goods from the employer's shop, followed her into the public street and accused her in the presence of others. The employee was actuated by the desire either to recover the goods or to obtain payment. It was held that a qualified privilege which might have attached was destroyed because the words were not spoken in furtherance of the civil duty of procuring the arrest and prosecution of a suspected thief.

Fair and Accurate Report

A fair and accurate report published in any newspaper or broadcast within the State of proceedings publicly heard before any court exercising judicial authority within the State, where published or broadcast contemporaneously with such proceedings, is privileged. So are the following: the findings or decisions of associations promoting art, science, religion, learning, or sport; reports of lawful public meetings, reports of a local authority, or of any commission, tribunal or person appointed for the purpose of any inquiry under statutory authority; reports of general meetings of public companies; copies and accurate reports, or summaries of notices, issued by Government departments, local authorities, and the Commissioner of the Garda Síochána.

The plaintiff spoke defamatory words, in *Nevin v Roddy and Carthy* (1935), about the second defendant, at a meeting of a local authority, of which both parties were members. These were published in a newspaper by the first defendant, who later published a letter from Mr Carthy claiming that the allegations made were spoken falsely and maliciously. An action against the publisher failed on the ground that the letter, written without malice, was a statement of contradiction.

Where the person against whom the defamatory remarks are made proves malice on the part of the maker, the defence of fair and accurate reporting will be defeated.

Offer of Amends

At common law an apology by the maker of defamatory remarks was no defence, nor did it mitigate the damages a court might award. A special defence is contained in the *Defamation Act 1961* in cases of unintentional defamation where the party publishing the statement claims it was published innocently. An innocent publication is one that the publisher did not intend to publish concerning the plaintiff, and that no circumstances were known in which it might be understood to refer to the plaintiff, or that the words were not defamatory on their face, and that the publisher knew of no circumstances in which the statement might be understood to be defamatory of the plaintiff and that in either case the publisher exercised all reasonable care in relation to the publication.

Where the publication is innocent, the publisher may make an offer of amends by offering to publish a suitable correction and a sufficient apology to the injured party. Where this offer is accepted and performed by the publisher, the aggrieved party cannot subsequently sue. In publishing an offer of amends it may be necessary to republish the defamatory words. It was decided in *Willis v Irish Press Ltd* (1938) that such an apology was subject to qualified privilege.

Fair Comment

A defence of fair comment may be pleaded. To succeed, it must be proved that any statement of fact on which the comment is based is true, or substantially true, that it is a matter of public interest, and that the comment was made honestly. In *Lefroy v Burnside* (1879) it was alleged that a civil servant abused his position in revealing information to a newspaper before it was officially published. The defence of fair comment failed because there were no facts to sustain it.

To constitute fair comment the statement must not contain imputations of corrupt or dishonourable motives on the part of the person whose conduct or work is criticised, unless such imputations are warranted by the facts. This defence of fair comment will fail if some important fact is omitted which, if stated, would falsify or alter the complexion of the stated facts. In *Foley v Independent Newspapers Ltd* (1993) a senior counsel was appointed as one of two inspectors to investigate a company. A newspaper criticised the level of fees charged by him, though the article failed to mention that these fees had been negotiated soon after his appointment. The High Court ruled that an ordinary reader, unaware of the facts, would have understood the article to mean that the inspector had submitted a claim for fees without any prior agreement as to the manner in which they should be calculated. Since the facts had not been truly stated the defence of fair comment failed.

Justification

A plea of justification is a claim that the allegations made are substantially true. Where successful, it is an absolute defence because the law does not accord to a person a character he or she either does not have, or ought not to possess. A person convicted of murder can be called a murderer; a rapist can be called a rapist.

The onus of establishing justification rests on the defendant. Where this defence fails, the defendant has prejudiced a chance to mitigate the injury because the defamatory allegation has been repeated and insisted upon during the trial. The court may, in such circumstances, award exemplary damages: see *Kennedy v Hearne* (1988) discussed earlier. For this reason it is a rare defence, though this may also be because those against whom true allegations are made have no cause of action.

Chapter 21

ECONOMIC TORTS

Nature of Such Torts

The torts of trespass, nuisance, defamation and negligence protect the individual from direct personal or property attacks. There are other interests protected in the law of torts. Interference with intangible interests in property, or with contractual relations, and fraud are torts. These wrongs are known as economic torts.

PASSING OFF

Nature of Passing Off

Passing off is unfair competition whereby one party, by using deception, attempts to obtain the economic benefit of the reputation which another has established in trade or business.

The principle underlying this tort is that one party cannot have a right to represent his or her goods as those of another. Where the trader's goods are sold under a particular name or description, or have been identified by some particular mark in such a way that in the course of time the goods so named, described or marked have become generally identified in the mind of the public as the goods of that trader, it is actionable for another party to sell goods under that, or some similar name, description or mark, where the result will be that a purchaser is likely to be misled.

Intention to Deceive not Necessary

In a passing off action, it need not be proved that the wrongdoer was fraudulent, or that someone was actually deceived, or that loss was actually suffered. What must be proved is merely that the goods were marked up, made up, or described in such a manner as to be calculated to mislead ordinary purchasers and to lead them to mistake the product of the defendant for the product of the plaintiff.

Protection of a Trading Name

Where a similar activity is carried on by different parties and one party has acquired a reputation under a particular name from which economic gain is derived, it may be passing off for another party to use the same name, or one so closely akin to it as to be calculated to mislead. One distillery, in *Jameson v Dublin Distillers Co.* (1900), traded under the name of 'John Jameson', while another traded under the name of 'William Jameson'. The latter changed the label name of its product to 'Jameson's Whiskey'. In an action to restrain the sale of whiskey under that name without the prefix William, or some other distinctive indication that the whiskey was not manufactured by the plaintiff, the High Court was of opinion that the name 'Jameson's Whiskey' had become so identified with the plaintiff's whiskey, that the use of it by the defendants without qualifying words was likely to mislead purchasers and an injunction was granted.

An injunction was granted, in *Griffin v Kelly's Strand Hotel* (1980) to the owner of the Rosslare Harbour Hotel, to prevent another hotelier who had traded for many years in Rosslare Strand without using the word 'Rosslare', from incorporating Rosslare into its name unless the word 'Strand' immediately followed the word 'Rosslare'. Rosslare Strand is five miles from Rosslare Harbour. An injunction was granted, in *An Post v Irish Permanent plc* (1995), to prevent the sale by the defendant of 'saving certificates' on the ground that, since it appeared that 'saving certificates' emanated only from a Government source, some confusion had been caused to the general public. On the other hand, in *B.& S. Ltd v Irish Auto Trader Ltd* (1995), an injunction was refused to prevent the sale in Ireland of a British magazine, the *Auto Trader*, on a complaint by the publisher of *Buy and Sell* magazine, whose cover page heading included the word 'auto-trader'. The High Court ruled that the defendant had acted *bona fide* by merely seeking to extend its business from Britain and that it would be unrealistic to produce a separate magazine for Ireland, that it was unlikely that traders would be confused between the two magazines, and that, while a purchaser might buy the defendant's magazine believing it to be the plaintiff's, it was probable that mistake would only happen once as the buyer would quickly realise that it was not the same magazine.

The fact that a party does not trade within the State is not a reason for denying a remedy, provided some goodwill has been acquired. A chain store in the retail garment business, trading in Britain and Northern Ireland, acquired a reputation in this State and sought, in *C & A Modes v C & A (Waterford) Ltd* (1979), to prevent the use of a description similar to its own. The Supreme Court agreed: 'Goodwill', according to Henchy J., 'does not stop at a frontier.'

Misleading Packaging

The packaging used by a party may be calculated to deceive a purchaser into believing that when buying that product, packaged as it is, the buyer is acquiring the product of another. The general get-up of the packaging is crucial. The size, shape, materials used, combination of colours, the decoration and lettering, the arrangement of labels and the spacing of the words must all be considered.

An injunction was granted, in *Polycell Products Ltd v O'Carroll* (1959), against the sale of an adhesive in packages similar in colour and design to those of the plaintiff. The fact that the brand name was dissimilar — 'Clingcell' as opposed to 'Polycell' — was insufficient to prevent the risk of confusion in the minds of purchasers. In *United Biscuits Ltd v Irish Biscuits Ltd* (1971) biscuits called 'Cottage Creams' were similar in size and design to biscuits known as 'College Creams'. The High Court refused an injunction because the packages in which the biscuits were sold were entirely different in design and colour. It was immaterial that the appearance, size and texture of the biscuits were similar.

The manufacturer of king size cigarettes in a distinctive blue wrapping successfully sought an injunction, in *Player & Wills (Ireland) Ltd v Gallagher (Dublin) Ltd* (1983), against another manufacturer who introduced club-size cigarettes in a similar distinctive blue wrapping, although the colour was not identical. The High Court held that the all-blue packaging was such as to amount to a badge of origin and that buyers asking for 'blues' could be deceived into thinking that they had received the plaintiff's product, when in fact they had received that of the defendant. The manufacturer of dairy products, in *Mitchelstown Co-operative Agricultural Society Ltd v Goldenvale Food Product Ltd* (1985), marketed butter under the brand name, 'Dairygold', in a gold-coloured tub with five colours and the symbol of a yellow flower. Subsequently the defendants marketed butter in a gold coloured tub using the brand name, 'Easigold'. The tub was identical in size, shape and dimensions with the plaintiff's, though the shade of gold was slightly different. The symbol of a yellow flower was used, though it was not the same type as that used by the plaintiff. The High Court held, in granting an injunction, that in ten months the plaintiff had acquired a sufficient reputation on which to bring an action for passing off.

Misleading Design

A manufacturer's product may be designed in such a way as to amount to passing off. This was the issue in *Adidas Sportschuhfabriken Adi Dassler KA v Charles O'Neill Ltd* (1983) where the well-known German sports company, Adidas, sought an injunction against an Irish company which had been making sportswear for some years. It was claimed that the use of three stripes on sports clothes by the defendant amounted to passing off, since the plaintiff's products had become well known for using that design. The

Supreme Court, in dismissing the action, held that the use of stripes of varying colours and numbers on sportswear was a fashion in the trade and that in responding to fashionable demands, the defendant had not attempted to deceive or pass off and had not in fact done so.

INTERFERENCE WITH CONTRACTUAL RELATIONS

Nature of this Tort

The infliction of economic loss in the course of business or industrial affairs was not necessarily a tort at common law. It is not a tort to induce one party to refrain from entering a commercial contract, or to induce a party in contract with another to terminate it lawfully. But it is a tort for a party, without justification, knowingly and intentionally to interfere with a contract between two other parties. Knowledge of the contract, coupled with an intention to interfere with one of the party's rights under that contract is essential to attach liability.

The High Court held, in *Hynes v Conlon* (1939), that trade union officials who had informed employers that an employee was not a member of the union and should be dismissed in accordance with an agreement between the union and the employer, was not actionable because there were no threats, no warnings and no violence. In *Cooper v Millea* (1938) railway employees who were trade union officials threatened an immediate strike if a fellow employee and former union member was allowed to work with them. The High Court awarded damages against the officials for unlawfully interfering with an employment contract because an immediate strike was in breach of contract, and a threat of unlawful action constituted illegal means.

In a dispute with a harbour authority the employees' trade union blacked the port and telegrammed its members aboard a ship in the port instructing them not to sail, and to give notice to the captain. The High Court held, in *B & I Steampacket Co. Ltd v Branigan* (1958), in an action by the shipowner, that the union had conspired to induce breaches of contract. While the instruction was contradictory, the telegram taken as a whole was an instruction to cease work.

A supplier of bottled gas, in *Flogas Ltd v Ergas Ltd* (1985) entered into exclusive dealing contracts (see page 116) with customers. Another supplier of bottled gas, without knowledge of these contracts, entered into similar contracts with the same customers. The High Court dismissed an action for procuring breaches of contracts because the contracts were entered into without actual or constructive knowledge of the prior inconsistent contracts. The failure to terminate the contracts on being informed of the prior contracts was not an actionable interference with contractual relations.

An injunction was granted, in *HB Ice Cream Ltd v Masterfoods Ltd t/a Mars Ireland* (1993), to prevent Mars from inducing, inciting, procuring or persuading HB's customers to breach cabinet agreements made between HB and its customers. HB supplied freezer cabinets to customers on free loan or hire for the exclusive storage of HB ice-cream products. There was evidence that customers were storing Mars products in the freezers, having been assured by Mars employees that 'HB would not mind'.

FRAUD

Nature of this Tort

'What will constitute fraud in a civil action', said Henchy J. in the Supreme Court, in *Banco Ambrosiano SPA v Ansbacher & Co. Ltd* (1987), 'is not easy to state in advance, for fraud usually hides behind conduct which is disguised, devious and dishonest, so that it may assume an infinite variety of forms.'

To establish the tort of deceit or fraud, a number of facts must be proved. The first is that the wrongdoer made a false statement of fact. A true statement cannot be fraudulent even though the effect of making it will induce a party to act to his or her detriment. The statement must be of fact and not of opinion. The second ingredient is that the statement must have been made fraudulently, in that it was made knowingly, or without belief in its truth, or recklessly or carelessly, whether it was true or false. A careless statement which the maker honestly believes to be true cannot be fraud, though it may be negligent misstatement (page 199). The right of action in fraud is confined to parties who intended to act on the statement. The last essential is that a party must act on the statement to his or her detriment.

It was held, in *Lombard Bank Ltd v P. McElligot & Sons Ltd* (1965), that a finance company was entitled to damages for fraud against motor dealers who had misstated the cash price of a car in a hire-purchase transaction. A number of promoters, in *Northern Bank Finance Corporation Ltd v Charleton* (1979), wished to acquire a public company. The bank agreed to act on their behalf and to advance a portion of the purchase money to acquire the shares, though only after each of the promoters' monies, which were to be contributed in equal shares and kept on deposit with the bank, were expended. When the purchasing of the shares commenced the bank knew, and failed to communicate to the other promoters that one of their number had withdrawn money from the bank. The bank, in the course of later dealings, misrepresented the financial state of the promoter who had withdrawn his contribution. The venture continued and when the shares proved to be worthless, the promoters successfully sued the bank for fraud.

Most of the instances of fraud are based on breach of contract, and reference should be made to Fraudulent Misrepresentation on page 108.

Part Five
EQUITY AND TRUSTS

Chapter 22

PRINCIPLES OF EQUITY

Nature of Equity

Equity is spoken of as a gloss upon the common law: the common law represents an ancient and venerable text and equity is its supplement. Equity was developed to 'supply the defects' of the common law. It represents the attempt by the English legal system to resolve a problem which confronts all legal systems at a certain stage of development, that of rigidity which results in the denial of justice by allowing wrongs to go without remedies. The common law had been developed by civil lawyers, whereas equity was the creation of canon lawyers. Inevitably, the two systems were doomed to confront each other. This confrontation, when it came, stifled the blossoming of equity into a full body of laws. Instead, equity remained fragmentary, with the consequence that it is impossible to establish a general theory of equity.

Definition of Equity

As with other legal concepts, equity has a broad popular meaning and a narrow technical one. In its broad sense equity corresponds in a general way to natural justice. But it is comprised solely of that part of natural justice which the common law omitted to enforce. In its narrower sense equity is defined as those rules administered by the Court of Chancery before the fusion of the courts by the *Judicature (Ireland) Act 1877.*

The Birth of Equity

In earlier times the primary source of the common law was the decisions of judges as to what the general custom of the English realm was. Certainty was achieved by the application of uniform rules throughout the realm. This certainty was achieved at the expense of flexibility, a necessary ingredient of a living, developing legal system.

The common law judges, rather than administering justice in a particular case, applied rigid rules of law. This, of course, led to injustices and the complainant turned to the Crown, who, as the perceived fountain of justice, stood at the pinnacle of the judicial system. Pressure of state affairs compelled the Crown to pass these petitions to the Chancellor as Keeper of the Crown's conscience. As a churchman he decided these petitions on the basis of justice rather than in accordance with narrow and technical legal rules.

The Writ System

The Chancellor had acquired control over the administration of justice even prior to the time when the Crown passed petitions to the Chancellor for decision. The commencement of proceedings in the common law courts was done by obtaining a writ, a command in the Crown's name to the other party to the dispute to appear and answer the complaint. These writs were issued out of Chancery and new writs were created as the necessity arose.

The Barons of England forced Henry III by the *Provisions of Oxford* in 1258 to forbid the creation of new writs. This caused hardship and was amended by the *Statute of Westminster II*, known as *In Consimili Casu*, in 1285, which permitted the Chancellor to issue new writs where one in a like case already existed. This statute proved inadequate and by an Ordinance of Edward III in 1349, all matters of grace could be referred directly to the Chancellor. In the beginning the Chancellor acted in the name of the Crown in Council, but in 1474 a decree was engrossed on his own authority and this practice continued. In this way the Chancellor acquired a permanent jurisdiction, distinct from the common law courts, which empowered a grant of relief in cases which called for extraordinary remedy.

The Court of Chancery

Because the Chancellor refused to be bound by legal technicalities, the Court of Chancery became extremely popular. Those possessed of a moral right to a remedy, which was not enforced in the common law courts because no legal rule had been breached, came for relief to the Court of Chancery. The Chancellor acquired a jurisdiction parallel to that of the common law courts. He was independent of these courts and the Court of Chancery provided the forum to allow equity to develop some form of a system of laws supplementing and often competing with the common law.

Conflict of Equity with the Common Law

The popularity enjoyed by the Court of Chancery led to bitter disputes with the Court of King's Bench, the principle common law court. To resolve this tension, which reached a peak in the *Earl of Oxford's* case (1615), James I ordered Lord Chancellor Ellesmere and Lord Chief Justice Coke, two very formidable opponents, to present the matter for arbitration to the Attorney General, Sir Francis Bacon. The King ordered, on Bacon's recommendation, that whenever the two systems conflicted, the rules of equity were to prevail.

Formalisation and Fusion of Equity

As the jurisdiction of equity developed and became settled, it adopted the doctrine of precedent, the very doctrine which had led to rigidity in the common law. The work of the systematisation of equity began with Lord Ellesmere and was completed in the early part of the nineteenth century. By that time the rules of equity became as fixed as those of the common law.

The *Judicature (Ireland) Act 1877* reformed the administration of justice by reorganising the court system. The Court of King's Bench and the Court of Chancery were amalgamated into the High Court of Justice. It was provided that 'in every civil cause or matter commenced in the High Court of Justice law and equity shall be administered . . .'

THE SCOPE OF EQUITY

The Inventiveness of Equity

Prior to reform the Court of Chancery was active in three broad areas. Its exclusive jurisdiction acknowledged new rights which the common law had ignored: the prime example is the recognition given to trusts. Its concurrent jurisdiction invented new remedies, such as Specific Performance and Injunction (see page 228), which complemented the common law remedy of damages. Prior to the fusion of the systems, separate actions had to be litigated in the two courts, where different remedies were sought. Its auxiliary jurisdiction adopted new procedures by having a more flexible approach to legal administration: equity refused to follow the common law rule which precluded a defendant from giving evidence.

Discretionary Equity

At common law a party who proved the commission of a legal wrong was entitled, as of right, to a remedy, generally damages, and could enforce that remedy by execution, without regard to his or her own misconduct, or however unfair the result. But the Court of Chancery exercised a discretion in granting its remedies. An equitable remedy might be refused where the party seeking its assistance had acted unfairly, or was unwilling to act fairly, or had delayed. A party refused an equitable remedy would have to seek whatever legal remedy the common law would grant.

THE MAXIMS OF EQUITY

The Court of Chancery strove to ensure that justice and fair play triumphed over rigid rules of law. The spirit of equity was expressed in the maxims of equity which exhibited not rules of law, but trends and principles which guided the judges of Chancery in their quest for justice. An understanding of the maxims provides a knowledge of the meaning of equity.

1. Equity acts *in personam*. The common law courts enforced judgments by either their putting the person entitled to property into possession, or by seizing goods where a party refused to pay an award of damages. The common law acted *in rem*. On the other hand, equity enforced its judgments by imprisoning a disobedient party: equity acted *in personam.*

2. Equity would not suffer a wrong to go without a remedy. This idea is the foundation of equity. The failure of the common law to grant new remedies led to the invention of equity, though every moral wrong was not redressed by equity: only wrongs considered suitable by canon lawyers for enforcement were provided with remedies.

3. Equity follows the law. The literal construction of this maxim would make equity synonymous with common law. The maxim means that where the case was governed by common law, equity was bound by the rule unless some important circumstance warranted a departure. 'Equity follows the law', said one American judge, 'but not slavishly nor too much.' An example of equity following the law was the recognition of the division of estates and interests in property; and the observance of the common law succession rules. On the other hand, equity recognised certain future interests in property which the common law did not.

4. Where the equities are equal, the law prevails. Where two equal equitable claims are made in relation to the same property, with one party having the advantage of a legal title, then equity steps to the sideline and allows the legal title to prevail.

5. Where the equities are equal, the first in time prevails. Where both parties have equal equitable interests in the same property, the first in time is recognised against the later claim. The rule is: *qui prior est tempore potior est jure*, whoever is first in time is strongest in law.

6. A party coming to equity must come with clean hands. A party at common law was entitled to succeed no matter how badly he or she had behaved. But equity only grants a remedy to those acting equitably and fairly in the transaction under dispute.

7. The party seeking equity must do equity. This maxim looks to the future. A party seeking the assistance of equity must in return be prepared to act fairly and equitably before a remedy is granted. For example, where a donor of property gives it to a donee and purports to give property of the donee to another, the donee will only be allowed to accept the gift on condition that the donee's property is given to that other. This is the doctrine of election, discussed later.

8. Equity aids the vigilant and not the indolent: *vigilantibus non dormientibus, jura subveniunt.* Delay defeats equity. Assistance is refused to stale demands where a party has slept on rights. The *Statute of Limitations 1957*, as amended (see pages 122 and 161), lays down time periods within which some actions must be brought, though this maxim continues to apply to situations not covered by the statute.

9. Equality is equity. Where rival claimants to jointly owned property sought the assistance of equity in a dispute *inter se*, the Court of Chancery favoured its division into equal shares.

10. Equity looks to the intention rather than the form. Equity examined the spirit of a legal document rather than its strict letter. For example, where a contract for the sale of property was not completed on the appointed day the common law acknowledged a breach of contract, whereas equity usually permitted its completion within a reasonable time thereafter.

11. Equity regards as done that which ought to be done. Where parties agree to perform some act which has legal consequences, equity considers it already done. For example, contracts for value are considered as performed as and from the time they ought to have been performed.

12. Equity imputes an intention to fulfil an obligation. Where a party is obliged to do some act, and another act is done which can be construed as a fulfilment of that obligation, equity will so construe it.

THE DOCTRINES OF EQUITY

Conversion

Conversion is an imaginary change of property from real to personal, or from personal to real, so that each is considered in its new character, even though in reality no actual conversion has been made. This is an example of the maxim that equity regards as done that which ought to be done. For example, where there is a binding contract for the sale of property, equity considers that the sale has already taken place and that the purchase price to be paid is changed into land and vice versa.

Reconversion

This is another imaginary process, whereby a prior conversion is annulled. For example, where a father leaves land on trust for sale to a child until that child reaches majority, that land, under the doctrine of conversion, is converted into money which is personal property. Where the trustees do not sell the land, the child on coming of age, may elect to take the land or compel the trustees to sell it and take the money. Where the child takes the land, that act reconverts it from personal to real property.

Performance

Under this doctrine the purchase of, or succession to, property operates as a complete, or *pro tanto*, discharge of a previous obligation. Performance is another application of the maxim that equity imputes an intention to fulfil an obligation. For example, where a person agrees to purchase and settle lands on trust and purchases lands of the same type as those agreed to be purchased and settled, equity will presume that the lands purchased were in satisfaction of that obligation.

This doctrine is illustrated in *In re Finnegan* (1925) where a husband entered into a bond on marriage whereby, on his death during his wife's lifetime, a sum of money was to be paid to her. On the husband's death it was held that the bond was to be regarded as satisfaction *pro tanto* of the widow's share of her husband's estate. This presumption of performance may be rebutted by contrary evidence, as in *In re Hood* (1923), where a husband placed money on deposit in the joint names of himself and his wife. When he died intestate, the question was whether this money was in satisfaction of a wife's share on intestacy. It was held that it was not, because the husband, when he deposited the money, was not acting under any obligation.

Satisfaction

Satisfaction is the doctrine whereby a transfer of property, if accepted by the transferee, operates as a complete, or *pro tanto*, discharge of a previous legal obligation. According to this doctrine a person places justice before generosity. For example, in *Ellard v Phelan* (1914), it was held that a bequest to a servant was in satisfaction of wages due by the testator on his death.

Election

The doctrine of election imposes an obligation on a party to choose between two inconsistent or alternative claims or rights. The party must choose because equity will not permit the receipt of both. Where a testator gives £30,000 to a son and gives his daughter a house owned by the son, the doctrine of election forces the son either to take against the will by keeping the house and giving his sister the value of it out of the £30,000, or to take under the will by giving the house to his sister and claiming the £30,000.

This doctrine operated in *In re Sullivan* (1917) where a testator, whose property (exclusive of certain stocks and shares standing in the joint names of the testator and his wife, which at his death became her absolute property) amounted to £1,858. He gave a legacy to his wife of £3,000, which if claimed by her, and bearing in mind that she already had the shares, would have resulted in the wife taking all the estate, leaving nothing for other beneficiaries. But if, as the court insisted, she had to elect between the shares or the legacy, she would take some property and others would have the remainder.

THE EQUITABLE REMEDIES

Nature of Equitable Remedies

The sole common law relief granted to a wronged party was an award of damages as compensation. This single remedy was inappropriate, or inadequate, in many situations. Equity invented a diversity of additional remedies which supplemented the common law remedy. Equity, acting *in personam*, ordered the wrongdoer to do what the court considered just, and failure to obey would lead to imprisonment. But equitable relief was refused to those who came to court with unclean hands, that is, those unwilling to do equity, and to those who had 'slept on their rights'. Equitable remedies were discretionary. A party unable to obtain an equitable remedy was left to find whatever remedy was available at common law. Indeed, the availability of common law relief was often sufficient reason for equity refusing to interfere. Equity invented a number of remedies: specific performance (page 127); rescission (page 127); rectification (page 128); injunction and receivers are considered below.

Injunction

An injunction is a court order which directs a party to do, or to refrain from doing, some particular act. Once an injunction is granted it is ultimately enforced by committal to prison if disobeyed.

In cases of urgency an application may be made *ex parte*, that is, without notice to the offending party, for an interim injunction. This application is heard on affidavit and, where granted, is effective for a few days while the offending party is given time to come to court and present a case. The court, having heard both sides, may discharge the injunction or grant an interlocutory injunction which continues in force until the action is heard. The test for granting interlocutory relief was laid down in *Campus Oil Ltd v Minister for Energy* (1983) by the Supreme Court. O'Higgins CJ. explained: 'Interlocutory relief is granted to an applicant where what he complains of is continuing and is causing him harm or injury which may be irreparable in the sense that it may not be possible to compensate him fairly or properly by an award of damages. Such relief is given because a period must necessarily elapse before the action can come for trial and for the purpose of keeping matters in status quo until the hearing.... Not only will the court have regard to what is complained of and whether damages would be an appropriate remedy but it will consider what inconvenience, loss and damage might be caused to the other party, and will enquire whether the applicant has shown that the balance of convenience is in his favour.'

Following a full hearing the court may, where the facts warrant, grant a perpetual injunction which may take either of two forms. A prohibitory injunction prohibits the doing of some unlawful act. In the *Educational Co. of Ireland v Fitzpatrick* (1961) (page 95) such an injunction was granted to an employer to prevent unlawful picketing by employees. A mandatory injunction commands the performance of some wrongful omission. A mandatory injunction was granted, in *Gaw v CIE* (1953) (page 258), to enforce the execution of repairs to a footpath.

In recent years the scope of the injunction has been extended to grant a remedy to a creditor against a debtor who was prepared to depart the country or dissipate assets in defiance of the creditor's rights. An injunction of this type became known as a mareva injunction, which is an *ad personam* order, restraining the defendant from dealing with assets in which the plaintiff has no claim whatsoever, and which does not give the plaintiff any precedence over other creditors with respect to the frozen assets. A mareva injunction will only be granted if there is a combination of two circumstances established by the plaintiff: (a) that he or she has an arguable case that will succeed in the action, and (b) the anticipated disposal of a defendant's assets is for the purpose of preventing a plaintiff from recovering damages and not merely for the purpose of carrying on a business or discharging lawful debts. An application by employees, in *Fleming v Ranks (Ireland) Ltd* (1983), for a mareva injunction to prevent their employer from dealing with its assets so as to evade its legal obligations to them, was refused by the High Court, on the ground that the anticipated disposal was for the purposes of carrying on the business and in discharge of lawful debts, and not for the purpose of preventing the employees from recovering their lawful entitlements. The Supreme Court, in *O'Mahony v Horgan* (1996), where a liquidator of an insolvent company claimed that its directors were guilty of fraudulent trading and thus personally liable for the debts of the company (see page 427), refused to grant a mareva injunction over a policy of insurance due to one director because the liquidator had not shown that the use to which the proceeds of the policy would be put, the replacement of destroyed property or the payment of lawful debts, was done with the intention of evading payment to him. But, in *Powerscourt Estates v Gallagher* (1984), a mareva injunction was granted restraining the disposal of assets up to the value of the plaintiff's claim.

The remedy of injunction was discussed when considering the prevention of the executive from acting *ultra vires* the Constitution (page 37) and as a remedy in contract law (page 127).

Appointment of Receiver

The High Court has the jurisdiction to appoint a receiver by way of equitable execution, though in many cases receivers are appointed by a party acting under some statutory or contractual power. For example, where a company borrows money the deed invariably provides for the appointment by the lender of a receiver in default of repayments.

The main function of a receiver is to collect and apply the income of property, which is the subject of the authority, and preserve the outstanding assets. A party, in *Garrahan v Garrahan* (1959), who had obtained a judgment which remained unsatisfied, obtained the appointment of a receiver over a Garda Síochána pension. A company, awarded compensation under the planning law which remained unpaid in *Grange Developments Ltd v Dublin County Council* (1989), had a receiver appointed over the assets of the local authority. In *Ahern v Michael O'Brien & Co. Ltd* (1989) a receiver was appointed over rents due by a party who had failed to satisfy a court judgment made against it.

Chapter 23
TRUSTS

The Nature of a Trust

A trust is the relationship which exists when one party, called a trustee, is compelled by law to hold property for the benefit of another, called the beneficiary, or for objects permitted by law, so that the real benefit accrues to the beneficiary.

Trusts are divided, according to their purpose, into two groups. A private trust is for the benefit of a person, or a group of persons. A trust for the promotion of some public welfare, or for the benefit of a large and fluctuating group is a public, or charitable trust.

CREATION OF TRUSTS

Express Trusts

A donor may create an express trust. This may be done during the donor's lifetime to take effect immediately, or it may be created by will. Where a trust consists of personal property no formalities are necessary. Such a trust may be created verbally. Where land or premises are the subject of a trust, there must be, according to the *Statute of Frauds (Ireland) 1695*, some evidence in writing, signed by the donor (page 93). Equity never allowed this statute to be used 'as an engine of fraud'. The courts have recognised trusts not created in accordance with the statute. These are known as secret trusts (page 234). Generally, an express trust is irrevocable unless a clause to that effect is contained in the trust document.

Implied Trusts

The courts may presume from the conduct of the parties and the circumstances of the transaction that an implied trust exists. For example, where property is held in the name of one party, an implied trust is presumed in favour of the party supplying the purchase money. Another implied trust arises where two persons, often a husband and wife but not necessarily so, execute mutual wills by disposing of their property in the same manner. Equity will compel the survivor to hold the property on trust in accordance with that will, and refuse to recognise any subsequent will.

Resulting Trusts

A resulting trust arises where an express trust fails. The trustee is bound to hold the property in trust for the donor. Historically, the concept of the resulting trust was an invention of equity to defeat the misappropriation of property as a consequence of potentially fraudulent or improvident transactions. In *Lynch v Burke* (1995) an aunt opened a joint deposit account with her niece. The Supreme Court decided, overruling an earlier decision of the Supreme Court, that on the death of the aunt, the niece did not hold the money on a resulting trust for the aunt's estate but that the niece had a legal interest in the money.

Constructive Trusts

A constructive trust is imposed by law to satisfy the demands of justice without reference to the express or implied intentions of the parties. It arises by operation of law to prevent fraud or unfair advantage. For example, a party who receives trust property from a trustee knowing it has been disposed of in breach of trust, is forced by equity to hold that property as constructive trustee for the beneficiaries.

Void Trusts

A properly created trust may be void because it offends the common good. A trust in favour of the testator's grandchildren, in *In re Blake* (1955), which provided that they must be reared in a particular religion, was void because it restricted the constitutional right of parents to educate their children.

Voidable Trusts

A properly created trust may be avoided in certain circumstances. A donor forced to create a trust may have it set aside by the courts on the grounds that it was induced by mistake, or fraud, or undue influence. The law prevents debtors from cheating their creditors by providing, in the *Statute of Fraudulent Conveyances (Ireland) 1634*, that a conveyance of property made with the intention of defrauding creditors is voidable at the instance of the party prejudiced. The *Bankruptcy (Ireland) Amendment Act 1872* makes similar provisions in the event of bankruptcy. Protected in both cases is a *bona fide* purchaser for value with no notice of the intention to defraud. In *In re Lowe* (1988), a sale of premises by a bankrupt to his daughter was set aside by the High Court because, while she was a purchaser for value, the conveyance was made with the intent to hinder, delay and defraud creditors of which the daughter was aware. Therefore the transaction was not made in good faith. The onus of proving that a voluntary conveyance, one for natural love and affection, was made *bona fide* and without fraudulent intent lies, according to *National Bank v Behan* (1913), on the party seeking to uphold the voluntary transaction.

PRIVATE TRUSTS

Nature of Private Trust

A private trust is one expressly created by the donor, either *inter vivos* or by will, for the benefit of a particular person, or a group of persons.

Types of Private Trusts

The purpose of a strict settlement is to secure the property for successive generations of beneficiaries. The duty of the trustees is to retain the property with the consequence that it remains in the one family for many years. Because of the *Settled Land Acts 1882–90* (page 248), strict settlements of real property are rarely created.

In a trust for sale a duty is placed on the trustees to sell the property though this may not be exercised until they think advisable. Once the sale is made, the trustees will either distribute the proceeds among the beneficiaries or hold the proceeds on their behalf.

A discretionary trust is one in which the beneficiary has no right to any part of the trust property. The trustees are given a discretionary power to apply such part of the property as they think fit for the benefit of the beneficiary.

As was seen earlier, it is contrary to the law to dispose of property in trust to defeat bankruptcy or creditors. However, a donor may grant property on trust until bankruptcy by way of a protective trust. A protective trust is usually combined with a discretionary trust. Property is given until bankruptcy with a discretionary trust in favour of other beneficiaries.

Requirements of a Valid Private Trust

For an express private trust to be valid, the document establishing it must contain what are known as 'the three certainties'. According to O'Byrne J. in *Chambers v Fahy* (1931): 'The subject-matter must be certain, the objects of the trust must be certain, and the words relied upon as creating the trust must have been used in an imperative sense, so as to show that the [creator] intended to create an obligation.'

There is certainty of subject-matter when the property to be the subject of the trust is sufficiently identified. The share each beneficiary is to receive must be certain. Certainty of objects is achieved when those to benefit under the trust are clearly identified. The High Court held, in *In re Prescott* (1990), that property left to the 'Russian Orthodox Church abroad in Ireland' failed for uncertainty of objects because at the date of the will that Church could not be considered a community in that it was priestless and without a church, had no records, no dues, very infrequent communications with clergy, no record of meetings and most infrequent services.

Certainty of words means that there must be imposed on the trustees a definite duty to carry out a trust. Mere precatory words are insufficient, as in *In re McIntosh* (1933), where a testator left property by will to his wife until their son reached the age of twenty-five years and added that 'in the meantime she may utilise it in any way she deems best for the improvement, education and general welfare of my three daughters'. The High Court held that no trust was created in favour of the daughters.

The trust, in the absence of words or subject matter, fails and the beneficiary takes the property absolutely. Where there is uncertainty of objects the trust fails, with the trustees holding the property on a resulting trust for the donor or the donor's heirs.

SECRET TRUSTS

Nature of Secret Trusts

The requirement of the *Statute of Frauds (Ireland) 1695* that a trust be evidenced in writing was intended to prevent fraud. But the failure to observe the statutory requirement is not necessarily fatal because the courts have consistently refused to allow this statute to be used as 'an engine of fraud'. The real application of this doctrine led the courts to acknowledge secret trusts.

Fully Secret Trust

A fully secret trust arises when a testator fails to disclose by will that the property is subject to a trust, though some party has already accepted the position of trustee. There must have been an intention by the testator to impose a trust, which must have been communicated to the trustee before the testator's death. The trustee must have acquiesced with the testator's wishes. A fully secret trust was declared to exist in *Revenue Commissioners v Stapleton* (1937) where a testator by will bequested a sum of money to his executors 'to be disposed of by them as I shall verbally direct them'. Verbal instructions, communicated contemporaneously with the making of the will, were to pay this sum to his widow.

Half-Secret Trust

A half-secret trust arises where property is given by will to trustees, but the particular trust is not disclosed in the will but by some independent manner.

A testator, prior to the making of a will, in *In re Brown* (1944), asked a friend to act as executor and to carry out his wishes. The will contained the words, 'I hereby give and bequeath unto [the friend] all my property, I relying on his carrying out the wishes which I have expressed to him, or may do so hereafter.' The testator showed his friend the will and informed him that his wishes were contained in 'Instructions', which were explained. The High Court held that a half-secret trust had been created. The fact that the trust was only communicated after the making of the will was of no importance: the crucial factor was its communication and acceptance by the friend during the testator's lifetime.

PUBLIC OR CHARITABLE TRUST

Definition of Public or Charitable Trust

A charitable or public trust is for the benefit of the community at large, or for a fair portion of the public. It is distinguished from a private trust which merely benefits a particular person, or a group of persons.

Statutory Classification

The preamble of the *Statute of Charitable Uses (Ireland) 1634* lists charitable objects which have furnished the courts with a guide to what a legal public charity is. This enumeration is not exhaustive and the courts from time to time have added objects which were considered to be within the spirit and intentment of the statute.

The statute, reflecting the social conditions of its time, included the following activities which are to be considered charitable: the relief of the aged, impotent and poor persons; the maintenance of sick and maimed soldiers, sailors and mariners; the maintenance of schools of learning, free schools and scholars in universities; the education and preferment of orphans; the relief and maintenance of correction and the relief and redemption of prisoners and captives; the marriage of poor maidens; the support, aid and help to young tradesmen and persons decayed; the maintenance of any preacher or minister of the word of God; and the relief of bridges, ports, havens, causeways, churches, sea-banks and highways.

Judicial Classification

The courts, since the enactment of the *Statute of Charitable Uses (Ireland) 1634*, have classified charitable trusts into four broad categories, a division accepted by the Supreme Court in the case of *Barrington's Hospital v Commissioner of Valuation* (1957), a case discussed later.

The first category of charitable trusts acknowledged by the courts is that for the advancement of religion. This category is not confined to the Christian religion, but includes the advancement of any religion. In *In re Greene* (1914) a gift for the decoration of the Carmelite Fathers' Church at Clarendon Street in Dublin was a valid charitable trust. A gift for Masses is also valid as a charitable gift.

The second category of charitable trusts is for the relief of poverty which, in this respect, does not mean destitution, but has a wider and more indefinite meaning.

The third category of charitable trusts is that for the advancement of education. Educational establishments, such as schools and universities, are included, but these trusts are not confined to learning in formal institutions. There must be some element of instruction or improvement. A university, because of its objects, user and financial accountability, was held to be exclusively used for charitable purposes, in *University College Cork v Commissioner of Valuation* (1911), even though students paid admittance fees. A school, in *Wesley College v Commissioner of Valuation* (1984), which provided general education on a fee-paying basis, which made a profit and which gave preference to children of a particular religion, was held by the Supreme Court not to be for public or charitable purposes. The High Court ruled, in *In re Worth* (1994), that the gift of a library is not charitable *per se*, though such a gift can have charitable status if it is for the public benefit, by being opened to the public or conducive to the attainment of other charitable objects.

The fourth category is that for other charitable purposes not included in the other three categories. Numerous gifts covering a wide variety of causes have been upheld by the courts as coming within this category. The words creating the trust may be vague, but the objectives of the gift must fall within the spirit and intentment of the *Statute of Charitable Uses.* The Supreme Court held, in *Barrington's Hospital v Commissioner of Valuation* (1957), that a hospital was a charitable trust even though some patients paid for treatment. The High Court held, in *In re MacCarthy* (1958), that a gift to assist the sick to travel to Lourdes was charitable.

The Doctrine of Cy-pres

Charitable trusts are subject to the same legal rules as private trusts, though there are important differences. The major distinction is this: once there is a general intention of charity to be gathered from a trust document, the trust, unlike a private trust, will not fail for uncertainty. This is known as the doctrine of *cy-pres,* or an application of the property to the next nearest purpose. A testator, in *In re McGwire* (1941), left property to the Society of St Vincent de Paul for use as a sanatorium. The High Court held, when the property proved to be unsuitable, that a general charitable intention was disclosed and applied the gift *cy-pres*. In *In re Worth* (1994) a library was left by will in 1732 to Dr Steevens' Hospital for the use and benefit of the physician, chaplain and surgeon. The books were kept there in what was known as the 'Worth Library' until the hospital closed in 1988. The High Court ruled that as the hospital no longer existed, the original purpose of this absolute and perpetual charitable bequest could not be carried out according to the directions and spirit of the gift, and it was appropriate to alter the original purpose so as to allow the property to be applied *cy-pres*.

Public Appeals

The *Charities Act 1961* provides a procedure for disposing of funds gathered after a public appeal, which either became impossible to apply for that purpose, or where a surplus remained after an application of the funds had been made. For example, a public collection might be made for the benefit of an accident victim, but the victim may die before the funds can be applied in that cause, or there may be funds remaining after the victim's needs have been satisfied. The Act provides that where the donors of the fund cannot be found, after reasonable advertisement and inquiries have been made, the fund may be applied *cy-pres*.

Supervision of Charitable Trusts

The authority responsible for the general supervision of charities are the Commissioners of Charitable Donations and Bequests for Ireland. Their general function is to promote the more effective use of charitable resources by encouraging better administration by making advice and information available to the trustees of public charities.

ADMINISTRATION OF TRUSTS

Nature of Trustee

A trustee is the owner of property who deals with it as owner, subject only to the equitable obligation to account to another to whom that party stands in the relation of trustee, and who are his or her *cestui que trust*. A sane adult may hold the office of trustee. A trust corporation has no special status, except that under the *Succession Act 1965*, it holds property on trust for a minor as a sole trustee.

Appointment of Trustees

The creator of the trust generally appoints the first trustees. There is no limit to the number that can be appointed, though it is usually two. Once the trust is established, the donor has no further power in this regard unless such a power is reserved in the trust document. Where a trust is established by will, the testator appoints the first trustees. The *Trustee Act 1893* allows the following to appoint new or additional trustees: the person nominated to do so in the trust document; a surviving trustee; the personal representative of the last trustee; the beneficiaries, provided all are of full age and entitled to the entire beneficial interest in the property; and the High Court, applying the maxim that 'equity never wants for a trustee'.

Where a minor is entitled to any share in a deceased's estate the *Succession Act 1965* permits the personal representatives of that estate to appoint trustees over that property. The Commissioners of Charitable Donations and Bequests for Ireland may appoint trustees of a charity: *Charities Act 1961.*

Powers of Trustees

Trustees must have sufficient powers to adequately administer the trust. Originally the donor granted the appropriate powers in the trust document to the trustees. The *Trustee Act 1893* provides trustees with a wide selection of powers, such as powers of sale, which are in addition to those, if any, contained in the trust document. The trust document may negative any power given by this statute. The *Charities Act 1961* grants powers to trustees of charitable trusts, and the *Succession Act 1965* grants powers to trustees of minors' property.

Duties of Trustees

The position of trustee is exacting and should not be undertaken lightly. The first duty is to take control of the trust property. Failure to do so may render the trustees liable to make good any loss suffered. Having done so, the trustees must administer the trust according to the trust document. In *Stacy v Branch* (1995) a settlor by will created a trust over property in favour of his minor son until the son attained twenty-one years. The trustee put a caretaker into the property, who, while obliged to maintain the property and pay all outgoings, was not obliged to pay rent. The trustee was not prepared to let the property to a succession of tenants, which would have resulted in significant wear and tear and possible malicious damage. While approximately £20,000 was lost in rental income, the property had been well preserved over fourteen years. The High Court refused to hold the trustee in breach of trust because his decision had been made honestly and in exercise of the discretion which the settlor had conferred on him.

Proper income and capital accounts must be maintained and supplied to the beneficiaries periodically. Capital must be invested to preserve its value and to provide a steady flow of income. The trust document may grant complete freedom of investment to the trustees. Where this does not occur, investment can only be made in accordance with the *Trustee (Authorised Investment) Act 1958*, which sets out a list of securities into which the trustees may invest trust monies. This list may be altered by statutory instrument.

With certain exceptions, it is the general rule that trustees cannot make a profit from the trust. A trustee must not place himself or herself in a position where duty to the trust and personal interest conflict. Applying this rule, a trustee is not entitled to remuneration as of right. But the trust document may authorise payment and this it usually does where persons, such as solicitors and bankers, are appointed. The High Court may order payment, or the beneficiaries may agree to payment, provided all are of full age and are entitled to the entire property.

Another application of this rule is the inability of the trustees to purchase the trust property. This rule is applied irrespective of how honest and fair the transaction actually is. To this rule there are the usual exceptions such as the right to purchase, where it is contained in the trust document, or permission is granted by the High Court, or where all the beneficiaries agree to the transaction. When exercising their powers the trustees must not favour one beneficiary over another, or one class of beneficiaries to the detriment of another class.

Because of the special fiduciary relationship which exists between trustees and beneficiaries, the general rule dictates that a trustee cannot delegate these duties and powers to another. The maxim *delegatus non potest delegare*: a delegate must not delegate, is applied. Once again, there are the usual exceptions. The *Trustee Act 1893* provides a statutory indemnity for trustees with regard to acts of neglect committed by the other trustees, and bankers and stockbrokers with whom the trust monies are deposited.

Breach of Trust

A trustee must compensate the trust for any breach of trust committed by that trustee. Liability does not extend to the actions of co-trustees unless the trustee contributed by wilful default, which means a deliberate breach of trust or reckless carelessness as to whether any particular conduct is, or is not, a breach of trust. It is breach of trust for one trustee to allow the trust property to remain under the control of co-trustees, or to ignore their breach of trust. Should a trustee make an unauthorised investment, all the funds must be replaced, together with any profit which may have accrued from that investment.

Where trustees jointly commit a breach of trust, each is personally liable for the total loss though a claim for fair contribution may be made against the others. A beneficiary may be disbarred from suing the trustees where he or she participated in the breach or where a breach comes to his or her attention and he or she confirms or acquiesces in it. In certain circumstances the High Court may relieve a trustee from liability where the action was honest and reasonable and ought fairly to be excused as a breach of trust.

In the event of a breach of trust, the beneficiaries may sue the trustees for compensation, though this remedy may be useless where the trustees are insolvent or have disappeared. A more useful remedy is a tracing order which allows the beneficiaries to pursue and recover trust property wrongfully held by any person. However, this remedy cannot be used against a *bona fide* purchaser for value without notice of the breach of trust.

Removal and Retirement of Trustees

A trustee may be removed, where such a power is contained in the trust document, or the beneficiaries may remove a trustee, provided all are of full age and entitled to the entire property. The High Court has this power and exercised it in *Arnott v Arnott* (1924) where one trustee refused to agree to any suggestion by the other trustees. Equity places the welfare of beneficiaries above all else. The High Court, in *Spencer v Kinsella* (1996), adjourned an application to remove the trustees of a trust relating to the show-grounds in Gorey, which had become dilapidated, to allow the rulings made by the court to be implemented. These were the appointment of trustees who were, as far as was possible, impartial as between the users of the ground, the execution of agreements with such users, and the appointment of a management committee.

Once a trustee has accepted office, the sole method of relinquishing it is by retirement. Where the trust document so permits, a trustee may retire without any particular formality, or a trustee may retire with the consent of all the beneficiaries, provided all are of full age and entitled to the entire property. A trustee may agree with co-trustees to retire and this is done by deed, or an application may be made to the High Court to release a trustee from the trust.

Part Six
LAND LAW

Chapter 24
PROPERTY IN GENERAL

The Constitution and Property

The Constitution declares that man has the natural right, which is superior to positive law, to the private ownership of property. This right is considered under fundamental rights in Chapter 6, page 72.

Categories of Property

The lay person uses the term 'property' to mean land and premises, though the law uses it to mean everything capable of ownership. Our law recognises two categories of property: realty and personalty. Freehold interests in land and premises are realty, or real or immovable property. Other kinds of property are personalty, such as cars, jewellery, clothing, money on bank deposit, or copyright in a song. Contractual rights, important property rights, are considered in Part Two: The Law of Contract, in Part Six: Commercial Law, and in Part Nine: Employment Law.

Leasehold interests in land and premises, which should naturally fall into the category of realty, are personalty. Where a deceased person willed 'my realty to my son and my personalty to my daughter', the son takes the freehold property and the daughter inherits all else including the deceased's leasehold property.

For practical purposes the law relating to freehold and leasehold property is combined under the general title of land law. This subject is an obscure and difficult one, and in the following chapters only the barest outline can be covered.

Ownership and Possession

To understand legal principles relating to property in general, it is crucial to distinguish between ownership and possession. These terms are not synonymous. The exercise of all legal and equitable rights over property is an attribute of ownership. When the physical property is parted with, for example when leased, possession passes to the tenant. In such a case ownership continues to vest in the landlord despite the surrender of exclusive possession to the tenant. Possession in preference to ownership is recognised by law in some instances. For example, tortious actions relating to land and goods are actionable by the possessor rather than the owner: indeed the possessor may bring an action against the owner (see Chapter 17).

Ownership and Interest

Another important distinction is between ownership and interest. Ownership has already been explained: interest is a right, or title, to property. While there is only one owner, there may be many parties with different interests in one piece of property, each with distinct rights and liabilities. Suppose the owner of premises lets them for five years to John. The law creates the relationship of landlord and tenant: each has rights and liabilities under the lease. Suppose then that John sublets part of the premises to Mary for three years. Again the relationship of landlord and tenant is created, but between different parties. Suppose the owner mortgages the premises to a bank. Now all four, the owner, John, Mary and the bank, have an interest, albeit different ones, in the premises. The law permits an infinite number of parties to have interests in the same property. This multiplicity of interests is one reason why the study and practice of land law is complicated.

Acquiring Ownership

Property ownership may be acquired in three ways. First, a party may acquire ownership originally by asserting a right of ownership and possession over some item not previously owned by another, or by asserting ownership over an item abandoned by the previous owner. Second, a party acquiring property by consent from a previous owner obtains it derivatively. Third, a party acquires property by succession, where it is inherited from another. Statute has, in some circumstances, provided that ownership can be compulsorily acquired. For example, local authorities can compulsorily acquire property to carry out various public works.

Remedies for Dispossession

A party wrongfully dispossessed of property has a choice of remedies depending on the type of property involved. Where the property is freehold or leasehold, a real action, or an action *in rem*, is taken to recover the property. Where the property is personal, a personal action, or an action *in personam*, a claim for damages for compensation rather than a claim to recover the property, is brought.

Legal Rights and Equitable Interests

Property rights protected by common law are called legal rights. These include the right to ownership and possession. But the common law did not protect all interests in property. For example, the right of a beneficiary under a trust was not protected because the common law recognised no interest worthy of protection. But equity did (see Chapter 23, page 222). Rights protected in this way became known as equitable interests. In time it was recognised that every legal estate had an equitable counterpart: there is a legal fee simple and an equitable fee simple. Generally, both are held by the one party but on occasion each may vest in different parties. For example, where a fee simple is subject to a trust, the legal fee simple vests in the trustee, whereas the equitable fee simple vests in the beneficiary.

Chapter 25
FREEHOLD ESTATES

FEE SIMPLE

Nature and Creation of Fee Simple

The greatest estate in real property acknowledged in law is the freehold known as the fee simple. It is the nearest equivalent to absolute ownership that can be found. The fee simple owner holds it free from all obligations: no rent is due, no covenants restrict it and it has a perpetual existence. At common law a fee simple was transferred by the exchange of a sod of the land but statute provides for transfer by deed, which is a document under seal.

A party knows, when acquiring property, that the fee simple is being transferred because of the use of the proper words of limitation. When the fee simple is transferred *inter vivos*, between living persons, the proper words must be either 'and his heirs' or 'in fee simple' after the name of the grantee: thus to 'Eamon Byrne and his heirs', or 'to Eamon Byrne in fee simple'. The use of either phrase denotes the passing of the fee simple. No other words will suffice.

The fee simple continues as long as the original grantee and any of the heirs survive. A fee simple owner can alienate the property by transferring it by sale or otherwise and the fee simple continues as long as there are heirs of the new holder, and so on, irrespective of any failure of heirs of the original grantee. Thus, a fee simple is potentially perpetual. It is crucial to note that the use of the word 'heirs' gives no interest to the heirs of the grantee. The heirs cannot prevent the grantee from alienating the property. The word 'heirs' denotes the interest granted.

At common law no formal words of limitation were required in a will to pass the fee simple. What was necessary was an intention to do so. The *Succession Act 1965* formalised this rule in statute.

Acquiring the Fee Simple

A fee simple can be acquired originally, derivatively and by succession. The private individual may, under statutory power, compulsorily acquire the fee simple of land on which his or her house stands and which is held under leasehold. The leaseholder is enabled to acquire the fee simple, thus terminating the duty to pay rent. This is achieved by converting the long lease into a fee simple. Once the proper procedures are followed the party in possession is entitled as of right, on the payment of compensation, to acquire the fee simple, and the landlord to whom ground rent is payable must grant the fee simple. Statute has prohibited the creation of new ground rents.

Fee Farm Grant

A fee farm grant is a fee simple subject to the payment of a perpetual rent. This estate has the same characteristics as the fee simple but is burdened with a reserved rent. Fee farm grants are uniquely Irish.

FEE TAIL

Nature of Fee Tail

A fee tail is a freehold estate which continues as long as the original grantee and any descendants survive. In earlier times conditional fee simples were granted subject to their terminating when all the direct descendants of the original grantee were dead. The common law courts decided that once an heir was born, the condition was fulfilled and the estate was thereafter an ordinary fee simple. It could be alienated and continue almost forever.

To negative the common law rule, the *Statute De Donis Conditionalibus 1285* provided that an estate granted in fee tail could only descend to the heirs of the grantee and must revert to the grantor when the last descendant died. The result was that the grantee had the property merely for life and could not alienate. This particular estate was popular in family settlements because the property could potentially be kept within one family for generations in succession. Statute, as we will see later, has frustrated this type of arrangement.

Creating a Fee Tail

The common law requires particular words of limitation to create a fee tail. The word 'heirs' followed by some other words of procreation are essential. These words of procreation must confine the heirs to descendants of the grantee: thus 'to Eamon Byrne and the heirs of his body' will suffice. Words of procreation are required because heirs include relatives other than descendants, such as brothers and sisters, uncles and aunts.

An entail, another description of a fee tail, can only pass to descendants. The addition of suitable words can further restrict the classes of descendants to benefit: thus 'to Eamon Byrne and the heirs male of his body' creates a tail male. The words of limitation grant no interest to the heirs except a *spes successionis*, or a hope of succession.

Only the holder of a fee simple can create a fee tail. Statute provides that the alternative expression 'in tail' may be used to create this estate. Where the grant was by will, prior to the *Succession Act 1965*, the appropriate intention, and not the particular words of limitation, would suffice. This rule has been altered by that statute: a testator wishing to create a fee tail must use the proper words of limitation.

Barring the Entail

The common law considered it desirable that property should be capable of alienation. Ways were found to allow fee tail estates to be disposed of by the party in possession. This became known as barring the entail. Two methods, one known as 'suffering a recovery' and the other as 'levying a fine', were used widely to bar entails. Statute abolished both and substituted a single simple method of achieving the same purpose. An entail is now barred by the party in possession executing a disentailing assurance and enrolling it within six months of its execution in the central office of the High Court. This is the sole recognised method. An attempt to bar the entail by will is not recognised.

Fee Tail Estates in Modern Times

An estate in fee tail is rarely created in modern times because of the easy method of barring the entail. These estates are of interest because, from time to time, the courts are called on to adjudicate on them. For example, in *In re Fallon* (1956), the High Court had to decide whether such an estate was created by a will; and in *Bank of Ireland v Domville* (1956) the High Court considered a fee tail created in 1854.

LIFE ESTATE

Nature of Life Estate

The life estate is the third freehold estate and, unlike the fee simple and fee tail, is not an estate of inheritance. There are two kinds of life estate. The ordinary life estate is for the duration of the life of the tenant: thus 'to Eamon Byrne for life'. The second type of life estate is the estate *pur autre vie* which endures for the life of a person other than the tenant: thus 'to Eamon Byrne for the life of John Murphy'. In this example John Murphy is known as the *cestui que vie.*

A life estate ceases automatically on the death of a tenant, and although an estate *pur autre vie* continues during the life of the *cestui que vie*, it does not descend to the heirs of the tenant. The *Statute of Frauds (Ireland) 1695* provides that a tenant *pur autre vie* can dispose of the remaining years by will. The *Succession Act 1965* provides that where such a tenant dies intestate, the interest in the remaining years devolves on the personal representative for distribution with the remainder of the estate.

Creation of a Life Estate

Only the holder of a fee simple, or a fee tail, can create a life estate. A life estate can be created by deed, or in a properly executed will by the use of the appropriate words of limitation such as 'for life', or 'for the life of X'. A life estate is created indirectly by the use of words insufficient to create a fee simple or a fee tail. An estate *pur autre vie* can be created indirectly by the tenant for life alienating that estate to another. This estate then lasts for the duration of the original tenant's life and the new tenant has an estate *pur autre vie* during the life of the old tenant.

Life Tenant and Waste

Any act which alters the nature of land or premises is technically waste, whether such alteration is for good or ill. The courts formulated rules regarding waste to prevent a life tenant from destroying the property to the detriment of those entitled in succession. There are four types of waste.

Alterations which improve the property, such as the conversion of a private dwelling into self-contained flats, is ameliorating waste and the courts are slow to prevent such improvements. It was held, in *Craig v Greer* (1899), that erecting a spirit grocery beside a villa residence in what had since become an urbanised district was not waste, though it obviously altered the character of that residence.

Permissible waste consists in negligently allowing property to decay without taking proper steps to halt such deterioration. A tenant for life is not liable for such waste unless it is so expressly stipulated in the deed granting the property. The life tenant is thus not impeachable for waste.

Voluntary waste is active damage. The tenant is generally liable for this type of waste unless excused by the grant. It was decided, in *Templemore v Moore* (1862), that to remove earth from the land was voluntary waste. At common law it was voluntary waste to cut down ripe timber, except that needed for personal use, and to open mines, though it was not waste to work a mine already in operation. These prohibitions have been greatly modified by statute.

Equitable waste is an act of wanton destruction which a prudent person would not do in the management of property. A tenant for life is liable for equitable waste unless the deed excludes such liability.

Fixtures

A fixture is a thing of an accessory character attaching to property which does not constitute part of the principal subject, such as a wall, but which is in actual union or connection with it, such as railings, and not merely brought into contact with the property, such as a picture hanging on hooks against the wall. The general rule is that fixtures form part of the property and cannot be removed by a life tenant. Exceptions are made for trade, agricultural and ornamental fixtures which can be removed by the life tenant.

Emblements

Emblements are the profits of a crop, such as wheat, which was sown by a tenant while in possession. The general rule as to emblements sown by an outgoing tenant whose estate has ended before harvest time is that the tenant can have the crop where the tenancy was terminated by some action of the landlord, or through the efflux of time. On the other hand, should the tenancy be ended by some act of the tenant, the crop could be harvested by the landlord.

LEASE FOR LIVES

Lease for Lives Renewable for Ever

One of the commonest forms of land-holding in this country was the lease for lives renewable for ever. The lease, originally granted for the term of lives, usually three, contained a clause that when any of the lives dropped out through death, the grantor would grant a renewal of the lease by substituting a new life on payment of a sum of money called a renewable fine. A leasehold was created between the parties but the interest granted was a freehold one. In effect it was an estate *pur autre vie*. Statute provides that the holder of such a lease has the right to convert it to a fee farm grant.

SETTLED LAND

Settlements

A settlement makes provision out of property for two or more persons in succession. A strict settlement of property was the traditional method of keeping property within one family for generations. Use was made of the life estate and the fee tail. The freehold owner, invariably the father as head of the family, would leave the property by will to his eldest son for life, followed by a fee tail to the eldest son of that son. Other family members, such as his wife, daughters and younger sons, were given portions, which was a sum of money out of the profits of the property to set these family members up in life. In this way every family member was given something.

The eldest son had a life interest which was useless as a commercial asset, because it could not be sold, leased or mortgaged. His eldest son was in no better position while his father was alive, though he could bar the entail sometime in the future. But when the eldest son, the grandson of the settlor, came of age, his father would encourage him successfully, by the offer of a sum of money, to bar the entail, give the father a life interest with another life interest to himself, and with the remainder to his own eldest son in fee tail. In this way the property was secured within the family for another generation.

This process of settlement and resettlement kept property, particularly a large estate of agricultural land, within the one family for generations. The land deteriorated with each passing generation. The life tenant had no great interest in developing it because the benefits accrued to others after his death. The common law, and later those made rich by the industrial revolution, disliked this practice of inalienability, though once the proper legal formalities were observed, nothing could be done to break the circle.

Settled Land Acts

The British Parliament intervened with the *Settled Land Acts 1882* and *1890*. These statutes effectively ended recurring settlements and released large tracts of land on to the open market.

For the purposes of these statutes a settlement exists where property stands limited to, or in trust for, any person by way of succession. One party, known as the tenant for life, is empowered to exercise various statutory powers given exclusively to the tenant for life who cannot assign or curtail them because that would defeat the intentment of the legislation. These powers may be exercised despite any restrictions imposed in the settlement deed. The tenant for life may sell, exchange, lease, mortgage or carry out a range of improvements.

While the tenant for life may deal with the property in a variety of ways, any capital monies raised must be paid over to trustees of the settlement for investment for the benefit of the tenant for life and those entitled to the property in succession. While those with succession rights lose their interest in the property, they are compensated with a corresponding interest in the capital monies.

REGISTRATION OF TITLE

Investigation of Title

When a sale of real property is proposed, the purchaser must ensure that the interest being transferred is the interest that the vendor has the right to dispose of. This investigation of title can be complicated because each previous transaction has to be vetted. To avoid a particular investigation of title each time the property changes hands, statute has provided a system of registration of title. The value of such registration, apart from streamlining the procedure, is that the State guarantees the title. Registration is governed by the *Registration of Title Act 1964*, though the practice dates back to the last century.

The Register and the Land Registry

The register consists of a series of folios with a separate numbered folio relating to each registered title. Each folio is divided into three sections. The first describes the land registered, including all easements, mines and mineral rights, and the date the land certificate was issued, together with a reference to the registry map. The second part contains the owner's name, description and address. The third section contains registered burdens and charges, such as mortgages.

The register, open to public inspection, is prepared and maintained in the Land Registry situated in Dublin. Three separate registers are maintained: one for freehold interests, another for leasehold interests and a third for incorporeal hereditaments, which are other interests such as easements (page 257).

Compulsory Registration

To make the investigation of title simple, the statute provides that some transactions must be registered. At present compulsory registration must be made in three situations. First, all freeholds and leasehold property acquired by local authorities and semi-State bodies must be registered. Second, freehold property purchased under various *Land Purchase Acts*, which enabled tenant farmers to purchase their lands from landlords, must be registered. Third, any county or county borough may be designated as a compulsory registration area. The counties of Carlow, Laoise and Meath have been so declared. Every acquisition of real property in those counties must be registered.

Advantages of Registration

Because of the advantages of registration, a large number of acquisitions, not subject to compulsory registration, are voluntarily registered. Where property is registered, a purchaser or other interested party can discover from an inspection of the register the vendor or owner's title. More importantly, the register will disclose what encumbrances, if any, bind the property. The register is conclusive evidence of the title of the person whose name appears on the register and a purchaser or other party acquiring an interest is not affected by any interest not registered. Where a party suffers loss by reason of official errors, compensation can be obtained from the State. The courts may order rectification of the register on the grounds of mistake or fraud.

On the other hand, a purchaser or other interested party has no simple method of discovering the title of unregistered real property. In such cases the purchaser must be satisfied from the abstract of title, the various deeds, the requisitions of title, searches and an inspection of the property, that the vendor has the power to sell the property which is not subject to undisclosed encumbrances.

Registration of Deeds

Unregistered property, that is, real property not registered in the Land Registry, can, however, be registered in the Registry of Deeds, established in 1707 and situated in Dublin. Registration is not compulsory and deeds affecting unregistered property together with other documents may be registered. The register may be searched by interested parties and the public. A purchaser, when acquiring an interest in unregistered land must search the Registry of Deeds to ascertain what burdens, if any, affect the property. The problem of priorities between different parties dealing with the same property is discussed on page 264, when dealing with mortgages. The ultimate aim is to provide a system where all real property in the State is registered property. When that objective is achieved the registration of deeds will be redundant.

Chapter 26

LEASEHOLD INTERESTS

Nature of Lease

A lease is a document creating an interest in real property for a fixed period of time usually, though not necessarily, in consideration of a fine, which is a sum of money paid by the tenant to the landlord on the creation of the interest, and always on the payment of periodic rent. The expression 'lease' denotes occasions where the interest is to continue for some time, whereas the expression 'tenancy' is normally used to describe interests which last a relatively short period. A tenancy agreement may be in writing, though it has the same effect as a lease. To create the relationship of landlord and tenant, the parties must so intend. The *Landlord and Tenant (Ireland) Act 1860*, known as *Deasy's Act*, provides that every lease created for any definite period of time, not being one from year to year, or a lesser period, must be by deed, or by a note in writing signed by the landlord, or an agent.

Types of Leases

There are different types of leases and tenancies. A lease may be granted for a fixed period which must be of certain duration and can be for a long period, such as 999 years, or a very short period. Both the commencement and duration must be certain. In earlier times, when money values were constant, these long leases were common, whereas in modern times leases tend to be of much shorter duration, say thirty-five years.

A tenancy may be periodic, such as from year to year, or from month to month, or from week to week. Such a tenancy may be expressly created or it may arise from the payment of rent measured with reference to a year, month or week. In such tenancies there is no certainty of duration beyond the particular period created, though where neither party takes action to terminate the tenancy, a new tenancy is created at the end of the initial period for a similar period on the same conditions. So a tenancy from week to week can continue for years, though it always remains a weekly tenancy.

A tenancy at will arises whenever a tenant, with the consent of the landlord, occupies premises on the terms that either party may terminate the tenancy at any time. A tenancy at sufferance arises where a tenant, having entered the property under a valid tenancy, holds over without the assent or dissent of the landlord after the original tenancy has terminated.

Conacre and Agistment

There are two common types of grants of land in this country which do not create a tenancy. The first is a letting in conacre, which is a licence to till the land, sow the crop and reap the harvest together with the right to enter the land to exercise these rights. The second is a letting in agistment, which is a licence to graze livestock. Neither of these lettings creates the relationship of landlord and tenant.

Statutory Tenant

A number of statutes grant protections to tenants. In such instances the tenant is known as the statutory tenant. For example, the *Landlord and Tenant (Amendment) Act 1980* gives security of tenure in business leases by providing the tenant with a statutory renewal of the lease at a marketable rent.

RELATIONSHIP OF LANDLORD AND TENANT

Creation of this Relationship

The relationship of landlord and tenant may be created under a lease, or a tenancy agreement. Where it is by lease, the duties and liabilities of each is set out in the deed. Where the agreement is a verbal one, which is generally the case in weekly or monthly tenancies of domestic premises, it may be silent on everything except the rent and duration. In such circumstances the law implies certain terms into the tenancy agreement (page 94).

Rights and Liabilities

The landlord, the party letting the premises, is under a duty not to interfere with the enjoyment by the tenant of the premises. Exclusive possession is the distinguishing feature of a lease, or tenancy, and a landlord must not interfere with the tenant's possession. In general, a landlord gives no implied undertaking that the premises are, or will be, fit for human habitation (but see page 201), nor is the landlord liable to repair them. The onus is on the tenant to inspect the premises before accepting the lease or tenancy.

The tenant is obliged to pay the rent when it becomes due, and not damage the premises over and above normal wear and tear. The tenant must allow the landlord to enter the premises from time to time to examine its condition.

Usual Covenants

When executing a lease, or entering a tenancy, the parties may agree to be bound by the usual covenants. A covenant is a clause which binds a party to do, or to refrain from doing some act. The usual covenants differ little from those mentioned above. On the landlord's part, there is a covenant to quiet enjoyment by the tenant. On the part of the tenant there are covenants to pay the rent and rates, if applicable; to keep the premises in repair; to deliver up the premises in good condition at the end of the term; to permit the landlord to enter and inspect the premises from time to time; and a right of the landlord to re-enter the premises for the non-payment of the rent, but not for the breach of any other covenant.

Assignment and Subletting

A tenant under a lease may dispose of the interest, where permitted under the lease, in either of two ways. An assignment involves a complete transfer of the remaining interest and, as a consequence, the tenant retains no interest in the property. The assignee, or new tenant, becomes subject to the same rights and liabilities as the assignor, or old tenant.

The subletting is a subgrant for a period less than that granted to the tenant. The tenant retains a reversion on the sublease and remains liable for the covenants in the lease. In effect, a new lease is created between the tenant, who in turn becomes a landlord, and the subtenant.

Termination of Leases

A lease, or tenancy, may come to an end in a number of ways. A lease or tenancy for a fixed period automatically expires when that period ends. This is known as termination by efflux of time. In some cases the tenant may, by virtue of a statute, claim a new lease: see earlier under Statutory Tenant. A lease or tenancy for a fixed period of time cannot be determined by a notice to quit unless expressly reserved in the lease. But a yearly, monthly, weekly or other periodic tenancy can be terminated by a notice to quit.

The right of a landlord to forfeit a lease, or to enforce a forfeiture, is usually contained in the lease. As already explained, every lease contains a list of actions which a tenant must not do. These are framed as either covenants or conditions. Where the forbidden action is framed as a covenant, the landlord has no right to forfeit unless the lease expressly grants such a right. On the other hand, where the action is worded as a condition, the lease may be forfeited even in the absence of a forfeiture clause.

A landlord has a right to forfeit for non-payment of rent. Before doing so the landlord must make a formal demand for payment. Where the rent remains unpaid, the landlord may not be able to enforce this condition because of intervention of equity. Equity considers that a right of forfeiture is merely a security for rent and where the tenant pays the amount due, together with expenses incurred by the landlord, it is just and equitable that the tenant should be restored to the original position despite the forfeiture of the lease.

Where a tenant surrenders the lease to the landlord, the lease merges in the interest of the landlord and is extinguished. Where a tenant acquires the landlord's interest, or where a third party acquires the interests of both landlord and tenant, the lease is merged in the larger interest and is destroyed. A lease may be determined by enlargement. Some statutes, for example, the *Landlord and Tenant (Ground Rents) Act 1978*, allow the tenant to enlarge the lease into a fee simple by requiring the landlord to transfer the fee simple to the tenant.

Chapter 27

CO-OWNERSHIP, EASEMENTS AND POWERS

Nature of Co-ownership

On page 242 we dealt with the principle that different parties may have different interests in the one property. Co-ownership, on the other hand, deals with concurrent interests in the same property. The two principle co-ownership interests are joint tenancy and tenancy in common. The word tenancy in this regard must not be confused with its use in relation to leaseholds. In this context it is used to denote an interest, and all estates, freehold and leasehold, may be held in this way.

Joint Tenancy

Where property is granted to two or more parties without words of severance, the property is held in joint tenancy and each is theoretically entitled to the entire property. A grant to 'Declan and Derek jointly', or simply to 'Eileen and Sheila' creates a joint tenancy. Joint tenancy has two distinctive features: the right of survivorship and the four unities.

The right of survivorship, or the *jus accrescendi*, provides that on the death of one joint tenant that interest passes to the other joint tenants, and this process continues until there is one survivor who then holds the property as sole owner. A joint tenancy cannot pass under a will or intestacy because the deceased left no inheritable interest. At the moment of death the interest possessed in life passes to the other joint tenants. A joint tenancy can be created by will.

The common law decided that a corporation, because of its perpetual existence, could not be a joint tenant because the other party, a natural person, would have no effective right of survivorship. The *Bodies Corporate (Joint Tenancy) Act 1899* reversed this rule. This reform was necessary because banks were becoming trustees and needed to hold property on trust as joint tenants. Because of the convenience of permitting the trust property to pass to the surviving trustees when one or more die, trustees are joint tenants of the trust property.

Four features, known as the four unities, must be present for a joint tenancy to arise. There must be unity of possession. Each joint tenant must be entitled to possession of the whole property: each cannot claim any particular part of the property. Where the property is a house, each joint tenant is entitled to use the entire premises. There must be unity of interest. The interest of each joint tenant must be the same in extent, nature and duration. There cannot be a joint tenancy where one party holds the freehold and another holds the leasehold. There must be unity of title. All the joint tenants must have acquired their interest under the same act or title. There cannot be a joint tenancy where one party acquires title under a will and another acquires title under a deed. There must be unity of time. The interest of each tenant must vest at the same time.

Tenancy in Common

A tenancy in common exists where property is granted which suggests that it is intended to be received as distinct shares, though the property remains physically undivided. Thus property given to 'Deirdre and Emma equally', or to 'Clare and Eamon in undivided shares' creates, in each case, a tenancy in common. Words conveying such a suggestion are known as words of severance.

A tenant in common has no right of survivorship because each party is possessed of a distinct part of the property. Only one unity is required for a tenancy in common: that is the unity of possession, though other unities may be present. The common law favoured joint tenancy whereas equity preferred tenancy in common because one of its maxims dictated 'equality is equity'.

EASEMENTS

Nature of Easement

An easement is a right attaching to property which allows the owner either to use the property of another in a particular way or to restrict its use to a particular extent. Examples of the former are rights of way and rights to enter and take water from the property of another. Examples of the latter are rights to lights and rights to support.

There are four essential features of an easement. First, there must be a dominant and a servient tenement. This means that the easement must be annexed to, or of benefit to, some property. Easements run with the land rather than with the owner: an easement cannot exist in gross, that is independently of property. Second, an easement must accommodate the dominant tenement: it must not only benefit the owner personally but must benefit the property. A right which confers a personal benefit on the owner of the property is not an easement. Third, the dominant and servient tenements must be owned and occupied by different parties because an easement is a right in *alieno solo*, in the soil of another, which obviously cannot exist unless there are separate owners. Fourth, an easement must originate in a grant.

Acquiring an Easement

An easement is acquired in a number of ways. It may be conferred by statute. This was done when the right of support was granted to canals and railways. The most usual method of creating an easement is by deed. In *Gaw v CIE* (1953) the parties' predecessors in title agreed that the occupiers of adjacent premises would have a right of way across a railway line. An easement may be created by an implied grant. This fiction is recognised by the courts out of necessity. A right of way of necessity was litigated in *McDonagh v Mulholland* (1931) where seven houses had been built by the same person and had remained for many years in the ownership of one family. A severance took place and a side door in the wall of one house was opened into an avenue leading to the defendant's house and out to the public highway. The High Court refused to recognise an implied grant because the door was opened not out of necessity but rather for convenience.

An easement may be acquired by a presumed grant where, at some time in the past, the easement had been granted by deed but the deed has been lost and cannot be produced. This is known as the doctrine of lost modern grant.

An easement may be acquired by prescription. This is the acquiescence by the servient owner in the open assertion of a right against the property by the dominant owner. The law infers that a grant is the only possible explanation of such a long continued acquiescence. The servient owner must prove that the easement was *nec vi, nec clam, nec precario*: that is without force, without secrecy, and without permission.

The legislators took notice of the common law rules pertaining to prescription and lost modern grant. The *Prescription Act 1832*, extended to Ireland in 1858, lays down two periods of user whereby an easement may be acquired. A claim to an easement, other than to light, may be based on proof of user for either twenty or forty years, depending on the circumstances of the case. Because an easement to light is more difficult to prove, the statute provides that where light has been enjoyed by any dwelling, workshop or other building for twenty years without interference, the right becomes absolute.

Extinguishing an Easement

An easement may be extinguished in three ways. Statutes which give power to compulsorily acquire property usually provide that all easements affecting the property are thereby extinguished. The owner of an easement may release it either expressly or by implication. Where expressly done, it must be by deed. An implied release arises where an intention to abandon exists, which may be presumed from the non-user of the easement for a long period of time. According to the High Court, in *Carroll v Sheridan* (1984), evidence of abandonment must be supported by conduct or intention adverse to the exercise of the right. In that case the servient tenant asserted that any right of way which had existed over a mile-long path, linking two public roads, had been extinguished by non-user. The owner of the dominant interest successfully refuted such a claim.

An easement may be extinguished where the dominant and servient tenements are acquired by the same person: there is then unity of ownership and possession.

At this point it is useful to refer to page 180 which discusses nuisance to easements.

Profits à Prendre

Though not an easement, a *profit à prendre* is a right exercised by one party over the soil of another coupled with participation in the profit of the soil thereof. There are a number of recognised *profits à prendre*, such as the right to graze animals on another's land, known as pasturage. The digging and taking away of turf for fuel is turbary. A *profit à prendre* may exist in a fishery. Sporting rights, such as hunting or shooting wild animals and fowl is another common profit. The right to take timber from another's land is the right to estovers.

POWERS

Nature of a Power

A power is an authority granted to a party, called the donee, to dispose of property which is owned by another, called the donor. The exercise of the power is called an appointment and the persons in whose favour an appointment is made are known as the objects of the power.

Kinds of Power

There are three kinds of power. A collateral power grants no interest in the property to the donee: thus 'to Ronan and Cristian on trust for whichever as my brother Noel shall appoint'. The sole right granted to Noel is to appoint between two named parties.

A power may be in gross where the donee is granted an interest in the property, but its exercise cannot affect that interest: thus 'to David for life, with power to appoint among whichever of his children as he chooses'. David is granted a life interest and his power, when exercised, can only become effective after his interest terminates.

A power is appendant where the exercise of the power can affect the interest of the donee: thus 'to Niamh with power to appoint by deed or will amongst her children in whatever shares she thinks proper'. Once Niamh exercises the power during her lifetime, the interest in the property passes to the appointee or appointees.

Power of Appointment

A power of appointment permits the donee to appoint the property to which the power relates in accordance with the terms of the power. These powers are generally granted under a settlement, trust or will. Such a power may be general, giving the donee the power to appoint as he or she thinks fit, or special, giving the power to appoint in favour of some or all of a specific group. Most powers are followed by a provision for some particular person or persons to take in default of the power being exercised. Where no party is mentioned, the donor takes any unappointed property.

Powers of Attorney

A power of attorney is an authority granted by one party to another, to act for that party in matters in which the donor has power to act. It is a special form of agency. For example, a power of attorney may be executed when the donor intends to be absent from the country for some time. In general, a power of attorney continues until the death, revocation or the onset of mental incapacity of the donor. The attorney may execute any document or deed in his or her own name under the authority of the power, and every such act done is as effective in law as if the act had been performed by the donor.

The *Powers of Attorney Act 1996* allows the creation, for the first time, of an enduring power of attorney, which will be effective during the donor's subsequent mental incapacity. Such a power must be executed, in the form provided for by law, by four persons: the donor, the attorney, a solicitor, who must state that he or she is satisfied that the donor understood the effect of creating the enduring power, and a registered medical practitioner, who must state his or her opinion that the donor had the mental capacity to understand the effect of creating the power. Certain parties must be notified of the making of the power and to be effective the enduring power must be registered with the Registrar of Wards of Court.

Chapter 28
MORTGAGES

Nature of Mortgage
A mortgage is a conveyance of an interest in real property to a creditor as security for a debt, subject to the proviso that on its repayment the mortgage will be void. The borrower is known as the mortgagor and the lender as the mortgagee. The essential feature of a mortgage is the concept of security. The commercial practice, when a loan of money is sought, is to require the borrower to give some security for the loan, generally real property, so that on non-payment of the loan the property can be sold to satisfy the debt.

In former times the mortgagor would lease the property to the mortgagee who would enter into possession and enjoy the benefits of the property. The characteristic of a modern mortgage is that possession of the mortgaged property remains vested in the mortgagor until the debt becomes overdue.

The Equity of Redemption
The common law construed the mortgage contract strictly by holding that where the mortgagor defaulted in repayments by the agreed date, the property was lost to the mortgagor. Equity saw the transaction as a loan security and not as a covert means of acquiring property and refused to follow this strict rule. Equity allowed the mortgagor to redeem the mortgage on repaying the sum borrowed and interest long after the fixed date for redemption had passed. This is known as the equity of redemption and any hindrance on this right of redemption, known as clogs on the equity, was void.

Mortgage of Freehold
The creation of a legal mortgage of freehold property depends on whether it is registered or unregistered. The sole way the registered owner of property can create a legal mortgage is by executing a charge which must be registered in the Land Registry on the folio of the property. Where the property is unregistered, alternative methods may be used. First, the mortgagor may convey the freehold to the mortgagee subject to the proviso for redemption. Secondly, the mortgagor may create a leasehold out of the freehold in favour of the mortgagee. The duration will equal the term of years of the loan.

Mortgage of Leasehold

Where the mortgagor has a leasehold interest, a choice of methods may be used to create a mortgage. First, the mortgagor can assign the term of years in the lease to the mortgagee subject to the proviso of redemption. This is unusual because such an assignment renders the mortgagee liable for the covenants and conditions, such as rent and repairs, imposed by the lease on the mortgagor. Second, the mortgagor can sublease in favour of the mortgagee for a term of years shorter than the original lease. While the relationship of landlord and tenant is created between the mortgagor and the mortgagee, no such relationship is created between the head landlord and the mortgagee. This is the common method of mortgaging leaseholds.

Equitable Mortgage

An equitable mortgage can arise in two ways. First, where the interest held by the mortgagor is an equitable one, such as an interest under a trust, the mortgage can only be an equitable one. A second or subsequent mortgage of a legal interest is an equitable mortgage. Second, an equitable mortgage is created where title deeds are deposited with the mortgagee. Such a deposit is *prima facie* an equitable mortgage.

Equity of Redemption

The most important right of a mortgagor is to redeem the property on the repayment of the loan. This entitles the mortgagor to a discharge from the mortgage on the repayment of the loan borrowed, together with any interest. The mortgagor has a legal right to redeem on the date fixed, and an equitable right to redeem thereafter.

Possession

It is the practice to allow the mortgagor to remain in possession of the property during the continuance of the mortgage. The mortgagor is entitled to rents and profits which the property may produce and must discharge all outgoings such as rates. The mortgagor may commit waste (see page 247) though damage which renders the property an inadequate security is forbidden. The mortgagor may take legal action to protect the property from wrongful acts, such as trespass, nuisance and negligence.

Title Documents

The mortgagee is entitled to possess the title documents for the duration of the mortgage. Statute grants the mortgagor the right to inspect and to make copies of these documents, provided the appropriate fees are tendered and the request is made at reasonable times. As a consequence, further dealings with the property are severely restricted. The inability of an owner to produce documents of title raises the suspicion that the property is mortgaged. Once the mortgage ends, the mortgagor is entitled to the return of the documents of title.

Sale of the Property

The mortgagor can dispose of the property subject to the mortgage. There is no legal prohibition to prevent the mortgagor from transferring the equity of redemption to another, though the mortgagor remains personally liable for the debt unless the mortgagee consents to the transfer.

Insurance

The mortgagee has a statutory right to insure the mortgaged property against loss or damage by fire. The premiums are usually paid by the mortgagor. This right to insure is limited to the reinstatement value of the property set out in the mortgage deed and as the value increases or decreases, so does the sum insured.

Action for Sums Due

A mortgage is a special type of contract, and where money owed on foot of the mortgage remains unpaid, the mortgagee can sue to recover it.

Enforcing the Security

The equity of redemption does not prohibit the mortgagee from realising the mortgaged property to satisfy the loan secured. The law leans on the side of the mortgagor by affording every opportunity to retain the property; but there must be occasions when the mortgagor cannot fulfil the mortgage obligations. There are a number of ways the mortgagee can realise the property to satisfy the mortgage.

The first is to seek a court order for possession and sale out of court. The mortgagor is ordered to surrender possession and a sale is conducted under the supervision of the court. The second method permits the mortgagee to sell the property without court intervention, though this remedy is useless unless vacant possession of the property can be obtained. The third course of action is for the mortgagee to seek from the courts an order for sale without seeking an order of possession. The sale is supervised by the court. The fourth remedy is for the mortgagee to take possession of the property without anything further, though this is only of limited usefulness because the mortgagee is liable to account strictly to the mortgagor for any damage caused. The fifth course of action is for the mortgagee to appoint a receiver, that is, someone of business experience to manage the property for the benefit of the mortgagee by raising the capital and interest on monies due (see page 230).

The High Court held, in *Gale v First National Building Society* (1985), that an express provision in a mortgage, which permitted the mortgagee to take possession in the event of default by the mortgagor, created a contractual licence between the parties, under which the mortgagor may, on such default, take possession of the property without the necessity of a court order.

PRIORITY OF MORTGAGES

Multiplicity of Mortgages

Before a mortgage of property is finalised, the mortgagee inquires as to whether the property is sufficient to satisfy the loan. Where the mortgagor creates a number of mortgages, it is possible that the funds obtained when the property is sold may be insufficient to satisfy all the mortgagees. In such a case it is imperative to ascertain which mortgage has first claim on the property and on the proceeds from its sale. The courts have evolved a number of rules in this regard, which are known as the doctrine of priorities.

The Doctrine of Priorities

The application of the doctrine of priorities depends on whether the property is registered or unregistered. With registered property the position is governed by the *Registration of Title Act 1964*. Mortgages of registered property take precedence in the order of their registration in the Land Registry, irrespective of when created: the first registered takes priority over the first created where the latter was not registered first.

With regard to unregistered property, the question is governed by the registration of deeds. (A glance at page 251 at this point might be useful.) Between mortgages of unregistered property, the rule is that they take precedence in the order of registration irrespective of when created. The first registered takes first priority. Each registered mortgage takes precedence over all unregistered mortgages.

Special rules apply to mortgages created by companies (see page 417).

Legal and Equitable Mortgages

The law developed rules regulating priorities before the intervention of statute and the notion of registered and unregistered property. Where both the mortgages are legal, a very rare occurrence, the first in time has priority. A legal mortgage takes priority over an equitable mortgage even if created after the equitable one. This is an application of the equitable maxim 'where the equities are equal the law prevails' and 'where the equities are equal', where two or more equitable mortgages exist, 'the first in time prevails'.

JUDGMENT MORTGAGES

Nature of Judgment Mortgage

A judgment mortgage is a type of mortgage created by statute which allows a litigant who has recovered damages and obtains a judgment against the owner of real property to convert that judgment into a mortgage against the property. Judgments of the Supreme Court, the High Court and in some instances the Circuit Court can be converted in this way.

The judgment mortgage grants the judgment creditor some remedy against the judgment debtor. The judgment creditor cannot force a sale of the property, though the existence of a judgment mortgage hinders its disposal because a prospective purchaser has notice that the property is mortgaged. The purchaser has the option to withdraw from the sale or to purchase the property subject to the mortgage, or to request the seller to satisfy the mortgage before the sale is completed. It is the latter consequence that encourages creditors to convert judgments into judgment mortgages.

Chapter 29

PLANNING AND ENVIRONMENT LAW

PLANNING

Planning Authorities

The *Local Government (Planning and Development) Act 1963*, as amended, constitutes county council and borough corporations as planning authorities. The planning authority has four broad functions: first, it prepares and revises development plans; second, it decides on individual applications for planning permission; third, it has planning control enforcement powers; and fourth, it is granted various powers to ensure the effectiveness of the statutory planning scheme.

Development Plan

The planning authority prepares and publishes a development plan, which is revised every five years, indicating the development objectives for the area in question. The plan consists of a statement which may be illustrated by maps. It must give notice to the public that the plan may be inspected and that objections and representations will be taken into account before variations are made.

The planning authority is bound by its own development plan. A material contravention of the development plan may occur where the proper procedure is followed. The planning authority, in *O'Leary v Dublin County Council* (1988), proposed a travellers' halting site in an area designated in the development plan as a high amenity area, without adopting the statutory procedures for effecting variations in the plan. The High Court held that the creation of a halting site in a high amenity area amounted to a material contravention of the development plan.

Special Amenities Order

The planning authority can make a special amenity area order which must be confirmed by the Minister for the Environment.

Planning Register

The planning authority must keep and maintain a planning register in which all relevant planning information is recorded and is obliged to publish a weekly list of planning decisions.

Development

Development is defined as the carrying out of any work on, in, or under land, or the making of any material change in the use of any structures or other land. The High Court held, in *Patterson v Murphy* (1978), that the installation of machinery, which resulted in intensive operations at a quarry where primitive intermittent activities had taken place previously, was a material change of use. The Supreme Court ruled, in *Cork Corporation v O'Connell* (1982) that a change of use from a retail hardware store to an amusement arcade was material.

Exempted Development

Exempted development is development which may be carried out without planning permission. There are many exempted developments; the following are a sample, though most are subject to some restriction: the use of land for agriculture and forestry; work carried out for the maintenance, improvement or other alteration of any structure which affects its interior, or which does not materially affect the external appearance of the structure as to render such appearance inconsistent with the character of the structure, or of neighbouring structures; an extension to the rear of a dwellinghouse or the conversion for use as part of a dwellinghouse of any garage, shed or other similar structure attached to the rear or side of the dwellinghouse; the provision as part of a central heating system of a dwellinghouse of a chimney, boiler house or oil storage tank; any tent, awning, shade, greenhouse, shed or other similar structure; a television or wireless aerial on the roof of a dwellinghouse; the erection within or bounding a dwellinghouse of a gate, railing, wooden fence or a wall; and the keeping or storing of not more than one caravan or boat within the curtilage of a dwellinghouse.

Planning Permission

Planning permission is required for development unless commenced before 1 October 1964 (the date on which the 1963 Act came into operation) or it is exempt development. There are regulations governing the making of applications for planning permission and the submission of appeals. The failure to comply with these regulations may or may not be fatal. A planning authority when granting permission may impose conditions. A planning permission is an appendage to the title of land; it endures for the benefit of the land and of all persons having an interest in it. A planning permission will lapse unless the development is commenced within five years.

Appeals

A planning decision may be appealed to An Bord Pleanála, or to the Minister for the Environment in certain instances. Appeals may be made against decisions for development, or to refuse permission. The entire application is reconsidered. Certain appeals must be heard on oral hearing. In the generality of cases the decision to hold an oral hearing is at the discretion of the Bord.

Appeal to Courts

The High Court has jurisdiction over a planning authority and An Bord Pleanála, and may grant relief by way of judicial review (see page 45). In general such legal action must be taken within two months of the decision being given.

Enforcement of Planning Control

A party who carries out development which requires planning permission without first obtaining that permission commits a criminal offence. The planning authority may serve an enforcement notice requiring that specific steps be taken within a specified time to remedy that breach. It is an offence not to comply with such notice.

The enforcement of planning control is by means of an order in the nature of an injunction by the High Court. In *Morris v Garvey* (1982) a block of flats was being built otherwise than in accordance with the planning permission. The High Court ordered the demolition of the partially built structure.

Compensation

Where it is shown that as a consequence of a refusal to grant planning permission to develop land, or such permission is subject to conditions, the value of an interest in the property is reduced, compensation for such reduction in value, and in the case of the occupier of the land, the damage to trade, business or profession carried on on the land, must be paid by the planning authority. A planning authority may recover compensation paid where significant development occurs on the property within fourteen years of its payment. A dissatisfied applicant for planning permission may require the planning authority to acquire the property.

Environmental Impact Assessment

Before planning permission is granted to projects which are likely to have a significant effect on the environment by virtue of their nature, size or location, an assessment must be made with regard to their effects.

ENVIRONMENT

General Protection

The common law, particularly through the law relating to nuisance (see page 174), controlled some abuses to the environment. But these rules were of very limited application because they were mainly concerned with preserving the enjoyment of private property. In recent years, it has become obvious that rules of a more general application were necessary if the wider environment was to be preserved and if risks arising from abuses to the environment were to be prevented, for the general well-being of the community. Accordingly, there has been a plethora of international conventions, EU regulations and directives, and a great number of statutes and statutory instruments. Volume and complexity is now the order of the day: an outline of the major areas of regulations is set out below.

Water

The *Public Health (Ireland) Act 1878* places a statutory obligation on a local authority to furnish a sufficient supply of drinking water fit for human consumption for public and private purposes.

Local authorities, under the *Local Government (Water Pollution) Acts 1977–1990*, have the major responsibility for ensuring the preservation, protection and improvement of water quality. Waters are defined as any river, stream, lake, canal, reservoir, aquifer, pond, watercourse or other inland waters, whether natural or artificial, tidal waters and any breach, river bank and salt marsh or other area which is for the time being dry but does not include a sewer. Polluting matters include any poisonous and noxious matter and any substances, including explosive, liquid or gas, the entry or discharge of which into any waters is liable to render those poisonous or injurious to fish, spawning grounds or the food of any fish, to injure fish in their value as human food, or to impair the usefulness of the bed and soil of any waters as spawning grounds or their capacity to produce the food of fish, or to render such waters harmful or detrimental to public health or to domestic, commercial, industrial, agricultural or recreational uses.

It is an offence to cause or permit any polluting matter to enter waters. It is a defence to prove that all reasonable care was taken to prevent the prohibited entry by providing, maintaining, using, operating and supervising facilities, or by employing practices or methods of operation, that were suitable for the purpose of such prevention.

It is an offence to discharge or cause to permit the discharge of any trade effluent or sewage effluence to any waters except in accordance with a licence. Trade effluent is material from any works, apparatus, plant or drainage pipe use for the disposal to waters or to a sewer of any liquid, whether treated or untreated, either with or without particular of matter, which is discharged from premises used for carrying on any trade or industry, including mining, but does not include domestic sewage or storm water. Such matter may be discharged provided a licence is obtained from the local authority. This is obtained following a process similar to a planning application. A number of activities are exempted from the licensing requirements.

The discharge of agricultural effluents into waters from premises such as silos, livestock housing, slurry tanks and dungsteads are prohibited, as is the discharge of dangerous substances.

With regard to marine waters, the *Sea Pollution Act 1991*, the *Oil Pollution of the Sea Acts 1956–1977*, and the *Dumping at Sea Act 1981* contain the major legal controls and enact into domestic law a number of international conventions on the subject.

The *Fisheries Acts 1959–1990* control inland and marine waters, including fish-farming, which requires an operating licence.

Air

The major statutory provision for the control of air pollution is the *Air Pollution Act 1987*. The responsibility and enforcement again rests with local authorities. Air pollution is defined as a condition of the atmosphere in which a pollutant is present in such a quality as to be (i) be injurious to public health, (ii) have a deleterious effect on flora or fauna or damage property, (iii) impair or interfere with amenities or with the environment. Pollutant means any substances specified in the Act or any other substance, including a substance which gives rise to odour, or energy which, when emitted into the atmosphere either by itself or in combination with any other substance, may cause air pollution.

The occupier of any premises, other than a private dwelling, is under a duty to use the best practicable means to limit and, where possible, to prevent an emission from such premises. It is an offence for the occupier of any premises, including a private dwelling, to cause or permit an emission from such premises in such a quantity, or in such a manner, as to be a nuisance. An emission is defined as an emission of a pollutant into the atmosphere. The Act provides a number of defences, such as that the best practicable means have been used to limit or prevent the emission concerned.

Industrial plant, which began to operate after 1 January 1989, must be licensed and the process is similar to a planning application. Industrial plant operating before that date must comply with emission standards as laid down.

Regulations may be made for the purpose of preventing or limiting air pollution, including regulations relating to standards, specifications, compositions and the contents of fuel used in fireplaces and mechanically propelled vehicles.

Waste Disposal

The major statute in this area is the *Waste Management Act 1996*. Local authorities are under a legal requirement to draw up a waste management plan and can take measures for promoting, supporting and facilitating the prevention or minimisation of waste.

Statutory responsibility for controlling waste disposal rests with the local authorities who must provide fit buildings and places for the deposit of any matter collected by them. Permits to collect waste by other parties may be granted. Local authorities may provide sites for waste disposal and accordingly the authority must carry out its duty in such a way as not to cause a nuisance (see page 180).

Environmental Protection Agency

This body was created by the *Environmental Protection Agency Act 1992.* It has a wide variety of activities, the main ones are: (a) the licensing, regulating and controlling of activities for the purposes of environmental protection; (b) monitoring environmental quality and disseminating such information; (c) providing support and advisory services to local and public authorities in relation to the performance of their functions; and (d) promoting and co-ordinating environmental research.

Part Seven
FAMILY LAW AND SUCCESSION

Chapter 30
MARRIAGE

Constitutional Protection of Marriage

Article 41 of the Constitution pledges the State to guard with special care the institution of marriage, on which the family is founded, and to protect it against attack. This guarantee justified striking down parts of the income tax code, in *Murphy v Attorney General* (1982), which taxed a married couple living together more heavily than two single persons with similar incomes living together. The Supreme Court ruled that the nature and progressive extent of the taxation burden amounted to a breach of this pledge by the State. This constitutional pledge was also breached in *Hyland v Minister for Social Welfare* (1990) where the Supreme Court held that the social welfare code, which granted lesser benefits to a married couple and their child living together than to an unmarried couple with a child living together, penalised the married state.

The Supreme Court ruled, in *McKinley v Minister for Defence* (1992), that the common law rule which granted to a husband a right to sue a third party for the loss of the consortium of his wife, and denied a similar action to a wife who had lost the consortium of her husband, was in breach of the guarantee of equality. The special place given to marriage in the Constitution emphasises the need to afford equal rights to both spouses. As a result both spouses can sue for the loss of consortium. The same court ruled, in *T.F. v Ireland* (1995), that the *Judicial Separation and Family Law Reform Act 1989* (see page 280), which attempted to deal with the consequences of marital breakdown, was not an attack on the institution of marriage because of the various safeguards contained in the statute.

Communications passing between spouses and a marriage counsellor are privileged against disclosure where a marriage is in difficulties, on the ground that the State guarantees to protect marriage and the family. This was decided by the High Court in *E.R. v J.R.* (1981) though the privilege could be waived by the mutual consent of the spouses. This rule is reinforced by the *Family Law (Divorce) Act 1996* which provides that any communication between spouses and a third party for the purpose of seeking assistance to effect a reconciliation, or to reach an agreement on the terms of a separation or a divorce, shall not be admissible as evidence in any court.

The High Court ruled, in *Ennis v Butterly* (1997), that given the place of marriage and the family under the Constitution, the public policy of the State ordained that non-marital cohabitation could not have the same constitutional status as marriage.

Marriage

Marriage is defined neither in the Constitution nor in statute law. The common law defined marriage as the voluntary union for life of one man and one woman to the exclusion of all others. Costello J. in *Murray v Attorney General* (1985) said: 'The concept and nature of marriage which [the Constitution] enshrines is derived from the Christian notion of a partnership based on an irrevocable personal consent, given by both spouses which establishes a unique and very special life-long relationship.'

The Constitution does not expressly acknowledge the right to marry though it is generally regarded as an implied personal right. Since persons marry for a great many different reasons, the law, in general, is not concerned with the reason why a person marries. Barrington J. explained this view, in *R.S.J. v J.S.J* (1982), (the facts are given on page 277) when he said: 'People have entered into . . . marriage for all sorts of reasons, and their motives have not always been of the highest. The motive for the marriage may have been policy, convenience, or self-interest. In these circumstances . . . one could not say that a marriage is void merely because one party did not love or had not the capacity to love the other.'

To contract a valid marriage the parties must comply with the prevailing legal requirements. For this purpose a distinction must be made between the capacity to marry, which is governed by the law of each party's pre-nuptial domicile, and the formalities of marriage, which is governed by the law where the marriage was solemnised.

Capacity to Marry

The *Family Law Act 1995* provides that a marriage solemnised between persons either of whom is under the age of eighteen years shall not be valid in law unless an exemption has been obtained from the High Court. This rule applies to any marriage solemnised in the State, irrespective of where the spouses, or either of them, are ordinarily resident, or outside the State, if at the solemnisation of the marriage the spouses, or either of them, are ordinarily resident in the State.

The parties must not be within the prohibited degrees of relationship either by consanguinity, meaning blood relationship, or affinity, meaning relationship by marriage. At present there are twenty-eight prohibited relationships.

Each party must freely consent to the marriage. The courts may look at the circumstances surrounding the marriage to determine whether the apparent consent was a true consent or whether the ceremony was a sham to achieve some other end. The High Court ruled, in *Kelly v Ireland* (1996), that a passport could not be refused to a non-citizen woman who had gone through a marriage ceremony in London with an Irish citizen (see page 9) because the State had not established that the marriage was a sham and had been arranged merely to prevent the woman from being deported from the United Kingdom.

A valid marriage cannot be contracted if either party is already married. The High Court ruled, in *W. v S.(Otherwise W.) (1987),* that a divorce obtained by the wife in England could not be recognised because the parties were domiciled in Ireland when the divorce was obtained (see page 279 for Recognition of Foreign Divorces). Since the wife was already married she could not validly have entered into the subsequent marriage. A second marriage between spouses is not rendered void by virtue of a first marriage between them. The High Court so decided, in *B.v R.* (1995), where the parties, married in a civil ceremony in the United States, subsequently married each other in Ireland in a full religious ceremony. The Supreme Court decided, in *Conlon v Mohammed* (1989), where the parties went through a valid Islamic ceremony in South Africa, that the marriage was invalid because it was potentially polygamous.

In order for a marriage to be valid, one party must be male and the other party female.

Formalities of Marriage

The formalities to be observed for the creation of a valid marriage depend on the religion of the parties. There are different formalities between the Christian religions, which have been created by statute in deference to minority religions and for those with no religious beliefs. The common law required the presence of a clergyman in holy orders at the time the marriage was solemnised. The presence of witnesses was not essential. The modern rule is that for a religious marriage to be valid it must be solemnised in a church in the presence of two or more witnesses after the banns have been notified to the public. In *Ussher v Ussher* (1912) a marriage took place in a private house between Catholics, solemnised by a priest in the presence of a witness. This was not in accordance with the Catholic rite which required two formal witnesses. The marriage was valid because it was celebrated in accordance with the common law. A marriage may be contracted by civil ceremony before a registrar appointed for that purpose.

For a marriage celebrated abroad to be recognised, the formalities must comply with the *lex loci celebrationis*, the law of the place where the marriage was celebrated. In this regard the *Marriage Act 1972* regularised certain marriages celebrated in Lourdes which had not complied with the formalities of French law. These marriages were irregular in that only religious ceremonies, and not the required state ceremonies, had been conducted.

Parental Consent

Parental consent must be obtained by those under the age of twenty-one years who wish to marry. The *Age of Majority Act 1985* which lowered the age of majority generally to eighteen years expressly excluded marriage in this regard. Consent is a formality and not a matter of capacity. Where both parents of an under-aged party are alive both must consent. Where only one parent is surviving, and no guardian has been appointed, the surviving parent must consent. Where both parents are deceased the consent of a guardian is required. Where there is no guardian, the consent of the President of the High Court is necessary.

The foregoing rules apply to legitimate children. Where a party intending to marry is illegitimate the mother's consent is required. Where she is deceased consent by a guardian, where there is one, is sufficient. Otherwise, an application must be made to the President of the High Court.

Notification of Intention to Marry

The *Family Law Act 1995* provides that a marriage shall not be valid unless the persons concerned notified the Registrar of Marriage for the appropriate district not less than three months prior to the date on which the marriage is to be solemnised. An exemption from this requirement may be obtained from the High Court. There is no obligation on the Registrar to make this information publicly available.

NULLITY OF MARRIAGE

Nature of Nullity of Marriage

A petition for nullity of marriage is a matrimonial action to obtain a judicial decree declaring that a supposed marriage is null and void. A decree of nullity is a declaration that no valid marriage existed between the parties. Nullity must be distinguished from divorce, which is a decree terminating a valid marriage. The parties to a successful nullity action can remarry because in law each is regarded as unmarried.

The High Court and the Circuit Family Court are vested with the jurisdiction to grant an annulment of marriage. This section details the principles of law applicable to civil or State annulments, and has no bearing whatever on annulments granted by any particular Church. Such an annulment is not recognised by law and a subsequent marriage is bigamous unless a divorce is obtained, and the issue of any such union are illegitimate.

In nullity law the alleged marriage may be either void or voidable. There are important differences between marriages alleged to be void and those alleged to be voidable. Firstly, in the case of a voidable marriage a decree of nullity is required, whereas in a void marriage no decree is necessary though it is advisable. Secondly, the validity of a void marriage may be challenged by any person with a sufficient interest, even after the death of the parties, whereas a voidable marriage may be challenged only by one of the parties during their lifetimes. Thirdly, a void marriage had never any legal effect whereas a voidable marriage is valid until it is annulled by decree. Fourthly, children of a void marriage are illegitimate whereas children of a voidable marriage are legitimate unless and until the marriage is annulled.

Void Marriages

A marriage may be void for a number of reasons. The lack of capacity where either, or both, parties are already married (see *W. v S.(Otherwise W.)* page 274), or are within the prohibited degree of consanguinity, or are under the age of eighteen years and the consent of the High Court has not been obtained, renders a marriage void. The non-observance of the appropriate formalities may render a marriage void. For example, a ceremony which fails to observe the proper legal requirements is void (see *Ussher v Ussher* page 274).

Because marriage is a voluntary union, the consent of each party must be freely and fully given. The lack of consent in one, or both of the parties renders a marriage void. A consent obtained by duress, mistake, misrepresentation or fraud is void. In *Griffith v Griffith* (1944) a nineteen-year-old man married a seventeen-year-old woman following untrue threats that acts of alleged intercourse, which were illegal because the woman was under the age of legal consent, would be reported to the gardaí. The High Court annulled the marriage on the ground that a consent obtained by a combination of fraud and fear was not a binding consent. In *S. v O'S.* (1978) the woman sought an annulment on the ground of emotional duress by the man, who suffered from Munchausen's Periodic Syndrome at the time of the marriage, whereby he exaggerated a feigned illness which he claimed could only be cured by early marriage. The High Court annulled the marriage because the freedom of will necessary to enter into a valid marriage was one particularly associated with emotion, and a person in the emotional bondage of another could not consciously have that freedom of will. The threat to commit suicide by the man, who was extremely jealous, possessive and domineering, if marriage was not agreed to, amounted to duress in *O'K.(Otherwise P.) v P.* (1985).

Parental duress was successfully pleaded in *McK.(Otherwise McC.) v McC.* (1982). The parties had met as teenagers, associated regularly for two years and pregnancy resulted after a single act of intercourse. Both sets of parents applied pressure to marry. The High Court annulled the marriage on the ground that the wills of the parties were overborne by the compulsion of persons to whom the parties had always been subjected in the parent and child relationship, and that the duress exercised was of a character that each was unable to withstand. In *N.(Otherwise K.) v K.* (1985) the wife, a quiet, unassertive and obedient girl had become pregnant as a result of a short and casual relationship. Her parents took the view that the parties should marry. The Supreme Court held that where the decision to marry has been caused by external pressure or influence, whether falsely or honestly applied, to such an extent as to lose the character of a fully free act of that person's will no valid marriage has occurred. But annulment was refused in *L. v L.* (1982), where the parties were older when they met, had lived together and had a child before marriage, and married because of parental pressure. The High Court ruled that without parental persuasion the parties would have married, but not as soon as they did.

Voidable Marriages

The first ground for avoiding a marriage is where either party is without the mental capacity to marry. Mental illness alone is not the sole ground for annulment: the inability to sustain a lasting marriage is required. The High Court held, in *R.S.J. v J.S.J.* (1982), that while the man suffered from some sort of personality defect similar to schizophrenia which made the likelihood of a successful marriage difficult, there was insufficient evidence that on the wedding day he was so incapacitated as to make the marriage voidable. It was proved, in *D. v C.* (1984), that the man suffered from a psychiatric illness, a manic-depressive disorder which resulted in a disturbance in mood states, which affected his personality and behaviour at the time of the marriage. This condition prevented him from entering into an emotional and psychological relationship, which marriage was, and sustaining that relationship. The High Court ruled that the marriage was voidable. In *E. v E.* (1987) the marriage was null and void because at the time of its solemnisation, the man was incapable by reason psychiatric illness of giving a full, free and informed consent, and was incapable of entering into and sustaining a normal marriage relationship.

A homosexual relationship by the man prior to the marriage may not be sufficient reason to annul a marriage. The High Court refused an annulment, in *Mc.D.(Otherwise O'R.) v O'R.* (1984), because the sexual relationship between the parties to the marriage was satisfactory and normal and the marriage had been consummated. But in *F. (Otherwise C.) v C.* (1991), where the man was a homosexual prior to, at the date of, and subsequent to the marriage, had a homosexual relationship, and was of a homosexual nature and temperament, the Supreme Court held that he lacked the capacity to form and maintain a normal marital relationship.

The second ground for avoiding a marriage is impotency, which is the inability to perform the act of sexual intercourse. Impotence must exist at the time of marriage, may be physical or psychological in nature, and must be incurable. Impotency occurring after the marriage is not a ground for nullity. An absolute impotency, that is the inability to have sexual intercourse *simpliciter*, renders a marriage invalid, as in *N. v C.* (1985), where the man regarded the sexual act as wrongful and repugnant, was unable to bring himself to perform the act and was unable psychologically to overcome this attitude. The inability of the man to inseminate the woman was not, in *M.(Otherwise G.) v M.* (1986), a ground for annulment.

An annulment may be sought on the ground of a qualified impotency, that is the inability to have sexual intercourse with the partner of the alleged marriage. The parties, in *S. v S.* (1976), had intercourse before the marriage and the man had intercourse with other women after the marriage but not with his partner of the alleged marriage. This was due, not to any perverseness or wilfulness, but to a revulsion he felt towards his partner which had begun shortly before the marriage. The Supreme Court granted nullity. The High Court annulled the marriage in *R.(Otherwise W.) v W.* (1980), where the parties had intercourse before marriage but failed to consummate the marriage due to the woman's invincible repugnance to her partner's advances. This revulsion was not to intercourse *per se* because the woman had formed a relationship with another man and had a child.

DIVORCE

Nature of Divorce

Divorce *a vinculo matrimonii* is the judicial termination of a valid marriage other than by death. The marriage is thereby dissolved and each party may marry again.

Grounds for Divorce

The *Family Law (Divorce) Act 1996* provides that the High Court or the Circuit Family Court may grant a decree of divorce where it is satisfied that, at the date of the institution of the divorce proceedings, the spouses have lived apart from one another for a period of, or periods amounting to, at least four years during the previous five years, that there is no reasonable prospect of a reconciliation between the spouses, and that such provision as the court considers proper, having regard to the circumstances, exists or will be made for the spouses and any dependent members of the family. A divorce may only be granted where either of the spouses is domiciled (see page 11), or was ordinarily resident throughout the previous year, in this State.

Alternatives to Divorce and Reconciliation

There is a duty on a solicitor acting for either party in divorce proceedings to discuss with the party the possibility of reconciliation, and to give the names and addresses of persons qualified to help effect a reconciliation between spouses who have become estranged, and to discuss the possibility of engaging in mediation to help effect an agreed separation (see page 281), and ensure that the party is aware of judicial separation (see page 280) as an alternative to divorce. The court may adjourn proceedings to allow spouses to consider the possibility of a reconciliation, with or without the assistance of a third party.

Recognition of Foreign Divorces

The *Domicile and Recognition of Foreign Divorces Act 1986* provides that a foreign divorce will be recognised in this State if either spouse is domiciled (see page 11) in a jurisdiction which granted it. The High Court decided, in *L.B. v H.B.* (1980), that a foreign divorce obtained by fraud would not be recognised.

Recognition of Foreign Ancillary Orders

A separate issue is whether our courts should recognise ancillary orders made subsequent to foreign decrees of divorce. In recent years the courts recognised and enforced in this State such ancillary orders obtained elsewhere. For example, in *G. v G.* (1984), an ex-wife successfully sued her ex-husband in this country, the parties having separately moved here, for maintenance for their child on foot of an American court order made eighteen months before the couple's divorce decree was granted. This judicial practice has been reinforced by the *Family Law Act 1995* which empowers the courts to make certain ancillary orders, such as maintenance orders, in certain circumstances, following the granting of a foreign divorce or legal separation which would be recognised in this country.

JUDICIAL SEPARATION

Nature of Judicial Separation

The courts may grant a decree of judicial separation which relieves the parties from the obligation to cohabit. This decree neither dissolves the marriage nor entitles either party to remarry. With the introduction of a no-fault divorce law it is likely that the reliance on judicial separation by spouses in difficult matrimonial situations will decrease in number and importance as a matrimonial remedy.

Grounds for Judicial Separation

The *Judicial Separation and Family Law Reform Act 1989* sets out the grounds on which judicial separation may be granted. The first ground is adultery which is voluntary sexual intercourse during the subsistence of a valid marriage with a person of the opposite sex who is not the spouse. Where spouses have lived together for more than a year after it became known that one had committed adultery, the other spouse is not entitled to rely on the adultery to obtain relief, though it may be one of the factors which may be relied on together with other matters. Where the defending spouse proves that the adultery was committed with the connivance of the other spouse, the court may refuse the application.

The second ground is that a spouse has behaved in such a way that the other spouse cannot reasonably be expected to live with that spouse. Severe alcoholism in either spouse, or pregnancy by a man other than the husband probably constitutes unreasonable behaviour. The High Court granted relief where the wife proved, in *Murphy v Murphy* (1962), that her husband constantly beat her, locked her out of the family home and refused to maintain her and the children. The High Court granted relief in *McA. v McA.*(1981) on the ground of cruelty though there were no acts of physical violence. The acts complained of were failure to communicate, the refusal to co-operate in trying to resolve their marital difficulties and the withdrawal of all emotional feelings. Where the spouses have cohabited for a period or periods after the date of the occurrence of the final incident relied on and held by the court to support an allegation of unreasonable behaviour, such cohabitation shall be disregarded in determining the issue where the length of the cohabitation was six months or less.

The third ground is desertion for a continuous period of at least a year. Desertion includes conduct on the part of a spouse which results in the other spouse, with just cause, leaving and living apart from that other spouse.

The fourth ground is where the spouses have lived apart for a continuous period of at least a year and the other spouse consents to a decree being granted.

The fifth ground is where the spouses have lived apart for a continuous period of at least three years. In computing these periods no account must be taken of any period not exceeding six months, or any two or more periods not exceeding six months in all, during which the spouses resumed living with each other, though this rule only applies where the spouses are living apart when the application is made. Spouses are to be treated as living apart unless they are living with each other in the same household.

The sixth ground is where the marriage has broken down to the extent that the court is satisfied in all the circumstances that a normal marital relationship has not existed between the spouses for a period of at least one year immediately preceding the date of the application.

Alternatives to Legal Separation and Reconciliation

There is a duty on a solicitor acting for either party in judicial separation proceedings to discuss with the party the possibility of reconciliation, and to give the names and addresses of persons qualified to help effect a reconciliation between spouses who have become estranged, and to discuss the possibility of engaging in mediation to help effect a separation on an agreed basis with an estranged spouse, and to discuss with the party the possibility of effecting a separation by the negotiation and conclusion of a separation agreement. The court may adjourn proceedings to allow spouses to consider the possibility of a reconciliation, with or without the assistance of a third party.

Rescission of Judicial Separation Decree

Either spouse may at any future date apply to the court to rescind the decree of judicial separation. Such an order must be made where the court is satisfied that a reconciliation has taken place and that the spouses have resumed or wish to resume cohabiting as husband and wife.

SEPARATION AGREEMENTS

Meaning of Separation Agreement

A separation agreement is made between a husband and wife when each agrees not to molest or interfere with the other, and to dispense with the duty of cohabitation which marriage brings, in return for some consideration. The common law tended not to recognise such agreements because of the cohabitation duty and because such agreements might be an impetus to terminate marriages rather than encourage parties to make successes of their marriages. But in modern times separation agreements are recognised because it is better for the parties to regulate their separation in private rather than in legal proceedings. Statute now recognises such agreements and lays down rules for their enforcement.

Terms of Separation Agreement

Such agreements generally contain terms relating to the living apart of the parties and an acknowledgement that each party will not molest or interfere with the other. Where there are children of the marriage, a term relating to their custody will be inserted. The issue of maintenance will be decided and how family property is to be dealt with will be set out.

Statutory Protection

Because parties to a separation agreement may not be of equal standing, statute has intervened to protect economically vulnerable spouses. The *Family Law (Maintenance of Spouses and Children) Act 1976* enables one spouse to obtain maintenance against the other spouse. Any agreement is void where it excludes or limits the operation of this statute. Separation agreements cannot be used to oust the provisions of this statute and a maintenance order cannot be resisted simply because maintenance has been provided for in the separation agreement.

A separation agreement may be made a rule of court where the court, before which the agreement comes, is satisfied that it is fair and reasonable and protects the interests of both spouses and dependent children.

Chapter 31
THE FAMILY

The Family and the Constitution

Article 41 of the Constitution recognises the family as the natural primary and fundamental unit group of society and as a moral institution possessed of inalienable and imprescriptible rights which are antecedent and superior to all positive law. The State guarantees to protect the family in its constitution and authority as the necessary basis of social order, and as indispensable to the welfare of the Nation and the State.

Definition of Family

The family is not defined in the Constitution. The courts have declared in a number of cases that the constitutional family is based, and exclusively based, on the institution of marriage. 'Unmarried persons cohabiting together and the children of their union', said Walsh J. in the Supreme Court in *The State (Nicolaou) v An Bord Uchtála* (1966), 'may often be referred to as a family and have many, if not all, of the outward appearance of a family and may indeed for the purposes of a particular law be regarded as such, nevertheless so far as Article 41 is concerned the guarantees . . . are confined to families based upon marriage.' This emphasis on marriage also appeared in *In re J., an infant* (1966) where Henchy J. in the High Court explained: 'The first question to be decided is whether the father, mother and child together constitute a family. I am of the opinion that they do. It is true that the child was born illegitimate and, therefore outside a family, but by its parents' marriage it has clearly become a legitimate child of the marriage.' In *Murray v Attorney General* (1985) Costello J. in the High Court said: 'The words used . . . to describe the "family" are . . . apt to describe both a married couple with children and a married couple without children.'

Family Rights

The family is possessed of a collection of rights loosely described as family rights. These include marital privacy in family planning, the right to consort together, the right to procreate, education rights, religious rights, guardianship, adoption, maintenance and succession rights.

An implied constitutional right is that of marital privacy. In *McGee v Attorney General* (1974) in the Supreme Court, Walsh J. explained: 'It is a matter exclusively for the husband and wife to decide how many children they wish to have; it would be quite outside the competence of the State to dictate or prescribe the number of children which they might have or should have ... the husband and wife have a correlative right to agree to have no children ...' The court held unconstitutional a law which prevented married couples from having access to artificial family planning.

Members of a family have the constitutional right to consort together to enjoy each other's company. Many of the express rights belonging to the family are based on this assumption. This right may be curtailed, for example, where a family member is lawfully imprisoned. A father was awarded damages, in *Cosgrove v Ireland* (1982), when passports for the children were granted, in disregard of the father's wishes, and without a court order dispensing with such consent. The mother removed the children from the State thus infringing the father's right to joint guardianship of his children.

Where one, or both spouses are non-citizens, are married, and have lived together in this country for some time, and have children who are Irish citizens, the Supreme Court ruled, in *Fajujonu v Minister for Justice* (1990), that while the State could issue deportation orders, it could only do so on being satisfied, after due and proper consideration, that the interests of the common good and the protections of the State and its society justified an interference with the constitutional right of the children to reside within the State.

The High Court ruled, in *Murray v Attorney General* (1985), that while married couples have a constitutional right to procreate, restrictions placed by the State on the exercise of this right by the spouses, both convicted prisoners serving long prison sentences, were constitutionally permissible.

LEGITIMACY, LEGITIMATION AND ILLEGITIMACY

Meaning of Legitimacy

A person is legitimate where that person's parents were married to each other at the time of conception, or at the time of that person's birth. A child born after the marriage has ended by the death of his or her father is legitimate, as is a person conceived before marriage but born during its continuance.

The *Status of Children Act 1987* provides that any presumption of law as to the legitimacy or illegitimacy of any person is abrogated. The statute introduced new rules in this regard. Where a woman gives birth to a child during a subsisting marriage to which she is a party, or within the period of ten months after the termination by death or otherwise of a marriage to which she is a party, then the husband of the marriage shall be presumed to be the child's father unless the contrary is proved on the balance of probabilities.

Where a married woman who is living apart from her husband, under a decree of divorce *a mensa et thoro* or a deed of separation, gives birth to a child more than ten months after the decree was granted or the deed was executed, her husband shall be presumed not to be the child's father unless the contrary is proved on the balance of probabilities. Where the birth of a child is registered, the person's name entered as the father on the register shall be presumed to be the child's father unless the contrary is proved on the balance of probabilities.

Children born of a void marriage are illegitimate from birth and children born of a voidable marriage are illegitimate from the granting of the annulment (see page 275).

Legitimation

The *Legitimacy Act 1931*, as amended, enlarged the common law definition of legitimacy by introducing the concept of legitimation *per subsequens matrimonium*. An illegitimate child is legitimated by the subsequent marriage of its parents. This rule is subject to the proviso that the father is domiciled in this country at the time of such marriage. The child is legitimated from the date of the marriage and not from the date of birth.

A legitimated child has almost the same rights as a legitimate child though while the latter acquires rights from the moment of birth, the former may only acquire some rights from the moment of the parents' marriage. 'I find it impossible', said Henchy J. in *In re J., an infant* (1966), 'to distinguish between the constitutional position of a child whose legitimacy stems from the fact that he was born the day after his parents were married, and that of a child whose legitimacy stems from the fact that his parents were married the day after he was born. In the former case the child is legitimate and a member of the family from birth by operation of the common law: in the latter case, by operation of the statute, from the date of his parents' marriage. The crucial fact in each case is that the child's legitimacy and consequent membership of the family are founded on the parents' marriage.'

Meaning of Illegitimacy

A child born outside wedlock is illegitimate. At common law such a child was *fillius nullius*, or the child of no one, with no parents and no relations. The legal rights and duties which flowed from the relationship of parent and legitimate child did not attach to either the illegitimate child or its natural parents. Major mitigation of the common law has been enacted in the *Status of Children Act 1987*, though the distinction between legitimate and illegitimate remains.

The Non-Marital Family

As already explained the family protected in the Constitution is that founded on marriage. The non-marital family is a grouping of unmarried parents, or at least not married to each other, and child or children, or a sole unmarried parent and child, or children. While individually each member of such a grouping is possessed of constitutional rights, this group as a unit has no constitutional protection and does not have legal rights to the same extent as the married family, though in recent years legislation has tended to create greater equality between the family founded on marriage and the non-marital family.

The Supreme Court held, in *G. v An Bord Uchtála* (1980), that the unmarried mother had a constitutional right to the custody and control of her child. The unmarried father initially fared worse, though his position is gradually improving. The Supreme Court ruled, in *The State (Nicolaou) v An Bord Uchtála* (1966), that the adoption of an illegitimate child without the father's consent was constitutional, though a change in the law in this regard is contained in the *Adoption Act 1998* which was necessitated by the decision of the European Court of Human Rights in *Keegan v Ireland* (1994) (see page 63).

An illegitimate child has the same constitutional rights as a legitimate child though not necessarily the same legal rights. The law may secure for the illegitimate child legal rights similar to those possessed by legitimate children. The *Status of Children Act 1987* is one such instance where laws have tended to place children on an equal footing.

ADOPTION

Meaning of Adoption

A legal adoption is a procedure by which the rights and duties of the natural parents of a child are extinguished while the equivalent rights and duties become vested in the adoptive parent or parents, to whom the child then stands in all respects as if born to them in lawful wedlock. At common law an irrevocable transfer of the rights and duties of a parent to a stranger was not recognised. But the Oireachtas, by enacting the *Adoption Act 1952*, and amendments, has altered this rule.

The adoption procedure affects three sets of rights and duties. Firstly, the rights and duties of the natural parents over the child are extinguished. Secondly, the status of the child is altered. Thirdly, the adopters acquire rights and duties with regard to the child.

The Adopted Child within the Family

The adoption of a child does not affect the rights of the family as a group or the rights of the natural children of the marriage. 'The adoption of a child by the parents of a family', stated Walsh J. in the Supreme Court in *The State (Nicolaou) v An Bord Uchtála* (1966), 'in no way diminishes for the other members of that family the rights guaranteed by the Constitution. Rights of succession, right to compensation for the death of a parent and such matters may properly be the subject of legislation, and the extension of such rights by legislation to benefit an adopted child does not encroach upon any of the inalienable and imprescriptible rights guaranteed by the Constitution to the family or its members or upon the natural and imprescriptible rights of children . . . .'

Legal Requirements of Adoption

Under the *Adoption Act 1952* adoption was restricted to orphans and illegitimate children, who must be at least six weeks old and, if over the age of seven years, be consulted.

The *Adoption Act 1987* permits the adoption of legitimate children where the parents for physical or moral reasons have failed in their duty towards their children. The Supreme Court advised the President that this Bill was constitutional: *Article 26 and Adoption Bill 1987*. The High Court in authorising an adoption order with regard to a legitimate child, in *Southern Health Board v An Bord Uchtála* (1995), ruled that the child had been the subject of gross physical abuse and neglect over a considerable period of time by his parents and that this was likely to continue until the child attained eighteen years and that this amounted to parental failure. On the other hand, in *Western Health Board v An Bord Uchtála* (1996), an adoption order was not authorised where the father, while having little or no contact with, or control over, the child, was expressly reluctant to give up his daughter and expressly claimed her custody. The court ruled that his conduct did not amount to a total and final abandonment of his rights as a parent.

An adoption order cannot be made where the person is over the age of eighteen years: *Adoption Act 1988*. When considering an adoption application the Adoption Board (An Bord Uchtála) must 'regard the welfare of the child as the first and paramount consideration': *Adoption (Amendment) Act 1974*.

An adoption order cannot be made unless the applicants are a married couple living together; or the applicant is the mother or father or a relative of the child; or the applicant is a widow or widower; or the Board is satisfied that, in the particular circumstances of the case, it is desirable that an adoption order be made in favour of the applicant who is a person not specifically mentioned already. An adoption order cannot be made to a married applicant without the consent of the other spouse, unless the couple are living apart under a decree of divorce *a mensa et thoro*, or a decree of judicial separation, or a deed of separation, or the spouse has deserted the applicant, or conduct on the part of the spouse resulted in the applicant, with just cause, leaving and living separately and apart.

Generally the applicant or applicants must have attained the age of twenty-one years. No upper age limit is set by the law. An adoption order cannot be made unless every person whose consent is necessary knows the religion of the applicant, or applicants. This rule allows the party to refuse consent where the applicant, or applicants, have a different religion to that of the child.

An applicant or applicants must be ordinarily resident in the State, must be of good moral character, have sufficient means to support the child and be a suitable person to have parental rights and duties in respect of the child.

An adoption order cannot be made unless the consent of the child's mother, or guardian or other person having control over the child, is given. The *Adoption Act 1998* provides a procedure for consulting the father of a child born outside of marriage before the child is placed for adoption. A consent is invalid if given before the child is six weeks old, or if given at any time before three months of the adoption application. The nature of this consent was considered by the Supreme Court in *G. v An Bord Uchtála* (1980), the facts of which are given later. According to Walsh J. 'the consent, if given, must be such as to amount to a fully informed, free and willing surrender or an abandonment of these rights'.

Before the final adoption order is made, the consent may be withdrawn. The withdrawal of the consent coupled with the marriage of the child's parents alters the circumstances considerably in that parents and child constitute a family within Article 41 of the Constitution. This occurred in *In re J.H., an infant,* (1985), where the parents sought the return of the child which had been placed for adoption. The Supreme Court ruled that the proper test in such cases was that the best interest of the child was served within the natural family unit except in exceptional circumstances.

The Adoption Board can dispense with consent where it is satisfied that the person whose consent is required is mentally unfit or cannot be found. The *Adoption Act 1974* provides that where a child is placed for adoption and the appropriate person fails, neglects or refuses consent, or withdraws a consent already given, the person or persons who have applied for an adoption order may apply to the High Court for an order authorising the Adoption Board to dispense with such consent. In *G. v An Bord Uchtála* (1980) the baby was born in November, placed for adoption the following January and consent was withdrawn in February after the mother had told her parents of the birth and found them supportive. The Supreme Court refused an order dispensing with consent on the ground that the consent had not been capriciously or irresponsibly withdrawn. However, the High Court in *McC.v An Bord Uchtála* (1982), made an order dispensing with consent where the mother gave two consents, one in February and the other in April, regarding a child born in January, and where the mother sought its return the following June. The Supreme Court ruled, in *M.O'C. v Sacred Heart Adoption Society* (1996), that a mother must be made aware that while she may withdraw her consent or refuse to consent further to the adoption, the possibility existed that the court could conclude that it was in the best interest of the child to dispense with her consent and that she could accordingly lose custody of the child forever.

Recognition of Foreign Adoptions

The *Adoption Act 1991* makes provision for the recognition in this State of certain adoptions effected outside the State. The statute covers two broad classes of foreign adoptions, those effected before 1 July 1991 and those effected thereafter. With regard to foreign adoptions effected after that date, and where the adopter or adopters are ordinarily resident in the State, the Adoption Board must declare in writing before the adoption is effected that it is satisfied the adopter or adopters are persons coming within the classes of persons in whose favour an adoption order could be made in Ireland (set out above), and that an assessment report by the appropriate health board or a registered adoption society has been carried out which complies with the law.

The Adoption Board shall make an entry in the Register of Foreign Adoptions in respect of an adoption effected outside the State to which the Act applies, on an application by the person adopted, or by the adopter or adopters, or any other person having an interest in the matter.

GUARDIANSHIP OF MINORS

Meaning of Guardianship

A guardian is one with charge or custody of another person who is not considered in law capable of managing his or her own affairs. In law a minor is a person who has not attained the age of eighteen years or is or has been married: *Age of Majority Act 1985*, though for guardianship purposes the common law age of twenty-one years remains unaltered. In general the rights and duties relating to minors rest with both parents, where married to each other, but persons, other than parents, may become guardians by appointment in a deed or will, or by an appropriate court.

The Constitution and Guardianship

The family rights contained in Article 41 of the Constitution have been interpreted to grant equality between the parents. This rule was stated in *In re Frost, infants* (1947) when Sullivan CJ. said that the courts 'must regard the family as a unit, the control and management of which is vested in both parents while both are living, and on the death of either of them, in the parent who survives'. The court held that the child also has natural rights under the Constitution and that the courts have jurisdiction, in appropriate cases, to control the exercise of parental rights.

Regulation by Statute

The Supreme Court view in *Frost* and other cases, were reduced into the *Guardianship of Infants Act 1964*, as amended. All matters concerning guardianship and custody of children must be decided on the basis of the welfare of the child and on the constitutional principle that parents have equal right to, and are joint guardians of, their children. This legal right to joint guardianship was breached by the State in *Cosgrove v Ireland* (1982) (see page 284).

Custody Disputes

With regard to the custody of children there are two types of disputes; the first are disputes between parents, and the second are between the parents or parent and a stranger, to use the legal term, though the latter may be a relative of the parents, parent or child. In general young children are given into the custody of the mother. Where the children are older their views as to which parent they would prefer to reside with are considered. The courts have had particular difficulty where the party seeking custody is living in an adulterous relationship. In custody cases the courts must consider the physical, intellectual, religious, social and moral welfare of the children.

In general, parents or a parent, will be granted custody against a stranger or against the State. In *In re O'Brien* (1954) a father who through long-term illness gave his daughter to her grandmother, the mother having died, had his daughter restored to him. Whereas, in *The State (McP.) v G.* (1965) a father was refused custody of his seventeen-year-old daughter given to her maternal aunt when she was an infant of some few months.

But the terms custody and guardianship are not synonymous. 'If one parent is given custody', said Walsh J. in the Supreme Court in *B. v B.* (1975), 'of an infant to the exclusion, whether total or partial, of the other parent, that does not mean that the parent who loses the custody is deprived of the other rights which accrue to him (or her) as guardian of the infant. A parent so deprived of custody can continue to exercise the rights of a guardian and . . . must be consulted on all matters affecting the "welfare" of the child . . . It is when parents do not agree on these matters that it may be necessary to apply to the court. . . .' In that case it was decided that a custody order is interlocutory in nature which may be altered whenever the child's welfare demands.

Guardianship of Illegitimate Children

The *Guardianship of Infants Act 1964* provides that the mother of an illegitimate child is its guardian. It was decided in *G. v An Bord Uchtála* (1980) that the mother of an illegitimate child has a constitutional right to the custody of that child which she may abandon by placing the child for adoption. Under the *Status of Children Act 1987* the court may on the application of the father appoint him guardian of the child. In *K.v W.* (1989) the parties had a relationship which ended shortly after the mother's planned pregnancy was discovered. When the mother placed the child for adoption the father applied for guardianship. The Supreme Court ruled that the statute gave the father a right to apply to be appointed guardian, as distinct from a defeasible right to be guardian, and that the discretion of the court must be exercised regarding the welfare of the child as the first and paramount consideration. Later the High Court refused the application. The European Court of Human Rights has ruled that this law breached the family rights of the father under the European Convention of Human Rights. That case was decided on its facts, particularly the father's absence from the child's nurturing. Where the father has played a role in the child's upbringing, a court might grant a guardianship application.

Access

When custody is awarded to one parent, and the parents are living apart, the court usually grants the right of access at particular times, or on particular occasions, to the other parent. This right of access may be lost through the misbehaviour of the parent to whom it is granted. In the case of an illegitimate child the natural father can apply for the right of access.

Protection Against International Child Abduction

The *Child Abduction and Enforcement of Custody Orders Act 1991*, based on a number of international conventions, has the objective of securing the prompt return of children wrongfully removed or retained, to the State of their habitual residence and to secure protection for rights of access. The culprit is generally a parent who takes the children from one jurisdiction to another jurisdiction.

Where a child has been wrongfully removed or retained, and at the date of the commencement of the legal proceedings a period of less than one year has elapsed from the date of the wrongful removal or retention, the courts in this country must order the return of the child forthwith. Where more than one year has elapsed the courts must order the return of the child unless it is demonstrated that the child was now settled in its new environment. The court is not bound to order the return of the child if there is a grave risk that the return would expose the child to physical or psychological harm, or otherwise place the child in an intolerable situation, or if the child objects to being returned and has attained an appropriate age and degree of maturity.

The courts in this country will not consider the issues of custody and access while a hearing under this statute is pending. Nor are the courts of this country concerned with the correctness or otherwise of custody and access orders made by the courts in the country of the child's habitual residence.

EDUCATION

Constitutional Right of Parents

The Constitution, in Article 42, declares that the primary and natural educator of the child is the family and the State guarantees to respect the inalienable right and duty of parents to provide, according to their means, for the religious and moral, intellectual, physical and social education of their children. Parents are free to provide this education in their homes or in private schools or in schools recognised or provided by the State. The State shall not oblige parents in violation of their conscience and lawful preference to send their children to schools established by the State or to any particular type of school designated by the State but, as guardian of the common good, the State may require children to receive a certain minimum education. 'We are of opinion', said Sullivan CJ. in the Supreme Court in *Article 26 and the School Attendance Bill 1942*, 'that the State, acting in its legislative capacity through the Oireachtas, has power to define [a certain minimum education]... which expression . . . indicates a minimum standard of elementary education of general application.' The court rejected as unconstitutional a statute which permitted the executive arm of government to define such a standard. To the present day the Oireachtas has not laid down a minimum standard of education.

The Constitution provides that in exceptional cases, where the parents for physical or moral reasons fail in their duty towards their children, the State, as guardian of the common good, by appropriate means shall endeavour to supply the place of the parents, but always with due regard for the natural and imprescriptible rights of the child. Thus, where a child has special needs which cannot be provided by the parents, the State is obliged to cater for such needs in order to vindicate the child's constitutional right to free primary education. This was decided by the High Court, in *Comerford v Minister for Education* (1997), where an eleven-year-old child who came from a dysfunctional family was diagnosed as having special needs which could best be catered for in residential care but which had not been provided by the appropriate State agencies.

Parents jointly decide on the education of their children. Where parents are unable to agree, the courts must decide the issue. While the State cannot dictate the education of a child, neither it seems, can anyone else. The High Court, in *Burke v Burke* (1951), declared invalid a condition attached to a gift by will to a child that it be educated in a school of a particular religious denomination because it abrogated the right of parents to educate their children.

Role of the State in Education

Article 42 of the Constitution also provides that the State shall provide for free primary education and shall endeavour to supplement and give reasonable aid to private and corporate educational initiative, and when the public good requires it, provide other educational facilities or institutions with due regard for the rights of parents, especially in the matter of religious and moral formation.

It was clarified by the Supreme Court in *Crowley v Ireland* (1980) that the State's duty is to provide for free primary education and not to provide it. In that case teachers in a school were on strike and the State arranged buses to bring the pupils to and from schools in neighbouring parishes. A pupil unsuccessfully sought an order directing the State to provide free primary education within the parish. Arising from that trade dispute a pupil, in *Conway v INTO* (1991), was awarded damages against the teachers' union which had instructed its members not to accept pupils from the school affected by the strike into their schools thus unlawfully interfering with the pupil's constitutional right to receive free primary education.

In the case of the *Campaign to Separate Church and State Ltd v Minister for Education* (1996), it was decided that the payment out of State funds to chaplains in certain schools to assist in the religious formation of children in accordance with their parents' wishes was constitutionally permissible.

Article 44 of the Constitution provides that legislation granting aid for schools must not discriminate between schools under the management of different religious denominations, nor should such legislation affect prejudicially the right of any child to attend a school receiving public money without attending religious instruction at that school.

RELIGION

Religion and the Family

As already noted the State acknowledges that the family is the primary and natural educator of the child, including religious education. Parents have the constitutional right to decide the religion of their children and the State cannot interfere. The principle was explained by Murnaghan J. in the Supreme Court in *In re Tilson, infants* (1951). 'The parents — father and mother — have a joint power and duty in respect of the religious education of their children. If they together make a decision and put it into practice it is not in the power of the father — nor is it in the power of the mother — to revoke such decision against the will of the other party . . . if a difference between father and mother leads to a situation in which the child is neglected, the State, through the courts, is to endeavour to supply the place of the parents.' In that case the parents were of differing religions and the husband before marriage signed an ante-nuptial agreement that the children would be brought up in the wife's religion. When each of the children were born this agreement was observed until differences arose between the parties. The husband placed the children in an institution of his religion and the wife was awarded custody of the children.

The *Guardianship of Infants Act 1964*, as amended, allows the court to make a custody order which secures the religious upbringing of the children. The High Court decided, in *H. v H.* (1976), among other grounds, to grant custody of a two-year-old boy baptised a Catholic to the father and not to the mother, who had formed an attachment with a Jewish man whom she proposed to marry, had received instruction in that faith and intended to alter the child's religion accordingly.

While the State cannot dictate the religion in which parents are to instruct their children, neither it seems, can anyone else, see *In re Blake* (1955) on page 232.

CHAPTER 32

FINANCE AND PROPERTY

FINANCIAL SUPPORT

Scope of Statutory Regulation

Following the social recognition of marital breakdown over the last decade or so, our legislative code now caters for three such distinct situations. The first, where spouses may continue to live together, or live separately within the one household, or live apart, and the sole issue is maintenance, is governed by the *Family Law (Maintenance of Spouses and Children) Act 1976*. The second, where judicial separation (see page 280) is granted, is governed by the *Family Law Act 1995*. The third, where divorce (see page 278) is granted, is governed by the *Family Law (Divorce) Act 1996*. Since maintenance is quite distinct it is considered separately but because of the almost identical rules governing the various financial arrangements consequent on judicial separation and divorce these are considered together. The rules relating to spouses and ex-spouses, and those rules relating to children are dealt with separately.

The court, when considering financial support orders, shall endeavour to ensure that the arrangements are adequate and reasonable having regard to all the circumstances of the case. In particular it must examine the income, the earning capacity, the property and other financial resources of the spouses and dependent children, including income or benefits to which the spouses or children are entitled by statute, and the financial and other responsibilities of the spouses towards the dependent children.

FINANCIAL SUPPORT OF SPOUSES AND EX-SPOUSES

Maintenance Orders

The *Family Law (Maintenance of Spouses and Children) Act 1976* permits the court to make a maintenance order where it appears that 'the other spouse has failed to provide such maintenance for the applicant spouse as is proper in the circumstances'. The applicant spouse is the maintenance creditor and the spouse ordered to pay maintenance is the maintenance debtor. A husband can claim maintenance from his wife though such applications are rare. With the greater involvement of married women in the labour market, such applications may increase in future years.

The court cannot grant a maintenance order for the support of an applicant spouse who is proved to have deserted the other spouse. Likewise, it has power to rescind a maintenance order already granted if it appears that the maintenance creditor has deserted the maintenance debtor. Desertion is the cessation of cohabitation and consists of two elements, namely, the fact of separation and the intention to desert. The simplest form of desertion is one spouse leaving the matrimonial home and not returning. However, the spouse who physically leaves the other is not necessarily the deserter, because that spouse may be forced to leave by the actions of the other spouse. It is desertion by a spouse if he or she causes the other spouse to live separate and apart. The spouse who intends to bring the cohabitation to an end and whose conduct causes its termination commits the act of desertion. The wife, in *R.K. v M.K.* (1978), left the family home because her husband was insensitive to her, committed adultery during a short period of separation, was uncaring during a pregnancy and unfeeling after the wife was diagnosed as suffering from motor nuerone disease. In the High Court, Finlay P. said: 'I am satisfied that in the civil law of this country . . . in which this marriage took place the obligation of a husband or a wife are not obviated but may be heightened by the sickness of the spouse. From the diagnosis of the wife's illness and her progressive incapacity caused by it the husband showed a gross lack of attention to and sympathy with her real needs which amounted to cruelty justifying her departure from the house.'

Where the applicant has committed adultery, the court may refuse a maintenance order unless the other spouse has connived or condoned or by wilful neglect or misconduct conduced to the adultery. In *L.v L.* (1979), the wife, who committed adultery twice after the parties had separated, was granted maintenance on the ground that her husband had by wilful conduct conduced to the wife's adultery in that he had an adulterous relationship while the marriage was still subsisting. Whereas in *O.C. v T.C.* (1981) a maintenance order was refused to the wife, who was in her own right financially independent and living in America, on the ground that her adultery could not be attributed to any wilful neglect on the husband's behalf.

But the *Judicial Separation and Family Law Reform Act 1989* provides that maintenance may be granted to the adulterous party where the court is of opinion that it would be repugnant to justice not to make such an order.

Financial Orders on Judicial Separation and Divorce

The first order which the court may make following the granting of judicial separation or divorce is a periodic payments order which is similar to a maintenance order. This is the payment of such amounts, during such periods and at such times as is considered reasonable. In some circumstances the court may order that the periodic payments order should be secured, presumably out of assets and property, held by the spouse against whom the order is made.

The second order which a court may make is a lump sum order, which may be paid by instalment, to meet liabilities or expenses reasonably incurred by the other spouse, or ex-spouse.

The third order which a court may grant is a financial compensation order, which is intended to provide for the financial security of the spouse, or ex-spouse. In particular, the court may direct that a policy of life insurance be effected by the other spouse for the benefit of the applicant spouse, or ex-spouse, or that an existing policy be assigned to that spouse, or ex-spouse.

The fourth order which a court may grant is a pension adjustment order which designates a portion of the retirement pension of one spouse for payment to the other spouse, or ex-spouse.

All these orders only continue during the lifetime of the spouse, or ex-spouse, in favour of whom the order has been made. They also cease on the remarriage of that spouse, or ex-spouse, following divorce.

FINANCIAL SUPPORT OF CHILDREN

Maintenance of Children

The *Guardianship of Infants Act 1964*, as amended, provides that a parent in whose custody a child is, can apply to the courts for a maintenance order requiring the other parent to provide financial support for that child. The *Family Law (Maintenance of Spouses and Children) Act 1976* provides that a spouse, when applying for maintenance, may join a claim in relation to dependent children. The *Family Law Act 1995* and the *Family Law (Divorce) Act 1996* make extensive provision for dependent members of the family consequent on the granting of a judicial separation or divorce to their parents.

A dependent member of a family means any child under the age of eighteen years of (a) both spouses or adopted by both spouses under Irish law, or in relation to whom both spouses are *in loco parentis*, or (b) a child of either spouse or adopted by either spouse under Irish law or in relation to whom either spouse is *in loco parentis* where the other spouse, being aware that he or she is not the parent of the child, has treated that child as a member of the family. A child over the age of eighteen years is dependent if receiving full-time education or instruction at any university, college, school or other educational establishment and is under the age of twenty-three years, or is suffering from some mental or physical handicap which prevents the child from maintaining himself or herself fully.

MATRIMONIAL PROPERTY

Right of Both Spouses to Hold Property

At common law a husband was capable of holding property and making contracts. The *Married Women's Status Act 1957* provides that a married woman is competent to acquire, hold and dispose of property, and is capable of contracting, and consequently liable in respect of debts incurred. The current law treats a husband and wife as separate persons for the purposes of acquiring, holding and disposing of property, and of making contracts.

Property in the Name of One Spouse

Few problems arise where spouses come to the marriage with their own separate properties. However, problems do arise where spouses acquire property during the marriage. Where one spouse purchases and maintains the property it remains the sole property of that spouse. Direct contributions by a spouse towards improvements in the family home held in the sole name of the other spouse cannot, in the absence of an express or implied agreement, create any interest in the property, according to the High Court in *W. v W.* (1981). The Supreme Court decided, in *L. v L.* (1992), that a wife who had made no direct or indirect financial contribution to the acquisition of a family home and substantial farm, was not entitled on the basis of her constitutional role as wife and mother in the home to any interest in the property.

A legislative proposal for the creation of mandatory joint equal interests by the spouses in the family home, irrespective of the decisions which may have been jointly made by them with regard to the family home, was held to be repugnant to the Constitution by the Supreme Court because it interfered with the right of a married couple to make a joint decision as to the ownership of the matrimonial home, which was one of the family rights recognised in Article 41 of the Constitution: *Article 26 and the Matrimonial Home Bill 1993.*

Contributions by Both Spouses

Where both spouses have directly or indirectly contributed, in equal or unequal amounts, to the purchase money, or expended money directly or indirectly, in equal or unequal amounts, in the repayment of mortgages, the *Married Women's Status Act 1957* provides that 'disputes between husband and wife as to the title, or possession of, any property' may be resolved as the court thinks proper and just. Resort to this procedure is usually when parties have separated though this is not a prerequisite to seeking the court's assistance. The principles to be applied in such cases were laid down by Kenny J. in the High Court in *C. v C.* (1976). 'In many cases... the wife contributes to the purchase or mortgage instalments. Her contribution may be either by payment to the husband of moneys she has inherited or earned, or by paying the expenses of the household so that he has money which makes it possible for him to pay the mortgage instalments... I think that the correct and most useful approach to these difficult cases is to apply the concept of a trust to the legal relationship which arises when a wife makes payment towards the purchase of a house, or the repayment of the mortgage instalments, when the house is in the sole name of the husband. When this is done, he becomes a trustee for her of a share in the house and the size of that share depends upon the amount of the contributions which she has made towards the purchase or the repayment of the mortgage.' In that case the court held that the wife was the beneficial owner of one half of the house where her contributions, by way of assistance towards the deposit and towards the mortgage instalments, amounted to one half of the purchase price. The Supreme Court decided, in *N. v N.* (1992), that the wife's management of apartments situated in the same building as the family home throughout the entire period of sole ownership by the husband and her contributions to the family fund out of which the mortgages were discharged, entitled her to a one-half share in the property.

Protection of Non-Owning Spouse

At common law a non-owning spouse, unless protected as described in the previous paragraph, never acquired property rights in the matrimonial home owned by the other spouse irrespective of the period of residence. The owning spouse could dispose of the matrimonial home at any time thus 'selling the roof' over the other spouse's head. No notice or consent was necessary. The *Family Home Protection Act 1976* prevents the owning spouse from disposing of the family home without the written consent of the other spouse.

This statute only applies where one spouse has 'any estate, right, title or other interest, legal or equitable' in the family home which is defined as 'primarily, a dwelling in which a married couple ordinarily reside'. The High Court, in *L.B. v H.B.* (1980), held that a house, owned by a company in which the husband was the major shareholder, was the family home. On the other hand, the High Court held, in *C. v C.* (1983), that a house, owned by a company in which the husband had no interest, was not the family home.

Where spouses have an interest in the family home, and agree to dispose of it, one spouse cannot later object to the sale on the ground that a consent in writing had not been obtained. The Supreme Court, in *Nestor v Murphy*

(1979), decided that the purpose of the statute was to prevent a unilateral alienation by one spouse. Where both spouses join in the transaction, the evil which the statute was enacted to prevent does not arise.

Void Disposition

The Act provides that where a spouse conveys any interest in the family home to a third party, such conveyance is void unless the prior consent in writing of the other spouse has been given. The consent must be fully informed and the spouse giving the consent must know to what his or her consent pertains. The Supreme Court so ruled, in *Bank of Ireland v Smyth* (1996), and held that a mortgage of land on which the family home stood was void on the ground that the non-owning spouse believed that the mortgage affected only the land and not the family home despite having given a written consent to the mortgage. This protection cannot be used to defeat the claim of a *bona fide* purchase for value of the family home. This exception may seem to negative the protection, though in practice this is not so because to be *bona fide* the purchaser must make such inquiries and inspections as are reasonable in the circumstances. For example, one spouse may register in the Registry of Deeds the fact that he or she is married to a person owning particular property.

Dispensing with Consent

The Act provides that where a spouse omits or refuses to consent to a disposal of the family home, the court may order the dispensing with such consent. For example, where the non-owning spouse deserts the owning spouse, the court may dispense with the deserting spouse's consent. The High Court, in *R. v R.* (1978), refused to dispense with the consent of the wife, where the husband wished to mortgage the family home to set up another residence, where the marriage had broken down, on the ground that the husband's earnings would be insufficient to repay the mortgage on another house he proposed purchasing.

Additional Protection

Where it appears to the court, on the application of a spouse, that the other spouse is engaging in such conduct as may lead to the loss of any interest in the family home, or may render it unsuitable for habitation as a family home with the intention of depriving the applicant spouse or a dependent child of residence in the family home, the court may make such order as is just and equitable. Before a court could construe the word intention as being equivalent to the implied or imputed intention which can arise from the natural and probable consequences of an act or omission, there must first be an element of deliberate conduct involved. The High Court, in *S. v S.* (1983), per McWilliam J. explained that '. . . the husband appears to have looked after his wife and children to the best of his ability, possibly to a large extent on borrowed money. Although he may have acted improvidently and, possibly, dishonestly, and the natural and probable consequences of his actions may have been that the family home would be a target for his various creditors, it appears to me that it is unlikely that he formed any intention of depriving his wife and children of their residence in the family home and that it is much more likely that he left the country to escape the attention of his creditors and other more distressing pursuers.'

In *G.P.P. v I.H.P.* (1984) the husband was given permission by the High Court to mortgage the family home for the purpose of setting up a business. Instead he applied the money for his own purposes. He was ordered to transfer his interest in the family home to his wife. The parties, in *O'N. v O'N.* (1989), owned the family home in equal shares. The wife left her husband to live with another man and borrowed money to purchase furniture. She failed to repay the loan and a judgment mortgage (see page 265) was registered against her interest in the family home. The High Court held that the wife was putting the family home at risk by making no effort to pay off the debt and the possibility of further borrowings reinforced that conclusion. She was ordered to transfer her share to the husband.

The Act further provides that where it appears that one spouse has by conduct deprived the other spouse or a dependent child of the family home, or rendered it unsuitable for habitation as a family home, the court may order that spouse or any other person to pay proper compensation or to make such order as it may appear just and equitable. In *A.D. v D.D.* (1983) the husband mortgaged the family home with the wife's consent. After the parties separated, the wife consented to its sale, and after repaying the mortgage the balance was to be expended on a house for the wife and children. When the house was sold and the mortgage repaid there was no outstanding balance. The wife sought compensation. Relief was refused because the High Court held that the failure to implement the terms of the agreement arose through lack of finance and not as a result of any action on the part of the husband.

Reliefs on Judicial Separation and Divorce

The court may make, in addition to those outlined above, a number of different orders relating to property consequent on the granting of judicial separation, under the *Family Law Act 1995*, and on divorce, under the *Family Law (Divorce) Act 1996.*

The first such order may confer on a spouse, or ex-spouse, the right to occupy the family home to the exclusion of the other spouse for life or such other specified period. In exercising this jurisdiction the court must consider whether it is not possible for the spouses to continue to reside together and that proper and secure accommodation should, where practicable, be provided for a spouse which is wholly or mainly dependent on the other spouse.

The second such order is a property adjustment order. In such instances, the court may direct a spouse with an interest in any property to either transfer or settle it on the other spouse, or ex-spouse, or any dependent child. This relief extends to all property owned by the spouses, not merely the family home.

The third such relief is for the court to order the sale of the family home and the disposal of the proceeds of the sale between the spouses. In addition, the court may order the sale of any property in which either spouse has an interest and direct how the proceeds are to be dealt with.

Each of these reliefs may only be granted during the life-time of the applicant spouse and is lost on remarriage following divorce.

Barring Orders

At common law an owner of property could not be excluded from it by any known legal process. This rule was eroded in matrimonial matters by the use of the injunction. In *C. v C.* (1976), Kenny J. in the High Court held that: 'the husband's behaviour has been so outrageous and has such a bad effect on the children that I propose to grant an injunction restraining him from entering the matrimonial home although he is the owner of a half share in it . . .'.

The *Family Law (Maintenance of Spouses and Children) Act 1976*, as amended, gives statutory effect to the power to exclude the owner of matrimonial premises from them. The court can grant a barring order, which prevents an owning spouse from entering the family home, even where that spouse is the owner, either wholly or in part. The court can make such order where it is of opinion that there are reasonable grounds for believing that the safety and welfare of the other spouse, and any dependent child of the family, requires it. The Supreme Court, in the leading case of *O'B. v O'B.* (1984), laid down the guidelines for granting a barring order. 'The making of such an order,' said O'Higgins CJ. 'requires serious misconduct on the part of the offending spouse — something wilful and avoidable which causes, or is likely to cause, hurt or harm, not as a single occurrence but as something which is continuing or repetitive in its nature. Violence or threats of violence may clearly invoke the jurisdiction. However, when one enters the area of tension or of mere disharmony in the home, even if clear incompatibility between the two spouses is established, can the existence of such a situation justify one spouse in barring the other merely because the situation would be much easier if only one spouse lived in the house? Or can the fact that the marriage has broken down — even irretrievably — justify the removal from the home of one of the spouses because it is difficult for both to live together in the same house? None of these situations, taken alone, justify the making of a barring order.'

The *Domestic Violence Act 1996* extends the protection of the barring order to persons who have lived together as husband and wife for a period of at least six months in aggregate during the immediate nine-month period and to the parents of children of full age.

Household Allowance

Where one spouse gives the other housekeeping money the property acquired by it, or any money remaining, belonged at common law to the spouse giving it. The *Family Law (Maintenance of Spouses and Children) Act 1976* provides that such money, or property acquired by it, or money remaining, belongs to the spouses as joint owners unless the spouses agreed to some different arrangement.

CHAPTER 33

SUCCESSION

Meaning of Succession

The branch of law governing devolution of property on the owner's death is the law of succession. The Constitution declares that the State guarantees to pass no law abolishing the general right to bequeath or inherit property, though the regulation of such rights ought, in civil society, to be governed by the principles of social justice. The relevant statute law is the *Succession Act 1965.*

The transmission of property ownership from the deceased to the succeeding owner is in two stages. The deceased's property devolves on death, notwithstanding the existence of a will, to personal representatives who subsequently transfer it to the beneficiaries.

Forms of Succession

The succession process takes two forms depending on whether the deceased left a will. The process is known as testate succession, where a will exists, and the personal representatives, known as executors, are appointed by the will. The process known as intestate succession operates where the deceased did not leave a will, or where it cannot be found, or the will made has been declared invalid by the High Court. In such cases the personal representatives, known as administrators, are appointed by the court. Both processes are utilised where a deceased makes a will but fails to dispose of all property. This is known as partial succession.

TESTATE SUCCESSION

Use of a Will

It was impossible by law, prior to 1634, to dispose of property by a document made during a lifetime. The *Statute of Wills (Ireland) 1634* permitted the free passing of property on death in accordance with instructions made during life. The document used is known as a will.

Capacity to Make a Will

A valid will can be made by any person over the age of eighteen years, or who was, or is married, and is of sound disposing mind. It was decided in *In re Mitten* (1934) that, for this purpose, a deaf mute is *prima facie* an insane person. A woman, in *In re Farrell* (1954), executed a will when suffering from two insane delusions. In her doctor's opinion she was, apart from these, capable of transacting other business. The High Court ruled the will valid. But in *In re Corboy* (1969) the will of a person, suffering from stereo-sclerosis for two years prior to its making, was held invalid. The Supreme Court ruled, in *In re Glynn* (1989), that a testator who, before suffering a massive stroke, had given instructions for the drawing up of a will which was executed after the attack, when he was unable to speak or write, fully appreciated that the document on which he placed his mark represented what he wanted done with his property.

Requirements of a Valid Will

Certain formalities must be observed for a will to be valid. It must be in writing. No special words need be used provided the document is intelligible and indicates an intention to be considered a will.

A will must be signed by the testator, that is the person making the will, or by some person in the testator's presence and at the testator's direction. The will of a blind man signed by a neighbour was, in *In re Dowling* (1933), deemed valid. The signature may take any form. It was held, in *In re Kiernan* (1933), that two indecipherable scrawls were sufficient although not the testator's signature, or his usual mark, or his initials. There must be evidence that the signature is that of the deceased. A will was invalid on this ground in *Clarke v Early* (1980) where a document, produced two years after the testator's death, and letters of administration, were not applied for until sixteen years after the death, when both the alleged witnesses were deceased, and there was some evidence that the disputed signature was not the deceased's true signature.

The signature must be at the foot or end of the will. This rule caused difficulty from time to time and the *Succession Act 1965* sets out elaborate provisions permitting a certain amount of latitude.

The testator must make or acknowledge his or her signature in the presence of two or more witnesses, who must be present together. Each witness attests by his or her signature, the signature of the testator in his or her presence, though the witnesses need not sign in each other's presence. The witnesses need not know that they are witnessing a will; all they need know is that they are witnessing a signature.

A witness to a will, and a spouse of that witness, cannot benefit in any way under that will. An executor may act as a witness though, of course, cannot benefit under the will.

Any alteration to a will after its execution, that is its signing and witnessing, is invalid unless executed in like manner. Such alteration needs the testator's signature and that of each witness, who need not be the original witnesses, in the margin or on some part of the will opposite or near the alteration. In *In re Rudd* (1945), an alteration written in the testator's handwriting in different ink and more cramped than the rest and squeezed into a space less than was normally required, was rejected as a valid alteration though the remainder of the will was acceptable.

Revocation

A will is ambulatory in that it is revocable until the testator's death. Revocation is automatic on marriage unless the will was made in contemplation of that marriage. The High Court held, in *In re Baker* (1985), that a will executed in 1951 which left all the testator's property to his future wife, the parties marrying in 1954, was revoked by the marriage because there was no evidence that the will was made in contemplation of that marriage.

A will may be revoked by its destruction, which can be done by tearing or burning, either by the testator or another acting at the testator's direction in the testator's presence. There must be the *animus revocandi*, the intention to revoke it. An accidental tearing or partial burning is not a revocation. The will must be completely destroyed. The High Court, in *In re Bentley* (1930), accepted a will in its mutilated condition where a testator had cut and burned a strip from it. Alterations made after execution of a will, initialled by the testator, but not signed by witnesses, do not effect a revocation of a will or any part thereof. There is a rebuttable presumption that an alteration, obliteration or interlineation was made after execution. The High Court, in *In re Myles* (1993), held that a will was invalid where five of the six paragraphs were crossed out, there were notes in the margins, signed but not witnessed, and a witness was not sure if the deceased had crossed out part of the will before execution, or when the writing in the margins was made.

A will is revoked by a subsequent will, or codicil, a supplement which may add, explain, alter, or retract any clause in the will. It is the usual practice, though not essential, to insert a clause expressly revoking all prior wills. Where the testatrix made two wills on the same day, each containing a revocation clause though with no further evidence to suggest which was made last, as occurred in *In re Millar* (1931), the High Court rejected both wills.

GIFTS UNDER A WILL

Devises

A gift by will of real property is a devise which may be either specific or residuary. It is a specific devise where a gift is made of a particular piece of property to another: thus 'my cottage in Blessington in the County of Wicklow to my son John' is a specific devise. Where part of the real property is disposed of by specific devise, as in the example, and then a disposition is made of any remaining real property by general description, such as 'the residue of my real estate I leave to my daughter Mary', the testator creates a residuary devise.

The distinction is important for various reasons. One is that property not specifically devised forms a fund from which the funeral and other testamentary expenses are payable.

Legacies

A gift by will of personal property is a legacy or bequest. There are different types of legacy. A specific legacy grants a particular piece of property, such as 'all my monies on deposit with the Trustee Savings Bank'. A general legacy is a grant of personal property which has been not distinguished from other personal property of the same kind, such as a bequest of 'one of my paintings'. A bequest 'of my Jack B.Yeats' is a specific bequest where the testator had only one painting by that artist.

A pecuniary legacy is a bequest of money. A demonstrative legacy is satisfied out of a particular part of the personal property, such as a gift of 'one hundred shares to be made out of the shares which I hold in Allied Irish Banks plc'.

Failure of a Gift

A gift of property may fail for a number of reasons. The beneficiary may disclaim it. Where the beneficiary predeceases the testator, the gift fails. There is a major exception to this rule. No lapse occurs where property is given to a testator's child who predeceases the testator, but leaves children of his or her own living at the testator's death. In that event these children take the gift. A gift also fails where the beneficiary is unworthy to succeed, discussed later on page 312. A gift fails where the property devised or bequeathed has been disposed of during the testator's lifetime.

CONSTRUCTION OF A WILL

Intention of Testator

In construing a will the first objective of a court, where a dispute arises, is to give effect to the wishes of the testator as expressed in the will. 'It is a fundamental matter of public policy', said McCarthy J. in the Supreme Court in *In re Glynn* (1989), 'that a testator's wishes should be carried out however, at times, bizarre, eccentric or whimsical they may appear. One man's whimsy is another man's logic.' Words are given their ordinary meaning and technical words or legal expressions are given their technical or legal meaning. Where the will is vague, or where it admits of two constructions, the interpretation which makes the gift operative is preferred.

Extrinsic Evidence

The *Succession Act 1965* provides that extrinsic evidence is admissible to show the testator's intention and to assist in the construction of, or to explain any contradiction in a will. The Supreme Court held, in *Rowe v Law* (1978), that once the meaning of the words used were clear the statute did not authorise the introduction of extrinsic evidence for the purpose of construing the will.

RESTRICTIONS ON DISPOSITION

Freedom of Disposition

At common law the freedom of a testator to dispose of property was absolute. A testator could disinherit a spouse and children to the benefit of a stranger or a charity. Close relatives could be left penniless, homeless and a charge on the State. The *Succession Act 1965* negatives this rule in its application to spouses and children. By virtue of this statute a spouse and children cannot be disinherited: the statutory provisions prevail notwithstanding any contrary intention contained in a will.

Legal Right of Spouse

The share of a testator's estate to which a surviving spouse is entitled is known as the legal right. A surviving spouse is entitled to legal right out of the testator's estate. A dispute may arise as to the identity of a spouse for this purpose. In *Bank of Ireland v Caffin* (1971) the testator had twice married and each of the two surviving 'wives' claimed to be the spouse.

Where the spouse solely survives, the legal right is one-half of the estate. Where there are surviving children the legal right is reduced to one-third of the estate. The legal right takes effect in priority to every gift in a will. The legal right may be renounced in a written ante-nuptial agreement made between the parties to an intended marriage, or it may be renounced in writing after the marriage and during the lifetime of the parties.

A gift to a spouse in a will is taken in satisfaction of the legal right unless such a gift is expressed to be in addition to the legal right. In such a case the spouse must elect whether to take the gift or the legal right. In default of election the spouse is deemed to take the gift and forgo the legal right.

The personal representative must notify the spouse in writing of such an election. The right to elect ceases to be exercisable after the expiration of six months from the receipt by the spouse of such notification, or one year from the first taking out of representation of the deceased's estate, whichever is latest. The Supreme Court ruled, in *O'Dwyer v Keegan* (1997), that the legal right vests automatically in the surviving spouse on the death of the other spouse and is dependent on the surviving spouse having to claim the benefit of that right.

Extinction of the Legal Right

Under the *Family Law Act 1995*, the court, on granting a judicial separation (see page 280), may make an order extinguishing the legal right of a spouse provided adequate and reasonable financial provisions have or can be made, and that spouse has tried and failed to obtain a financial or property order (see page 296) and where it appeared likely that the court would refuse such order to that spouse.

Succession Rights Following Divorce

While the settling of property rights will generally occur on the granting of a divorce, the *Family Law (Divorce) Act 1996* provides that where an ex-spouse dies the other ex-spouse, within a specified time, may apply to the court for provision to be made out of the estate of the deceased ex-spouse. The court may only make such an order if it considers that proper provision had not been made for the applicant ex-spouse during the lifetime of the deceased ex-spouse and must have regard to the rights of other persons to share in that estate. This succession right is lost on remarriage.

Appropriation of Family Home

The *Succession Act 1965* provides the surviving spouse with another important benefit. Where the testator's property includes a dwelling, in which at the time of the testator's death the surviving spouse was ordinarily resident, that spouse may require the personal representatives to appropriate the dwelling, and all household chattels, in satisfaction of the legal right. Dwelling means an estate or interest in a building occupied as a separate dwelling or a part, so occupied, of any building and includes any garden or portion of ground attached to and usually occupied with the dwelling or otherwise required for the amenity or convenience of the dwelling. In *Hamilton v Armstrong* (1984) a surviving spouse sought to appropriate a bungalow and a surrounding five acre field. The claim to the field was resisted. The High Court appropriated the field because the septic tank serving the bungalow was situated there, together with the well from which water was piped to the house. The deceased, when retired, used the field to fatten some cattle to supplement the family income.

The right to appropriate the dwelling cannot be exercised where the dwelling is held together with agricultural land, or is part of a hotel, guest or boarding house, or where a part of the dwelling was, at the time of the testator's death, used for purposes other than domestic purposes. Such a claim may be allowed by the High Court where it is satisfied that the exercise of the right is unlikely to diminish the value of the property, other than the dwelling, or make it more difficult to dispose of all the property. The surviving spouse failed, in *H. v H.* (1978), to have the dwelling appropriated where it was bordered by 114 acres of farm land.

Provision for Children

Where an application is made by a testator's child or children for provision to be made out of the testator's property, the High Court may make whatever order it considers just in the circumstances The court acts where it is of opinion that the testator failed in his or her moral duty to make provision for the child in accordance with the testator's means. The application is considered from the point of view of a prudent and just parent, taking into account the position of each of the testator's children. The scope of this moral duty was explained in *F.M. v T.A.M* (1970) in the High Court by Kenny J.: 'The obligation to make proper provision may be fulfilled by will or otherwise and so gifts or settlements made during the lifetime of the testator in favour of a child or the provision of an expensive education for the child when the others have not received this may discharge the moral duty. It follows . . . that the relationship of parent and child does not of itself and without regard to other circumstances create a moral duty to leave anything by will to the child.' In that case the court held there was a failure of moral duty where the testator left nothing to his only son, who was informally adopted in 1941 and legally adopted in 1954, and whose education and upkeep were provided by the testator's wife.

The High Court held, in *In re N.S.M.* (1973), there was a failure of moral duty where the testator with a wealthy estate excluded his two married daughters on the ground that they were adequately provided for. The High

Court, in *L.v L.* (1984), held that there was a failure of moral duty where a testator, who had provided no assistance towards the maintenance or education of his only daughter during her lifetime because the parties to the marriage had separated within two years of the marriage, and had left his daughter only £2,000 in his will.

Such an order to benefit a child, or children, cannot be made where it diminishes the legal right of the surviving spouse, or any devise or bequest to that spouse or any share to which that spouse is entitled on intestacy. An application must be made within twelve months from the first taking out of representation to the deceased's estate.

INTESTATE SUCCESSION

Meaning of Intestacy

A person dies intestate where he or she dies without leaving a will, or where it cannot be found, or where the will was declared invalid by the High Court. On partial intestacy, where a will exists but not all the property is disposed of under it, the remainder is distributed as if the deceased died intestate.

Distribution on Intestacy

The *Succession Act 1965* provides that the property to which a deceased was entitled is to be distributed, after all debts and testamentary expenses are paid, in accordance with the statute where a deceased dies intestate. The statute sets out a detailed set of statutory rules for the distribution of an intestate estate.

Where there are no children the surviving spouse takes all the property. Where there are children the spouse takes two-thirds and the remainder is divided equally among the children. Where there is no surviving spouse and only children, the property is divided equally among them.

Where the intestate dies without leaving a spouse or children, the property is divided equally between the deceased's parents, where both survive the deceased. Where one parent survives, that parent takes all the property.

Where the deceased dies without leaving a spouse, children or parents, the property is divided equally between brothers and sisters. Where any brother or sister predeceases the deceased but leaves children, the parent's share is divided equally between them. Where no brother or sister survives the property is divided equally among the surviving nephews and nieces.

Where the deceased dies without leaving a spouse, children, parents, brother, sisters, nephews or nieces, the property is divided equally among the next-of-kin, which are persons who, at the deceased's death, stood nearest in blood relationship.

In default of any person taking the property, the State, as ultimate intestate successor, takes it, though the Minister for Finance may waive this right on behalf of the State in favour of any person as is thought proper in all the circumstances.

Advancement

Any advancement made to a child during the intestate's life must be brought into account, or into hotchpot as it is known, when reckoning the share of that child. An advancement includes a gift to establish the child in a profession, trade or business; a portion on the child's marriage; and payments made towards the child's education to a standard higher than that provided for the deceased's other children. A father, in *Baines v McLean* (1934), bought a ticket in a sweepstake and for luck inserted his young daughter's name. When the ticket won a prize the father claimed that his daughter held the prize in trust for him. The court held that the ticket was an advancement and accordingly the prize money was the daughter's property.

The value of an advancement is calculated at the date it was given. Where the value is greater than, or equal to the child's share on intestacy, that child receives no further benefit. Where the value is less than the child's share, the child only benefits by the difference between the two.

UNWORTHINESS TO SUCCEED

Preclusion from Inheritance

The *Succession Act 1965* precludes categories of persons from inheriting a deceased's estate on the ground of unworthiness to succeed. These preclusions exist because it is considered to be contrary to the common good to permit succession in such circumstances. The deceased's property is distributed, in such cases, as if the person in question had predeceased the deceased. These rules of preclusion apply to both testate and intestate succession.

A sane person, guilty of murder, attempted murder, or manslaughter of the deceased cannot benefit from that deceased's estate unless a will, leaving the culprit a share, was executed after the offence was committed. A child guilty of having committed any of these offences against a parent is precluded from applying to the High Court to have provisions made out of that parent's estate. Any person guilty of any offence against the deceased, his or her spouse, or child, which is punishable by imprisonment for a maximum of at least two years, or a more severe penalty, is precluded from taking any share in the estate of the deceased.

A spouse guilty of desertion (see page 280) is precluded from claiming any benefit from the deceased's estate.

ADMINISTRATION OF ESTATES

Nature of Administration of Estates

The administration of estates is concerned with the administration of the deceased's property from the moment of death. The process involves the collection of all property owned by the deceased, the payment of funeral, testamentary and other debts, and the distribution of the property amongst the persons entitled under the statute, the will, or on intestacy.

Personal Representatives

It is a fundamental principle of law that property should never be without an owner. When a person possessed of property dies, that property immediately devolves on the deceased's personal representatives. Where the deceased died testate, the property devolves on executor(s) appointed by the deceased in the will. Where the deceased died intestate, or where the executors appointed by the will have predeceased the deceased, the property vests in the President of the High Court until personal representatives, known as administrators, are appointed.

Grant of Representation

Prior to executing any function, the personal representatives must obtain a grant of representation. Where the deceased died testate, a grant of probate is necessary. Letters of administration are granted where the deceased died intestate.

The jurisdiction over the property of deceased persons is vested in the High Court. To seek a grant of probate, application is made to the Probate Office in Dublin, or to a District Probate Registry in which the deceased had a fixed abode at the time of death. The original will must be deposited when the application is made.

The High Court has jurisdiction to grant letters of administration to whomsoever it thinks fit, but every person to whom this grant is made must lodge an administration bond, obtained from an insurance company approved by the President of the High Court, generally twice the value of the estate.

All matters of contention arising during the administration of an estate must be referred to the High Court for decision. The Circuit Court has concurrent jurisdiction in certain aspects of the administration of estates.

Personal Representatives are Trustees

The personal representatives hold the property in trust for those entitled to it under the statute, or a will, or on intestacy. They are also trustees for the deceased's creditors. The rules which apply to trustees are applied to personal representatives (see page 238).

Duties and Powers of Personal Representatives

The first duty of the personal representatives, having gathered in as much of the property as they can, is to pay debts and discharge the liabilities of the deceased together with the funeral and other testamentary expenses. A clause to the contrary in a will is void.

The next duty is to distribute the estate amongst those entitled. It is a rule that personal representatives have a year from the deceased's death to complete the administration and cannot be sued by a beneficiary within the executor's year.

The actual transfer of the property to the beneficiaries from the personal representatives is by way of assent. Where the estate consists of personal property the assent may be verbal coupled with delivery of the property. Where the estate consists of real property the assent must be in writing.

The personal representatives may sell all, or any, of the property which may be necessary to discharge the deceased's liabilities or to facilitate the distribution of the estate. Before this is done the wishes of the beneficiaries must be ascertained, provided they are adults. Where agreement cannot be reached, the wishes of the majority, according to their combined interests, prevail.

A *bona fide* purchaser of any property from personal representatives holds that property free from all claims made by beneficiaries entitled to it. The purchaser is not under a duty to ensure that the purchase money is properly applied. The claim of the beneficiaries is overreached and from then on attaches to the purchase money. Apart from selling the property, the personal representatives may grant leases and may mortgage it. They have power to settle claims and disputes in relation to the property.

A debtor of the deceased making a payment to the personal representatives under a grant of representation is indemnified and protected despite any defect in the grant. This protection is only available where the debtor acts *bona fide.* Where a grant is revoked by the court, all payments made in good faith to the personal representatives, before the revocation, are a valid discharge of those debts.

Tracing Property

The *Succession Act 1965* confers power on the High Court to deal with a disposal of property which was made by the deceased with the purpose of defeating, or substantially diminishing, the legal right of a spouse, or the share of a child. The court may order that such property is to form part of the deceased's estate and that the party who took the property from the deceased is to be a debtor of the estate. Where the party who took the property purchased it, the order may instead be made against the purchase money.

The *Succession Act 1965* also grants an important protection to creditors of the deceased. They may follow the property after it has been distributed to the beneficiaries. Where the personal representatives have conveyed the property to any person, other than a *bona fide* purchaser for value, the property, so long as it remains vested in that person, remains liable to answer the deceased's liabilities.

Part Eight
BUSINESS LAW

Chapter 34
AGENCY

Nature of Agency

For practical and commercial reasons the common law permitted a party to act through an agent. The maxim *qui facit per alium facit per se*: he who does something through another does it through himself, was applied. Exceptions exist to this general rule. The law of agency has no application in a contract which requires personal performance. For example, where an employment contract exists, an ill employee cannot send a relative to do the work. Moreover, some statutes require an action to be personally performed. For example, the *Consumer Credit Act 1995* provides that the hirer must sign the agreement in person (see page 361).

Definition of Agency

Agency is the relationship which arises when one party, called the agent, acts on behalf of another party called the principal, and which affects the legal position of the principal with regard to a third party. An agent in practice is a party employed to bring the principal into contractual relations with a third party. The most important and vital feature of agency is this power to effect the relations of the principal with third parties. Generally, once the agent has performed the contracted task, the agent departs and the principal and third party continue with the contract. Thus, a travel agent, acting on behalf of an airline, brings the principal and customer into contractual relations. Once the ticket is sold the agent drops out and subsequent relations are directly between the airline and the passenger.

Formalities for Creating Agency

Generally, the law does not require any particular formality to be observed in the appointment of an agent. It may be created verbally, or in writing or by conduct. The major exception exists where an agent is appointed to execute a deed. In such a case the agency must also be created by deed which is known as a power of attorney (see page 260).

Capacity and Consideration

Because an agent does not contract on his or her own behalf, the agent is not required to have full contractual capacity. A minor appointed an agent binds the principal, though the minor may avoid the contract with the principal under the general rules of contract law (see page 101). The principal must have the capacity to make the particular contract. Can a minor appoint an agent? It seems so, though the minor may avoid the contract during minority, or within a reasonable time after reaching majority, provided the contract is harsh and oppressive.

In most instances of agency there is some agreement, either express or implied, as to payment by the principal of the agent. But consideration is not essential and the courts have recognised gratuitous agencies.

Kinds of Agency

Universal agency occurs where a principal appoints an agent to handle all his or her affairs. This is rare though it may happen where a person is going abroad for a lengthy period. A general agency occurs where the principal appoints the agent to represent him or her in all matters of a particular kind. Such an agent has implied authority to represent the principal in all matters incidental to the agency. For example, a sporting or show business personality may appoint an agent to manage his or her business affairs. Such an agent has no role in the principal's personal affairs.

A special agent is appointed by the principal for a particular purpose and the authority given is confined to matters directly affecting that purpose. For example, an auctioneer may be retained to find a purchaser for the principal's property. No multiplication of acts as a special agent converts a special agent into a general agent. In *Barrett v Irvine* (1907) a horse was sold to a minor on the representation that his mother would pay for it. The minor had on former occasions, to the seller's knowledge, purchased horses for which his mother afterwards paid. In an action against the mother for the price, it was contended that the mother's conduct in relation to her son's former purchases constituted him her general agent for the purchase of horses. The action was dismissed as there was no evidence of general agency in the son.

CREATION OF AGENCY

Express Authority

An express authority may be given by the principal to the agent either verbally or in writing. The extent of an agent's express authority depends on a true construction of the words of appointment. Where these are vague or ambiguous the principal may be bound where the agent, in good faith, interprets them in a manner not intended by the principal.

Implied Authority

An agent has implied authority to do everything necessary for, or incidental to, the execution of the express authority. An implied agency may arise because of a particular relationship. At common law the law implied an agency in favour of a wife living with her husband, whereby she was entitled to pledge his credit to purchase necessaries, though this may no longer be applicable in modern times.

Usual Authority

Where an agent carries on a particular trade, profession or calling, the agent has an implied authority to perform such acts as are usual in that trade, profession or calling. This is also known as customary authority. The principal is bound by the custom even if unaware of it. Usual authority also applies where the agent is employed to perform the act in a particular place. In such cases the usual rules or customs of the place apply unless these are unreasonable or unlawful. An example of an agent dealing in a particular place is a stockbroker dealing in the Stock Exchange.

Apparent Authority

Where a party represents to another that he or she has authorised an agent to act on his or her behalf, that party will not be allowed to deny the truth of that representation and will be bound by the agent's act whether it is authorised or not. This is known as apparent or ostensible authority. The parties, in *Kilgobbin Mink & Stud Farms Ltd v National Credit Co. Ltd* (1980), in compromising legal proceedings, agreed to the surrender of a lease in return for a payment. When the plaintiff's chairman delivered possession of the premises to the defendant he directed that the money be paid to another company which was a subsidiary of the plaintiff. When a receiver was appointed to the plaintiff company he claimed that the defendant continued to be indebted to the plaintiff. In dismissing the claim, the High Court held that the chairman had apparent authority to request the defendant to pay the money to the other company and that the plaintiff was estopped from revoking that authority.

The High Court stressed in *Essfood Eksportlagtiernes Sallgforening v Crown Shipping (Ireland) Ltd* (1991) that the representation must be made by the principal and no representation by an agent can amount to a 'holding out' by the principal. In that case the contract entered into by a carrier with the defendant was entered into pursuant to a contractual obligation owed to the plaintiff to ensure that the goods were shipped to Japan. It was not made under any relationship of agency existing between the carrier and the plaintiff. Therefore, the defendant could not rely on any liability arising from the doctrine of ostensible authority (see page 206 for other cases on agency).

Authority by Necessity

A party who acts to save the property of another, or to perform some obligation of another, may as a matter of law have authority of necessity. There is no express or implied authority to perform the act in question. For the agent's action to be binding on the principal four conditions must be present. Firstly, there must be a genuine emergency; secondly, it must be impossible to obtain the authority of the principal before the action is performed; thirdly, the action must be done in good faith; and fourthly, the action must be done for the benefit of the principal and not simply for the convenience of the agent.

An agency of necessity arises where a party goes to the aid of a ship in distress at sea and saves life or property: that party is entitled to a reward. In *Walsh v Bord Iascaigh Mhara* (1981) the crew of the Valentia lifeboat saved a trawler which was drifting towards rocks off the Kerry coast, after the engine had failed in a moderate sea driven by a gale force 6. The crew was awarded £1,500 salvage.

Agency by Ratification

Where a properly appointed agent exceeds authority, or a person having no authority purports to act as an agent, the principal incurs no liability on the concluded contract. But in such situations the principal may ratify the transaction and consequently becomes liable and bound by it. It is a case of express authority given after the event has occurred.

For ratification to operate successfully a number of conditions must be satisfied. The principal must have been in existence when the act was performed; the principal must have been identified by name, or other means, because an undisclosed principal can never ratify; the principal must have had full contractual capacity at the time the agent made the contract and at the time of ratification. A principal cannot ratify a contract unless aware of all the material facts. A valid ratification is generally retrospective to the date of the original act.

A solicitor was engaged by a bank, in *Barclay's Bank v Breen* (1962), to act on its behalf in dealing with the legal formalities in connection with the disposal of a property. The solicitor sold the property, issued a receipt for the deposit, and having been paid the balance became insolvent. He had only paid part of the balance to the bank and the bank claimed the remainder of the price from the purchaser. The purchaser claimed he had paid the full price to the solicitor as the bank's agent. The Supreme Court, in granting specific performance, held that even if the solicitor had no actual authority, the bank, with knowledge of the facts, had ratified the transaction by accepting the deposit.

In *Brennan v O'Connell* (1980) an estate agent, having procured a purchaser for a farm, entered into a written agreement to sell without the authority of the principal. However, when the principal was informed of these events he replied that he was well pleased though when he expressed his approval he did not know that there had been another inquiry about the property. When he discovered this fact he refused to complete the sale and the purchaser sought specific performance. The Supreme Court granted the order holding that the ratification of the contract was not invalidated by the principal's ignorance of the inquiry.

Nature of Scope of Agency

When an agent makes a contract on behalf of the principal with a third party, the transaction gives rise to legal effects between (a) the principal and the agent; (b) the principal and the third party; and (c) the agent and the third party.

PRINCIPAL AND AGENT RELATIONSHIP

Duties of the Agent

Where the agency is based on contract the agent is bound to perform the agency in accordance with its terms. Where that is not done the agent is liable to the principal in damages. An agent is never required to perform an illegal act. Where the agency is gratuitous the agent is not liable for a failure to perform its terms, though once the agent begins to perform them liability attaches for failure to complete.

An agent must exercise due care and diligence on behalf of the principal: *spondes pertiam artis*, a person professing a special skill must show an appropriate degree of skill. Insurance brokers, in *Chariot Inns Ltd v Assicurazioni Generali SPA* (1981), employed by a publican, advised the principal not to disclose certain information on an insurance proposal form. When the insurers avoided the policy after a fire in the premises, the insurance brokers were held liable in negligence to the principal (see also page 368).

An agent must disclose to the principal any material information acquired while performing the agency. The complementary duty of not disclosing to others confidential information entrusted to the agent by the principal exists.

Because the relationship of principal and agent is essentially one where the personal quality and particular skill or trust are vital, the general rule is that the agent must perform the obligations personally. The agent cannot delegate: *delegatus non potest delegare*, a delegate cannot delegate. This restriction is not strictly applied and the agent may, with the principal's permission or in the interest of commercial necessity, delegate.

An agent stands in a fiduciary relationship with the principal. It follows that the agent must act in good faith and not allow a situation to occur where duty to the principal conflicts with personal interest. In the absence of full disclosure, therefore, an agent who is employed to sell cannot sell to himself or herself and an agent employed to buy cannot buy from himself or herself. Should an agent be permitted to make a secret profit, or to take a bribe, self-interest would be in conflict with duty.

An agent is bound to pay to the principal all sums received in the course of the agency. In order to do so, proper accounts must be kept and the principal's property should be held separately from the agents.

Remuneration

The agent can only claim remuneration where there is an express or implied term to that effect in the contract. The amount of remuneration depends on the terms of the contract. In default of an agreed sum, a reasonable sum is payable.

Frequently payment is by commission and claims for commission, especially by auctioneers, have been litigated on frequently. To help resolve this problem the court will ask two questions: has the actual event contracted for happened, and if it has was the agent the cause of that happening? Where the answer to both questions is yes, the agent is entitled to the agreed commission. In *Stokes & Quirke Ltd v Clohessy* (1957) the owner of a house instructed auctioneers to sell it. The auctioneers introduced a prospective buyer who agreed to purchase subject to certain repairs being carried out by the seller. Before a formal agreement was signed, the seller received a more advantageous offer from a person not introduced by the auctioneers which the seller accepted. A claim for commission failed because the High Court held that the contract between the parties provided for payment only where the auctioneers introduced a buyer who would actually complete the sale or sign a binding contract to do so. Since the auctioneers had not introduced such a person, the claim failed. In *Murphy, Buckley & Keogh Ltd v Pye (Ireland) Ltd* (1971) the seller of a factory appointed auctioneers its 'sole agents' in the sale. The day before this agreement the eventual purchaser made a first tentative enquiry from the seller and a sale was negotiated without informing the auctioneers. The auctioneers claimed commission. The High Court dismissed the claim because the auctioneers' exertions as sole agents had not played any part in effecting the sale, nor did the agreement contain any express term forbidding the seller to negotiate a sale during the continuance of the auctioneers' agency.

But in *Cusack v Bothwell* (1943) an auctioneer was instructed to find a buyer for lands. The agent was to receive a commission of 5 per cent. The agent introduced a buyer but the seller refused to sell and refused to pay the commission. The court gave the auctioneer a sum equivalent to 5 per cent of the fixed price because the auctioneer had done what was required of him. In *Henehan v Courtney* (1967) an auctioneer, who had effected the introduction of a buyer to the seller, was entitled to reasonable remuneration for work done where the parties had not expressly agreed terms.

A commission cannot be paid if the result would be to breach a statute. In *Somers v Nicholls* (1955) the plaintiff, having introduced a buyer to the defendant who was selling a hotel, sued for a commission. The High Court dismissed the claim because the plaintiff was not licensed to act as a house agent as required by the *Auctioneers and House Agents Act 1947.*

Remedies of the Principal for Breach of Duty by Agent

Where the agency is based on contract an agent in breach of its terms may be sued by the principal for damages for loss incurred. Where a secret profit had been made by the agent, the principal may sue for it. The principal may dismiss an agent in breach of the agency and is not bound to compensate the agent for loss of contract. Whether the principal must pay the agent for work already done will depend on the terms of the contract.

Duties of the Principal

Where an agent incurs liability, financial or otherwise, in the performance of the agency the principal must indemnify the agent unless the contract excludes such liability. Of course there can be no indemnity where the acts which incurred the liability were outside the scope of the agency, or where the liability arose because of the fault of the agent. The principal is not liable for the deceit of the agent. In *United Dominions Trust (Ireland) Ltd v Shannon Caravans Ltd* (1976) an employee of a hire-purchase company designed a scheme whereby a third party could obtain finance to purchase a van. This involved the defendant in the pretence that it was the owner of the van and on its sale to the hire-purchase company the latter would let it to the third party. The money obtained would be given to the third party so that the defendant never profited in any way. When the third party defaulted and the hire-purchase company became aware of the true facts, it sued the defendant who claimed that the company was bound by the deceit of its agent. The Supreme Court rejected this defence. It held that the agent was privy to an act of deceit against the principal and that the knowledge of that deceit could not be imputed to the principal.

THE PRINCIPAL AND THIRD PARTY RELATIONSHIP

Privity Between Principal and Third Party

Once an agent makes a contract on behalf of the principal, the agent generally drops out of the transaction and privity of contract exists between the principal and the third party. But the effect of a contract may depend on the actual circumstances of the particular case.

Rights of Principal

The rights of a principal against a third party depend in part on the distinction between disclosed principal and undisclosed principal. A disclosed principal is one whose existence the third party was aware of at the time of contracting. The principal is a named principal where the third party also knows his or her name, and is an unnamed principal where the third party is ignorant of that information. The general rule is that a disclosed principal can sue the third party.

An undisclosed principal is one of whose existence the third party is unaware at the time of contracting. An undisclosed principal can, in general, sue the third party.

Rights of Third Party

Under the doctrine of undisclosed principal the third party can either sue the agent or the principal, when the third party becomes aware of the identity of the principal. In *O'Keeffe v Horgan* (1897) the defendant ordered articles of furniture on credit which were fitted up in a room in a relative's house in which he was working. At the time of purchasing the goods he did not inform the seller of his agency. The seller successfully maintained an action against the defendant. The third party cannot sue both principal and agent. A seller of goods, in *Jordie & Co. v Gibson* (1894), obtained judgment for the price. At that time he was unaware that the buyer was acting as his father's agent. When he unsuccessfully attempted to enforce the judgment against the son, because of lack of goods, he sued the father. The case was dismissed. The court held that the right of election to sue either the agent or principal is determined where either is sued to judgment though the fact of the agency was not discovered until after the date of judgment.

THE AGENT AND THIRD PARTY RELATIONSHIP

The general principle, already explained, is that the agent can neither sue nor be sued on a contract entered into on behalf of the principal and third party.

The agent incurs neither rights nor liabilities. But there are exceptions to this rule. For example, where the agent is *de facto* the principal, or the agent exercises an authority not possessed. In both cases the agent is liable. An agent is liable under the doctrine of undisclosed principle already explained.

TERMINATION OF AGENCY

Performance

The usual method of terminating an agency is performance. An agent automatically terminates the agency when the terms of the agreement are successfully completed.

Acts of the Parties

An agency may be terminated by mutual agreement, or the principal may revoke at any time the authority of the agent. This revocation prevents the agent from entering into any contract which binds the principal.

By Operation of Law

Agency is automatically terminated in the following instances: (a) by the death of either the principal or agent; (b) by the bankruptcy or liquidation of the principal or agent: (c) by frustration; (d) by the insanity of either the principal or agent; (e) by the efflux of time, where the agency was created for a limited period; and (f) by an intervening illegality. Many of these topics are discussed in greater detail in Chapter 10 (page 122) when considering the principles relating to discharge of contract.

CHAPTER 35

SALES OF GOODS AND SUPPLY OF SERVICES

On Sales of Goods in General

A contract for the sale of goods is a particular kind of contract. The principles of contract law, discussed in Part Two, apply to such contracts. The reason these contracts are exceptional is that statute law has modified the rules of contract in major ways. The *Sale of Goods Act 1893*, the principle statute in this regard, codified the common law rules. The *Sale of Goods and Supply of Services Act 1980* amends the 1893 Act in important respects. In this chapter, where appropriate, these statutes are referred to as the 1893 Act and the 1980 Act. But where the 1980 Act substitutes certain sections in the 1893 Act, reference is made to the combined Acts.

A Sale of Goods Contract

A contract of sale is defined by the 1893 Act as: 'A contract whereby the seller transfers, or agrees to transfer, the property in the goods to the buyer for a money consideration called the price. There may be a contract of sale between one part owner and another.'

The definition of a contract of sale covers two distinct transactions: a sale and an agreement to sell. The 1893 Act provides that where 'the property in the goods is transferred from the seller to the buyer the contract is called a sale; but where the transfer of property is to take place at a future time, or subject to some condition thereafter to be fulfilled, the contract is called an agreement to sell'.

A sale of goods contract is one for goods which are defined as including all chattels personal other than things in action, which include such items as debts, shares, patents, cheques, bills of exchange, promissory notes, and money.

The consideration in a contract for the sale of goods must be money though not exclusively so. A contract of sale is valid where the consideration is partly goods and partly money. In an instance where a new car is sold and an old car is taken in part exchange, as in the case of *Clarke v Michael Reilly & Sons* (1962) discussed later, the transaction is clearly a contract for the sale of goods. A simple exchange of goods, known as barter, does not come within the ambit of the sale of goods. The price of the goods may be fixed by the contract, or by the course of dealing between the parties, or in a manner laid down by the contract. Where the price is not fixed by any of these methods the buyer is required to pay a reasonable price. Where necessaries are sold to a minor, or to a person of unsound mind, or to a person incompetent because of drunkenness, a reasonable price must be paid. Necessaries are goods suitable to the condition in life of that person and to that person's actual requirements at the time of sale and delivery (see page 101).

Formation of Sale of Goods Contracts

The general law of contracts governs the formation of a contract for the sale of goods. The 1893 Act provides that subject to statutory exceptions 'a contract of sale may be in writing . . . or by word of mouth, or may be implied from the conduct of the parties'. The 1980 Act permits the Minister for Industry and Commerce to order that contracts relating to goods of a specific type must be in writing.

Where goods are valued at £10 or over, the contract cannot be enforced unless one of the following conditions is fulfilled. Firstly, there has been acceptance and receipt of part of the goods by the buyer. Whether or not there is an acceptance of the goods is a question of fact in each case. Reference will be made later to the case of *Hopton v McCarthy* (1882). Secondly, the buyer must give something in earnest to bind the contract, or make part payment. It was decided in *Kirwan v Price* (1958) that a tendered but rejected cheque was not something in earnest to bind the contract nor part payment. Thirdly, there is a written note or memorandum containing the terms of the contract and signed by the party to be charged or an agent. In *Haughton v Morton* (1855) the buyer verbally ordered some grain which could not be delivered because the ship carrying it was lost at sea. The buyer sued for the non-delivery and in support proved an entry in a memorandum book which had not been signed by the seller and a letter written by the seller which admitted the sale but stated it was subject to certain conditions agreed on by the buyer. The court ruled that the entry in the book was not sufficient because it had not been signed by the seller, the party to be charged, nor was the letter a sufficient memorandum because it omitted an essential term of the contract. The same result occurred in *Mahalen v Dublin & Chapelizod Distillery Co. Ltd* (1877) where the parties verbally agreed on the sale of some whiskey which was to be paid for by cash within one month or by a bill of exchange at four months with interest (see page for 378 bills of exchange). When the buyer sued for non-delivery he relied on an invoice which represented the sale solely for cash as being a sufficient memorandum in writing. The court held that since the invoice differed from the agreement in an important particular, by omitting payment by bill of exchange, it was not a memorandum in writing of the verbal bargain.

PASSING OF THE PROPERTY IN GOODS

The Meaning of Property

A contract of sale exists where the seller transfers, or agrees to transfer, the property in the goods to the buyer for the price. Property, in this context, means ownership and is distinct from the mere physical possession of the goods.

In most transactions the buyer obtains property and possession of goods simultaneously, for example, where Paul pays for a motor bike and takes delivery of it. But the buyer may have property in the goods without possession, for example, where Paul pays for the motor bike and leaves it with the seller to have the registration plates fitted. In this instance the buyer has the property though the seller retains possession. Or, for example, Paul may have possession of the motor bike while the seller retains property in it: where Paul goes for a trial run on it. The kernel of a sale of goods transaction is the passing of the property and, as we shall see, the consequences of this determination are significant.

Consequences of the Passing of the Property

It is imporant to distinguish between the passing of the property and the passing of mere possession, because the passing of the property in goods has a number of consequences. Firstly, as a general rule, the risk of accidental loss or damage passes with the property. Secondly, the right of the buyer to claim the goods where the seller becomes a bankrupt, or a company is liquidated, depends on whether or not the property has passed to the buyer. Thirdly, once the property has passed, the seller can sue the buyer for the price. Fourthly, the passing of the property as between the seller and the buyer is important where the goods are to be transferred to a third party. A resale by the owner of goods always passes a good title to the third party, whereas a resale by a person with possession will generally not pass a good title. There are a number of exceptions to this rule which are discussed later in this chapter.

Classification of Goods

For the purposes of the passing of the property in goods it is necessary to divide goods into specific goods, ascertained goods and unascertained goods.

Specific goods, the only type defined by the 1893 Act, are 'goods identified and agreed upon at the time a contract is made'. Where the seller shows the buyer a garment, and the buyer agrees to buy it, that is a sale of specific goods.

Unascertained goods can be either purely generic goods, for example, an order of 100 cream cakes, or goods forming part of a larger consignment, for example, five sheep from a farmer's herd.

Ascertained goods means goods which are identified and agreed upon after the contract is made. An agreement by the seller to sell one pup of a litter not born, which the buyer may choose, is a contract for unascertained goods. Once the pups are born, and the buyer makes a choice, the goods become ascertained.

Passing of Property in Specific and Ascertained Goods

The crucial factor in determining when the property passes in a contract for specific or ascertained goods is the intention of the parties. Section 17 of the 1893 Act provides that the property in such goods 'is transferred to the buyer at such time as the parties to the contract intend it to be transferred. For the purpose of ascertaining the intention of the parties regard shall be had to the terms of the contract, the conduct of the parties, and the circumstances of the case'.

An example of the courts interpreting the intention of the parties is found in *Clarke v Michael Reilly & Sons* (1962). The parties contracted for the sale of a new car. The buyer agreed to 'trade in' his old car and pay the balance of the purchase price in cash to the seller, a motor trader. Before the new car was delivered and the old car traded in, the old car was seriously damaged in an accident. Because the car was then worthless the seller purported to repudiate the contract. The Circuit Court held that the property in the old car passed to the seller when the contract was made, that the buyer of the new car was given a right to use the old car pending the delivery of the new car, and that the seller must bear the loss.

Rules for Ascertaining Intention

In many cases the contract will be silent on the question of intention. Section 18 of the 1893 Act sets out five rules for ascertaining the intention of the parties. But, and this is vital, these rules only apply in the absence of a contrary intention between the parties. We will see later attempts by the parties to do this when reservation of the right of disposal is considered.

Rule 1: Where there is an unconditional contract for the sale of specific goods, in a deliverable state, the property in the goods passes to the buyer when the contract is made, and it is immaterial whether the time of payment and/or the time of delivery be postponed.

The significance of this rule is seen in the case of *Clarke v Michael Reilly & Sons*, discussed above. In that case delivery of the new car, and payment — the old car and additional cash — were postponed. But the court held that property in the old car passed to the seller when the contract was made.

Rule 2: Where there is a contract for the sale of specific goods and the seller is bound to do something to the goods, for the purpose of putting them into a deliverable state, the property does not pass until such thing be done, and the buyer had notice thereof. Two examples illustrate this rule. Where a store undertakes to alter a garment before the sale is agreed, the item is not in a deliverable state and property does not pass until the work is done and the buyer is notified. Therefore, should a buyer request a jeweller to engrave a purchased item, the property passes at the time of the sale because the goods are then in a deliverable state. The engraving is an additional contract.

Rule 3: Where there is a contract for the sale of specific goods in a deliverable state, but the seller is bound to weigh, measure, test, or do some other act or thing with reference to the goods for the purpose of ascertaining the price, the property does not pass until such act or thing is done, and the buyer has notice thereof.

This rule is self-explanatory though it only applies where something is to be done by the seller. Where the buyer has to weigh etc. the property passes when the contract is made.

Rule 4: When goods are delivered to the buyer on approval or 'on sale or return' or other similar terms the property passes to the buyer:

(a) when the buyer signifies approval or acceptance to the seller or does any other act adopting the transaction: or,

(b) if the buyer does not signify approval or acceptance to the seller but retains the goods without giving notice of rejection, then, if a time has been fixed for the return of the goods, on the expiration of such time, and, if no time has been fixed, on the expiration of a reasonable time. What is a reasonable time is a question of fact in each case.

A person who has received goods on sale or return has the option of becoming the owner of them in three different ways. Firstly, the goods may be paid for. Secondly, the goods may be retained beyond a reasonable time for their return. Thirdly, the buyer may do some act which signifies acceptance, such as a resale, a pledging, or a pawning of the goods.

Passing of Property in Unascertained Goods

As already explained, unascertained goods are those which have no separate identity at the time of the contract. Section 16 of the 1893 Act provides: 'Where there is a contract for the sale of unascertained goods no property in the goods is transferred to the buyer unless and until the goods are ascertained.' In practice, however, the passing of property in unascertained goods is governed by the next rule.

Rule 5: 1. Where there is a contract for the sale of unascertained or future goods by description, and goods of that description and in a deliverable state are unconditionally appropriated to the contract, either by the seller with the assent of the buyer, or by the buyer with the assent of the seller, the property in the goods thereupon passes to the buyer. Such assent may be either express or implied, and may be given either before or after the appropriation is made.

2. Where, in pursuance of the contract, the seller delivers the goods to the buyer or to a carrier or other bailee or custodier (whether named by the buyer or not) for the purpose of transmission to the buyer, and does not reserve the right of disposal, the seller is deemed to have unconditionally appropriated the goods to the contract.

The kernel of this rule is unconditional appropriation, which means that some act must be done by the seller, or, unlike Rules 2 and 3, by the buyer, whereby the goods are irrevocably earmarked to the contract.

Reservation of the Right of Disposal

Section 19 of the 1893 Act provides: 'Where there is a contract for the sale of specific goods or where goods are subsequently appropriated to the contract, the seller may, by the terms of the contract or appropriation, reserve the right of disposal of the goods until certain conditions are fulfilled.' Reservation of title, or retention of title, clauses have featured in a number of cases in recent years as sellers attempt to protect their interest in unpaid goods in the event of the buyer becoming insolvent. Whether or not the retention of title clause is effective for its purpose depends on the facts of each case. But the principle remains that the seller and buyer may include such a term in the contract.

Before a reservation of title clause can achieve its purpose, it must, like all terms, be incorporated into the contract. Where this is proved by the party relying on the clause, it is incorporated. This was the result in *Sugar Distributors Ltd v Monaghan Cash & Carry Ltd* (1982) where four years after the parties first did business, the seller printed on the front of its invoices a reservation of title clause. On the buyer's liquidation the seller sought the return of unsold goods. The High Court held that despite the seller's failure to prove that the reservation of title clause had been specifically drawn to the buyer's attention, the clause had been incorporated into the contract. This was because reasonable notice of it had been given in that the invoices received by the buyer for fifteen months contained the clause which was not intimidatory in complexity and which was printed on the front of these documents.

Where the party relying on the clause fails to prove that it was incorporated it cannot be relied on. This was the result in *Union Paper Co. Ltd v Sunday Tribune Ltd* (1983) where the High Court held that the manufacturer of newsprint had not established on the evidence that the general trade rules, which contained the reservation of title clause, had formed part of the contract between the parties and that therefore the property in the paper had passed to the buyer.

Reservation of title clauses need not be drafted in any particular form and, as the cases will illustrate, the seller may use any terminology which suits the circumstances of the case. In *In re Stokes and McKiernan Ltd* (1978) four different clauses used by four suppliers of goods were considered when the company went into receivership and disputes concerning the ownership of unsold goods arose. In the 'Oerlikon' clause, the relevant provision was that 'equitable and beneficial ownership shall remain with the seller until full payment has been received'; the 'Thor' clause stated that 'the title of goods sold shall not pass to the buyer until the full purchase price and any sums due have been paid by the buyer to the seller'; in the 'AET' clause it was provided that 'the property in the goods shall not pass to the customer until the full purchase price has been paid'; and in the 'Tecalemit' clause, the relevant provision was that 'all materials etc. shall remain the company's property until the whole purchase price has been paid'. The High Court decided that each seller was entitled to the return of the unsold goods which remained in the buyer's possession at the time the receiver was appointed.

The clause, in *Frigoscandia (Contracting) Ltd v Continental Irish Meats Ltd* (1982), provided that 'until all sums due to the seller have been fully paid the plant etc. supplied by the seller shall remain the seller's personal property' was sufficient to retain ownership in a machine used in the buyer's manufacturing processes on which the buyer defaulted in repayments. In *Sugar Distributors Ltd v Monaghan Cash & Carry Ltd* (1982) a clause which provided that 'the ownership of the sugar to be delivered as per invoice shall only be transferred to the purchaser when the full amount of the purchase price has been discharged' was sufficient to preserve the seller's title to goods which were in the buyer's possession where the buyer went into liquidation owing a portion of the purchase price. A clause, in *In re Galway Concrete Ltd* (1983), which stated that 'the complete plant with all attachments remain the seller's property until paid for in full' reserved the seller's title to machinery, which had been affixed to the buyer's premises, where the buyer had defaulted in payments and had gone into liquidation.

But a simple reservation of title clause may not be sufficient to retain the seller's property in goods which have changed their character during some process performed by the buyer. When the buyer went into receivership, in *Kruppstahl AG v Quitmann Products Ltd* (1982), the seller, relying on a reservation of title clause, sought the return of unworked steel and worked steel. The High Court held that the unworked steel in the buyer's possession remained the seller's property and could be reclaimed, but that with regard to the worked steel, the clause was not sufficiently complex to create a charge over future manufactured goods, the title to which could not exist at the date of the contract.

In *Uniacke v Cassidy Electrical Supply Co. Ltd* (1987) the clause provided: 'No property in any goods shall pass until full payment for all goods supplied has been received by the seller and until such payment has been received by the seller the buyer shall hold the goods in trust for the seller in a manner which enables them to be identified as the goods of the seller'. It was argued, despite the general wording of the clause, that the use of the words 'in trust' transferred the legal ownership in the goods to the buyer. The High Court rejected that argument and held that the seller was entitled to a return of the unsold goods.

It is possible for the seller to waive, or abandon, a retention of title clause which was initially incorporated into the contract for the seller's protection. In *S.A. Foundries du Lion MV v International Factors (Ireland) Ltd* (1985) the seller supplied goods under conditions of sale which included a retention of title clause. The buyer's successor in title argued that the seller in a telex message had waived the clause. The High Court held that on the evidence the seller had not waived the clause but accepted that it was permissible for a seller to waive the benefit of such a clause.

THE PASSING OF THE RISK

The General Rule

Section 20 of the 1893 Act provides: 'Unless otherwise agreed, the goods remain at the seller's risk until the property therein be transferred to the buyer, but when the property therein is transferred to the buyer the goods are at the buyer's risk, whether delivery has been made or not.' Thus the risk of accidental loss or damage falls on the owner of the goods, whether or not in possession of them. Section 33 reads: 'Where the seller of goods agrees to deliver them at his own risk at a place other than that where they are when sold, the buyer must, nevertheless, unless otherwise agreed, take any risk of deterioration in the goods necessarily incidental to the course of transit.' The seller must, however, bear the risk of extraordinary or unusual deterioration or loss.

This general rule is subject to the exception in section 20 which provides; 'where delivery has been delayed through the fault of either the buyer or seller, the goods are at the risk of the party in fault as regards any loss which might not have occurred but for such fault'.

The general rule that the risk passes with the property is illustrated by *Spicer-Cowan Ireland Ltd v Play Print Ltd* (1980) where the buyer, unable to take possession of goods due to lack of storage space, was ordered to pay for them although they were destroyed by fire in a warehouse, where they had been temporarily stored by the seller's carriers at the buyer's request.

But it is common practice for a seller of goods to provide, generally on such documents as invoices, delivery notes, etc., that the goods are at the buyer's risk despite the fact that the buyer does not have property in the goods. For example, in one of the four clauses in dispute in *In re Stokes & McKiernan Ltd*, discussed earlier under reservation of title clauses, it was provided that 'the risk in the goods passes to the buyer upon delivery but equitable and beneficial ownership shall remain with the seller until full payment has been received'.

Perishing of the Goods

Goods perish where they no longer exist in a commercial state. The obvious way in which goods perish is where they are completely destroyed, for example, by fire. But goods may perish though they fall short of complete destruction. For example, a cargo of fruit impregnated by sewage is not destroyed in a physical sense though it has certainly lost its commercial value.

Section 6 of the 1893 Act provides that where specific goods have perished, without the seller's knowledge when the contract was made, the contract is void. Section 7 provides that where an agreement to sell specific goods is made, and subsequently the goods, without any fault on the part of the seller or buyer, perish before the risk passes to the buyer, the agreement is avoided. This rule is of limited importance because it only applies where the risk does not pass immediately to the buyer. Usually, of course, the effect of section 18, rule 1 together with section 20, is to pass the risk immediately the contract is made. Or, the terms of the contract may provide that the goods are at the buyer's risk.

TERMS OF A CONTRACT OF SALE

Terms may be Express or Implied

A statement becomes a contractual term where the maker of it, expressly or by implication, warrants it to be true. Contractual terms may therefore be either express or implied. Express terms are those terms actually agreed upon by the parties. In verbal contracts such terms will include the goods to be sold, the price and possibly the details of delivery. In written contracts an attempt may be made to expressly reduce all the terms of the contract into a document. Implied terms are ones which the courts will import into a contract where a dispute arises. The courts approach these problems by asking what terms would the parties have agreed to had they alerted themselves to the terms (see page 96).

Implied Terms in Sale of Goods Contract

A contract for the sale of goods, like all contracts, may contain both express and implied terms. But there is a feature of these contracts which distinguishes them from other contracts. It is that statutes, namely the *Sale of Goods Act 1893* and the *Sale of Goods and Supply of Services Act 1980,* imply certain terms into contracts for the sale of goods. These implied terms give far-reaching protection to the buyer, and cannot, except in certain circumstances, be excluded. Statute, in this regard, interferes with the general principle of contract law that the parties are exclusively responsible for agreeing the terms of the contract: freedom of contract is curtailed. Each of these implied terms will be considered later in the chapter.

Unfair Terms

The *Consumer Communities (Unfair Terms in Consumer Contracts) Regulations 1995* (S.I. No.27 of 1995) regulates contractual terms, between a seller and/or supplier, defined as a person who acts for purposes related to his business, and a consumer, defined as a natural person who acts for purposes which are outside his business. These terms, known as standards terms, are those which have not been individually negotiated in that they were drafted in advance and the consumer has therefore not been able to influence its substance. A contractual term shall be regarded as unfair if, contrary to the requirement of good faith, it causes a significant imbalance in the parties' rights and obligations to the detriment of the consumer, taking into account the nature of goods and services for which the contract was concluded and all circumstances attending the conclusion of the contract and all other terms of the contract or of another contract on which it is dependent. Such a term is not binding on the consumer.

Conditions and Warranties

The combined Acts divide these statutory terms into conditions and warranties. A condition, though not defined by either statute, has been interpreted by the courts to mean a term vital to the contract. A warranty, defined by the 1893 Act, is a term collateral to the main purpose of the contract, and as such is of lesser importance than a condition. The word warranty, in the remainder of this chapter, is used in its legal sense and not in its commercial sense where it is used to denote a guarantee.

In general, whether a term is a condition or a warranty depends in each case, according to section 11 of the combined Acts, on the construction of the contract in its entirety. Thus a term may in fact be a condition though called a warranty and vice versa. The combined Acts expressly state whether any of the terms to be implied into sale of goods contracts are conditions or warranties.

Consequences of Breaching a Condition or Warranty

Why does the law draw a distinction between conditions and warranties? It does so because the consequences which flow from a breach of a condition differ from those which follow the breach of a warranty. The breach by a seller of a condition gives the buyer a choice of action. Firstly, the buyer can treat the contract as repudiated, return the goods or refuse to accept them, and request the return of the price, or refuse to pay it. There is an exception to this rule where the contract is not severable and the buyer has accepted the goods, or part thereof, the breach of a condition can only be treated as a breach of a warranty. Secondly, the buyer may treat the breach of condition as though it was a breach of warranty. The choice rests with the buyer and not the seller.

Section 53 of the combined Acts provides that where there is a breach of warranty by the seller the buyer is not entitled to reject the goods. Instead, the buyer may claim that the breach of warranty diminishes or extinguishes the price, or the buyer may sue the seller for damages for loss which results.

Where the buyer deals as a consumer, in the legal sense explained later in this chapter, an additional remedy is provided. The buyer, promptly on discovering the breach, may request the seller to either remedy the breach, or to replace the goods. Should the seller refuse or fail to comply with such a request within a reasonable time the buyer may either reject the goods or repudiate the contract, or have the defect remedied and sue the seller for the cost incurred.

IMPLIED CONDITIONS AND WARRANTIES IN CONTRACTS FOR SALES OF GOODS

Good Title

Section 12 of the combined Acts provides that there is on the seller's part an implied condition that the seller has a right to sell the goods. Generally, a seller not possessed of a good title to goods cannot pass a good title to the buyer. This is known as the *nemo dat* rule, discussed at the end of this chapter, and to which there are a number of exceptions. A buyer purchasing goods from a seller who has no title to them must return the goods to the true owner. The buyer can claim that there has been a total failure of consideration and recover the price paid for them from the seller. Such a buyer may also claim damages, such as the cost of necessary repairs carried out on the goods.

Section 12 also provides that there is an implied warranty that the buyer is to have quiet enjoyment of the goods and that the goods are free from any charge in favour of a third party which was not made known to the buyer either before, or at the time the contract was made. For example, the goods might have been the subject of a hire-purchase agreement.

Description

A sale is by description where words or images are used to identify the goods. Most goods are sold by description. A buyer's request for 'a box of matches', or 'a bottle of milk', or 'a tin of beans' are all sales by description. Section 13 of the combined Acts provides that: 'Where there is a contract for the sale of goods by description, there is an implied condition that the goods shall correspond with the description; and if the sale be by sample as well as description, it is not sufficient that the bulk of the goods correspond with the sample if the goods do not correspond with the description.'

There is a tendency for the courts to construe this condition as to description widely. The buyer, in *American Can Co. v Stewart* (1915), ordered adding machines which, according to the seller's representations and the book of instructions, would add together sums of money and would convert the total obtained from pence to shillings and from shillings to pounds in one simultaneous operation. However, it was necessary in certain combinations of figures to adopt a particular process which had been explained neither by the seller nor by the book of instructions. When the buyer discovered this he refused to accept or pay for the machines and the seller sued for the price. The court ruled that the seller had not supplied the articles contracted for and that the buyer was not liable to pay for them. In *O'Connor v Donnelly* (1944) the buyer purchased a tin of 'John West Middle Cut' salmon. After eating some of the fish the buyer suffered illness and sued the seller for damages. The court ruled that the sale was one by description and that the goods supplied did not correspond with the description.

In *Egan v McSweeney* (1956) the buyer purchased coal and after placing some on a fire an explosion occurred which caused the buyer a serious injury. It was probable there was some explosive matter in the coal. The buyer successfully claimed that the coal did not correspond with the description. 'I think it is reasonably clear', said Davitt P. in the High Court, 'that what (the buyer) wanted was coal and not coke, or turf, or anthracite or any other form of fuel.' Still less an unexploded detonator. A farmer, in *McDowell v E.P.Sholdice & Co. Ltd* (1969), ordered a particular named onion seed. The seller, unable to supply the type ordered, offered another instead. The buyer asked for information on this seed and consulted a number of advisors who were not familiar with the seed offered. After being informed that this seed had the same characteristics as the seed ordered the buyer purchased it. When the crop failed to mature the buyer suffered loss and sued the seller. The Supreme Court ruled that this was a sale by description and awarded damages.

The buyer, in *Webster Hardware (International) Ltd v Enfield Rolling Mills Ltd* (1981), purchased copper chippings which contained phosphorus to be used in a manufacturing process, a purpose made known to the seller. The buyer was not aware that there were different grades of copper chippings and that such copper containing phosphorus was unsuitable for its processes. The buyer sued for loss suffered on the ground that the goods supplied did not correspond with the description of the goods ordered. The High Court dismissed the case, holding that the goods supplied did correspond with the description of the goods ordered.

A sale of goods is a sale by description even where the goods are exposed for sale and are selected by the buyer. Sales in a self-service store, where there is no verbal request for the goods by the buyer, are covered by this section. A reference to goods on a label, carton, bottle or tin, or other descriptive matter accompanying the goods exposed for sale may form part of a description.

Quality and Fitness

Section 14 of the combined Acts opens with the words 'subject to the provisions of the Act and any other statute in that behalf, there is no implied condition or warranty as to the quality or fitness for any particular purpose of goods supplied under a contract of sale.'

These words embody the common law doctrine of *caveat emptor:* let the buyer beware. In *Wallis v Russell* (1902), the facts of which are discussed later, FitzGibbon LJ. explained: 'The maxim, *caveat emptor*, applies to the purchase of specific things upon which the buyer can and usually does exercise his own judgment... it applies also where, by usage or otherwise, it is a term of the contract express or implied that the buyer shall not rely on the skill and judgment of the seller but it has no application to any case in which the seller has undertaken and the buyer has left it to the seller to supply goods to be used for a purpose known to both parties at the time of the sale.'

This doctrine has been greatly curtailed though it has not been completely excluded. It has been refined and the reader must be alert to note the various nuances. In this regard the central consideration is the status of the seller. Where the seller acts in the course of a business the doctrine of *caveat emptor* has been greatly restricted and the buyer is protected by the implied condition as to quality and fitness. Conversely, where the seller is not acting in the course of a business the maxim applies and the buyer is forced to take care. Whether or not a seller acts in the course of a business is a question of fact in each case. For example, where a householder sells an old washing machine the buyer must protect himself or herself because the law, as regards quality and fitness, will not. On the other hand, where a householder buys, repairs and resells washing machines as a hobby, or part-time business, the householder acts in the course of a business when selling a washing machine and the buyer is protected by the law.

Merchantable Quality

Section 14(2) of the combined Acts provides that: 'Where the seller sells goods in the course of a business there is an implied condition that the goods supplied under the contract are of merchantable quality.' Merchantable quality means that goods must be fit for the purpose, or purposes, for which goods of that kind are commonly bought, and as durable as it is reasonable to expect having regard to any description applied to them, the price, if relevant, and all the other relevant circumstances. Thus clothes are intended to be worn; food is intended to be eaten. Clothes and food can be used for other purposes though they need not be of merchantable quality if they are put to a use which was not intended by the parties. Having regard to their nature, goods should be durable, hold their colour, shape and style for an appropriate time.

In many of the decided cases where a finding was made that goods were not of merchantable quality, there was also a finding that the goods were not fit for the purpose for which they were supplied. For convenience these cases are considered together later.

Under the section there are two situations in which there is no implied condition as to merchantable quality, despite the fact that the seller acts in the course of a business. The first is where the seller specifically draws the attention of the buyer to defects in the goods before the contract is made. Goods described as 'fire damaged', or 'seconds' come within this proviso in that the seller is putting the buyer on notice that the goods are in some way defective. The second is where the buyer examines the goods and fails to find any defect which such an examination ought to reveal. The buyer of an overcoat, which had one sleeve longer than the other, or had different colour shades, or had the buttons missing, or had no button holes, would have no remedy where the goods were on display and fitting was permitted. If, however, the defect is not discoverable on such an examination, the seller is liable.

Fitness

Section 14(4) of the combined Acts provides: 'Where the seller acts in the course of a business and the buyer, expressly or by implication, makes known to the seller any particular purpose for which the goods are being bought, there is an implied condition that the goods supplied under the contract are reasonably fit for that purpose, whether or not that is a purpose for which such goods are commonly supplied, except where the circumstances show that the buyer does not rely, or that it is unreasonable for him to rely, on the seller's skill or judgment.' In most contracts of sale for everyday goods the purpose for which the goods are purchased will be obvious: food for human consumption, clothes to be worn. Where goods have several purposes, the buyer must indicate the one required. For example, some seeds may be either sown, or eaten by birds. If they are purchased in a garden centre the buyer by implication is making known the purpose for which they are to be put, that is planting. If purchased in a pet shop the implication is that the seeds will be fed to birds. But seed purchased in the pet shop may not be fit for planting. Here, in order to gain the protection of the section, the buyer must expressly make known to the seller the purpose to which the seed is to be put.

In *Wallis v Russell* (1902) the buyer asked a fishmonger for two nice fresh crabs for tea. When a portion of the crabs was eaten it caused illness and the buyer sued for damages. It was held that the crabs were purchased for a particular purpose made known to the seller and that the buyer relied on the seller's skill and judgment. The buyer was awarded damages. In *Egan v McSweeney*, discussed earlier, it was held that the buyer relied on the seller's skill and judgment, and that the seller knew the purpose for which the coal was required, namely, domestic burning.

The buyer, in *T.O'Regan & Sons Ltd v Micro-Bio (Ireland) Ltd* (1980), required a vaccine to prevent infectious bronchitis in broiler chickens. A brand-named vaccine was recommended by the seller's employee, but when used the chickens suffered a high mortality rate. The buyer sued for damages for the unfitness of the vaccine. The defect alleged was that it was more potent than it should have been. The High Court held that there was a breach of the implied condition as to merchantable quality and fitness in that the buyer relied on the seller's skill and judgment to supply a vaccine for use against infectious bronchitis in broiler chickens under the conditions normally obtaining where such fowl were reared in this country.

The seller, in *McCullough Sales Ltd v Chetham Timber Co. (Ireland) Ltd* (1983), sold 'Celuform', which was a man-made material to be substituted for timber in architraves and skirtings. It required special nails for fixing to masonry. These nails were either not forthcoming or were not suitable for use in this country because the density of concrete used here was different to that used elsewhere. The High Court held that the goods were not reasonably fit for the purpose for which they were purchased and dismissed an action by the seller for the price of the goods.

This statutory protection may not be available where the buyer does not rely on the seller's skill and judgment. The ordering of goods by a brand name by the buyer may exonerate the seller in the event that the goods prove defective. But recommending or selling of a brand name product, not ordered by the buyer, may leave the seller open to liability. 'The goods', said McMahon J., in the *T.O'Regan* case, 'were described in the contract by their trade name but the contract was not for the sale of goods under their trade name but was for the sale of a vaccine which the sellers recommended to the buyer.'

The protection as to fitness may also be lost where the buyer is deemed to be possessed of an equal, or greater, amount of skill than the seller. In such a case it would be unreasonable to allow the buyer to rely on the seller's skill and judgment. A salesmaster, in *Draper v Rubenstein* (1925), sold cattle in the course of business in the Dublin Corporation Cattle Market to a buyer, who was skilled in the purchase of cattle. The cattle proved to be unfit for human consumption. The Circuit Court held that there was no implied condition that the cattle sold were suitable for any particular purpose.

Sale by Sample

Section 15 of the combined Acts provides that in a contract for sale by sample there is an implied condition that the bulk of the goods shall correspond with the sample as to quality. There is also an implied condition that the buyer shall have a reasonable opportunity of comparing the bulk with the sample; and there is an implied condition that the goods are free from any defects, rendering them unmerchantable, which would not be apparent on reasonable examination of the sample. Where the sale is by sample and by description, there is an implied condition that the goods correspond with both the sample and description.

EXCLUSION OF IMPLIED TERMS

Exemption Clauses

An exemption clause is a contractual stipulation which excludes or diminishes the liability of one party to the contract. Exemption clauses are fully considered on page 97. The question for consideration at this point is whether the implied conditions and warranties under the combined Acts can be excluded, or limited, in contracts for the sale of goods? If this were possible these statutory protections would be rendered worthless. The 1893 Act permitted the exclusion of all these implied terms. An example of such exclusion is found in *Tokn Grass Products Ltd v Sexton & Co. Ltd* (1983) (the facts occurred before 1980). Machinery was purchased under a written contract which contained a clause which provided: 'No condition as to quality is implied and no guarantee or warranty expressed or implied is given under the Sale of Goods Act 1893 or otherwise in respect of any goods, vehicles or equipment sold.' When the machinery proved to be faulty the buyer sued the seller for damages and was met with the exemption clause. The claim failed because, as Doyle J. in the High Court explained: 'Applying the strictest scrutiny to the wording of the clause I consider it to be sufficiently wide and explicit to exclude the provisions of [the Act].'

The Sale of Goods and Supply of Services Act 1980 radically curtails this right of exclusion. Whether a particular term can be excluded depends either on the term in question, or the status of the buyer.

Exclusion Prohibited

Section 55 of the combined Acts provides that a term in a contract of sale which excludes all, or any, of the provisions of section 12, which relates to the title of the goods, is void.

Exclusion Permitted

Section 55(4) of the combined Acts permits the exclusion of all the other implied terms subject to two major exceptions. To be effective such an exclusion clause must be by express agreement, or by the course of dealing between the parties, or by usage where the usage is such as to bind both parties to the contract.

The first exception provides that any term of a contract for sale of goods which excludes section 13, which deals with description; section 14, which deals with quality and fitness; and section 15, which deals with sale by sample, is void where the buyer deals as a consumer. The second exception provides that in other cases the contract of sale is unenforceable unless such exclusion is shown to be fair and reasonable.

Where the Buyer Deals as a Consumer

The reason these statutes grant extensive protections to the lay person is to prevent, in the first instance, the sale of shoddy goods and, in the event of such a sale, to grant effective remedies. Because the lay person has no special knowledge of the goods, or may not be accustomed to trading in goods, special protections are provided by statute. Here the law draws a crucial distinction between the lay person, referred to in the 1980 Act as a consumer, and others, who are considered to be possessed of such skill and knowledge as not to warrant special protection by law.

A party to a contract deals as a consumer in relation to the other party if that party does not make the contract in the course of a business and the other party does make the contract in the course of a business, and the goods supplied are of a type ordinarily supplied for private use or consumption. The expression 'consumer' is thus given a legal meaning which is different to its ordinary meaning. A householder purchasing goods in a local supermarket deals as a consumer. However, a person buying an old washing machine from a next-door-neighbour, or through a card placed in the window of the local grocer, does not deal as a consumer. Nor does a retailer buying goods from a wholesaler.

The owner of a take-away shop, in *O'Callaghan v Hamilton Leasing (Ireland) Ltd* (1984), leased a machine which dispensed fruit drinks. When it proved defective and the buyer sued for the return of instalments the defence was made that he was not a consumer and therefore not entitled to the protections of the statute. The High Court held, in dismissing the claim, that the contract was made in the course, and for the purpose, of the buyer's business despite the fact that the goods were not for resale. The owners of an agricultural college, in *Cunningham v Woodchester Investments Ltd* (1984), who had an internal telephone installed, were not deemed to be dealing as consumers because of the extensive agricultural activities which yielded high profits.

It must again be emphasised that where a buyer deals as a consumer none of the implied terms, in sections 13 to 15, can be excluded.

Exclusion which is Fair and Reasonable

An exemption clause in a contract of sale of goods, where it is not void, is valid only if it is fair and reasonable. In considering whether a term is fair and reasonable the court must have regard to the circumstances which were, or ought reasonably to have been, known to, or in the contemplation of, the parties when the contract was made. Particular regard should be had to: (a) the strength of the bargaining positions of the parties relative to each other, and the alternative methods by which the customer's requirements could have been met; (b) whether the customer received an inducement to agree to the term, or whether she or he had an opportunity of entering into a similar contract with other persons without having to accept the requirement of the term; (c) whether the customer knew, or ought to have known, of the existence and extent of the term; and (d) whether the goods supplied were manufactured, processed or adapted to the special order of the customer.

The discretion given to the courts in this regard is wide. For a seller to be certain of excluding liability the exemption clause must be brought to the buyer's attention at the time of the contract. We noted *Tokn Grass Products Ltd v Sexton & Co. Ltd* earlier on page 340. If that case had occurred after the enactment of the 1980 Act it might have been decided in the same way because the exclusions had been brought to the attention of the buyer. Note that neither party was dealing as a consumer.

Statements Purporting to Exclude Rights

Section 11 of the 1980 Act makes certain activities criminal offences. It is an offence to display a notice on any part of the premises, or publish an advertisement, or supply goods with a label, or otherwise furnish a document which contains a statement which indicates that a right arising under sections 12 to 15 of the combined Acts can be restricted or excluded, otherwise than under section 55 of the combined Acts. It follows that a statement explaining, or simply stating, section 55 would not be an offence.

Implied Condition on Sale of Motor Vehicle

In every contract for the sale of a motor vehicle, except where the buyer is a person whose business it is to deal in motor vehicles, there is an implied condition that at the time of delivery the vehicle is free from any defect which would render it a danger to the public, including persons travelling in it. This condition is not to be implied where the parties agree that the vehicle is not intended for use in the condition in which it is to be delivered to the buyer, and a document to that effect is signed by the seller, or someone on the seller's behalf, and the buyer, and given to the buyer prior to, or at the time of, delivery, and it is shown that the agreement is fair and reasonable.

In every other case of a sale of a motor vehicle by a person whose business it is to deal in motor vehicles, a certificate in writing shall be given to the buyer by the seller to the effect that the vehicle is, at the time of delivery, free from any defect which would render it a danger to the public, including persons travelling in it. Where this certificate is not given it is to be presumed until the contrary is proven that the defect existed at the time of delivery. Any term of a contract exempting all, or any, of these provisions is void.

GUARANTEES

Definition and Terms of a Guarantee

A guarantee is any document, notice or other written statement supplied by a manufacturer, or other supplier, other than a retailer, in connection with the supply of any goods and indicating that the manufacturer, or other supplier will service, repair or otherwise deal with the goods following the purchase.

A guarantee must be clearly legible and must refer to the specific goods, or to one category of goods; it must state clearly the name and address of the person supplying the guarantee; it must state clearly its duration from the date of purchase, and different periods may be stated for different components; it must state clearly the procedure for presenting a claim; and it must state clearly what the manufacturer, or other supplier, undertakes to do in relation to the goods and what charges, if any, the buyer must meet.

Liability of Seller under a Manufacturer's Guarantee

Where the seller of goods delivers a guarantee to the buyer which has been supplied by the manufacturer, the seller is liable to the buyer for the observance of its terms unless it is expressly indicated to the buyer at the time of delivery. For example, in *Tokn Grass Products Ltd v Sexton & Co. Ltd*, the seller's invoices contained at the bottom the following printed words: 'The company holds itself free from any liability in respect of manufacturer's guarantees.' In a letter to the buyer was the sentence: 'We are unable to avail of the manufacturer's warranty on the motor.' While nothing in the case turned on these terms, they would clearly have been sufficient to exclude the manufacturer's guarantee.

Where the seller is a retailer and gives to the buyer a written undertaking that the seller will service, repair or otherwise deal with the goods following purchase, it is presumed unless the contrary is proven, that the seller is not liable under the manufacturer's guarantee.

Exclusion of Implied Rights

Prior to the 1980 Act the acceptance by the buyer of a manufacturer's guarantee was usually in exchange for the surrender of the protections provided by that Act. The 1980 Act provides that a guarantee is not an alternative to the implied rights granted by the statute: it is an addition to them. Any guarantee which purports to exclude or limit the rights of the buyer at common law or under statute law is void.

Right of Action under the Guarantee

The buyer of goods may sue a manufacturer, or other supplier, who fails to observe any of the terms of the guarantee as if that manufacturer, or other supplier, had sold the goods to the buyer and had committed a breach of warranty. The court may order the manufacturer, or other supplier, to take such action as is necessary to observe the terms of the guarantee, to the satisfaction of the court and within a specified time limit, or the court may award damages.

In this regard the word buyer includes all parties acquiring title to the goods within the duration of the guarantee. Where goods are imported the manufacturer is construed as including the importer.

DELIVERY AND ACCEPTANCE AND PAYMENT

General Rule

Section 27 of the 1893 Act provides that: 'It is the duty of the seller to deliver the goods and of the buyer to accept and pay for them in accordance with the terms of the contract for sale.' Section 28 adds: 'Unless otherwise agreed, delivery of the goods, and payment of the price are concurrent conditions, that is to say, the seller must be ready and willing to give possession of the goods to the buyer in exchange for the price, and the buyer must be ready and willing to pay the price in exchange for possession of the goods.'

From these provisions it can be seen that the passing of the property does not necessarily give the buyer the right to possession. Should the buyer want possession the buyer must be ready and willing to pay the price, or be able to show that the seller agreed to grant credit.

Meaning of Delivery

Section 62 of the 1893 Act defines delivery as the 'voluntary transfer of possession'. Thus, the legal meaning of delivery does not correspond with the popular meaning, which is that the seller must physically deliver the goods to the buyer's premises.

The mere selection of goods does not constitute delivery. It was held in *Bonner v Whelan* (1905) that the marking and weighing of cattle by the buyer did not constitute delivery under the statute.

Kinds of Delivery

There are five possible ways of effecting delivery.

1. There is the physical transfer of the goods. This is the most usual method.
2. There is the physical transfer of a document of title. Imported or exported goods are delivered when the bill of lading is transferred.
3. There is the physical transfer of the means of control. Thus giving the buyer a key of a warehouse where goods are stored, constitutes delivery.
4. There is delivery by attornement, which is explained in section 29 of the 1893 Act: 'Where the goods, at the time of sale, are in the possession of a third party, there is no delivery by the seller to the buyer, unless and until such third party acknowledges to the buyer that he holds the goods on his behalf; provided that nothing in this section shall effect the operation of the issue or transfer of any document of title to goods.'
5. Delivery takes place where there is an alteration in the character of the seller's possession. This would occur should the seller agree to store the goods for the buyer until the latter requires them. In such a case the seller becomes a bailee for the buyer.

Place of Delivery

Whether the buyer must come and take possession of the goods, or whether the seller must send them to the buyer depends on the terms of the contract. In *Board of Ordnance v Lewis* (1955) a seller was held in breach of contract for not delivering the goods at the places specified in the agreement.

In the absence of agreement, section 20 of the 1893 Act states: 'The place of delivery is the seller's place of business, if he has one, and if not, his residence, provided that, if the contract be for the sale of specific goods, which to the knowledge of the parties when the contract is made, are in some other place, that place is the place of delivery.'

Time and Cost of Delivery

The time for delivery is usually governed by express agreement of the parties. In commercial contracts the time of delivery is usually a vital term: it is a condition. Section 29 of the 1893 Act provides: 'Where under the contract of sale the seller is bound to send the goods to the buyer, but no time for sending them is fixed, the seller is bound to send them within a reasonable time.' A tender of delivery is ineffectual unless it is made at a reasonable hour. The same section further provides: 'Unless otherwise agreed, the expenses of, and incidental to, putting the goods into a deliverable state must be borne by the seller.'

Delivery of Wrong Quantity

Section 30 of the 1893 Act provides: 'Where the seller delivers to the buyer a quantity of goods less than he contracted to sell, the buyer may reject them, but if the buyer accepts the goods so delivered he must pay for them at the contract rate.' Section 31 states: 'Unless otherwise agreed, the buyer of goods is not bound to accept delivery thereof by instalments.' The buyer, in *Norwell & Co. Ltd v Black* (1931), ordered furniture and carpets. When the goods were delivered the invoice did not sufficiently correspond with the order, in that all the goods were not being delivered, and the buyer refused to accept delivery. A claim by the seller for loss which occurred on the resale of the goods failed because the Circuit Court held that the contract was not one by instalment.

Section 30 further provides that: 'Where the seller delivers to the buyer a quantity of goods larger than he contracted to sell, the buyer may accept the goods included in the contract and reject the rest, or he may reject the whole. If the buyer accepts the whole of the goods so delivered he must pay for them at the contract rate.' In *Wilkinson v McCann, Verdon & Co.* (1901) the seller delivered £65 worth of flags instead of the £28 worth ordered by the buyer, who rejected them, and a claim by the seller failed.

Delivery to a Carrier

Frequently a seller agrees to send goods to the buyer by some form of transport supplied by another. In such a case, section 32 of the 1893 Act provides: 'Delivery of the goods to a carrier, whether named by the buyer or not, for the purpose of transmission to the buyer, is *prima facie* deemed to be a delivery of the goods to the buyer.' If, in fact, the carrier is the seller's agent, delivery to the carrier is not deemed delivery to the buyer. In *Michel Freres SA v Kilkenny*

Woollen Mills Ltd (1961), a cost, insurance and freight (c.i.f.) contract, Irish post, cash against documents, it was held that the French sellers had not delivered the goods until the carriers had landed the goods at Dublin, which was after the delivery date, so that the Irish buyer was entitled to reject them.

Section 32 of the 1893 Act provides: 'Unless otherwise authorised by the buyer, the seller must make a contract with the carrier on behalf of the buyer as may be reasonable having regard to the nature of the goods and the other circumstances of the case.' The seller in such a case makes the contract as agent for the buyer, so the buyer is able to sue the carrier on the contract. 'If the seller omits to do so', says section 32, 'and the goods are lost or damaged in course of transit, the buyer may decline to treat delivery to the carrier as a delivery to himself, or may decline to treat delivery to the carrier as a delivery to himself, or may hold the seller responsible in damages.' But in *Spicer-Cowan Ireland Ltd v Play Print Ltd* (1980) the buyer, who was unable to take possession of the goods due to lack of storage space, was held liable to pay for the goods although they were destroyed in a fire in a warehouse, where they had been temporarily stored by the seller's carriers at the buyer's request.

Section 30 also provides: 'Unless otherwise agreed, where goods are sent by the seller to the buyer by a route involving sea transit, under circumstances in which it is usual to insure them during their sea transit, and, if the seller fails to do so, the goods shall be deemed to be at his risk during such sea transit.'

Acceptance

Section 35 of the combined Acts provides: 'The buyer is deemed to have accepted the goods when he intimates to the seller that he has accepted them, or subject to section 34 of these Acts, when the goods have been delivered to him, and he does any act in relation to them which is inconsistent with the ownership of the seller, or when without good and sufficient reason, he retains the goods without intimating to the seller that he has rejected them.'

As can be seen from this section there are three occasions on which the buyer accepts the goods. The first occurs where the buyer accepts the goods which is a question of fact in each case. In *Hopton v McCarthy* (1882) goods were verbally ordered. When the invoice arrived it was returned immediately stating that it did not correspond with the order. It was held that there was no acceptance of the goods and in the absence of a written contract an action for the price of the goods failed. The second one occurs where the buyer resells the goods, or converts raw material into finished products. These are acts inconsistent with the seller's ownership. The third one was invoked in *Gill v Heiton & Co. Ltd* (1943) where a buyer lost his right to reject goods by allowing the unloading of the goods to continue after it became obvious that they were not of the quality demanded under the contract.

Section 36 of the 1893 Act provides: 'Unless otherwise agreed, where goods are delivered to the buyer, and he refuses to accept them having the right to do so, he is not bound to return them to the seller, but it is sufficient if he intimates to the seller that he refuses to accept them.'

Right to Examine the Goods

Section 34 of the combined Acts provides: 'Where goods are delivered to the buyer, which he has not previously examined, he is not deemed to have accepted them unless and until he has had a reasonable opportunity of examining them for the purpose of ascertaining whether they are in conformity with the contract', and 'unless otherwise agreed, when the seller tenders delivery of the goods to the buyer, he is bound, on request, to afford the buyer a reasonable opportunity of examining them for the purpose of ascertaining whether they are in conformity with the contract.'

It was held, in *Marry v Merville Dairy Ltd* (1954), to be reasonable for a dairy, where the contract did not expressly specify where or when an examination of milk was to take place, to defer acceptance of the milk until tested at the buyer's premises. But in *White Sewing Machine Co. v Fitzgerald* (1895) the buyer was deemed to have accepted the goods where there was a failure to return faulty goods immediately.

Payment

We have already seen that section 27 of the 1893 Act provides that 'it is the duty of the buyer to accept and pay' for the goods in accordance with the contract. Delivery of the goods and payment are concurrent conditions, though it must be remembered that the property in the goods may pass to the buyer despite delivery and payment being postponed. Section 10 of the 1893 Act provides: 'Unless a different intention appears from the terms of the contract, stipulations as to time of payment are not deemed to be of the essence of the contract of sale.' A default in payment, unless otherwise agreed, does not entitle the seller to repudiate the contract.

REMEDIES FOR BREACH OF A CONTRACT OF SALE

Remedies of the Buyer

1. The buyer may, where there has been a breach of a condition, repudiate the contract.
2. The buyer may sue for the return of the price where the consideration for that payment has failed.
3. Where there is a breach of warranty the buyer may sue for the loss directly and naturally resulting, in the ordinary course of events, from that breach. We

saw in *Egan v McSweeney* (1956) (page 336) damages awarded for personal injuries where the goods supplied proved to be faulty and caused injury.

4. Where the buyer deals as a consumer, the buyer may, promptly on discovering the breach of a condition, request the seller either to remedy the breach, or to replace the goods. Failure by the seller to do so permits the buyer either to reject the goods, or to have the defect remedied elsewhere and sue the seller for the cost incurred.

5. The buyer may seek an order for specific performance where the contract is for specific or ascertained goods. The court has a discretion in this regard and in practice specific performance is only ordered where damages would be inadequate.

6. The buyer can bring an action against the seller for failure to deliver the goods. Where there is an available market for the goods in question the measure of damages is *prima facie* to be ascertained by the difference between the contract price and the market price. In *MacAuley v Horgan* (1925) the damages awarded to the buyer for failure by a Kerry seller to deliver wool was based on the price of the wool on the Dublin market, less the cost of carriage to Dublin at the time of refusal to deliver.

Remedies of the Seller

1. The seller may bring an action for the price of the goods. This can only be done where the seller is ready and willing to deliver the goods. This rule is subject to two exceptions. In the first instance, the buyer must pay the price where the goods have been accidentally destroyed, provided the property has passed to the buyer. In *Spicer-Cowan Ireland Ltd v Play Print Ltd* (1980) (see page 332), the buyer was ordered to pay despite the goods having been destroyed in an accidental fire at the carrier's premises because the goods had become the buyer's property. In the second instance, where the contract provides that payment must be made on a specified date, the seller may bring an action for the price, even though the goods had not been appropriated to the contract.

2. The seller has a right to sue the buyer for damages for non-acceptance where the buyer wrongfully neglects or refuses to accept and pay for the goods. The amount of damages is the estimated loss directly and naturally resulting from the buyer's breach of contract.

3. Either or both of these remedies may be of little value to the seller where the buyer is insolvent. The 1893 Act gives extensive rights over the goods to the unpaid seller, who according to section 38, exists if 'the whole of the price has not been paid or tendered'. We examined on page 330 the ability of the seller to insert a reservation of title clause into the contract and the effectiveness of this in cases where buyers are insolvent.

4. The unpaid seller has a lien over the goods where the goods have been sold without any stipulation as to credit, or where the goods have been sold on credit, but the terms of the credit had expired, or where the buyer has become insolvent. The unpaid seller exercising this lien is entitled to retain the goods until the price is paid or tendered. This right of retention terminates on delivery of the goods to a carrier without reserving a right of disposal, or when the buyer or agent lawfully obtains possession of the goods, or where the seller waives this lien. Of course, the lien is discharged where the buyer pays the price.

5. Where a seller delivers the goods to a carrier for transmission to the buyer the unpaid seller's lien is normally at an end. But where the buyer becomes insolvent while the goods are in transit, the unpaid seller is given a right of stoppage *in transitu*. The seller can, by exercising this right, recover possession of the goods from the carrier but the seller must bear the cost of redelivery.

6. The unpaid seller, according to section 48 of the 1893 Act, 'who has exercised his right of lien, or stoppage *in transitu* resells the goods, the buyer acquires a good title thereto as against the original buyer'. Where the goods are of a perishable nature, or where the unpaid seller gives notice of his intention to resell, and the buyer does not within a reasonable time pay or tender the price, the unpaid seller may resell the goods and recover from the original buyer damages for any loss occasioned by this breach of contract. Where the seller expressly reserves the right of resale the original contract is rescinded.

UNSOLICITED GOODS

A business practice, which caused considerable legal difficulties, was the sending of unsolicited goods. The recipient was unclear as to the legal obligations, if any, which arose. The position has been clarified by section 47 of the *Sale of Goods and Supply of Services Act 1980.* The statute defines unsolicited goods as goods sent, without prior request, to any person.

A person who receives unsolicited goods who has neither agreed to acquire, nor return them, may treat them as an unconditional gift, provided either (a) six months have expired since receiving the goods and the seller has not attempted to take possession of them, or (b) not less than thirty days before the expiration of that period the recipient gave notice to the sender in writing, stating his or her name and address and that the goods are unsolicited, and the sender did not, during the following thirty days take possession of the goods, and the recipient did not unreasonably refuse to permit the sender to take them.

It is an offence for a sender of unsolicited goods to demand payment, threaten legal proceedings or to subject the recipient to certain debt collection procedures.

THE SUPPLY OF SERVICES

Implied Undertaking as to Service

The *Sale of Goods and Supply of Services Act 1980* provides that in every contract for the supply of a service, where the supplier is acting in the course of business, the following terms are implied: (a) that the supplier has the necessary skill to render the service; (b) that it will be supplied with due skill, care and diligence; (c) that, where materials are used, they will be sound and reasonably fit for the purpose for which they are required; and, (d) that, where goods are supplied under the contract, they will be of merchantable quality.

The High Court ruled, in *Irish Telephone Rentals Ltd v Irish Civil Service Building Society* (1991), that a telephone communications system hired from the plaintiff was not fit for the purpose of providing a reasonably efficient telephone system.

Exclusion of Implied Terms

Any term of a contract implied by the Act may be negatived or varied by an express term of the contract, or by the course of dealing between the parties, or by usage. Where, however, the recipient of the service deals as a consumer it must be shown that the exclusion is fair and reasonable and has been specifically brought to the recipient's attention. In *McCarthy v Joe Walsh Tours Ltd* (1991) a provision in an arbitration clause in the contract for a holiday, which excluded recovery of damages in respect of personal injury and limited liability for any claim to £5,000 was held to be a term varying the defendants' liability under the terms implied by the statute. Because the arbitration clause had not been specifically brought to the attention of the plaintiff, who had dealt as a consumer, the High Court ruled that this term was void when the plaintiff sued for damages for an unsuccessful holiday.

CONSUMER INFORMATION

False Trade Description

Under the *Mercantile Marks Act 1887*, as amended by the *Consumer Information Act 1978* and supplemented by the *European Communities (Misleading Advertising) Regulations 1988* (S.I. No.134 of 1988), every person who, in the course of any trade, business, or profession applies any false or misleading trade description to goods, or causes another to apply such a description, is guilty of an offence. Every person who sells, or who exposes for sale, or who has in his or her possession for sale, in the course of any business, trade, or profession, any goods to which a false or misleading trade description is applied is guilty of an offence.

Trade description is defined as any description, statement, or other indication, direct or indirect, concerning almost every aspect of the goods such as attributes, quality, origin, fitness, composition, history, and other features. A false trade description is a trade description which is false to a material degree, and includes a trade description which is misleading to a material degree.

False or Misleading Advertisements

The *Consumer Information Act 1978*, as supplemented by the *European Communities (Misleading Advertising) Regulations 1988*, provides that a person who publishes, or causes to be published, an advertisement in relation to the supply or provision in the course or for the purpose of a trade, business or profession, of goods, services or facilities, which is likely to mislead and thereby causes loss, damages, or injury to members of the public is guilty of an offence.

The Director of Consumer Affairs and Fair Trade may, upon giving notice to any person, apply to the High Court for an injunction prohibiting the publication, or the further publication, of a misleading advertisement.

False Statements as to Services and Prices

It is an offence under the *Consumer Information Act 1978* for a person knowingly, or recklessly, to make a false statement as to any service, accommodation, or facilities provided, where the statement is made, and the service, accommodation, or facilities are provided in connection with a trade, business or profession. In the *Director of Consumer Affairs v Sunshine Holidays Ltd* (1984) a travel agency which continued to accept bookings, and moneys, for holidays in apartments in Spain, knowing that these apartments were no longer available, was convicted of this offence.

It is an offence for a person to give false or misleading indications of the present, or previous, prices of goods or services.

Defences

The *Consumer Information Act 1978* provides a number of defences to a party charged with an offence under its provisions. These include mistake or reliance on information supplied to the person charged, the act or default of another, accident or some cause beyond that party's control, provided all reasonable precautions and due diligence were taken to avoid the offence. In some defences seven days' notice of relying on it must be given.

THE DIRECTOR OF CONSUMER AFFAIRS AND FAIR TRADE

The *Consumer Information Act 1978*, as amended by the *Restrictive Practices (Amendment) Act 1987* establishes the office of the Director of Consumer Affairs and Fair Trade, a civil service post with a five-year renewable contract. The Director is appointed, and removable, by the Minister for Trade and Employment and is independent in the performance of the functions of the office.

The Director is required under the *Sale of Goods and Supply of Services Act 1980* to review, examine and influence practices or proposed practices in respect of the obligations imposed on persons by any of the provisions of that statute. The Director must, under the *Consumer Information Act 1978*, keep under general review practices in relation to advertisements; encourage and promote the establishment and adoption of codes of standards in relation to advertisements; ensure that consumer legislation is brought to public attention; and prosecute certain offences. The Director must report annually to the Minister for Industry and Commerce.

TRANSFER OF TITLE BY NON-OWNER

A Legal Quandary

We saw earlier that there is an implied condition that the seller has a right to sell the goods. In other words, the seller can pass a good title in them to the buyer. What happens where the seller is not the owner of the goods which are purportedly being sold? For example, a thief might sell stolen goods to an innocent buyer, or a dry-cleaner might sell a garment which has been deposited for dry-cleaning. In these instances should the law protect the property rights of the true owner and leave the innocent purchaser with nothing except a remedy against the seller? Or, should the law protect the commercial transaction, so that the true owner loses title to the goods permanently and merely has a remedy against the seller? This dilemma has been resolved by the development of the *nemo dat* rule.

The Nemo Dat Rule

There is a common law maxim: *nemo dat quod non habet*, which declares that a party cannot give what that party has not got. Here we mean ownership or property and not merely possession. Only the party with ownership can pass ownership. This rule is reflected in section 21 of the 1893 Act which provides: 'Where goods are sold by a person who is not the owner thereof, and who does not sell them under the authority, or with the consent of the owner, the buyer acquires no better title to the goods than the seller had, unless the owner of the goods is by his conduct precluded from denying the seller's authority to sell.'

There are a number of exceptions to this rule and these bite deeply into this general principle of law.

Agency

Where the owner of goods appoints another to sell them to the buyer, any sale in accordance with the principal's instructions passes a good title to the buyer. An auctioneer selling goods passes a good title to them despite the fact that he or she is not the owner of the goods (see page 316).

Estoppel

Where the owner of goods by conduct leads a buyer to believe that a certain fact is true and the buyer alters his or her position because of it, the owner is later precluded, or estopped, from denying that fact is true. An example will illustrate how estoppel operates. Suppose the prospective buyer of a motor car refuses to purchase it from a particular seller because in the past he has sold faulty cars. The seller, to effect a sale, pretends that he does not own the car but says it is owned by a party whom the buyer trusts, and that party goes along with the pretence. The buyer purchases the car by paying the third party who absconds with the money. The seller will be estopped from denying that the third party was the owner, and a claim against the buyer for the return of the car, or the purchase price, will fail.

Disposition by a Mercantile Agent

Section 1 of the *Factors Act 1889* defines a mercantile agent as one 'having in the ordinary course of business as such agent authority to either sell goods, or consign goods for the purpose of sale, or to buy goods, or to raise money on the security of goods'. A stockbroker is a mercantile agent. Section 2 provides: 'Where a mercantile agent is, with the consent of the owner, in possession of goods, or of the document of title to goods, a sale, pledge, or other disposition of the goods made by him when acting in the ordinary course of business of a mercantile agent, shall . . . be valid as if he were expressly authorised by the owner of the goods to make the same; provided that the person taking under the disposition acts in good faith and has not at the time of the disposition notice that the person making the disposition has not authority to make the same.' So a stockbroker selling a client's shares gives a good title to them despite acting without the client's knowledge provided the buyer acts in good faith.

Sale under a Common Law or Statutory Power

Both at common law and under various statutes there are a number of instances whereby a non-owner of goods is entitled to sell, and such a sale will pass a good title in the goods to the buyer. For example, at common law the finder of goods who has made a reasonable effort to find the true owner, may keep the goods and pass a good title to them. Under statute, carriers, hotel proprietors, sheriffs and pawnbrokers can pass good title to goods which come lawfully into their possession.

Sale under an Order of the Court

Rules of court authorise courts to order a sale of goods which are the subject of legal proceedings.

Sale in Market Overt

Section 22 of the 1893 Act provides: 'Where goods are sold in market overt, according to the usage of the market, the buyer acquires a good title for the goods, provided he buys them in good faith and without notice of any defect or want of title on the part of the seller.' A market overt means any open, public and legally constituted market where goods are sold. Market, in this respect, is any place where buying and selling openly takes place and is not confined to open-air market places. The buyer of goods in such circumstances acquires a good title whereas those who buy clandestinely are not protected.

Sale under a Voidable Title

The term voidable means that the contract is fully binding until steps are taken to set it aside. Section 23 of the 1893 Act provides: 'Where the seller of goods has a voidable title thereto, but his title has not been avoided at the time of sale, the buyer acquires a good title to the goods, provided he buys them in good faith and without notice of the seller's defect of title.' Examples of those with voidable titles are minors, and those coerced into contracts.

This type of situation is illustrated by the case of *Anderson v Ryan* (1967). The owner, D, of a mini car answered an advertisement which offered a Sprite car for sale. This car was brought by X to D for inspection and the parties agreed to exchange cars. In fact X was not the owner of the Sprite, which had been stolen. Later X, representing himself as D, sold the mini to the defendant who bought it in good faith and without notice of the defect in X's title. The defendant sold the car to the plaintiff who paid for it and some time later it was seized by the gardaí. The plaintiff sued the defendant for the price. The High Court held that X had acquired a voidable title to the mini as a result of the exchange, which title had not been avoided by D at the time when the sale by X to the defendant was completed. The court concluded therefore that the defendant had acquired a good title under section 23 and it followed that the plaintiff had acquired a good title to the mini, and the claim was dismissed.

Disposition by a Seller in Possession

A sale of goods may be complete and valid though the goods remain in the seller's possession. What happens if the seller sells the same goods to another buyer? Does the first buyer lose the goods to the second buyer? The answer is yes provided the second transaction is an innocent one. In *Hanley v ICC Finance Ltd* (1996) the defendant purchased a car from a motor retailer and in a series of contracts it was agreed that the dealer would later repurchase the car. The dealer, who was registered in the tax book as the owner, regularly taxed the car though never repurchased it. Later, the dealer openly sold the car to the plaintiff and fifteen months later it was seized by the defendant who claimed ownership and stated that the dealer had no authority to sell the car. The High Court, ruling that the car be returned to the plaintiff, held that while the dealer did not have legal title to the car, it gave a good title to the plaintiff by virtue of section 25 of the *Sale of Goods Act 1893.*

Disposition by a Buyer in Possession

This is the converse of the previous situation. Does the seller who has property in goods, but parts with possession, run the risk of losing the goods? The answer is yes, provided the new buyer acts in good faith. The new buyer acquires a good title to the goods which the seller leaves in the buyer's possession.

Disposition under a Hire-Purchase Agreement

Section 70 of the *Consumer Credit Act 1995* provides: 'Where goods of any class or description are let under a hire-purchase agreement to a dealer in goods of that class or description and the dealer sells the goods when ostensibly acting in the ordinary course of his business, the sale shall be valid as if the dealer were expressly authorised by the owner to make the sale, provided that the buyer acts in good faith and has not at the time of the sale notice that the hirer has no authority to make the sale.'

In cases covered by this section the buyer acquires a good title to the goods; but its application is restricted to dealers in like goods. For example, an auctioneer of used cars gives a good title to the buyer where a car he has on hire-purchase is auctioned. But a hirer of goods does not give a good title to them where they are sold before the hire-purchase agreement has been terminated.

Holder in Due Course of Bill of Exchange

A holder in due course of a bill of exchange acquires a better title to it than the transferor had. This is discussed more fully on page 378 when examining negotiable instruments.

CHAPTER 36

CREDIT AND SECURITY

Credit as a Feature of Business

Credit is a central feature of business. The consumer society operates on the basis that the consumer, without the ability to pay immediately from his or her own resources, can acquire and enjoy the benefits of a huge variety of goods and services. This is effected by obtaining credit from those in the business of lending money and then purchasing the goods or services, or by obtaining the goods or services on credit granted by the supplier of the goods or services. The loan is repaid or the goods or services are paid for by periodic payments which are tailored to the consumer's resources. The lender benefits by charging interest and the supplier obtains a sale which might otherwise not have been forthcoming had credit not been available.

Credit is allied to security. Depending on the amount of the loan, security may be demanded by the lender. The business community has developed different forms of security to suit the needs of the occasion. Thus, in return for a loan to purchase land or premises, the land or premises may be mortgaged in favour of the lender (see page 261), or the assets of a company may be charged (see page 416), or the seller of goods on credit may use a reservation of title clause to protect his property rights (see page 330). The commonest forms of credit are examined in this chapter.

LOANS AND GUARANTEES

Loans

A loan, or credit agreement to use the legal term, from a lending institution, such as a bank, is one of the most common forms of credit. The *Consumer Credit Act 1995* defines a credit agreement as an agreement whereby a creditor grants or promises to grant to a consumer a credit in the form of a deferred payment, a cash loan or other similar financial accommodation. Since the transaction is based on contract, such topics as the amount and duration of the loan and the repayments details will be expressly agreed between the parties.

While the terms of the credit agreement are not controlled by law, the form of the agreement is regulated by the *Consumer Credit Act 1995*. The credit agreement must be in writing, be signed by the consumer and by, or on behalf of, the other party. A credit agreement for a cash loan must contain such details as: (a) the amount of the credit; (b) the date on which it is to be advanced; (c) the number, amount and date on which each repayment instalment is due; (d) the rate of interest charged and the annual percentage rate (APR); (e) the total amount repayable; (f) the expiry date of the loan; and (g) details of any other charges to be paid by the consumer.

A copy of the credit agreement must be given to the consumer either in person on the making of the agreement or by delivering it within ten days of making it.

The credit agreement must contain a statement that the consumer has a cooling-off period of ten days from the date of receipt of the agreement in which to withdraw from the agreement, without penalty, by giving written notice to the creditor.

A creditor may not be entitled to enforce a credit agreement unless these statutory requirements have been complied with, though where a court is satisfied that the omission was not deliberate, did not prejudice the consumer and that it would be just and equitable to dispense with the requirements, and subject to any condition that it may impose, it may decide that the agreement is enforceable. But this discretion cannot be exercised where the requirement as to writing has been ignored.

Guarantees

Where a loan of money is sought it is commonplace for the lender to seek some form of collateral or security for its repayment. If the borrower cannot provide this the lender may demand that a third party is found to guarantee the loan. Thus, a contract of guarantee is a collateral contract whereby a third party, known as the surety, undertakes to be answerable to the lender for the debt or default of the borrower. The guarantee may be for one transaction, in which case it expires when the principal contract is discharged, or it may extend to a series of transactions and be called a continuing guarantee.

The *Statute of Frauds (Ireland) 1695* provides that contracts of guarantee must be evidenced in writing (see page 93) and the *Consumer Credit Act 1995* provides that certain guarantees, such as those relating to credit agreements, must be in writing.

The liability of the surety does not arise until the borrower has defaulted. The guarantee must be strictly construed and the lender cannot hold the surety liable for more than the agreed undertaking. The liability of the surety arises when the debtor makes default without the need for notice or a request for payment, and the lender need not sue the borrower, or even make a request for payment, unless the guarantee provides otherwise. When the debt becomes due, and even before the borrower has been asked to pay, the surety may require the lender to call on the borrower to meet his obligations. The surety may pay the lender and then sue the borrower who is liable for all payments made by the surety in respect of the guarantee.

As soon as the surety becomes liable to pay the guaranteed debt to the lender, the surety is entitled to call on the borrower to pay off the debt. Should the borrower fail to pay the surety may obtain a court order to compel him or her to do so. When the surety has paid money to the lender under the guarantee, the surety becomes, to that extent, the creditor of the borrower. The surety is entitled to the sum actually paid, with interest, though if he or she has suffered damage beyond that amount this too may be recovered. The surety is discharged by full payment to the lender by either the borrower or the surety.

A fidelity guarantee or bond is a contract whereby a surety guarantees that a party holding a particular office will faithfully discharge his or her duties to another person who would suffer loss if they are not so discharged. Needless to say, the surety is not liable for acts done by the office holder outside the scope of the office.

OBTAINING GOODS ON CREDIT

Credit-sale agreement

Instead of acquiring a loan to pay for the goods or services, the consumer might enter into a credit-sale agreement with the buyer whereby the goods are transferred immediately and paid for by instalments. The *Consumer Credit Act 1995* defines a credit-sale agreement as a credit agreement for the sale of goods under which the purchase price or part of it is payable in instalments and the property in the goods (see page 327) passes to the buyer immediately on the making of the agreement.

Before any credit-sale agreement is entered into the seller shall state in writing the cash price to the buyer otherwise than in the agreement. This rule is satisfied if the cash price was clearly stated when the buyer either inspected the goods or selected them from a catalogue or advertisement.

Since a credit-sale agreement is a credit agreement the statutory rules as to writing, cooling-off period and enforceability, as set out above, are equally applicable. In particular, the credit-sale agreement must contain a statement of: (a) the total cost of credit; (b) the cash price of the goods; (c) details of the instalments; (d) a description of the goods; and, (e) the rate of interest charged and the annual percentage rate (APR) charged.

Hire-purchase

According to the *Consumer Credit Act 1995*, a hire-purchase agreement is defined as an agreement for the bailment of goods under which the hirer may buy the goods, or under which the property in the goods will, if the terms of the agreement are complied with, pass to the hirer in return for periodic payments.

Before any hire-purchase agreement is entered into the owner shall state in writing the cash price to the hirer otherwise than in the agreement. This rule is satisfied if the hirer has either inspected the goods or selected them from a catalogue or advertisement and the cash price was clearly stated.

The hire-purchase agreement must be in writing, signed by the hirer personally and by, or on behalf of, the owner. A copy of the agreement must be delivered or sent to the hirer within ten days of the making of the agreement which must contain details of: (a) the cash price; (b) the hire-purchase price; (c) details of the instalments; (d) a list of the goods; (e) details of any costs or penalties to which the hirer may be liable on the failure to comply with the agreement; (f) a notice, as prominent as the rest of the agreement, which relates to the hirer's right to terminate the agreement once half the hire-purchase price has been paid and restrictions on the owner's right to recover the goods once one-third of the hire-purchase price has been paid; and, (g) a statement, in respect of the cooling-off period, that the hirer has a right to withdraw from the agreement without penalty by giving written notice to this effect within a period of ten days after the receipt of a copy of the agreement, or a signed separate statement to the effect that the hirer does not wish to exercise this right.

An owner of goods letting them on hire-purchase without complying with the requirements of the statute will be heavily penalised. While the agreement remains a valid one, the owner is placed under severe disabilities, in that the owner cannot enforce the agreement, or raise any security or guarantee, or exercise any right to recover the goods from the hirer. The onus of proving that the statutory requirements have been observed rests with the owner. The severity of these disabilities is modified by allowing the court a discretion to waive some of the requirements, where the court is satisfied that non-compliance has not prejudiced the hirer and that it would be just and equitable to grant relief. However, no relief can be granted where the agreement has not been personally signed by the hirer and by, or on behalf of, the owner. The High Court held, in *British Wagon Credit Co. v Henebry* (1963), that to satisfy the statute it must be proved that the agreement contained the statutory details at the time it was signed by the hirer. In that case the claim by the owner for outstanding instalments, which the hirer had refused to pay when the goods proved defective, was dismissed because there was evidence that the statutory details had been inserted after the agreement was signed by the hirer. In

United Dominions Trust (Commercial) Ltd v Nestor (1962) the parties to a hire-purchase agreement, which complied with the statutory requirements, made a subsequent oral agreement covering the balance due on some of the hired goods. There was no note or memorandum in writing of this verbal contract and the High Court held that the requirement could not be dispensed with and dismissed the owner's action for the return of the goods, or their value and payment of the outstanding instalments.

The rigours of the statute are illustrated by the *Mercantile Credit Co. of Ireland v Cahill* (1964) where the hirer took a car on hire-purchase. When the agreement was signed by the hirer the statutory particulars were left vacant and when they were filled in, these differed considerably from those originally agreed. When the hirer refused to pay the instalments, the owner brought an action to recover the full amount due. The Circuit Court held that since the statutory requirements had not been complied with, it would be unjust and inequitable to dispense with them. The hirer was lawfully in possession of the car, no order was made for its return, and the claim was dismissed.

A hirer can terminate a hire-purchase agreement at any time before the last instalment falls due. This is done by notifying the owner, or the person authorised to receive the hire rent, in writing. In this situation the hirer's liability is that all outstanding sums must be paid, and such further sum, if any, which will bring the total repayments up to one-half of the hire-purchase price. Where the hirer has failed to take reasonable care of the goods, which must be something more than ordinary wear and tear, damages may be payable for such failure. Lastly, the hirer must allow the owner to take possession of the goods. Where the hirer, having terminated the agreement, wrongfully retains possession of the goods, the court shall, unless it is satisfied that having regard to the circumstances of the case it would not be just and equitable so to do, order the goods to be delivered to the owner without giving the hirer an option to pay the value of the goods. A clause in the agreement which excludes or restricts the right of the hirer to terminate the agreement is void.

Any provision in a hire-purchase agreement whereby the owner, or a person acting on the owner's behalf, is authorised to enter premises for the purpose of taking possession of the goods is void, except that the agreement may authorise the entry into premises, other than a house used as a dwelling or any building within the curtilage of the house, for the purpose of taking possession of the motor vehicle. The owner cannot enforce any right to recover possession of the goods from the hirer otherwise than by a court action where one-third of the hire-purchase price has been paid or tendered by the hirer, or the guarantor. Where the owner seizes the goods without a court order, the consequences are serious for the owner. Firstly, the agreement comes to an end; secondly, the hirer or guarantor can recover all sums already paid under the agreement; and thirdly, the hirer and guarantor are no longer liable under the agreement. Where the owner has commenced legal proceedings to recover possession of a motor vehicle, let under a hire-purchase agreement, and it has been abandoned or left unattended in circumstances which have resulted, or are immediately likely to result in damage, the owner has a right to recover, and retain possession, pending the outcome of the proceedings.

Where a hirer voluntarily surrenders the goods there is no infringement of the restrictions already explained because the owner has not enforced any right. This was the result in *McDonald v Bowmaker (Ireland) Ltd* (1949) where the hirer, having paid more than one-third of the hire-purchase price, fell into arrears. The owner terminated the agreement and threatened to institute proceedings to recover the goods. Thereupon the hirer voluntarily returned the car and later brought an action against the owner claiming the return of the instalments. The High Court dismissed the action on the ground that the owners had not enforced a right to recover possession.

To protect the hirer against shoddy goods, implied conditions and warranties, similar to those contained in the *Sale of Goods and Supply of Services Act 1980*, are implied into most hire-purchase contracts (see page 93) and cannot be excluded. In *Butterly v United Dominions Trust (Commercial) Ltd* (1963) the hirer took delivery of a car in March and soon afterwards several minor defects became apparent. In May the car broke down due to a serious defect. The hirer claimed rescission of the contract, the return of the deposit and instalments and damages for consequential loss. The High Court found that the car was not of merchantable quality.

The court has considerable discretion in dealing with an action by the owner to recover possession of goods after one-third of the hire-purchase has been paid. The court may: (a) order the hirer to deliver the goods to the owner; or (b) order the delivery of the goods but postpone its operation subject to such condition as the court thinks fit; or (c) order the transfer to the hirer of part of the goods and deliver the remainder to the owner, subject to such conditions as the court thinks fit. The High Court decided, in *United Dominions Trust (Commercial) Ltd v Byrne* (1957), that where there is *prima facie* evidence that the goods are divisible, it is the duty of the owner to prove whether or not the goods are divisible and, if so, what are the relative values of the parts into which the goods may be divided. The failure of the owner to furnish such evidence may, where the balance due under the hire-purchase agreement is small, be a ground on which the court may, in its discretion, allow the hirer to retain the entire goods, subject to the payment of the balance due under the agreement.

Consumer-hire

The *Consumer Credit Act 1995* defines a consumer-hire agreement as an agreement for the bailment of goods, of more than three months duration, to a hirer under which the property in the goods remains with the owner. Since the statutory rules governing consumer-hire agreements are almost identical to those applicable to hire-purchase agreements, it is not necessary to repeat these and reference should be made to the preceding paragraphs.

Pledge

A pledge is a bailment of goods to another as security for a debt. In contrast to a lien, a pledge arises by way of a contract between the parties. While never becoming the owner of the goods the creditor has a right to sell them and be reimbursed from the proceeds. Where time for payment is fixed, the creditor may sell the goods forthwith following default in payment though, if no such time is fixed, the creditor must first demand payment and only then on default may the goods be sold. Any surplus over the debt must be retained for the debtor.

The *Pawnbrokers Act 1964*, as amended, contains detailed rules regarding the pawning of goods, a type of pledge, for amounts not exceeding £50.

Lien

A lien, in simple terms, is a right to retain possession of goods. A lien on goods is a possessory security, whereby a creditor obtaining possession of a debtor's property may retain possession of it until the debt has been repaid or other obligation has been discharged. A lien usually arises by implication of law, such as the lien held by a repairer of goods for the cost of repairs and a carrier in respect of the cost of carriage. The *Sale of Goods Act 1893* gives an unpaid seller a lien over the goods in respect of the purchase price (see page 350).

The creditor holding the lien has no right to sell the goods and be reimbursed from the proceeds but where the goods are deteriorating a court order to sell may be obtained. The creditor has no right to use or damage the goods and may, in this respect, be responsible to the debtor.

CHAPTER 37

INSURANCE

Nature of Insurance

The individual, and those engaged in business, may suffer loss through the occurrence of some unforeseen event. To offset this loss the commercial world developed the contract of insurance. In return for a fee the individual, or the business enterprise, would be indemnified for the loss suffered on the occurrence of the event insured against. Contracts of insurance cover a wide field such as life assurance, personal accident, public liability, damage to property and general liability insurance.

A contract of insurance is a contract whereby one party, called the insurer, agrees in return for a payment called the premium, to pay a sum of money to another, called the insured, on the occurrence of a certain event, or to indemnify the insured against the loss caused by the risk which is insured against. Policies of insurance are of two broad types: life assurance, which insures against an event which must happen, namely, death; and liability insurance which insures against events which may happen.

A contract of insurance may be in any form, such as by deed, in writing, or verbal. In practice such a contract is embodied in a written document called a policy which expressly states all the terms of the contract.

Insurance and Arbitration

Disputes between the parties to a contract of insurance are rarely litigated in the courts because most policies provide that such disputes should be resolved by arbitration. This process provides a more informal, more private and less expensive method of resolving disputes than legal proceedings. The *Arbitration Act 1954*, as amended, applies to such disputes. The High Court decided, in *Church & General Insurance Co. v Connolly* (1981), that it had jurisdiction to set aside an arbitration award where there was an error of law in the decision.

But the conduct of the parties may exclude the obligation to go to arbitration. In *Coen v Employers Liability Assurance Corporation* (1962) a clause in a motor insurance policy stated that all disputes arising under the policy should be referred to arbitration and that if the insurers should disclaim liability to indemnify the insured, such a dispute must go to arbitration within twelve months or the right would be lost. The High Court held that the insurers, having disclaimed liability on the ground that no valid contract of insurance existed, were not entitled at the same time to rely on the insurer's failure to refer such a disclaimer to arbitration as an abandonment of all claims under the contract. Accordingly, the insurer was entitled to have the matters in dispute resolved by the court.

Insurers

Insurance business is carried on principally by registered friendly societies, who deal in life assurance and are governed by the *Friendly Societies Acts 1896–1977*, and by insurance companies, who engage in life assurance and general insurance and are governed by the *Insurance Acts 1909–1989*. Both statutes attempt to provide some supervision by the State so as to safeguard the interest of policy holders. Insurance companies must hold a licence, maintain a bond with the High Court and make annual returns.

Proposal Form

The usual procedure for a party seeking insurance is to first complete a proposal form and submit it to the insurers. Where the proposal is rejected that is an end of the matter and there is no contract. The insurer is not bound to give reasons why the proposal was rejected: see *Carna Foods Ltd v Eagle Star Insurance Co. (Ireland) Ltd*, later. Where the proposal is accepted a contract may come into existence. The precise moment of its creation will depend on the particular events. It often happens that the policy does not become operative until the first premium is paid; this occurred in *Harney v Century Insurance Co. Ltd* (1983), a case discussed later, where it was declared that 'this policy is not in force until the first premium has been paid to the company . . .' In such cases the parties are free to withdraw from their commitments between lodging the proposal form and the payment of the first premium.

Role of Agent

In many instances preliminary negotiations will take place between a person seeking insurance and the insurance company's agent. Where the role of the agent extends to filling up the proposal form the agent is the company's agent in the matter. But should the duty of the agent fall short of this function, and the agent in fact fills out the proposal form, the agent may become the agent of the proposer. The consequences of the agent carrying out this function can be far-reaching. The insurer's agent, in *Connors v London & Provincial Assurance Co.* (1913), with full knowledge of the true facts, carelessly filled out a proposal form, after obtaining the proposer's signature. When the insurer avoided the policy on discovering the true facts, an action by the proposer failed on the ground that the authority of the agent was confined to submitting the proposal form and that the insurer was not bound by any statement or representation made by the agent.

Cover Note

A person who wishes immediate insurance while the proposal form is being considered is generally given temporary cover by the issue of a cover note. This is in effect a separate contract and is distinct from the policy. A cover note will contain such terms as are appropriate to a short-term contract. The cover note is operative for a given period, usually a month, unless in the meantime the insurers decline the proposal.

Renewal of the Policy

Most life assurance policies give the insured a right to renew the policy on payment of the premium. Most other policies of insurance make renewal conditional on the insured obtaining the consent of the insurer. The insured, before renewing, must make disclosure of matters which occurred since the last renewal, in order to either allow the insurer to reject the renewal or to refix the premium. The Supreme Court refused, in *Carna Foods Ltd v Eagle Star Insurance Co. (Ireland) Ltd* (1997), to imply a term into an insurance contract that, in the event of a declinature to renew a policy or the cancellation of a policy, the insurer was bound to state reasons.

Duty of Disclosure

The general rule in contract matters that silence is golden has no place in the law of insurance because the courts hold such contracts to be of the utmost good faith, or, *uberrimae fidei*. This duty of disclosure is based on the sound principle that a party applying for insurance is in possession of the material information whereas the insurer knows nothing.

To redress this imbalance the insured is placed by the law under a duty to disclose all material facts of which the proposer knows, or ought to know, where questions are asked of the proposer. In practice this duty works harshly against the insured, as will be seen in the next paragraph, especially as there is no duty on the insurer to warn the proposer of this duty of disclosure, and the consequences of non-disclosure.

All material information which may influence the insurer in assessing the risk to be incurred, and whether the insurer should incur such risk, and what premium should be imposed where the risk is accepted, must be disclosed.

No Duty of Disclosure

But this duty of disclosure may only exist where the proposer is actually expected to answer questions. The advent of over-the-counter insurance has given the courts the opportunity to modify the *uberrimae fidei* rule somewhat. This the Supreme Court did, in *Aro Road & Land Vehicles Ltd v Insurance Corporation of Ireland Ltd* (1986), where an insurance policy was sold without the requirement of a proposal form being filled out. The court ruled that since no questions were asked of the proposal the insurers were not, in the absence of fraud, entitled to repudiate the policy on the ground of non-disclosure.

Consequences of Non-Disclosure

The consequences of non-disclosure by the insured, where such a duty exists, allow the insurer to avoid the policy, which means that the insurer may refuse to honour the contractual obligations. Avoidance is the sole remedy and it may be availed of before or after the occurrence of the loss. In the latter situation the consequences for the insured are most serious in that the insured may be left to face the loss without the protection of indemnity.

Failure to disclose a refusal to reinsure by another insurer was material in *Taylor v Yorkshire Insurance Co. Ltd* (1913). Failure to disclose previous damage was held, in *Furey v Eagle Star & British Dominions Insurance Co.* (1922), to be a wilful misstatement and the insurer was entitled to avoid the policy. In *Irish National Assurance Co. Ltd v O'Callaghan* (1934) the insurer successfully avoided a policy where the proposer incorrectly stated the age of the life to be assured. The failure to disclose that the insured had tuberculosis was considered material, in *Griffin v Royal Liver Friendly Society* (1942), as was the omission, in *Curran v Norwich Union Life Insurance Society* (1987), that the insured had suffered an epileptic manifestation shortly before effecting the policy. The failure to state that the insured had been suffering from influenza was not material in *Harney v Century Insurance Co. Ltd* (1983). The failure to disclose that the insured had suffered loss in a previous fire was material in *Chariot Inns Ltd v Assicurazioni Generali SPA* (1981). Failure to disclose a petty criminal conviction recorded twenty years prior to effecting the policy was not material in *Aro Road & Land Vehicles Ltd v Insurance Corporation of Ireland Ltd* (1986).

It was decided in *Keating v New Ireland Assurance Co. plc* (1990) that a policy cannot be avoided on the ground of non-disclosure unless it is proved that the insured was aware of the material fact in issue. In that case the insured suffered from epigastric discomfort which was diagnosed as angina though the insured was never told of that condition. Before the proposal was accepted the insured was medically examined on the insurer's behalf and he made a full disclosure of his medical history and treatment as he understood it. The Supreme Court ruled that, in order to avoid the policy, the onus of proving that the insured knew the true condition rested with the insurer and that it was not sufficient to prove that he ought to have known the true position.

Where a proposal form is completed the duty of disclosure may continue up to the moment the proposal is accepted, or even later. In *Harney v Century Insurance Co. Ltd* (1983) the proposal form for a health insurance policy contained the sentence: 'The office must be notified of any changes in health and circumstances of the life to be insured prior to the assumption of risk.' When the policy was issued the 'date risk assumed' was 31 August. On 9 August the proposer attended the doctor with a head cold, was given antibiotics, and continued to attend work. His condition worsened and when the insured claimed payment the insurers avoided the policy. The High Court held that the non-disclosure of the cold in August was not material to the risk and that the insurers were not entitled to avoid the policy.

Contra Proferentem Rule

It is a general rule of contract law (see page 96) that a written contract is construed against the party drawing it up and insisting on its use as the basis of the contract. This is known as the *contra proferentem* rule and has been applied to insurance contracts. The rule goes some way towards mitigating the duty of disclosure. The courts use the rule to protect the weaker party to a contract of insurance because, while no duress is applied, it cannot be fairly said that the insurer and the insured stand on an equal footing in negotiations for an insurance contract. The insurer will generally adopt a 'take it or leave it' attitude and the party seeking the insurance will find similar terms when an approach is made to other insurers.

In *In re Sweeney and Kennedy's Arbitration* (1950), the proposer was asked in the proposal form: 'Are any of your drivers under twenty-one years of age or with less than twelve months' driving experience?' The answer given was 'No'. At the time that was factually correct and the proposer had no intention of employing staff to the contrary. After the policy was issued he employed an under twenty-one year old driver. When that driver had an accident, the insurers avoided the contract. The High Court refused to allow them to do so. The insured had acted in good faith, and as Kingsmill Moore J. remarked: 'The result of using ambiguous expressions is generally a decision against those who deal in such ambiguities.'

The Claim

When the insured suffers the loss insured against, he or she is normally required to make a formal claim and to give the insurer speedy notice of the loss. The question of notice is governed by the terms of the policy. Where the insured does not give notice in accordance with the policy the insurer may repudiate liability. In *In re Arbitration between Gaelcrann Teo and Payne* (1985) the insurer refused to indemnify the insured on the ground that there had been failure to comply with the condition of the policy which provided that immediate notice in writing of the happening of any occurrence which could give rise to a claim must be given. In that case an accident was reported to the insurer two years after the event.

Where the insured makes a fraudulent claim the duty to act in good faith is broken and the insurer can avoid liability under the policy though the insurer was at risk when the loss occurred. In *P.J. Carrigan Ltd v Norwich Union Fire Society Ltd* (1987) a claim under a fire policy was considered by the High Court to be fraudulent where it was proved that the fire had been deliberately started by a party who had a substantial interest in the company which owned the premises. The courts will not aid enforcement of a fraudulent claim even where the party seeking the assistance is an innocent party. In *Carey v W.H. Ryan Ltd* (1982) a claim by an employee against his employer for negligence was settled and a sum of money lodged in court. The insurers became aware of fraudulent misstatements made by the employer and avoided the policy. When the employee, on reaching majority, sought payment out of court the insurers sought repayment to them. The employee argued that since he was not a party to the fraud he should be allowed to have the money. The Supreme Court held that the subsequent events rendered the lodgement nugatory and the insurers were entitled to reclaim the money lodged in court.

An honest, but exaggerated, claim does not have a similar effect.

Insurable Interest

The essence of a contract of insurance is the protection of some interest of the insured. This is known as an insurable interest. To prevent contracts of insurance being used as instruments of gaming the law provides that insurance contracts are void unless the assured has some insurable interest in the life, or property, insured.

In some instances an insurable interest is required by statute: the main example is life assurance. The *Life Assurance Act 1774*, applied to this country by the *Life Insurance Act 1886*, and the *Gaming Act 1845* contained provisions designed to prevent insurance being used as a means of gaming and wagering. The 1774 Act provides that no contract of assurance can be made by a person on the life of another unless that person has an interest in the life of that other. Various statutes allow relatives of different degrees to be assured by other relatives but sets limits as to the amount of such insurance.

It is a well-established rule that one has an unlimited interest in one's own life. In cases other than insuring relatives, where a person proves some pecuniary and legally enforceable interest in the life of another then an insurable interest exists. For example, a creditor has an insurable interest in a debtor's life up to the amount of the debt. An employee has an insurable interest in the life of an employer up to the amount of remuneration. In life assurance the vital, and only, time for ascertaining whether an insurable interest exists is the date on which the policy is effective.

The owner of property has an insurable interest in that property, whether it is real or personal property. Because of the different interests which may exist in the one piece of real property (see page) various parties may have different insurable interests. The owner, a tenant, a mortgagee, and a prospective purchaser all have an insurable interest in the property.

Insurable Interest Required by the Policy

Whether a policy requires the insured to have an insurable interest is a matter of construction. While it is not unlawful for an insurer to pay on a policy where the insured has no insurable interest, the practice is that most policies require some proof of interest because of the important principles of indemnity, discussed later.

In *Coen v Employers Liability Assurance Corporation* (1962) the insurers attempted to disclaim liability under a motor policy on the ground that the insurer, not being the owner of the car, had no insurable interest. The High Court held that, on the evidence, the insured was the owner of the car and the disclaimer failed. In *Church & General Insurance Co. v Connolly* (1981) the committee of a youth club insured their premises, for which they were merely tenants at will, against fire. When a claim was made, following a fire which destroyed the premises, the insurers resisted on the ground of lack of insurable interest. The arbitrator found that the insured had an insurable interest in the premises because they were responsible for the maintenance of the premises while in occupation.

Indemnity

It is said by the law that contracts of insurance are construed as contracts of indemnity. This simply means that the insured cannot recover more than any actual loss. Of course, where there is no insurable interest there is no loss to be indemnified. An insured cannot make a profit from insurance. A number of rules have been developed to enforce this principle.

The Amount Recoverable

Under most policies of insurance the parties agree on a maximum figure up to which the policy is to operate. The premium is assessed by reference to this maximum figure, which is sometimes referred to as the sum assured, though this is misleading because the insurer's liability can never exceed this figure and in many cases will be a great deal less. Why is this? This is so because the contract usually provides that the insurer will pay the sum insured, or indemnify the actual loss suffered by the insured, whichever is the lesser amount.

Where there is a total loss of property, the insurers are only liable to pay its market value at the time of the loss, or the sum assured, whichever is the lesser, and not the market value at the time it was first insured. An example will illustrate this point. Suppose a car is insured for £12,000 against fire and its market value is only £7,000 when the car is destroyed two years later. The insurers are only bound to pay the latter sum even though the insured may have been paying the same premium each year. The onus is on the insured to reduce the sum insured as the property depreciates. Conversely, the insured should increase the cover as the property increases in value because, in the event of a total loss, the insurer is only liable to pay the amount insured.

This problem of the amount recoverable is illustrated in *St Alban's Investment Co. v Sun Alliance & London Insurance Co. Ltd* (1984) where an old disused warehouse was insured against fire for £250,000. The premises were destroyed by fire and the insured claimed the full amount which it was argued was necessary to reinstate the premises. The insurers argued that the amount to be paid, £65,000, was the market value of the premises at the time of the fire. The Supreme Court decided that, in the absence of an intention by the insured to rebuild the premises, the liability of the insurers only extended to paying the market value of the premises at the time of its destruction.

Average

Where there is a failure to insure the property for its full amount the insured must bear the remaining loss after receiving the sum insured. But what happens where there is only a partial loss of the property? It might be thought that the insurers must pay the total sum insured. In general, this is not so. To guard against partial loss under insurance it is common to find an average clause in a policy relating to property. Where the value of the property is greater than the sum insured, the insured is his or her own insurer for the difference and must bear a rateable share of the loss. If, for example, property worth £72,000 is insured for £24,000 under a policy containing an average clause and damage is caused which totals £18,000, the insurer is only liable up to the sum of £6,000, thus:

$$\frac{£18,000}{£72,000} \times £24,000 = £6,000$$

Valued Policy

The one exception to the rule that an insured cannot recover more than an actual loss arises under a so-called valued policy. This kind of policy is used where the parties wish to determine with certainty the sum of money to be payable in the event of a loss. This sum is agreed at the time of contract. Where a total loss occurs the sum representing the agreed value is paid, despite the fact that it exceeds the insured's actual loss.

Reinstatement

The primary obligation of the insurer is to provide a cash indemnity where a successful claim is made. In practice many policies give the insurer the option to either replace the value of the property with a sum of money, or to reinstate the property as it existed before the damage. For example, in the *St Alban's Investment Co.* case, discussed earlier, the clause read: 'The company will pay to the insured the value of the property at the time of the happening of its destruction or the amount of such damage or, at its option, reinstate or replace such property or any part thereof.' Should the insured desire reinstatement of the building in the event of its destruction, a special clause to that effect, known as a reinstatement clause must be inserted in the policy.

Where the insurers opt to reinstate the premises they are under a duty to replace it in substantially the same condition as it was originally. This obligation is not limited to the sum insured. If, during the reinstatement, costs arise which compel the insurers to pay in excess of the sum insured they must complete the work. And of course, insurers may be liable in negligence where the reinstatement is done poorly, or if there is unreasonable delay.

Subrogation

The cardinal principle of insurance, that the insured cannot recover more than an indemnity, has been stressed. In other words, the insured cannot make a profit from insurance. Subrogation means that an insurer, who has paid an indemnity to an insured, assumes the rights of the insured, where the insured is capable of sustaining a claim against a third party. For example, where a house is insured against fire and is destroyed by the negligence of a third party, the insurer, having paid on the policy, can then sue the third party to recoup the amount paid to the insured. The action is brought in the name of the insured, who is compelled, under the terms of the policy, to lend his or her name to the proceedings. Once the insurer has been indemnified any surplus belongs to the insured.

However, the insurer is only subrogated when the insured is paid. This was explained in *Driscoll v Driscoll* (1918): 'A contract of insurance is only a contract of indemnity', said O'Connor MR., 'and I think that the foundation of the doctrine of subrogation is to be found in the principle that no man should be paid twice over in compensation for the same loss. The corollary to this is that a contract of indemnity against loss should not have the effect of preventing the insured from being paid once in full.'

Contribution

A party can generally insure as often as he or she pleases but where loss is suffered that party can only be compensated once. This is yet another example of the principle that a contract of insurance is a contract of indemnity. If the insured has double insurance of the same interest against the identical risk, an insurer who has paid on one of the policies can bring an action to recover a rateable contribution from the other insurer. Some policies exclude all liability where another policy is in force against the same risk.

Salvage

Where there is a total loss of the goods, as distinct from damage to property, the question of salvage does not arise. If, however, the goods are only partially destroyed and the insurer pays in full the insurer is entitled to claim the goods as salvage. This is a further application of the principle that an insured can only recoup actual losses.

The Risk Insured Against

It is important for the insured to understand exactly the risks covered by the policy. In general a policy covers a loss sustained because of the insured's negligence. But some types of losses are not covered. For example, damage caused by the insured's wilful act, such as the deliberate arson of the insured property (see *P.J. Carrigan Ltd v Norwich Union Fire Society Ltd* on page 370), or the killing of an assured relative, are not covered. And in holiday insurance policies risks which cause loss from trade disputes or acts of God are generally excluded.

Where property is insured against loss the insured will not be successful with a claim unless two facts can be proved. In the first place, the insured must prove that there has been a loss, and in the second place, the insured must show that the loss caused was covered by the risk insured against. Thus, if goods are insured against theft, no claim can be made where the goods are destroyed by fire.

This problem is illustrated by *Ashworth v General Accident Fire & General Assurance Corporation Ltd* (1955) where a ship, insured against the perils of the sea under a policy of marine insurance, was lost. The High Court ruled that the ship was not seaworthy, to the knowledge of the insured, when it put to sea, that the loss was due to that fact and not to any peril of the sea. In *Stanbridge v Healy* (1985) a policy of motor insurance, which covered the insured against negligence caused by the driving of a motor vehicle in a public place, and which was required by statute, was obtained by the insured. Injuries were caused to a passenger in a car driven by the insured on a driveway to a house and the insurer, when sued by the injured party, repudiated liability on the ground that the driveway was not a public place. The High Court ruled that the place where the accident happened was not a public place and therefore the insurer was entitled to repudiate liability.

The Premium

The premium is the consideration for the risk undertaken by the insurer. The method and time of payment depends on the terms of the policy. The insurer may sue for the premium where there is a binding contract to issue the policy. In practice, this is rarely possible because the policy usually provides that the insurers are not on risk until the premium is paid.

If the renewal of a policy requires the consent of the insurer, as it does in virtually all types of insurance, except life assurance, the insurer is not bound to accept a renewal premium. It is important to remember that in such renewals the duty of disclosure revives each time a renewal is to be made.

Subject to special rules as to fraud and illegality, a premium is recoverable where the risk never attaches because there has been a failure of consideration. If the policy was obtained by fraud the insurer cannot sue to recover the premium because it is contrary to the common good to allow a wrongdoer benefit from a wrongful action.

Assignments of Policies

In general, the only policy which can be assigned is one of life assurance. In practice, this is often done to secure a bank overdraft, or as security on a mortgage. A legal assignment of the policy enables the assignee to sue on the policy. Assignment is possible by either an endorsement on the policy itself, or by a separate document. The assignee must give notice to the insurer at its head office, and if there is more than one assignment, priority is governed by the date on which each notice is given. An intending assignee, in order to protect that interest, should inquire at the insurer's head office whether any previous notices have been received.

A contract of insurance, being a personal contract between the insured and the insurer, cannot be transferred without the consent of the insurer. Otherwise, the insurer might grant insurance cover to a party with which it might not otherwise deal. An insured with a spotless character might be replaced by a rogue.

Motor Insurance

The arrival of the motor car brought a sharp increase in accidents on the roads. A great many were caused by the negligence of persons who were unable to compensate the injured parties. To remedy this situation it is compulsory for the users of motor vehicles on public roadways to be covered by a policy of insurance. Part VI of the *Road Traffic Act 1961*, as amended, governs the position. Section 46 provides that a person must not use a motor vehicle in a public place unless a vehicle insurer is liable for injury caused to third parties by the negligent use of the vehicle. A person who contravenes this section is guilty of a criminal offence.

CHAPTER 38

NEGOTIABLE INSTRUMENTS

Nature of Chose in Action

Property which cannot be reduced into physical possession is a chose in action. Choses in action are intangible forms of personal property. The owner of such property must usually have some document of title as evidence that he or she has such a valuable right and to facilitate the transferability of that interest. These documents of title are called instruments and they operate as a contract between the parties. Instruments of title include share certificates, insurance policies, debentures, dividend warrants, bills of lading, postal orders, tickets, bills of exchange, promissory notes and cheques.

At common law choses in action were non-transferable. In time equity allowed transfer, or assignment, subject to two restrictions. First, the debtor had to be informed because when the debtor paid the assignor he or she could not be called upon to pay the assignee, and second, an assignment was usually subject to whatever defects existed in the assignor's title at the time of the transfer.

The business community disliked these restrictions and the practice arose, in relation to some mercantile documents, of free transferability. Once the transferee took in good faith and for value, without notice of any defect in the transferor's title the transferee obtained a full legal title although the transferor had either no title, or a defective one. These documents came to be known as negotiable instruments.

Certain types of choses in action may be assigned in the manner authorised by statute. These include company shares, policies of life assurance, copyright, patents, bills of lading, debts and negotiable instruments.

Definition of Negotiable Instrument

A negotiable instrument is a chose in action which can be freely transferred and in respect of which a transferee can acquire a better title than the transferor. The most important of the negotiable instruments are bills of exchange, cheques and promissory notes.

BILLS OF EXCHANGE

Definition of Bills of Exchange

The *Bills of Exchange Act 1882*, which codified the common law rules developed from the law of merchants and bankers, defines a bill of exchange as: 'An unconditional order in writing, addressed by one person to another, signed by the person giving it, requiring the person to whom it is addressed to pay on demand, or at a fixed or determinable future time, a sum certain in money, to, or to the order of, a specified person, or to bearer.'

Functions of a Bill of Exchange

A seller of goods is generally anxious to obtain payment as soon as possible whereas a buyer of goods may equally be anxious to defer payment until the goods have been resold and the proceeds collected. By making use of a bill of exchange it is possible for the seller to have payment and for the buyer to have credit at the one time.

Suppose that Murphy in Dublin sells goods to Roche in Paris, who requires a thirty-day credit period. Murphy will draw a bill of exchange on Roche ordering him to pay in thirty days' time. Should Roche agree to the terms of the bill, he signifies his agreement by accepting the bill, signing it and returning it to Murphy. Murphy can keep the bill until it matures, or if she wants to convert it to cash, she can sell the bill to a bank, or another party, at its face value, less a small discount. The bill is drawn as follows:

£20,000	Dublin 1 January 1999
30 days after date pay to my order Twenty Thousand Pounds (£20,000) value received.	
	Murphy
To Roche Paris	

Thus Murphy has the bulk of the money for the goods while Roche has credit for thirty days as agreed. The commercial world is further involved in that Murphy can transfer it to another party. When the time of payment arrives, the bill matures, and the holder of the bill will seek payment from Roche, who in that thirty days will hopefully have resold the goods and have funds to pay the party presenting the bill for payment.

Initially there are three parties to a bill. The person who gives the bill (Murphy in our example) is the drawer; the person to whom it is given (Roche in our example) is the drawee; and when he signs it he becomes the acceptor. Finally, the person to whom the bill is payable is called the payee (Murphy in our example, though when she transfers it the transferee is the payee).

Types of Bills

A bill of exchange may be drawn payable to bearer, or to the order of the drawer. A bearer bill is one payable to bearer, or one on which the only or last endorsement is an endorsement in blank, which is where the endorser merely adds a signature, or which is payable to a fictitious or non-existent party. A non-existent party is one who has never existed, whereas a fictitious party is one who does exist but was not the party intended by the drawer to receive the bill.

An order bill is one payable to order, or which is expressed to be payable to a particular party, and does not contain words prohibiting transfer. Should a bill be drawn 'Pay Mary Murphy or order' it is an order bill, and so would be a bill drawn 'Pay Mary Murphy' because the words 'or order' are implied. The distinction between a bearer bill and an order bill is that a bearer bill is negotiated by delivery whereas an order bill is negotiated by an endorsement coupled with delivery.

An inland bill is one which is both drawn and payable within Ireland and Britain and a foreign bill is any other bill of exchange.

Inchoate Bills

Where a party signs a blank piece of paper with the intention that it may be converted into a bill, it operates as authority to fill it up as a complete bill for any amount, using the signature already on it as that of the drawer, acceptor or endorser. Likewise, should a bill be wanting in any material particular the party in possession has authority to fill up the omission in any way the holder thinks fit.

Time of Payment

A bill of exchange must be payable on demand or at a fixed or determinable future time. A bill is payable on demand if it is expressed to be payable on demand, or at sight, or at presentation, or where no time for payment is expressed, or where it is accepted or endorsed when overdue.

A bill which is not payable on demand must be payable at a fixed or determinable future date. This means it must be payable at a fixed period after sight, or after date or at a fixed period after the occurrence of a specified event which is certain to happen, though the time of happening may be uncertain.

A bill of exchange may stipulate that it is to be paid at a fixed period after issue or after acceptance. In our example it was three months, which means three calendar months. Time begins to run from the day after issue, or from the date of acceptance, respectively.

The period mentioned in the bill may be extended by the addition of days of grace. Three days are added to the period in which the bill must be paid unless the bill provides to the contrary. When the last day of grace falls on a Sunday or other public holiday, the bill is payable on the preceding business day. When the day of grace is a bank holiday, the bill is due on the following business day.

Acceptance of Bills

The drawee is under no liability unless the bill is signed in such a way as to signify acceptance of the duty to pay the sum of money stated in the bill. Acceptance may be either general or qualified. It is a general acceptance where the drawee accepts the bill as drawn without qualification.

Where the acceptance in some way varies the effect of the bill as drawn, it is known as a qualified acceptance. Section 19 of the 1882 Act specifies five types of qualified acceptance. It may be conditional: 'I accept if the bills of lading are handed over.' It may be partial if acceptance is made of only part of the sum specified. It may be local if it is accepted to be paid only at a particular place. It may be qualified as to time: accepted payable in four months whereas the bill specifies three months. Should the bill be accepted by one or more of the drawees but not all of them, it is a qualified acceptance. On receiving a qualified acceptance the holder has the option to refuse or take it.

This duty to present for acceptance only arises where the holder receives a bill which has not yet been accepted. In such a case the holder generally presents the bill to the drawee for acceptance, and when the bill matures the drawee presents it again but this time for payment. Where the bill is one payable on demand there is no reason why the bill should be presented twice. In practice it is only presented once, for payment.

However, what if the bill is a time bill? Presentation for acceptance is necessary only in three cases. Firstly, where the bill is payable after sight, presentation is necessary to fix the maturity of the bill. Secondly, where the bill is drawn payable elsewhere than at the residence, or place of business, of the drawee. Thirdly, where the bill expressly stipulates that it must be presented for acceptance.

Presentation is excluded, and the bill is treated as dishonoured, where the drawee is dead, a bankrupt, lacks capacity, is a fictitious party, or presentment is impossible, or acceptance is refused.

Presentation for Payment

A bill payable on demand must be presented for payment within a reasonable time of issue to make the drawer liable, and within a reasonable time of endorsement to make the endorser liable. A bill not payable on demand must, after it has been accepted, be presented for payment on the day it falls due. Presentment must be made at a reasonable hour. This is dispensed with if, after reasonable diligence, it cannot be effected, or where the drawee is a fictitious party, or where presentment is waived.

Dishonour

A bill is dishonoured by non-payment when it is duly presented for payment and payment is refused, or cannot be obtained, or where presentment is excused and the bill is overdue and unpaid. Such dishonour gives to the holder an immediate right of recourse against the drawer and endorser. Notice of dishonour must be given to the drawer and every endorser whom the holder may wish to hold liable. No special form of notice is required. It may be verbal, or in writing. It must clearly identify the bill which has been dishonoured. For example, the return of a dishonoured bill is sufficient notice. Notice must be given within a reasonable time of dishonour.

In *Spicer-Cowan Ireland Ltd v Play Print Ltd* (1980) the plaintiff sued the defendant for £7,293 on foot of a ninety-day bill of exchange, which had been drawn by the plaintiff and accepted by the defendant in a transaction involving the supply of paper by the plaintiff to the defendant. Before the bill matured, the paper was destroyed by fire (see page 332) and when presented for payment the bill was dishonoured. The action succeeded. In *Terex Equipment Ltd v Trunk and Machinery Sales Ltd* (1994) trucks were sold which were paid for by the seller accepting a number of bills of exchange drawn by the buyer in the seller's favour. Some bills were discharged and some were dishonoured. When sued by the seller the buyer alleged fraud in that vehicles which had been delivered were different to those which had been ordered. The High Court held in favour of the seller because the alleged fraud had occurred after the bills were accepted. Since the fraud had not induced the contract it could not be invoked to challenge the validity of the bills.

The Supreme Court held, in *Walek & Co. v Seafield Gentex Ltd* (1978), in an action on a dishonoured bill of exchange, that the practice of treating a bill as equivalent to cash would not be departed from and that the defendant would not be allowed to counterclaim for unliquidated damages.

Where a foreign bill of exchange is dishonoured, formal notice of dishonour must be given by the process of noting and protesting. A notary public must present the bill for payment and must note the reply obtained on the bill. The notary then issues a formal certificate of dishonour called the protest.

Lost Bills

Where a bill is lost before it is overdue the holder may apply to the drawer for a replacement and the drawer must comply. But the drawer may demand security from the holder against the possibility of the lost bill being found because the drawer is liable on both bills.

Discharge of a Bill

A bill is said to be discharged when all rights of action on it are extinguished. This occurs in a number of ways. The majority of bills are discharged by payment in due course. This means that payment is made at, or after, the maturity of the bill to the *bona fide* holder without notice that the title to the bill is defective. When the acceptor of the bill becomes the holder of it at, or before, its maturity, in his or her own rights, the bill is discharged. Should the holder of a bill at, or after, its maturity, absolutely and unconditionally renounce all rights against the acceptor, the bill is discharged. The renunciation must be in writing, unless the bill is delivered up to the acceptor. Should a bill of exchange be materially altered, without the assent of all the parties liable on the bill, the bill is discharged. The date, sum payable, and the time of payment are all material alterations.

Negotiation of Bills

A bill of exchange is negotiated when it is transferred in such a way as to constitute the transferee the holder of the bill. This is done by the delivery of a bearer bill, or by delivery and endorsement of an order bill. Negotiation may be prohibited by clear words written on the face of the bill. Words such as 'not negotiable' have this effect, though these words written on a cheque have a different consequence and are considered later.

Endorsements

Section 32 of the 1882 Act contains the requirements for a valid endorsement. It must be written on the bill, usually the back, and the signature of the endorser is sufficient without any further words indicating transfer. The manner of the endorsement must correspond with the drawing of the bill; if a payee's name is misspelt, the endorsement should be in that version with the correct version added if desired. The endorsement must relate to the total value of the bill and a partial endorsement is invalid. If there are several payees all must endorse unless one has authority to act on behalf of the others. Where there are two or more endorsements on a bill, each endorsement is deemed to have been made in the order in which it appears on the bill, until the contrary is proven.

Types of Endorsement

Where the endorser merely signs his or her name without specifying the transferee's name, it is a blank endorsement, and the bill becomes payable to the bearer. Any subsequent holder can convert it back into an order bill by endorsing it and adding the name of the person to whom the transfer is made. This is known as a special endorsement.

A restrictive endorsement is one which prohibits further transfer or limits transferability. An example would be an endorsement to: 'Pay Mary Murphy only — signed Gary Halpin'. Where the holder of a bill endorses it by writing: 'Pay Gary Halpin only if the bills of lading are handed over', it is a conditional endorsement. The payer has the option to disregard the condition and pay the endorsee, or to refuse payment until the condition has been fulfilled. Other common conditional endorsements are *sans recours* — a statement that the endorser accepts liability on the bill — and *sans frais* indicates that the endorser accepts liability for the value of the bill, but not for the expense of enforcing it. An endorsee is entitled to refuse any such endorsement but once it is accepted the endorsee is bound by its terms.

Holder of a Bill

A holder of a bill is the payee, or endorsee in possession of it, or the bearer of a bearer bill. The holder's rights will depend on whether the holder is a holder for value, or a holder in due course.

A holder in due course is one who has taken the bill, complete and regular on its face, before it was overdue, in good faith and for value and without any notice of any defect in the transferor's title. Such a holder is entitled to sue on the bill in his or her own name and defeats defences depending on defects of title, or arising from the relations of the parties prior to the taking of the bill. In other words, the holder in due course takes a better title than the transferor had to it. This is an important exception to the *nemo dat* rule (see page 353) and it lies at the very heart of the law relating to negotiable instruments.

A holder for value is one who has given, or is deemed to have given, valuable consideration for a bill. Such a holder is entitled to sue in his or her own name, but takes the bill subject to any defects in title arising because of fraud or illegality. A holder for value receives no better title to it than the transferor had. Where the holder obtains the bill from a holder in due course a perfect title is obtained. Generally speaking, a holder of a bill for which value has not been given cannot enforce it at all. But value is presumed to have been given for a bill, and a party seeking to defeat the claim of any holder on this ground must prove that value was not given.

Liability of the Parties

By drawing a bill the drawer agrees that it will be duly paid on presentment or, if it is dishonoured, the drawer will compensate the holder, or any endorser for any loss suffered. The Supreme Court held, in *Walek & Co. v Seafield Gentex Ltd* (1978), that the drawer of a dishonoured bill cannot defend the claim by seeking damages for breach of contract. As against a holder in due course the drawer is precluded from denying the existence and capacity of the payee.

The drawee is not liable to any holder before a bill is accepted though after acceptance the acceptor is the party primarily liable on the bill and agrees to pay in accordance with the terms of acceptance. As against a holder in due course the acceptor cannot deny the existence, capacity and signature of the drawer, or the existence and capacity of the payee of an order bill. The drawer, and endorser, only become liable on the bill should the acceptor fail to pay.

Any party who endorses a bill agrees that it will be duly paid on presentment, and that if it is dishonoured the endorser will compensate the holder or any party who endorses the bill subsequent to his or her endorsement who is compelled to pay it. The endorser is precluded from denying to a holder in due course the genuineness of the drawer's signature and of all endorsements prior to his or her own, and to a subsequent endorser that endorser is precluded from denying the validity of the bill, or of his or her title when he or she endorsed it.

Forgeries

Title to an order bill passes by endorsement coupled with delivery. A forged endorsement is wholly inoperative. Should an order bill bear a forgery as an essential endorsement no subsequent party can acquire a title to the bill. The holder in due course provisions do not apply because the party in possession is not even a holder. A forged endorsement on a bearer bill has no significance because such a bill does not require endorsement to pass title.

CHEQUES

Definition of a Cheque

Section 73 of the *Bills of Exchange Act 1882* states that a cheque is a bill of exchange drawn on a banker, payable on demand. When this definition is coupled with that of a bill of exchange the fuller definition reads: 'A cheque is an unconditional order in writing addressed by one person to a bank, signed by the person giving it, requiring the bank to pay on demand a certain sum in money to, or to the order of a specific person, or to bearer.'

The essential ingredients of a cheque are shown as follows:

		1 January 1999
Southern Bank Ltd Main Street, Dublin		
Pay Derek Feeney	or order	
Three hundred pounds only	£200	
		Mary Murphy

Obtaining Payment on a Cheque

Should Derek Feeney, or a subsequent endorser, wish to obtain payment on this cheque it can be done by either presenting it at Southern Bank at that address and obtaining payment over the counter, or by lodging it to his own bank which will present it to Southern Bank for payment. Where there are funds in Mary Murphy's account, or she is allowed to overdraw, the Southern Bank will pay on the cheque, cancel the drawer's signature and debit her account, while the collecting bank will credit the account of Derek Feeney, or the endorser.

Form of a Cheque

In the absence of contrary agreement the cheque need not take any particular form, provided it is in writing. A cheque written on a blank piece of paper, or the cheque issued by one branch of a bank can be altered so as to constitute a mandate to another bank. With the increased use of computerisation the banks are making strenuous efforts to prevent cheques, other than those given to customers for their particular use, from being used generally. Many cheque books contain the notice, on the inside cover: 'It is a condition of the issue of this cheque book by the bank that the cheque forms it contains will only be used for drawing cheques on the account for which the book is provided.' But this notice is not sufficient to prevent the practice.

Crossing Cheques

The object in crossing a cheque is to convey instructions to the drawer's bank that it is to be paid in a particular manner. Payment in a manner not in accordance with the crossing is a failure by the bank to obey the drawer's instructions and may leave the bank open to an action by the drawer.

A general crossing is made by drawing two transverse lines across the face of the cheque, with or without the addition of the words '& Co.' between the lines. The effect of such a crossing is to make the cheque payable only through a collecting banker. A general crossing is an instruction to the drawer's bank only to pay to another bank and not to pay across the counter.

In addition to the ordinary general crossing indicating payment through a banker there are two common general crossings regularly used. The words 'not negotiable' may be inserted between the transverse lines. These words, contrary to their ordinary meaning, do not deprive the cheque of its negotiability. What they do is to deprive the person taking it from having a better title to it than the person giving it.

Where the words 'account payee only' are inserted between the transverse lines they act as an instruction to the collecting bank to credit the payee's account with the proceeds of a cheque. A collecting banker is put on notice where such a cheque is presented for collection by someone other than the payee.

A special crossing is made by adding the name of a particular bank, with or without the addition of the two transverse lines.

Duty of Banker as to Crossed Cheques

A banker is liable to the true owner for any loss which is suffered where the banker pays on a cheque which is crossed, though a banker is not liable should the bank act in good faith and without negligence by paying on a cheque which did not on presentment appear to have been crossed, or to have had a crossing which had been obliterated.

Alteration of a Cheque

Generally, a visibly altered cheque is void against all parties who have not assented to the alteration. A banker paying on such a cheque is liable to the party suffering loss. Where the alteration is not apparent, and has been facilitated by the drawer's carelessness, the bank is not liable. This may happen where the drawer does not properly draw a cheque.

Position of Paying Bank

The paying banker is under a duty to pay customers' cheques and to do so quickly. In so doing the banker runs the risk of paying to the wrong party and where this is done the banker cannot debit the customer's account and is liable to the true owner for the cheque's face value. But a banker who pays has four possible protections provided by the statute. By section 60 of the 1882 Act the banker is not liable where an endorsement is forged, provided the banker acts in good faith and in the ordinary course of business. This section only applies to forged endorsements and not where the drawer's signature is forged.

By section 59 of the 1882 Act, where a banker pays the holder of the cheque, in good faith and without notice that the holder's title is defective, the payment is valid and the banker is entitled to debit the customer's account. As was noted earlier it is the duty of a paying bank to pay a crossed cheque in accordance with the crossing. It follows that where the banker pays a crossed cheque in accordance with the crossing the banker is protected from liability.

It was a long established practice by bankers to refuse to pay a cheque unless it was endorsed at the bank by the party presenting it for payment. This rule applied even where the party was lodging cheques to a personal bank account. This practice was considered tiresome both by the business community and the banks. Section 1 of the *Cheques Act 1959* now provides: 'Where a banker, in good faith, and in the ordinary course of business, pays a cheque drawn on him which is not endorsed, or is irregularly endorsed, he does not, in doing so, incur any liability by reason only of the absence of, or irregularity in, endorsement, and he is deemed to have paid it in due course.' But the banks still in practice, despite this protection, require endorsement of cheques unless paid into a bank account for the credit of the payee.

Position of Collecting Bank

Should a banker collect payment on behalf of a party who is not the true owner, the banker is exposed to the possibility of an action by the owner for any loss suffered. But the collecting bank is given two statutory protections. Section 4 of the *Cheques Act 1959* provides that a collecting banker is protected from liability where the banker receives payment for a customer who has no title, or a defective title, provided the banker acts in good faith and without negligence. This protection is only afforded where a customer of the bank is involved. A party becomes a customer by opening a bank account. Where a banker obliges a party, not having an account at that bank, by cashing cheques over the counter from time to time that party is not a customer. The second statutory protection exists where it can be proved that the banker has become a holder in due course.

Cheques and Bills of Exchange Compared

Subject to some exceptions, which have already been noted, the rules governing cheques and bills of exchange are identical. However, there are a number of important differences:

1. The rules relating to acceptance do not apply to cheques.
2. The rules relating to negotiation while they apply, have little practical relevance because the majority of cheques are not negotiated.
3. Delay in presenting a cheque for payment does not discharge the drawer, unless loss is suffered by that delay.
4. The rules relating to crossings are confined to cheques and do not apply to bills of exchange.

5. The payment of an order cheque bearing a forged endorsement discharges a banker, whereas in similar circumstances the acceptor of a bill is not discharged.
6. A number of obligations arise between a banker and customer by virtue of the contractual relationship between them which do not arise between the parties to a bill of exchange.

THE RELATIONSHIP OF BANKER AND CUSTOMER

Relationship of Debtor and Creditor

The relationship of banker and customer is a simple contractual relationship of debtor and creditor. The bank is the debtor and the customer is the creditor. The relationship is not a fiduciary one (see page 109).

Duties of Banker

A banker owes a contractual duty to take reasonable care in his or her conduct of the customer's account. A banker owes a duty to pay cheques properly drawn on the customer's account, provided the account is in credit or within the permitted overdraft limits allowed by the banker. This duty is owed to the customer and not to any other party. In *Dublin Port and Docks Board v Bank of Ireland* (1976) a drawer drew cheques on his bank in favour of the plaintiffs at a time when the account was in credit. Because of a strike by the bank staff at the time when the cheques came to be paid, there were not sufficient funds to meet it. These cheques were dishonoured and an action by the plaintiffs failed because the Supreme Court held that the bank owed no duty to the payee. Equally, should a banker wrongly refuse to honour a customer's cheque the banker is liable to the customer in contract and possibly in defamation (see page 211), and not to the payee, or endorser.

The duty and authority of a banker to pay a cheque drawn on the bank is terminated in a number of ways. The customer may countermand the payment. A banker will be liable for wrongly paying a countermanded cheque. A customer, in *Reade v Royal Bank of Ireland* (1922), who had a current account which was in funds, drew a cheque in payment of a gambling debt. Prior to its presentation for payment the customer countermanded payment by telegram which was ignored by the bank. It was decided that the bank was in breach of its duty and that the customer was entitled to recover from the bank the amount of the cheque.

The banker's duty is terminated by notice of the death of the customer. In *Bank of Ireland v Hussey* (1965) the banker was unable to recover from a payee sums of money paid on cheques the day before the banker's authority to honour cheques was withdrawn due to the drawer's mental illness. The banker's duty is also terminated on notice of the presentation of a bankruptcy petition, or a petition for the liquidation of a company.

The relationship of banker and customer is confidential. The banker must not divulge any information relating to the customer which the banker discovers while acting in the capacity of banker. The *Bankers' Books Evidence Act 1897* provides that a court may make an order authorising a party to litigation to inspect, and take copies of, entries in the books of a bank. The *Finance Act 1983* gives the High Court wide powers to force a banker to reveal the affairs of a customer and in addition, under certain circumstances, vests a discretion to freeze the bank account of a customer, who is a taxpayer.

Duties of Customer

The customer owes a duty towards the banker to take reasonable care in drawing cheques so as to guard against alterations. The giving of a blank cheque, signed by the customer, is not a prudent practice and the customer may have to compensate the bank for any negligence in this regard.

PROMISSORY NOTES

Definition of Promissory Note

The *Bills of Exchange Act 1882*, defines a promissory note as: 'An unconditional promise in writing, made by one person to another signed by the maker, engaging to pay, on demand or at a fixed or determinable future time, a sum certain in money, or to the order of, a specified person, or to bearer.'

An example of a promissory note:

Dublin
1 January 1999

I promise to pay Eamon Byrne the sum of £3,000 on 1 August 1999 value received

Mary Murphy

Promissory Note and Bills of Exchange

The difference between a promissory note and a bill of exchange is that the former is a promise to pay, while the latter is an order to pay. Apart from this distinction, both are negotiable instruments and most of the rules which apply to bills of exchange apply also to promissory notes.

Collateral Security

A promissory note given by a borrower of money is frequently accompanied by additional security, such as a deposit of title deeds of property, or company shares. A promissory note is not invalid by reason only that it contains a pledge of collateral security with authority to sell, or otherwise dispose of the property.

Requirements as to Time

In the definition of a promissory note one of the requirements is that it is to be paid 'on demand, or at a fixed or determinable future time'. A question arose in *Creation Press Ltd v Harman* (1973) whether an instrument which was to be paid 'on, or before 1 November 1970' was a promissory note. The High Court held that it was because while the makers of the note could have been paid before the date mentioned, which payment the plaintiffs would have been bound to accept, this did not mean that the makers had not engaged to pay money at a fixed future time.

Presentation for Payment

To make the drawer of the note liable the promissory note must be presented for payment though it need not be presented for acceptance.

CHAPTER 39

PARTNERSHIP

Nature of Partnership

A party wishing to engage in business can do so in any of three ways. First, that party may operate as a sole trader. In such case that party is, in every respect, the complete controller of his or her destiny. The sole trader enjoys great freedom of action and great privacy in the running of the commercial concern.

However, a person may join with others in a business or professional enterprise. In return for the benefits received, such as extra capital and expertise from the others engaged jointly in the venture, that party must in return share the profits and information. This type of relationship is called partnership.

The third method by which a party may engage in business is within the registered company. In this case the individual receives certain benefits in return for making information about the company public. Companies are considered in the next chapter.

Definition of Partnership

Section 1 of the *Partnership Act 1890* defines partnership as: 'The relationship which subsists between persons carrying on a business in common with a view to profit.' A business means a series of acts which, if successful, will produce profit or gain. Those engaged in voluntary or charitable organisations are not partnerships. Person means a legal person and includes both human and artificial, or corporate persons. It is possible for an individual to enter into partnership with a registered company.

Formation of Partnership

A partnership may arise in two possible ways. Where two or more persons form a business association for the purpose of sharing profits, they form a partnership whether they realise it or not. Many partnerships are the result of an express agreement of the partners, generally contained in a partnership contract. A formal document is not necessary, that is, it is possible to form a partnership without putting anything in writing. This is known as a partnership at will. Where two or more persons work together in such a way as to bring their relationship within the definition of partnership they are partners in the eyes of the law. This is implied partnership.

The defendant, in *Greenham v Gray* (1855), owned a mill in Drogheda. Under an agreement between the parties the plaintiff was to have full control and management of the mill, was to be paid an annual salary and was to have one-fifth of the profits. The defendant was to receive rent, interest on his capital and the remainder of the profits. After some months the defendant forcibly expelled the plaintiff from the mill, which the plaintiff claimed was unlawful in that the parties were in partnership, whereas the defendant claimed the plaintiff was merely an employee. The court held that although the word partnership had not been used, and the only contribution made by the plaintiff was his expertise, the legal effect was to create a partnership. In *Shaw v Galt* (1864) the plaintiff drew bills of exchange on the firm and when the firm became bankrupt, the plaintiff claimed the defendant was a partner in the firm and was liable. The defendant who had control of the manufacturing department of the firm, was paid an annual salary, and was to receive one-third of the profits for three years. The court held that no partnership existed. Participation in the profits was not the sole test, control was crucial. In this case the defendant acted under the firm's control.

The skipper of a fishing vessel, in *DPP v McLoughlin* (1986), engaged the crew members before setting out on each weekly voyage. The crew members were entitled to a share in the profits, if any, though they were not required to contribute to any losses sustained on any voyage. When it was alleged that the skipper, as an employer had failed to comply with the income tax and social welfare codes, it was argued that a partnership existed between the skipper and crew members. The High Court upheld that claim. The fact that each weekly voyage was a separate venture, that the crew members were entitled to a share in the net profits, and that the skipper did not determine the rate of remuneration outweighed the fact that the proceeds of the sale of the catch were paid directly to the skipper, and the element of control exercised by the skipper. In *O'Kelly v Darragh* (1988) the plaintiff was chief biochemist and the defendant was a director of a project which provided drug testing to drug companies. A special bank account was opened and all cheques drawn on that account were signed by both parties. Periodically, a sum of money in the nature of a dividend was withdrawn and divided equally between the parties. The High Court held that a partnership did not exist. Looking at the arrangement as a whole there was insufficient evidence that the plaintiff was a partner in the enterprise. While he was a key person, in the sense of qualification and ability, nevertheless he was an employee and while entitled to be paid a share of the profits this remuneration was to an employee and not to a partner.

In *Macken v Revenue Commissioners* (1962) the question arose for tax purposes as to when the partnership came into existence. It was agreed in September that a painting contractor, his son and daughter should form a partnership to become effective from the following 1 January. The deed was executed in April. The High Court held that the partnership only came into existence from the date the deed was executed.

Rules of Determining Existence of Partnership

Section 2 of the 1890 Act declares that in determining whether a partnership exists regard must be had to the following factors:

1. The existence of a joint tenancy, tenancy in common, joint property, common property, or part ownership does not of itself create a partnership. (The nature of these interests is explained in Chapter 27, page 256.)
2. The sharing of gross returns does not of itself create a partnership.
3. The receipt by a person of a share of the profits of a business is *prima facie* evidence that that person is a partner in the business, but the receipt of a share, or of a payment contingent on, or varying with, the profits of a business, does not of itself make that person a partner; and in particular:
   (a) the receipt of a debt, or other amount by instalments, or otherwise, out of the profits; or
   (b) a contract for the remuneration of a servant or agent by a share of the profits of the business; or
   (c) a person, who is a widow or a child of a deceased partner, and receiving an annuity out of the profits; or
   (d) if a lender, in return for an advance of money, receives a rate of interest varying with the profits; or
   (e) a person receiving a portion of the profits of a business in consideration of the sale by him of the goodwill of the business, does not make that person a partner in the business.

Partnership Contracts

Most partnerships define the rights and obligations of each partner in a written document, known as a partnership contract or partnership articles. Provision is generally made for the following: (a) the nature of the business and the firm name; (b) the capital and property of the firm; (c) intended duration of the partnership; (d) provision for salaries; (e) rights and duties of individual partners; (f) provision for audit and accounts; (g) division of profits and losses; (h) powers of admission and expulsion of partners; (i) termination of partnership; (j) valuation of goodwill and assets on the sale, or death of a partner; and (k) an arbitration clause.

This arbitration clause is generally a feature of partnership agreements. The advantage of arbitration is that disputes can be settled by an informal procedure in private without the expense, formality and publicity of a court case. Arbitration procedure is governed by the *Arbitration Act 1954*, as amended.

Section 376 of the *Companies Act 1963*, as amended, provides that no partnership of more than twenty persons can be formed for the purpose of carrying on any business that has the acquisition of gain as its object. This restriction does not apply to bankers, solicitors or accountants.

Legal Status of Partnership

A partnership is simply a collection of individuals involved in some business activity. Each has individual responsibility for the actions and liabilities of the firm as a whole. In law a partnership is not regarded as a legal entity separate from its members. This is the greatest distinction between it and a registered company; this and other distinctions are noted in the next chapter (see page 403). A registered company has a legal entity separate from its shareholders.

Because all partners in a firm are usually bound by the actions done, and the liabilities incurred, by any one of the partners on behalf of the firm, it follows that all the partners may lose everything they possess through the recklessness of one partner. However, the shareholders of a company with limited liability are not in a similarly exposed position; they can only be held to account up to a limited amount unless they abuse this privilege of limited liability.

The Partnership Name

Section 4 of the 1890 Act provides that persons who enter into partnership are to be called collectively a firm, and the name under which the business is carried on is called the firm name. Generally, partners commence trading under their own names, but where they do not do so they must comply with the *Registration of Business Names Act 1963*. The registration of the identity of those behind a partnership name allows the public, and creditors, to know the parties with whom they are dealing.

PARTNERSHIP DEALINGS WITH THIRD PARTIES

A Type of Agency

A firm of partners will rely for its business activities with third parties on one or more of the partners. These latter partners are agents for the firm. The firm is the principal and the individual partners are the agents. The rules relating to agency, explained in Chapter 34 (page 316), are applicable to the relationship of each partner with the partnership, and could be referred to at this point.

Powers of Partners

Section 5 of the 1890 Act provides that each partner is an agent for the firm and can bind the firm to any contract made for the purpose of the firm's business and which appears to be in the ordinary course of that business. This implied authority does not apply where the partnership agreement negatives or restricts it; or, the contract appears to be outside the scope of that business and the third party knows that the partner has no authority to enter into it.

Section 6 of the 1890 Act has a bearing on transactions which are not usual and extends to cover partners and other persons, provided they have authority, either express or implied. It provides that an act, or instrument, relating to the business of the firm and done, or executed, in the firm's name, or in any other manner showing an intention to bind the firm, by any person so authorised, whether a partner or not, is binding on the firm and on all the partners.

Section 7 of the 1890 Act provides that where one partner pledges the credit of the firm for a purpose apparently not connected with the firm's ordinary business, the firm is not bound, unless that partner is specially authorised by the other partners. This section does not affect the personal liability incurred by the individual partner.

The firm is not bound by the action of a partner acting in excess of powers where, according to section 8 of the 1890 Act, the third party had notice of the restricted authority.

Liability of Partners

Each partner in a firm is jointly liable for all debts and obligations of the firm which are incurred while he or she is a partner. After that partner's death his or her estate is liable insofar as partnership liabilities remain unsatisfied though these are subject to the prior payment of separate debts.

Where any wrongful act or omission is done by any partner acting in the course of the firm's business, or with the authority of co-partners, which causes any loss, damage or injury to a third party, the firm is liable.

Where a partner, acting within the scope of apparent authority, receives money or property belonging to a third party, and misapplies it by fraudulently converting it to his or her own use, the firm is liable. It is not a defence to prove that the firm never received the proceeds, or that the other partners had no knowledge of the partner's fraud.

An admission, or representation, made by one partner concerning the partnership affairs and in the ordinary course of business, is evidence against the firm. The converse also applies in that notice to a partner, who habitually acts in the partnership business, or any matter relating to it, operates as notice to the firm, except in the case of a fraud on the firm committed by, or with the consent of, that partner.

Persons holding Themselves out as Partners

Section 14 of the 1890 Act provides that every person who knowingly by spoken or written words, or by conduct, represents, or who knowingly allows such a representation, that that person is a partner in a particular firm, is liable as a partner to any third party who has, on the faith of such representations, given credit to the firm. Thus, a person who is not a partner may become liable for a particular debt of the firm where he or she represents himself or herself to be a partner, or knowingly allows others to make such representation, and the creditor claiming the debt relied on these representations. This is another example of the doctrine of estoppel (see page 92).

This rule is restricted where, after a partner's death, the business is continued in the old firm name. It is provided that the continued use of that partner's name does not of itself make that partner's estate liable for any partnership debt incurred after the death. Should the deceased partner's personal representatives allow the deceased's name to be represented as being alive, the estate is liable.

RELATIONS OF PARTNERS *INTER SE*

Relationship of Trust

A partnership agreement is one of the utmost good faith, or *uberrimae fidei*, between the partners. Each partner has a duty to disclose fully to the other partners any information acquired which is relevant to the firm's business. Each partner must account to the firm for any benefit which is derived from the partnership, in other words, a partner cannot make a secret profit. Partners are bound to render true accounts of the proceeds of the partnership. Partners must not place themselves in positions where their personal interests clash with their duties to the partnership.

The position of a partner *qua* the other partners is similar to that of a trustee and a beneficiary under a trust (see page 238), or a principal and agent under an agency agreement (see page 320). It is a fiduciary relationship.

Variation of Agreement

Since partnership essentially is a relationship founded on contract, section 19 of the 1890 Act provides that mutual rights and duties of the partners can be varied by the consent of all the partners. Such consent may be express or implied from the course of dealing of the partners. Where the agreement is by deed, or in writing, the variations can be verbal, provided all partners concur.

Partnership Property

Partnership property means the property originally brought into the partnership, or acquired, whether by purchase or otherwise, on account of the firm, or for the purposes, and in the course of the partnership business. Such property must be held and applied by the partners exclusively for the purposes of the partnership, and in accordance with the partnership agreement. Unless the contrary intention appears, property bought with money belonging to the firm is deemed to have been bought on the firm's account.

The 1890 Act lays down a particular rule where land, or premises, belongs to the partnership. It provides that unless the contrary appears, the land or premises is to be treated, as between the partners themselves, as personal property. The statute notionally converts real property into personal property. This is a feature of equity (see page 226).

Before 1965 this conversion was made for practical purposes. Where a partner died intestate his or her real property would have devolved on an heir, while personal property passed to the next-of-kin. This statutory rule allowed the same mode of devolution for a partner's real and personal property. But the *Succession Act 1965* abolished the common law rules of descent and substituted new rules which apply to both real and personal property. The rule contained in the 1890 Act is of little relevance now.

Charging the Partnership Property

A partner can be liable for two distinct debts: on the one hand, the partnership debts, and on the other hand, personal debts. The 1890 Act provides that an execution order is not to issue against partnership property unless it is a judgment against the firm. Does this mean that a creditor of a partner cannot obtain satisfaction from the latter's assets in the partnership? The answer is no. The 1890 Act provides for the appointment of a receiver whose task it is to collect for the creditor all profits attributable to the partner/debtor's share of the business and to apply them in satisfaction of the debt. By this method the partnership continues and the other partners are unaffected by the intervention of the creditor, although in such a situation the other partners can dissolve the partnership.

Rights and Duties Inter Se

The rights and duties of partners *inter se* depend primarily on the terms of the partnership agreement. In the absence of express agreement, or where the agreement is silent on a particular matter, section 24 of the 1890 Act lays down draft rules which are to be applied.

All partners are entitled to share equally in the capital and profits of the business, and must contribute equally towards the losses, whether of capital or otherwise. The firm must indemnify each partner in respect of payments made, and personal liabilities incurred, in the ordinary and proper conduct of the business, or in anything necessarily done for the preservation of the business, or the firm.

A partner making, for the purpose of the partnership, any actual payment, or advance beyond the amount of capital which had been agreed upon, is entitled to interest at the rate of 5 per cent per annum, from the date of payment or advance. A partner is not entitled, before the ascertainment of profits, to interest on capital subscribed.

Each partner may take part in the management of the partnership business. No partner is entitled to remuneration for acting in the partnership. A partner is, of course, entitled to a share in the profits. A new partner cannot be introduced to the partnership without the consent of each of the existing partners.

The partnership books are to be kept at the firm's place of business, and each partner has a right of access to, and the power to inspect and take copies of, such records. The right of inspection can be exercised by the partner, or an agent, such as an accountant.

A majority of the partners cannot expel one of their number unless such a power has been conferred by express agreement between the partners. Where a power of expulsion is granted in the partnership agreement it must be exercised *bona fide.*

DISSOLUTION OF PARTNERSHIP

Meaning of Dissolution

Dissolution is the procedure whereby a partnership is brought to an end. It may occur in several ways. The 1890 Act covers two matters in this regard. In the first place it provides a number of ways by which a partnership may be dissolved and second, it states the consequences of a dissolution.

Retirement from Partnership at Will

Where no fixed terms have been agreed on for the duration of the partnership a partner may terminate the partnership in the same way it had been created, that is by agreement. But this can only be done where all the partners concur. Where one, or more, but not all, wish a mutual dissolution it cannot be effected this way. Once all the partners agree, dissolution is effective from the moment of agreement, or from some other date agreed on. A dissolution can be verbally agreed.

Dissolution by Efflux of Time

Subject to any contrary agreement between the partners, a partnership is dissolved, if entered into for a fixed term, by the expiration of that term. Where the partnership is formed for a single venture it is terminated when that venture has ended.

Where the arrangement is a partnership at will it may be terminated by any of the partners giving notice of intention to dissolve. In such cases the termination date is that mentioned in the notice, or where no date is mentioned the partnership terminates on the date of the communication of the notice to the other partners. The dissolution is effective from the relevant date despite the opposition from the other partners. A notice of dissolution once given, cannot be withdrawn.

Dissolution by Death or Bankruptcy

Subject to any agreement between the partners, a partnership is dissolved by the death or bankruptcy of any partner. As already explained, a partnership may be dissolved, at the option of the other partners, where any partner suffers his or her share of the partnership property to be charged for personal debts.

Dissolution by Intervening Illegality

A partnership is dissolved by the happening of any event which renders it unlawful for the business of the firm to be carried on, or for the members of the firm to carry on in partnership. Of course, should a partnership be formed for an illegal purpose it was illegal *ab initio* (from the beginning).

Dissolution by Court Order

On application by a partner the High Court may dissolve a partnership for any number of reasons. Should one partner, at any time during the partnership, become mentally ill so as to be incapable of managing his or her affairs, or those of the firm, another partner, or interested party, may apply to have the partnership dissolved. The court's principal concern will be the preservation of the incapacitated partner's interest.

A physical incapacity of a permanent nature is ground for applying to have the partnership dissolved. This application may only be made by one of the partners, and not by a stranger. It would be grounded on the fact that the incapable partner cannot perform the agreement. For example, where a partnership is formed for the driving of a racing car and the partner who drives becomes blind the other partner would have sufficient grounds for seeking the aid of the court.

Where a partner, other than the partner suing, is guilty of misconduct, which in the opinion of the court, and having regard to the nature of the business, is considered prejudicially to affect that business, the court may order dissolution. Misconduct means misconduct with regard to the business, though behaviour by the partner in private life, which reflects adversely upon the business, may be sufficient. Where a solicitor is struck off the roll of the Law Society for professional misconduct the other solicitors in the partnership could seek a dissolution. An example of the private life of a partner having a bearing on the partnership would be where one partner in a marriage bureau is convicted of a serious sexual offence.

Where a partner, other than the partner suing, wilfully and persistently breaks the partnership agreement, or persists in other conduct which makes it impractical for the other partners to carry on the business, the other partners may seek the assistance of the court. Where the business operates at a loss, a dissolution of the partnership by the court is permitted.

Apart from these specific reasons, where there arises in any partnership any circumstances which, in the opinion of the High Court, renders it just and equitable that the partnership be dissolved, the court may so order.

Notification of Dissolution

On the dissolution of partnership, or on the retirement of a partner, any of the partners may publicly notify the dissolution, and may require the other partners to concur in this. This is important because where a person deals with a firm after a change in its constitution that person is entitled to treat all apparent members of the old partnership as being members of the new firm until that person has notice of the change. And, of course, the liability of a partner may continue after the resignation, unless notice is given of the retirement.

In this respect a distinction must be made between old and new customers. A public notice is sufficient to place new customers on notice of any change, though existing customers should be notified personally.

Winding-up Process

After a dissolution, the authority of a partner, together with all rights and duties, continues so far as is necessary for the purpose of winding up the partnership. In comparison, the formalities in the winding up of a company are more demanding. For example, when winding up a partnership it is not necessary to appoint a liquidator.

A firm, however, is not bound by the acts of a bankrupt partner. Where a party, not a partner, holds himself or herself out as a partner of a bankrupt, that party is bound by the acts of such bankrupt, and cannot escape liability.

Distribution of Property and Profits on Dissolution

On the dissolution of a partnership, every partner is entitled to have the partnership property applied in the payment of the firm's debts. Any surplus is then divided among them according to their respective rights as to sharing.

Where a partner has died, or otherwise ceased to be a partner, and the surviving or continuing partners carry on the business of the firm with partnership assets, without any final settlement of accounts, then, in the absence of any agreement to the contrary, the outgoing partner, or a deceased partner's personal representatives, are entitled to claim a share of the profits since the dissolution, or interest at the rate of 5 per cent per annum. The Supreme Court decided, in *Meagher v Meagher* (1961), that in a partnership at will, which had been carried on by three partners for a number of years, the time for ascertaining the value of a deceased's partners was at the date of realisation and not the date of the death, and that where the partnership assets increase after a partner's death, that partner's estate was entitled to an appropriate share. However, if the choice made was the interest of 5 per cent, then the value of the partner's share must be calculated at the moment of death.

This rule only applies in the absence of a contrary intention. Two partners, in *Williams v Harris* (1980), retiring from a four-person partnership which operated a stud farm, claimed interest for a two-year period from the date of their retirement to the date of asset realisation. The claim failed because the partnership agreement declared that when any partner ceased to be a partner, that share in the partnership business should, from the date of retirement, be purchased and belong to the remaining partners. This provision, the Supreme Court held, was sufficient to exclude the general rule.

Rule for Distribution

In settling accounts between the partners after a dissolution, a number of rules apply, in the absence of a contrary agreement:

1. Losses, including losses and deficiencies of capital, are to be paid:
   (a) first, out of profits;
   (b) next, out of capital; and
   (c) lastly, by the partners in the proportion in which they were entitled to share in the profits.
2. The assets of the firm, including the sums, if any, contributed by the partners to make up the losses, are to be applied as follows:
   (a) in paying the firm's debts and liabilities to persons who are not partners; next
   (b) in paying to each partner rateably what is due for advances, as distinguished from capital; next
   (c) in paying to each partner rateably what is due from the firm in respect of capital; and lastly
   (d) in paying the ultimate residue, if any, among the partners in the proportion in which the profits are divisible.

LIMITED PARTNERSHIP

Nature of Limited Partnership

The common law refused to recognise limited liability among partners. To alter this position the *Limited Partnership Act 1907* was enacted. A limited partnership is a firm which has general partners, who have full managerial and financial liability, and limited partners, who have no managerial role in the firm and whose financial liability is limited to an agreed sum. Persons who simply invest money in a partnership and take no active part in management are often referred to as sleeping partners. The statutory protection is lost where the limited partners take any part in the firm's management, or where the proper formalities as to registration are not observed.

Registration of Limited Partnership

Every limited partnership must register a statement, signed by the partners, with the Registrar of Companies. It must contain: (a) the firm name; (b) the nature of the business; (c) the principal place of business; (d) the full name of each partner; (e) the term of the partnership; (f) the date of its commencement; (g) a statement that the partnership is limited; (h) a description of each limited partnership; (i) the amount of the contribution from each partner, and how this is to be paid.

The purpose behind the registration of limited partnership is that persons dealing with the firm can easily ascertain who the partners are, and what their liability is. However, this disclosure of information destroys one of the greatest advantages, that of privacy. Limited partnerships became a popular method of tax avoidance though legislative changes in this area have negatived this advantage.

Modification of Partnership Rules

The *Partnership Act 1890* applies to limited partnership unless modified by the 1907 Act. Modifications have been made in a number of ways. A limited partner cannot take part in management, cannot bind the firm, and cannot dissolve the partnership by notice, nor is the partnership dissolved by the death, bankruptcy or lunacy of that partner. A limited partner may inspect the firm's books, and may, with the consent of the other partners, assign his or her share in the partnership. The assignee becomes subject to all the rights and liabilities of the limited partner.

CHAPTER 40

COMPANY LAW

Nature of Registered Company

A company is an arrangement whereby parties form a partnership which is constantly changing, with the new partners succeeding to the assets and liabilities of the old partnership. Such a partnership becomes a registered company by complying with the provisions of the *Companies Act 1963*, as amended. A registered company may be formed for many purposes, and a proportion are formed for social and charitable purposes, though the majority are formed to carry on commercial enterprises.

There are other companies, such those created by charter and statute, which are outside the ambit of this chapter.

Separate Legal Personality of Registered Company

The outstanding feature of a registered company, and the reason for its widespread usage in the commercial world, is that it is recognised in law as a legal person independent of its members, a principle emphasised in the Supreme Court, in *Belton v Carlow County Council* (1997), by Keane J. when he said that 'It has been settled law . . . that the company on the one hand and its shareholders on the other are separate and distinct legal entities.' Thus a registered company, as an artificial person possesses its own legal personality, is capable of holding property, of entering into contractual relations and of suing and being sued. Its great advantage over the natural person is its potential perpetual existence.

Comparison of Registered Company with Partnership

Many registered companies are formed before the commercial enterprise begins though it commonly happens that a business, which commences as a partnership or a sole tradership, is formed into a registered company.

There are a great many differences between a partnership and a registered company, some of which are set out hereunder:

1. A registered company is formed by the registration of certain documents required by the *Companies Act 1963*, as amended; a partnership is formed by agreement, either express or implied, and without any special formalities.
2. A registered company has a separate corporate personality distinct from its members; a partnership has no separate personality apart from the partners.

3. A private registered company can have one to fifty members and a public registered company can have from seven members upwards; a partnership cannot have more than twenty partners unless it is one of solicitors, accountants or bankers.
4. In a registered company the liability of each member may be limited; in a partnership the liability of partners is unlimited, except in the case of limited partners.
5. The creditors of a registered company generally have no right of action against the members; the creditors of a partnership can sue the partnership in the firm's name with the partners jointly and severally liable, except in the case of limited partners.
6. The powers of a company are fixed by the memorandum of association, and its internal regulation by the articles of association, both of which can only be altered in accordance with the *Companies Act 1963*, as amended; the powers of a partnership and its internal regulation are fixed by the partnership agreement, if there is one, or by the *Partnership Act 1890* and these can be altered at any time by agreement.
7. The memorandum and articles of a registered company, and other documents which must be registered from time to time, are open to public inspection; the partnership agreement is not open to public inspection, except where there are limited partners some information must be registered.
8. A member of a registered company has no implied right to contract on the company's behalf; each partner, except a limited partner, has implied authority to bind the partnership in contract.
9. In a public registered company the shares are freely transferable whereas in a private registered company the consent of the directors must usually be obtained; in a partnership a partner cannot transfer a share without the agreement of the other partners.
10. A registered company is wound up in the manner provided by the *Companies Act 1963*, as amended, and is performed by a liquidator appointed by the High Court, or the members, or the creditors; a partnership is dissolved in the manner provided for in the agreement, or by the *Partnership Act 1890* and this is generally done by the partners.
11. The capital of a registered company can only be altered in accordance with the procedures set in the *Companies Act 1963*, as amended; the capital of a partnership can be altered freely by the partners at any time.
12. Disputes in a registered company are resolved by a vote among the members, and the *Companies Act 1963*, as amended, sets different quotas for different resolutions; in a partnership disputes are either resolved by a majority, or, in serious disputes, by an arbitrator.

13. A registered company can have perpetual existence in that the death of one, or more, members has no effect on its continuance; in a partnership generally the death, bankruptcy, or retirement of one partner dissolves a partnership.
14. A registered company is subject to special taxation codes; the taxation of partners is on the same basis as that of the sole trader.

Public Registered Company

The *Companies (Amendment) Act 1983*, section 2, provides that a public company is a limited liability company which states in its memorandum that it is a public company and is registered as such. A public company must have at least seven members and two directors.

Private Registered Company

In Ireland the overwhelming number of companies are registered, and a large amount of commercial activity is carried on by private companies. The *Companies Act 1963*, section 33, defines a private company as one which has a share capital, and which by its articles (a) restricts the right to transfer its shares; (b) limits the number of its members to fifty, excluding employees and past employees whose membership commenced whilst employed by the company; and, (c) prohibits any invitation to the public to subscribe for any shares, or debentures, in the company.

Prior to 1994, a private registered company had to have two members. The *European Communities (Single-Member Private Limited Companies) Regulations, 1994* (S.I. No.275 of 1994) recognises the single-member private company and provides that the rules relating to private companies are to be modified accordingly. All registered private companies must have at least two directors.

Registration of Documents

A disclosure of certain informations must be made when registering a company. This necessity for disclosure is the major disadvantage of incorporation. A company must register a memorandum, may register articles of association, must lodge details of the first directors and secretary and the location of the company's registered office, and a statutory declaration that the statutory requirements have been complied with. These must be lodged with the Registrar of Companies at Dublin Castle.

MEMORANDUM OF ASSOCIATION

Nature of Memorandum

Every company must file a printed memorandum of association, which is the company's charter, and regulates its external affairs. Inspection of the memorandum enables parties who invest in it, or creditors dealing with it, to ascertain certain basic informations concerning the business enterprise.

Name of the Company

The memorandum must state the name of the company which must be one which the Minister for Enterprise, Trade and Employment does not consider undesirable. An appeal from the refusal to register a particular name lies to the High Court. To ensure that parties dealing with the company know of its nature, the last word, in the name of a limited private company, must be limited, or teoranta, and the name of a public limited company must end with the words public limited company, or cuideachta phoibli teoranta. The abbreviations Ltd (or teo) and plc (or cpt) may be used respectively. The Minister may dispense with this requirement where satisfied that the company is formed for promoting commerce, art, science, religion, charity, or any other useful object, and that the company intends to apply its profits, if any, in promoting its objects, and prohibits the payment of a dividend to its members.

Where a company, through inadvertence or otherwise, registers a name which is similar to a company name already in existence, the Minister may order a change of name within six months of its being registered. A company may, by special resolution, and with the approval of the Minister, change its name.

The company's name must be: (a) affixed to the outside of its place of business; (b) engraved on its seal; and (c) mentioned on all of the company's business documents. The use of the company's name in an incorrect form may render the directors personally liable for a debt of the company.

Objects of the Company

A registered company must have an objects clause. This indicates the type of business the company will pursue and enables a party contemplating an investment to discover its field of enterprise. Investors can then decide whether to take the risk. It also allows a party contemplating contracting with the company to discover whether the proposed contract comes within the objects, though this, as will be seen presently, since statutory reform, has lost much of its importance.

Modified Ultra Vires Rule Since 1963

Where a company purported to perform some act outside its objects the act was said to be *ultra vires* (beyond its powers). Prior to 1963 the courts took a strict line in this regard and consistently ruled that all such transactions were null and void and the company could, on its own plea, escape its contractual obligations. This rule was probably fair where the outside party knew that the company was acting *ultra vires*. A bank, in *In re Cummins* (1939), granted a loan to a company to enable a new majority shareholder to purchase shares in that company, a purpose outside the company's general borrowing powers and therefore *ultra vires*. Since the bank had full knowledge of the loan's purpose, the High Court held the transaction was null and void and dismissed a claim by the bank to recover the money.

But the rule was equally applied to those who had no actual knowledge that the transaction was *ultra vires*. The courts applied the doctrine of constructive notice which declared that, since the memorandum of association was a public document, those dealing with the company could have perused the objects clause in the Companies Office and thereby would discovered that the company was acting *ultra vires*. The application of the rule is illustrated by the leading English case, *Ashbury Railway Carriage Co. Ltd v Riche* (1875) where the memorandum stated that the object was the making and selling of railway carriages. The company purchased a concession for constructing a railway. It was held that the contract was *ultra vires* and that the subsequent assent of all the shareholders could not ratify the transaction. Thus, the onus was placed on the party dealing with the company not to enter an *ultra vires* transaction with the company whereas the company was not placed under a similar duty. This case illustrates how unfair the *ultra vires* rule as applied by the courts was and statutory reform has gone a long way towards mitigating its harsh effects.

Section 8 of the 1963 Act provides: 'Any act or thing done by a company which if the company had been empowered to do the same would have been lawfully and effectively done, shall, notwithstanding that the company had no power to do such act or thing, be effective in favour of any person relying on such act or thing who is not shown to have been actually aware, at the time when he so relied thereon, that such act or thing was not within the powers of the company . . .' Now the position is this: where a third party enters into an *ultra vires* contract with the company it cannot be defeated by the company unless it can be shown that the party was actually aware that the company was acting *ultra vires*. The constructive notice rule has been abolished. This provision has since been supplemented, as far as limited companies are concerned, by the *European Communities (Companies) Regulations 1973* (S.I. No.163 of 1973) which states, in section 6 that: 'In favour of a person dealing with a company in good faith, any transaction entered into by any organ of the company, being its board of directors or any person registered under these regulations as a person authorised to bind the company shall be deemed to be within the capacity of the company and any limitation of the powers of that board . . . whether imposed by the memorandum or articles of association or otherwise, may not be relied upon as against any person so dealing with the company.' The registration of a person authorised to bind the company is effected by delivering to the Registrar of Companies a notice giving the name and description of the person concerned.

The much more fair effect of section 8 can be seen in *Northern Bank Finance Corporation Ltd v Quinn and Achates Investment Co.* (1979). The bank agreed to loan money to Quinn on condition that the company guaranteed the loan by mortgaging some of its property to the bank. The company supplied its memorandum and articles to the bank. These were perused by the bank's solicitor who failed to notice that the company had only power to guarantee the company's own loans and not those of third parties. When the borrower defaulted and the bank sought to enforce its security, the company argued that the guarantee was an *ultra vires* transaction of which the bank was actually aware, an argument upheld by the High Court, which dismissed the action. The section did not protect the bank since it was actually aware that the company was precluded from entering into the transaction. The fact that the bank's solicitor did not appreciate the implications in the memorandum did not alter the fact that the transaction was null and void. The bank could not rely on the *European Communities (Companies) Regulations 1973* because the company was unlimited.

Limitation of Liability

The third item which a memorandum must contain is a statement that the liability of the members is limited, if that is to be so. Limited liability provides that no member of the company is liable to contribute towards the payment of its debts and liabilities, on a winding up, a sum greater than the amount, if any, unpaid on the shares held by that member. Where the shares are fully paid the member incurs no further liability for the company's debts and liabilities. There are some exceptions to this rule. Where the membership of a public company falls below seven, and the company carries on business for more than six months after that event then every member who knows that the company is operating at the reduced membership becomes liable for all the debts incurred during that time. Limited liability may also be lost where it is proved that members, and others, knowingly carried on the business with the intent to defraud the company's creditors, or for any fraudulent purpose (see page 427).

Share Capital of the Company

The memorandum must state the amount of the share capital with which the company is to be registered, and its division into shares of a fixed amount. To register a public company the share capital must consist of the authorised minimum which is currently at £30,000.

Association Clause and Subscription

The memorandum of association ends with the association clause and subscription. In this clause the subscribers state they desire to be formed into a company and agree to take the number of shares set opposite their names. Then follow the subscribers' witnessed signatures.

Altering the Memorandum

A company may alter its memorandum. A company may by special resolution and with the approval of the Minister alter its name. A company may by special resolution abandon, restrict, or amend any existing object or adopt a new object. An application may be made by either: (a) the holders of not less, in the aggregate, than 15 per cent in nominal value of the company's issued share capital; or (b) the holders of not less than 15 per cent of any debenture stock to the High Court within twenty-one days for the cancellation of the alteration. Such application cannot be supported by a party who consented to, or voted for, the alteration. At the hearing the High Court may confirm or cancel the alteration, or may adjourn the application so that the shares of the dissenting members may be purchased. The alteration of capital is considered on page 414.

Effect of Memorandum

The memorandum when registered binds the company and the members to the same extent as if it had been signed and sealed by each member and contained covenants by each member to observe all its provisions.

ARTICLES OF ASSOCIATION

Nature of Articles

The articles of association are regulations for the internal arrangements and management of the company. The articles generally deal with such topics as the issue and transfer of shares, alterations of share capital, general meetings, voting rights, directors, secretary, dividends, accounts and audit, winding up and various other matters.

Registration of Articles

Articles of association may, in a company limited by shares, be registered with the memorandum. Where articles are not registered the model articles set out in Table A will automatically be the articles of the company. Where a company registers articles it should expressly exclude Table A because otherwise the provisions of Table A will apply insofar as they are not inconsistent with the articles registered.

Interpretation of Articles

The articles must not contain any matter that contravenes any principle of law. In the High Court, in *Roper v Ward* (1981), Carroll J. explained: 'In construing the articles, I am guided by the principles that they are subordinate to and controlled by the memorandum of association which is the dominant instrument. While the articles cannot alter or control the memorandum or be used to expand the objects of the company, they can be used to explain it generally or to explain an ambiguity in its terms.'

Alteration of Articles

A registered company may alter its articles by special resolution subject only to the provisions of the statutes and its memorandum. The 1963 Act provides that, subject to the contrary agreement in writing of a member, no alteration of the memorandum or articles can compel a member to take or subscribe for more shares in the company, or in any way to increase that member's liability to contribute to the share capital, or otherwise to pay more money to the company.

The courts have held that the power to alter the articles must be exercised *bona fide* for the benefit of the company as a whole.

Effect of Registration

The articles when registered bind the company and the members as if they had been signed and sealed by each member, and contained covenants on the part of each member to observe their provisions.

The articles place neither the company nor its members under any contractual obligation to a non-member. The case of *Securities Trust Ltd v Hugh Moore & Alexander Ltd* (1964) (see page 199), illustrates the principle that an outsider relying on the articles has no contractual relationship with the company.

MEMBERSHIP OF A COMPANY

Definition of Member

The members of a company consist of those parties who have subscribed to the memorandum, and others who have agreed to become members and whose names are entered in the company's register of members. A party may do this by agreeing to take an allotment of shares from a company, or by taking a transfer of shares from an existing member. In either case entry on the register of members is an essential prerequisite of membership.

Allotment of Shares

The *Companies (Amendment) Act 1983* provides that the directors of a company may not issue shares without express authority contained in the articles, or by a resolution in general meeting. Such authority may be given for a specific allotment or generally, and must state the maximum amount of the shares which may be issued. An authority granted by the articles expires after five years.

Pre-emption Rights

Under the *Companies (Amendment) Act 1983* ordinary shares in a company to be issued for cash must first be offered to existing ordinary members in proportion to the nominal value of their existing holdings. Any pre-emption offer must remain open for twenty-one days. Shares not taken up on the *pro rata* basis must be offered to the ordinary members generally. Private companies may exclude this pre-emption right in the articles.

Payment for Shares

The general rule is that the member must pay in full for the shares. However, payment in full need not be made where the company does not require it. For example, shares may be allotted on payment of part of the nominal amount and on a promise of payment of the remainder as and when required by the company. Such shares are partly paid shares.

Generally, payment must be in cash though payment in kind is permitted subject to important exceptions. The *Companies (Amendment) Act 1983* prohibits a public company from accepting as consideration for shares any undertaking which is to be performed more than five years after the date of allotment. Any allotment of shares in a public company for a non-cash consideration cannot be made unless a report of the value of the consideration has been made by an independent person qualified to be an auditor of the company. The report must state the amount payable on the shares, a description of the consideration and the valuation methods used, the date of valuation and the extent to which the shares are to be treated as paid up (a) by the consideration and (b) in cash. The report must be filed with the Registrar of Companies. A share may not be allotted, in a public limited company, unless it is paid up to at least 25 per cent of the nominal value of the shares.

Where shares are issued for a non-cash consideration in a private company the company must deliver to the Registrar of Companies, within one month of the allotments, either a copy of the written contract or written particulars of the allotment and a return stating the number and nominal amount of shares so allotted, the extent to which they are to be treated as paid up, and the consideration for which they were allotted.

Shares Issued at a Discount

The general rule is that shares must not be issued at a discount, that is at a price which is lower than the nominal value of the shares. Where shares are allotted at a discount the member is liable to pay the amount of the discount to the company together with interest. It is lawful to pay a commission of up to 10 per cent in consideration for a party's agreement to take the shares.

Shares Issued at a Premium

It is possible for a registered company to issue shares at a premium, which means at an amount exceeding their nominal value, e.g., a £1 share for £1.50. Where shares are issued at a premium a sum equal to the aggregate amount of the premium on these shares must be transferred to a special account known as the share premium account. This account may be used to pay up unissued shares to be issued as fully paid bonus shares to the members, or in writing off the preliminary expenses, or providing for the premiums payable on redemption of any of the company's redeemable preference shares or debentures.

Company Providing Assistance to Purchase its own Shares

In general a company is prohibited from giving financial assistance to a party for the purpose of buying shares in that company. This rule is excluded where such assistance is permitted by a special resolution passed within the previous twelve months and a copy of the statutory declaration made by the directors, giving the names of the parties to be assisted, the form of the assistance and the purpose of the assistance, is issued to each member of the company. An application to have the resolution cancelled may be made to the High Court by not less than the holders of an aggregate of 10 per cent of the nominal value of the issued capital.

A company is exempt from the necessity to pass a special resolution in a number of instances. Where a company lends money in the ordinary course of business it can lend money to a borrower to purchase shares in that lending company. An obvious example is a bank lending money to a customer for the purchase of shares in the bank. Where the shares are to be purchased for the benefit of present, or past, employees, the company can give financial assistance.

Restriction on Membership

The number of members of a private company cannot, according to section 33 of the 1963 Act, exceed fifty though this ceiling does not apply where present and past employees are members of the company. There is no restriction on the membership of a public company.

SHARE CAPITAL

Meaning of Share Capital

The word capital in connection with a company has several meanings. It may refer to the authorised or nominal capital, which is the amount of share capital the memorandum authorises the company to issue. Or, it may relate to the issued capital which is that portion of the authorised share capital that has been allotted to the members. The paid up capital is that portion of the authorised share capital in respect of which payment has been received. The uncalled capital is that portion of the issued capital which has not been called up and for which the member remains liable. The reserved capital is that portion of the company's uncalled capital which the company has by special resolution determined shall not be called up except in the event of the company being wound up.

Relationship between Share Capital and Assets

The share capital of a company need not, and generally does not, bear any ratio with the actual value of the company's assets. It is possible on the company's formation that the value of the assets may equal the value of capital but this relationship will quickly disappear. For example, the fixed assets of a company, such as land or premises, may appreciate at a greater rate than the value of the company's shares. A company with a £100 share capital may, or may not, have assets in excess of £100.

Shares of Different Classes

A company may issue different classes of shares with different rights. The memorandum, though more usually the articles, may authorise the company to issue shares of different classes. Where a company has different classes of shares they will usually be two: ordinary shares and preference shares.

The articles determine the rights which attach to each class of shares. An ordinary share is one which carries no special rights or privileges. The holders of preference shares usually are given preference over other classes of shares as regards dividends and the repayment of capital. Preference shares may be cumulative, which entitles the holders to arrears of dividends together with current dividends, or non-cumulative. Preference shares are usually redeemable at some future date though they may be non-redeemable. The articles usually provide that preference shareholders have no voting rights except in exceptional circumstances.

Purchase by Company of its Own Shares

Section 236 of the *Companies Act 1990* provides that a company may, where so authorised by its articles, purchase its own shares. Certain formalities must be observed before the purchases may be made.

Alteration of Share Capital

The 1963 Act provides that a company authorised by its articles may at a general meeting by resolution: (a) increase its share capital by the issue of new shares; (b) consolidate its shares into one of larger amounts; (c) convert any of its paid up shares into stock; (d) reconvert stock into shares; or, (e) cancel any shares which have not been taken up and thus diminish the company's authorised share capital. Notice of such alteration must be given to the Registrar of Companies within fifteen days where the capital has been increased, and in other cases notification must be given within one month.

A company may, if authorised by its articles, reduce its share capital by special resolution. Where such a resolution is passed it may apply to the High Court for confirmation. The High Court has a discretion whether or not to confirm the resolution. In reaching a decision the court must pay particular attention to the needs of existing creditors.

TRANSFER OF SHARES

Instrument of Transfer

For a transfer of shares to be lawful a proper instrument of transfer must be delivered to the company. The company must enter in its register of members the name of the transferee on the application of the transferor of any share (see Transferability of Shares below).

Share Certificate

A share certificate contains a statement by the company that the party mentioned therein is the registered holder of a specified number of shares. It states the extent to which the shares are paid up and where the shares have a distinguishing number the certificate records it. The possession of a share certificate made out in the holder's favour is only *prima facie* evidence of title. The true evidence of title is the holder's name entered on the members' register. The validity of an extraordinary general meeting called by the company was challenged, in *Kinsella v Alliance & Dublin Consumers Gas Co.* (1982), on the ground that the company had made a conscious decision to deprive persons, to whom stock had been transferred but whose names had not been entered in the register of members, of their rights to attend and vote at the meeting. The High Court held that the meeting was valid, that only those persons who were registered as shareholders had the right to attend and vote, and that the company had made every reasonable effort to effect the transfers.

A share certificate provides the member with documentary evidence of an interest in the company which can be used as collateral for a loan. The company's articles usually state that a share transfer will not take place unless the share certificate is produced.

Register of Members

Every registered company must maintain a register of members containing the names and addresses of members, a statement of the number of shares held by each member with its distinguishing numbers, and the amount paid up on the shares. The register must show the date on which a party became a member and the date that membership ceased. This register must be kept at the company's registered office.

Every public company must maintain an index of the names of members. The index must contain a sufficient indication to enable the account of each member to be readily found in the register proper.

Except on certain occasions the register of members, and the index where one is maintained, must be open for inspection by members free of charge and by the public on payment of a small fee.

Transferability of Shares

A member has an unfettered right to transfer shares unless the memorandum or articles provide otherwise. For the company to satisfy the definition of a private company its articles must impose restrictions on the transferability of its shares, which are discussed below.

A member intending to transfer shares executes a transfer and delivers this document and the share certificate to the transferee who executes and forwards it together with the share certificate to the company. The company in due course registers the transfer by substituting the transferee's name for that of the transferor in the members' register and issues a new share certificate in favour of the transferee.

Restrictions on Transfer of Shares

As already noted a private company must by its articles restrict the transferability of its shares. The extent of such restriction will depend on the wording of the articles. Two common types of clause are used. The first provides that the directors may, in their absolute discretion and without assigning any reason, decline to register any transfer of shares. This discretion must be exercised by the directors' *bona fide* in the company's best interests.

The second common restriction to be found in the articles of a private company is the pre-emption clause. This provides that a member intending to transfer shares must first offer them to the other members of the company at a price to be ascertained in accordance with a formula contained in the articles. Where existing members fail to exercise this right of pre-emption and purchase the shares that member may transfer the shares unhindered.

BORROWING

Power of Company to Borrow

A registered company may only borrow where its memorandum expressly or impliedly so provides. A trading company has an implied power to borrow as being incidental to the carrying on of the company's business. In such cases it is unnecessary to express such a power in the memorandum. A power to borrow brings with it the implied power to charge the company's property as security for the repayment of the loan. It was held by the High Court in *Northern Bank Finance Corporation v Quinn and Achates Investment Co.* (1979) (see page 408), that an unlimited investment company was not a trading company and consequently had no power either expressly or by implication to mortgage its property in relation to a loan by a party other than the company itself.

Specific Charge

A specific charge is a mortgage on some particular piece of property (for mortgages see page 261). The existence of a specific charge prevents the company from realising and disposing of that property without the consent of the holders of the charge.

Floating Charge

A specific charge is inappropriate where the company has a circulating capital, such as stock in trade, because the party taking the charge must consent before any item can be sold. A fixed charge over the circulating capital would paralyse the company's business.

To combat this difficulty use is made of the floating charge which is an equitable charge on the current assets of a going concern. It is a charge on the assets, or on a class of assets, both present and future. The charge floats over the assets, or remains dormant, until the time when it crystallises, or becomes fixed.

Until the charge crystallises the company can dispose of its assets in the ordinary course of business. The assets disposed of cease to be subject to the floating charge, whilst all new assets acquired by the company become subject to it. In general, a floating charge crystallises, and becomes fixed, when a receiver is appointed or when the company ceases to carry on its business and begins the winding-up process, though the deed creating the charge may provide for other occasions when the charge is to crystallise.

Distinction between Fixed and Floating Charge

It is essential to distinguish between fixed and floating charges because, in certain circumstances, floating charges may be invalid on the winding up of the company (see page 426).

The company, in *In re Keenan Bros. Ltd* (1985), created a charge over its present and future book debts to secure a loan. The company was obliged to pay all money it received in respect of such debts into a designated account with the bank. On the liquidation of the company within twelve months the question arose whether the charge was fixed or floating. The Supreme Court held that by requiring the mandatory lodgement of the book debts as received by the company to a special account, which funds could not be disposed of without the bank's permission, the bank had deprived the company of the use of the book debts in the ordinary course of business. Thus, the charge created was a fixed rather than a floating charge.

Registration of Charges

The *Companies Act 1963*, section 99, provides that every charge created by a company is void against the liquidator and any creditor of the company unless particulars are delivered to the Registrar of Companies for filing in the company's file within twenty-one days after its creation. Failure to register renders the charge void against the liquidator and creditors though this is without prejudice to any contract to repay any money due.

When the High Court is satisfied that the omission to register a charge within the twenty-one days was accidental or inadvertent, or because of some other sufficient cause, or is not of a nature to prejudice creditors or members, it may extend the time for registration. The practice in such cases, as happened in *In re Telford Motors Ltd* (1978), is for the High Court to extend the time for registration without prejudice to the rights, if any, acquired by parties prior to the time when particulars of the charge were actually registered. In that case the company borrowed money against a charge on land. When the company was about to be wound up two years later it was discovered that the charge has not been registered. An application to extend the time for registration was granted but subject to the proviso already explained.

COMPANY MANAGEMENT

Members and Management

In the discussion of a partnership on page 395 it was noted that every partner, except a limited partner, is entitled to partake in the management of the business. There is no such rule as regards the members of a company. An attraction of company membership is that it enables a party to invest money and enjoy its rewards without the responsibilities of management. Of course, there are many occasions when the members of the company will be its management. In many private companies the shares are held by a small number of persons who all play an active role in management, or where the majority are held by one party who is the management and the remaining member is registered merely to satisfy the definition of private company.

Directors

The management of a company is performed by its directors. The *Companies Act 1963*, section 174 provides that every company must have at least two directors. A director need not be a member of the company. The *Companies Act 1990* restricts directors of insolvent companies from becoming directors of other companies for five years. The High Court may lift this restriction where the director had acted honestly and responsibly in the conduct of the insolvent company's affairs. The restriction does not apply where the other company has an allotted share capital of £100,000 if a public limited company, or £20,000 if a private company, and the allotted share capital was fully paid up in cash.

The articles generally provide that the directors may exercise all such powers as are not by statute, or the articles, required to be exercised by the company in general meeting. The directors may, by the articles, be permitted to delegate any of their powers to committees consisting of such members of their body as they think fit. They may appoint one, or more of their body to the office of managing director and may confer any of the powers exercisable by them on such terms and conditions as they think fit.

Office of Director

The office of director is that of a paid servant of the company. A director is not bound to give continuous attention to the company's affairs. The duties are of an intermittent nature to be performed at periodic board meetings. A director is not bound to attend all board meetings though attendance should be as regular as is reasonably possible. It is only where a director combines this office with another post within the company, such as managing director or company secretary or accountant, that a substantial amount of time must be devoted to the company's affairs.

When acting on the company's behalf a director is its agent. The powers entrusted to directors are fiduciary powers which should only be exercised for the benefit of the company. Decisions must be made *bona fide* for the benefit of the company. In *Clarke v Workman* (1920) a resolution transferring a controlling interest in the company was declared invalid where the directors, holding 55 per cent of the shares, proposed to transfer their shares to a competitor while the directors holding the remainder of the shares, apprised of the meeting, were not told of its purpose. In *Nash v Lancegaye Safety Glass (Ireland) Ltd* (1958) it was held that an issue of a large block of shares to one director to strengthen his voting rights was not a *bona fide* exercise of their powers by the directors.

Directors must not place themselves in positions where their duty to the company clashes with their personal interests. Directors are accountable to the company for their breaches of trust. In *Jackson v The Munster Bank* (1885) the directors were held liable to the company for loans issued to a fellow director without security despite the fact that the directors had not sanctioned the loan but because they had remained passive after ascertaining the true position. The High Court held, in *Jones v Gunn* (1997), that where a company is clearly insolvent, the directors owe a fiduciary duty to the general creditors and may not make payments which benefit themselves personally to the detriment of the general and independent creditors.

Secretary of the Company

Every company must appoint a company secretary who may combine this office with that of director. The *Companies Act 1990* lays down qualifications which those holding a company secretaryship in a public limited company must hold.

MAJORITY RULE

General Meetings

The members have an opportunity at the general meetings of the company to control the directors. The principle of majority rule applies. The first general meeting of a company must be held within eighteen months of its incorporation. Thereafter, an annual general meeting must be held in each calendar year with an interval of not more than fifteen months between each.

The directors may summon other general meetings, known as extraordinary general meetings. Members, holding not less than one-tenth of the paid up capital which carries the right to vote at the company's general meetings, may requisition an extraordinary general meeting. On the directors' failure to do so, the members requisitioning the meeting may themselves do so.

If for any reason it is impracticable to call a meeting of a company, the High Court may on a director's or a member's application order a general meeting to be held.

Resolutions

Prima facie, an ordinary resolution at a company's general meeting binds the company. An ordinary resolution requires a simple majority to be passed. Statute, or the articles, may provide for the passing of a special resolution, which is one passed by a majority of not less than three-fourths of the members, to validate certain actions. Notice to move a special resolution must be given at least twenty-one days before the general meeting at which it is to be proposed. For example, resolutions to alter the company's objects or the articles must be by special resolution.

Voting

Members of a company with the right to vote, which is normally confined to ordinary shareholders, may attend general meetings and vote in person or may appoint a proxy. Every member, entitled to attend and vote at a general meeting, may appoint another party, whether a member of the company or not, to attend and vote.

Minority Protection

Those in control of a company, particularly in a private company, may take advantage of their position to oppress the minority. Those oppressed may apply to the High Court for relief. The High Court may, where oppression is proved, order that the company be wound up under section 213 of the 1963 Act. The High Court, in *In re Murph's Restaurants Ltd* (1979), ordered the winding up of a company where two directors and shareholders excluded a third director and shareholder from the company's management.

An alternative relief which the High Court may grant, under section 205 of the 1963 Act, is to order the other members of the company to purchase the shares of the oppressed members. In *In re Greenore Trading Co. Ltd* (1980), when resigning, one of the three directors sold his shares to a fellow director. Part of the purchase price came from company funds. When this fact was revealed to the third director he sought an order that his shares should be purchased by the remaining director. The High Court, holding that the original transaction was oppressive to the third director, granted the order.

COMPANY ACCOUNTS

Books of Accounts

Every company must keep proper books of accounts. Such documentation as is necessary to give a true and fair view of the state of the company's affairs, and to explain its transactions, must be kept. Account must be kept of: (a) all moneys received, and all moneys expended, by the company, and the matters in respect of which the receipt and expenditure takes place; (b) sales and purchases of goods by the company; and, (c) the assets and liabilities of the company.

The books of accounts must be kept at the company's registered office, or at such place as the directors think proper, and must at all times be open to inspection by the directors.

Presentation of Accounts to Members

The directors of a company must, within eighteen months after its incorporation, and subsequently at least once in every calendar year, lay before the company in general meeting a profit and loss account and a balance sheet. The balance sheet must give a true and fair view of the company's state of affairs as at the end of the financial year, and the profit and loss account must give a true and fair view of the profit and loss of the company for that financial year. These accounts must be signed by at least two of the company's directors. The *Companies (Amendment) Act 1986* provides the form in which financial information must be given to the members.

Filing of Accounts

Section 149 of the 1963 Act provides that public companies have to attach certain financial information to the annual return made to the Registrar of Companies. The *Companies (Amendment) Act 1986* extends this provision to private companies though concessions are made in respect of small and medium sized companies.

A small company is one with a balance sheet not exceeding £1.25 million, with a turnover not exceeding £2.5 million and an average number of employees not exceeding fifty. A small company must file a summarised balance sheet and limited notes to the accounts. A medium company is one with a balance sheet not exceeding £5 million, with a turnover not exceeding £10 million and an average number of employees not exceeding 250. A medium company is exempt from filing its turnover and cost of sales and the profit and loss account begins at gross profit.

COMPANY AUDIT

Auditors

Every company must, at each annual general meeting, appoint auditors to hold office until the conclusion of the next annual general meeting. The auditors must report to the members assembled in general meeting on the accounts examined by them and on every profit and loss account and balance sheet laid before the company in general meeting. This duty is fulfilled by forwarding their report to the company secretary. The auditors' report must be read to the company in general meeting and must be open to inspection by the members.

The report of the auditors must state whether in their opinion the company's accounts have been properly prepared in accordance with the statutory provisions and that they give a true and fair view of the state of affairs of the company in this regard.

Powers and Liabilities of Auditors

Auditors have a right of access at all times to the books and accounts of the company and are entitled to require from the officers of the company such information and explanation at they consider necessary for the proper performance of their functions. Auditors are entitled to attend the general meetings, receive all communications relating to any general meeting of the company and address a general meeting on any matter which concerns them as auditors.

Auditors are liable to the company for any loss occasioned it by their fraud or negligence in the performance of their functions. The auditors must exercise reasonable care and skill in making the appropriate inquiries and investigations. But it is not a function of the auditors to give advice to either the directors or members. Their task is to ascertain the true financial position of the company and it is of no concern to the auditors whether the company's business is being conducted prudently or profitably.

PROTECTION OF COMPANY BY THE COURT

Appointment of Examiner

Where it appears that a company is unable to pay its debts, and no notice of a resolution for its winding up has been given more than seven days before the application and no order had been made for its winding up, the High Court may appoint an examiner to the company for the purpose of examining the state of its affairs and to perform such duties as are imposed by the *Companies Act 1990*. The court may make an order where it considers that such action would be likely to facilitate the company's survival as a going concern.

The petition to appoint an examiner may be presented by the company, or the directors, or a creditor, or members holding not less than one-tenth of such of the paid up capital as carries the right of voting at general meetings.

Protection of Court

During the period beginning with the presentation of a petition and ending on the expiry of three months from that date or on the withdrawal or refusal of the petition, whichever first happens, the company is deemed to be under the protection of the court.

Effect of Court Protection

As long as a company is under the protection of the court: (a) no proceedings for its winding up may be commenced or resolution for winding up passed and any resolution so passed has no effect; (b) no receiver may be appointed; (c) no legal process can be put into force against its property without the examiner's consent; (d) no action may be taken to realise any security which is charged on its property without the examiner's consent; (e) no step may be taken to repossess goods in the company's possession under a hire-purchase agreement without the examiner's consent; and (f) where any person other than the company is liable to pay all or any part of the company's debts no legal process can be put in force against such person's property and no proceedings of any sort may be commenced against such person in respect of such debts.

Powers of Examiner

The examiner has, with the necessary modifications, the powers possessed by auditors. The examiner may convene, set the agenda, and preside at meetings of the directors and general meetings, and propose resolutions and give reports. An examiner is entitled to reasonable notice of, and to attend and be heard at, all meetings of the directors and all general meetings.

Where the examiner becomes aware of any actual or proposed action in relation to the income, assets or liabilities which is likely to be detrimental to that company the examiner, subject to the rights of parties acquired in good faith and for value, has full powers to take whatever steps are necessary to halt, prevent or rectify the effects of such action.

The examiner must conduct an examination of the company's affairs and report to the High Court within twenty-one days or such longer period as the court allows. A copy of the report must be given to the company. The report must contain a statement of the affairs of the company showing particulars of the company's assets, debts and liabilities. An opinion must be given as to whether the company is capable of survival as a going concern together with a statement of the conditions which it is felt are essential to ensure its survival whether as regards the internal management and controls of the company or otherwise. An opinion must be formed as to whether an attempt to continue the undertaking is likely to be more advantageous to the members as a whole, and the creditors as a whole, than the company's winding up.

An examiner may, and must where directed by the court, appoint a committee of creditors to assist in the performance of the duties of examiner.

Powers of the Court

The High Court may, following a hearing on the examiner's report, make such order as it deems fit. Amongst other actions it may: (a) order the discharge from the protection of the court of the whole or part of the company's assets; (b) impose such terms and conditions as it sees fit for the continuance of the protection of the court; (c) wind up the company; (d) order the sale of the whole or any part of the undertaking; (e) formulate proposals for a compromise or scheme of arrangement; or (f) order the calling, holding and conduct of a meeting of the directors or a general meeting to consider such matters as the court directs.

LIQUIDATION OF COMPANY

Perpetual Existence of Company

The advantage of a registered company is the possibility of perpetual existence. Members may dispose of shares and directors may die, resign or retire but the company may continue for ever. A company ceases to exist where it is dissolved. The process towards that end is known as liquidation or winding up.

Nature of Liquidation

Liquidation is the winding up of a company. It is a signal to members, creditors and the world at large that the company no longer wishes to exist as a legal entity. Section 206 of the 1963 Act provides that a winding up may be: (a) compulsory by the High Court; or, (b) voluntary by the members or creditors.

Compulsory Liquidation

A petition for the compulsory liquidation of a registered company may be presented to the High Court by: (a) the company; (b) a creditor; or (c) in certain circumstances, by a present or past member.

A registered company may be wound up where: (a) the company has passed a special resolution for compulsory liquidation; (b) the company does not commence its business within a year of incorporation or suspends its business for a whole year; (c) the number of members is reduced below seven, or below two in the case of a private company; (d) the company is unable to pay its debts; (e) the court is of opinion that it is just and equitable that the company should be wound up; or, (f) the court is satisfied that the company's affairs are being conducted, or the powers of the directors are being exercised, in a manner oppressive to any member of the company.

A company is unable to pay its debts where either a creditor proves that the company owes to that creditor more than £1,000, that a demand for payment in writing has been made and the company has for three weeks failed to comply, or a judgment creditor of the company has levied execution which remained unsatisfied. In a compulsory winding up the High Court appoints the liquidator.

Voluntary Liquidation

A company may be wound up voluntarily where: (a) the period, if any, fixed for the duration of the company by its articles expires, or an event, if any, takes place on the occurrence of which the articles provide that the company is to be liquidated, and a general meeting has resolved that the company be wound up voluntarily; (b) where the company resolves by special resolution that it be wound up voluntarily; or, (c) where the company in general meeting resolves that it cannot by reason of its liabilities continue its business and that it be wound up voluntarily.

Where a voluntary liquidation is proposed, the majority of the directors may make a statutory declaration that, having enquired fully into the company's affairs they have formed the opinion that the company will be able to pay its debts in full within a specified period not exceeding twelve months from the commencement of the liquidation. To be effective this declaration of solvency must be made within twenty-eight days of the winding up resolution, it must embody a statement of the assets and liabilities, it must have attached a report made by an independent person that the opinion of the directors and the statement of the assets and liabilities are reasonable, and must be delivered to the Registrar of Companies.

Where the declaration of solvency is made, the liquidation is known as a members' voluntary winding up and the company in general meeting appoints the liquidator.

Where the declaration of solvency is not made the liquidation is known as a creditors' voluntary winding up. In such a winding up the company must arrange a meeting of the creditors, to be held not later than the day after the company meeting at which the resolution for voluntary liquidation is proposed, at which the directors must make a full statement as to the company's financial position. Members and creditors, at their respective meetings, may nominate a person as liquidator. Where they nominate different persons the creditor's nomination is liquidator. At their meeting, the creditors may also appoint a committee of inspection to supervise the liquidator, to which the members of the company may appoint representatives.

Duties and Powers of Liquidator

The primary duty of a liquidator is to collect in the company's assets. Out of these the expenses of the liquidation and the debts and liabilities of the company are paid, and the remainder is distributed amongst the company's members.

In performing this duty the liquidator may do all, or any, of the following: (a) bring or defend any legal action in the name and on behalf of the company; (b) carry on the business of the company so far as that may be beneficial to the winding up; (c) appoint a solicitor to assist in the performance of the duties; (d) sell or mortgage the company's property; and (e) do all other acts which may be necessary for the winding up of the company's affairs.

Fraudulent Preference

Under section 286 of the 1963 Act any conveyance, mortgage, delivery of goods, payment, execution or other act relating to property, made or done by or against a company which is unable to pay its debts as they become due in favour of any creditor with a view to giving such creditor a preference over the other creditors is, if a winding up commences within six months, deemed a fraudulent preference of the creditors and is invalid. Certain other transactions made within two years before the commencement of the winding up are, unless the contrary is shown, deemed to have been made with a view to giving a preference over the other creditors and to be a fraudulent preference.

A payment is a fraudulent preference where it is made with the dominant intention of giving that creditor a preference over other creditors and it is the company's voluntary act. In *In re John Daly & Co. Ltd* (1886) the company's auditor advanced money to it which was to be repaid on a date when it was expected the members in a general meeting would authorise additional capital. Instead, the members resolved to wind up the company. After the petition was presented the company repaid the money. It was held to be a void preferential payment. In *In re Olderfleet Shipbuilding Co. Ltd* (1922) the granting of a mortgage to a bank to secure overdraft facilities was held not to be a fraudulent preference but a *bona fide* attempt to assist the company out of its difficulties.

Avoidance of Floating Charges

To prevent an insolvent company from creating a floating charge to secure past debts to the prejudice of its unsecured creditors, section 288 of the 1963 Act provides that where a company is being wound up, a floating charge on the undertaking or property of the company created within twelve months before the commencement of the winding up is invalid, unless the company was solvent immediately after the charge was created. Exceptions to this are money actually advanced or paid, or the actual price or value of goods or services sold or supplied to the company at the time of, or subsequent to the creation of, and in consideration for, the charge with interest at 5 per cent. Certain other floating charges are invalid where created within two years of the commencement of the winding up.

The Supreme Court, in *In re Creation Printing Co. Ltd* (1981), held invalid a floating charge in favour of a bank, which was given in forbearance to demand the immediate repayment of money, on the ground that immediately after its creation the company was insolvent. The onus of proving insolvency lies on the party asserting the validity of the floating charge.

The effect of section 288 is merely to invalidate the charge. The creditor remains an unsecured creditor.

Fraudulent Trading

Section 297 of the 1963 Act provides that if in the winding up of a company it appears that the business has been carried on with intent to defraud creditors, or for any fraudulent purpose, any person who was knowingly a party to the carrying on of the business is guilty of a criminal offence. Section 297A provides that if in the course of the winding up it appears that any person was, while an officer of the company, knowingly a party to the carrying of any business of the company in a reckless manner, or with intent to defraud creditors or for any fraudulent purpose, the High Court may, on the application of the liquidator, any creditor, or any member, if it thinks it proper to do so, declare that such person is to be personally liable without any limitation of liability for all, or any of the liabilities of the company. In effect, such persons lose the privilege of limited liability.

The High Court, in *In re Hunting Lodges Ltd* (1985), held the directors of the company and the purchaser of the main asset personally liable for the company's debts where one director, on the sale of the sole asset, deposited part of the sale price, paid by the purchaser by way of three bank drafts made out to fictitious persons, in a building society. The High Court, in *Mehigan v Duignan* (1997), held a director personally liable for £91,000, an expenditure which flowed from the huge amount of time the liquidator spent seeking to overcome deficiencies in the books and records of the company because of the failure by the company, wilfully authorised by the director, to keep proper books of account.

CHAPTER 41

COPYRIGHT, PATENTS AND TRADE MARKS

Nature of Intellectual Property

As explained elsewhere in this book property is divided into real property and personal property. Real property consists of interests in land and premises and personal property consists of all other types of property. One of the sub-categories of personal property is intellectual property, which encompasses copyright, patents and trade marks. In this regard the law protects the results of the individual's ingenuity and inventiveness. This facet of the individual's personality is considered capable of ownership and, therefore, protection by the law.

Protection of a Limited Nature

The protection of intellectual property is, as in other instances, the balancing of conflicting interests. On the one hand, the inventiveness of the individual warrants protection because it is just that endeavour and achievement are rewarded and the search for new ideas and inventions is encouraged. On the other hand, the inventiveness of one individual should benefit mankind and add to the store of human knowledge. To reconcile these conflicting interests the law grants, generally, a limited protection to the owners of intellectual property. For example, copyright continues during the lifetime of an author and fifty years thereafter. It does not continue forever. The owner of a patent has the exclusive benefit of it for a period of sixteen years. Again, the protection does not continue forever.

COPYRIGHT

Nature of Copyright

Copyright in relation to an original literary, musical or artistic work is the exclusive right to do, or to authorise other persons to do, certain acts in relation to that work. Such acts include reproducing it in any material form, publishing it, performing it in public, broadcasting it, or making an adaptation of it. This type of copyright subsists for a certain period of time. A party is not entitled to copyright except in accordance with the *Copyright Act 1963*, as amended.

Subjects of Copyright

Copyright subsists in every original literary, dramatic or musical work. Copyright does not exist over thoughts or ideas. It is the form in which such ideas or thoughts are expressed which is protected. For copyright to attach, the work must be original. This does not mean that the work must be the product of original or inventive thought. It only means that the expression of thought must have originated with the author.

Literary work includes all words in print or writing. The form of the work is protected without any consideration of style or quality. A letter, private or commercial, is the copyright property of the writer though the paper itself may pass to the recipient. The length of the work is unimportant. A single-worded invented title receives the same protection as a longer work.

Copyright subsists in dramatic work to include the dramatic incidents together with the words, if any. A dramatic work includes any piece of recitation, choreographic work or entertainment in mime, the scenic arrangement or acting form of which is fixed in writing or otherwise, and any cinematograph production where the arrangement or acting form, or combination of incidents represented, gives the work an original character. Copyright subsists in every musical work. This protection extends to all original musical work together with the rearranging of existing work or an adaptation. Copyright subsists in records and other contrivances by means of which sound is mechanically produced and extends to tapes. Artistic work includes works of painting, drawing, sculpture and artistic craftsmanship and architectural works of art and engraving and photographs. Engraving includes an etching, lithograph, woodcut, print or similar work not being a photograph. Sculpture includes any cast or model made for the purpose of sculpture.

Copyright subsists in every cinematograph and extends to the film together with the soundtrack.

Ownership of Copyright

The author of an original literary, dramatic or artistic work is entitled to the copyright subsisting in that work. Where such a work is made by the author in the course of employment under a contract of service for a newspaper, magazine or similar periodical the copyright subsists in the owner of the newspaper, magazine or periodical. Where a party commissions the taking of a photograph, or the printing or drawing of a portrait, or the making of an engraving, and pays, or agrees to pay, for it in money or money's worth and the work is made in pursuance of that commission, that party and not the author is entitled to the copyright.

The maker of a cinematograph film is entitled to the copyright in the film except where a party commissions its making, then that party is the copyright owner. The maker of a sound recording is entitled to the copyright in that sound recording. On a sound recording there may be two distinct copyrights, that of the author of the material and that of the maker of the recording. Copyright subsists in every television, and in every sound recording, broadcast.

Term of Copyright

The term of copyright in every original literary, dramatic or artistic work is the lifetime of the author and a period of fifty years from the end of the year in which the author died. In the case of a photograph the copyright continues for a period of fifty years from the end of the year in which the photograph was first published. Copyright subsisting in a cinematograph film continues for a period of fifty years. Copyright in a television broadcast or in a sound broadcast continues to subsist for fifty years from the end of the year in which the broadcast is first made.

Infringement of Copyright

Copyright in a work is infringed by a party who, without the copyright owner's consent, does anything with the work where the sole right to do such act is conferred on the copyright owner. A production, reproduction, performance, translation, adaptation or recording of the work, without the copyright owner's consent, is prohibited. The High Court ruled, in *Private Research Ltd v Brosnan* (1996), that, since the definition of a literary work includes any written table or compilation, the compilation of the annual returns of companies for a given period prepared by the plaintiff was protected by copyright and any substantial reproduction of it by the defendant was a breach of copyright. Copyright, unlike a patent, is not a monopoly. Where two independent works prove to be similar, such as two photographs of the same object, sole protection is not afforded to either author. Copyright merely prevents the appropriation by one party of the creative labours of others.

An infringement of copyright is actionable by the copyright owner. The remedies are damages, injunction and an order for account. In *Allibert SA v O'Connor* (1982) the High Court, in a successful action for breach of copyright in respect of the manufacture of boxes, awarded compensation for lost profits which the copyright owner would have made but for the infringement.

Where the infringement of copyright is innocent an award of damages cannot be made. The only remedy is an account of profits in respect of the infringement. Where there was a flagrant infringement, the court may award additional damages.

Where, on the application of the copyright owner, the District Court is satisfied on evidence that there are reasonable grounds for believing that goods are being hawked, copied or sold, it may authorise the gardaí to seize such copies without a warrant and to destroy them or deliver them up to the copyright owner under the *Copyright (Amendment) Act 1987*.

A number of criminal offences in relation to the infringement of copyright are created by the statutes.

Lawful Uses of Copyright Work

Some infringements of copyright are lawful. Any fair dealing with any work for the purpose of private study, research, criticism, review or newspaper summary is not an infringement of the copyright of that work. The copyright in a published literary or dramatic work is not infringed by reading or reciting in public, or in a broadcast, of a reasonable extract from it, provided the work is sufficiently acknowledged.

The publication in a collection, mainly composed of non-copyrighted matter, intended for use in schools and so described in the title and in any advertisement issued by the publisher, of short passages from published literary works, is not an infringement of copyright provided that not more than two of such passages from works by the same author are published by the same publisher within five years, and that the source from which such passages are taken is acknowledged.

The making of records of a musical work is not an infringement of the copyright where the party making the recording proves that records of the work have previously been made or imported into the State for the purpose of retail sale with the consent of the copyright owner. In such cases the recording maker must give notice to the copyright owner and pay a fair royalty.

Where copyright has subsisted in a cinematograph film and such copyright has, after the passage of fifty years, ceased to subsist, there is no infringement of the copyright in any literary, dramatic, musical or artistic work presented in the film where the film is shown in public. This would occur where the copyright owner of the work exhibited in the film is alive. In the case of a newsreel cinematograph film there is no infringement of copyright where it is shown in public provided more than fifty years have elapsed since the principal events depicted in the film have occurred.

Licences

The owner of the copyright may consent to the publication of the work. Such a consent, when given, is known as a licence and is generally granted on terms agreed between the parties. A licence may relate to all the rights comprised in the copyright or it may be confined to one or more of such rights.

PATENTS

Nature of Patent

A patent is a grant from the State of the exclusive right to make, use, exercise and sell the products of an invention. It is a true monopoly in that it enables the patentee to prevent all others, without consent, from making, using, exercising and selling the invention. Should another party independently of the patentee subsequently arrive at the same invention, the patentee can prevent that other party from using that invention.

The *Patents Act 1964*, as amended, is the relevant legislation.

Meaning of Invention

Invention is defined as any new and useful art, process, machine, manufacture or composition of matter, or any new and useful improvement in any art, process, machine, manufacture or composition of matter, and includes an alleged invention and also any new method or process of testing applicable to the improvement or control of manufacture. The invention, to be patented, must be the result of human ingenuity. A process of nature cannot be patented. In *Ranks Hovis McDougall Ltd v Controller of Patents* (1979) an application to patent a new strain of micro-organism, which when treated provided edible protein, was refused because the High Court held it was a form of life, albeit a very low form. The process by which the micro-organism was isolated from soil was patented.

Application for Patent

An application for a patent for an invention can be made either by a party claiming to be the true and first inventor, or any assignee of the party claiming to be the true and first inventor. A personal representative may make the application where the deceased would have been entitled to apply.

An application for a patent must be made in the prescribed form and be filed in the Patents Office. The application must state that the applicant is in possession of the invention and must state the name of the party claiming to be the true and first inventor.

Every application must be accompanied by either a complete specification or a provisional specification. Should it be the latter a complete specification must be filed within twelve months or the application is deemed to have been abandoned. Every specification must describe the invention.

Examination of Application

When a complete specification has been filed the application is referred to an examiner who investigates whether the invention has been published previously and whether the requirements of the statute have been fulfilled. An application will be refused where the invention has been published prior to the application.

Refusal of Application

Where it appears to the Controller of Patents that an application for a patent: (a) claims as an invention anything obviously contrary to well established natural laws; (b) that the use of the invention in respect of which the application is made would be contrary to public order or morality; or (c) that it claims as an invention a substance capable of being used as food or medicine which is only a mixture of known ingredients, the application may be refused.

Opposition to Application

When the requirements of the statute have been fulfilled the Controller accepts and publishes the fact that a complete specification has been accepted. Within three months from the date of publication any party interested may give notice of opposition to the grant of the patent on any of the following grounds: (a) that the opponent is the true inventor; (b) that the invention has been published in the State in either another specification or in any other document; (c) that the invention was used in the State prior to application; (d) that the invention is obvious and does not involve any inventive step; (e) that the subject of any application is not an invention; or, (f) that the complete specification does not sufficiently and fairly describe the invention or the method by which it is to be performed.

In *Beecham Group Ltd v Bristol Myers Co.* (1981) a pharmaceutical company applied to register a patent which related to a penicillin, known as amoxycillin, which could be orally administered to humans. A rival pharmaceutical company successfully opposed the application on two grounds. First, it was proved that the specification had been previously published, and second, that there was no ingenuity involved in producing the composition and that it lacked novelty.

Granting of Patent

The Controller of Patents grants and seals a patent. Such grant confers on the patentee the full, sole and exclusive right to make, use, exercise and sell in the State the invention in respect of which the patent is granted. The granting of the patent prohibits all others from making use of, or putting in practice, the said invention or to represent themselves as the inventor. The term of the patent is sixteen years from the date of the granting of the patent.

Where it appears that the patentee has been inadequately remunerated by the patent the term may be extended by five years or in exceptional circumstances by ten years. In *In re Fisons Pharmaceuticals Ltd* (1984) the patentee of INTAL, a large selling cromoglycate product used as a prophylactic for asthma, applied for an extension of the term, claiming it had not been adequately compensated in Ireland. The Supreme Court refused an extension on the ground that the sales in Ireland of the product had been good and that it would not be proper to deduct from such profits a proportion of the research and development costs incurred by the patentee, a multinational industrial giant. But the High Court, in *In re Technobiotic Ltd* (1989), granted the full ten-year extension to the patented drug Flutamide, which was used in the treatment of cancer.

Revocation of Patent

A patent may, on the application of the Attorney General or any interested party, be revoked by the High Court on any of the following grounds: (a) that the patent was granted to a party not entitled to it; (b) that the subject of the patent was not an invention; (c) that the invention is not novel; (d) that the invention is obvious and does not involve any inventive step; (e) that the invention was not useful; (f) that the complete specification did not sufficiently and fairly disclose or describe the invention; (g) that the patent was obtained on a false representation; or, (h) that the primary or intended use or exercise of the invention is contrary to public order or morality.

The defendant, in *Wavin Pipes Ltd v Hepworth Iron Co. Ltd* (1981), was granted a patent which related to pipe couplings. The plaintiff sought to revoke the patent on the grounds of lack of novelty and obviousness. Both grounds failed and the High Court refused to revoke the patent.

Licences of Right

At any time after the sealing of a patent the patentee may apply to the Controller for the patent to be endorsed with the words 'Licences of right'. Where a patent is so endorsed any party is entitled as of right to a licence under the patent on terms settled by the Controller, in default of agreement between the parties. In settling the terms the Controller shall endeavour to secure the widest possible use of the invention in the State consistent with the patentee's right to derive reasonable advantage from the patent.

Infringement of Patents

A patentee enforces the right under the patent by means of an action for an infringement of the patent. Damages and an injunction may be awarded. In such proceedings damages may not be awarded where the defendant proves that at the date of the infringement he or she was not aware, and had no reasonable grounds for supposing, that the patent existed. A party is not deemed to have been aware or to have reasonable grounds for supposing that the patent existed merely because of the application to an article of the word 'patent' or 'patented', or any words expressing or implying that a patent has been obtained for the article, unless the number of the patent accompanied the word or words in question.

Register of Patents

A register of patents is maintained at the office of the Controller of Patents and contains the particulars of patents in force, assignments and licences. The register is *prima facie* evidence of matters entered therein and is open to public inspection.

TRADE MARKS

Meaning of Trade Mark

A trade mark means any sign capable of being represented graphically which is capable of distinguishing the goods or services of one undertaking from those of other undertakings and may consist of words (including personal names), designs, letters, numerals or the shape of goods or their packaging.

The question arose, in *ITT World Directories Inc. v Controller of Patents* (1985), whether directories were goods and whether the applicants were acting in the course of trade. The applicants published, under a monopoly granted by the Minister for Posts and Telegraphs, the classified telephone directory of businesses known as *The Golden Pages.* Advertisements were carried for which the applicants were paid. The directory was distributed by the Minister and the applicants received no revenue from direct sales. The Supreme Court held that the directories were goods, and the definition of trade mark did not require that the connection in the course of trade between the goods and the person using the trade mark depended upon a sale effected or intended by the latter person. The devise sought to be registered was the expression *Golden Pages* surmounted by an open book, coloured yellow, above which, in silhouette, the handpiece of a telephone lay horizontally.

A registered trade mark is a property right which is obtained by registration of the mark under the *Trade Marks Act 1996* which entitled the owner to rights and certain remedies. No action may be maintained in relation to an unregistered trade mark though the law relating to passing off (see page 216) remains intact.

Registerable Trade Mark

The application to register a trade mark must state that the trade mark is being used by the applicant in relation to the specified goods or services or that the applicant has a *bona fide* intention that it should be so used. Where there is no present intention by the applicant to use the trade mark registration will be refused.

Marks whose Registration is Prohibited

The following shall not be registered:

1. Trade marks which are devoid of any distinctive character.
2. Trade marks which consist exclusively of signs or indications which may serve, in trade, to designate the kind, quality, quantity, intended purpose, value, geographical origin, the time of production of goods or of rendering of services, or other characteristics of goods or services.
3. Trade marks which consist exclusively of signs or indications which have become customary in the current language or in the *bona fide* and established practice of the trade.
4. A sign if it consists exclusively of the shape which results from the nature of the goods themselves or the shape of the goods which is necessary to obtain a technical result or the shape which gives substantial value to the goods.
5. A trade mark which is contrary to public policy or the accepted principles of morality or of such a nature as to deceive the public.
6. Trade marks which are identical or similar to an earlier trade mark and where the goods or services for which the trade mark is applied for are identical or similar to the goods or services for which the earlier trade mark is protected, and there exists a likelihood of confusion on the part of the public, which includes the likelihood of association of the later trade mark with the earlier trade mark.
7. Trade marks which are identical or similar to an earlier trade mark and, where the goods or services for which the trade mark is applied for are not similar to those for which the earlier trade mark is protected, shall not be registered if the trade mark has a reputation and the use of the later trade mark without due cause would take unfair advantage of, or be detrimental to, the distinctive character or reputation of the earlier trade mark.

An application made, in *Cola-Cola Co. v F. Cade & Sons Ltd* (1957), to register the mark Cada Cola in respect of non-alcoholic cola drinks was opposed by the registered owners of the mark Cola Cola on the ground that it was likely to deceive purchasers. The Supreme Court held there was no likelihood of the mark causing deception or confusion. In *Application of Mediline AG* (1970) an application to register the word Bidex as a trade mark for cosmetics and soaps was opposed by the registered owner of the trade mark Barbidex on the ground that the proposed mark was likely to deceive. The High Court held that there was no likelihood of deception or confusion. But the High Court held, in *P.J.Carroll & Co. v Philip Morris Inc.* (1970), that the word Paxona used on cigarette cartons, which was sought to be registered, would suggest a connection in the course of trade with cigarettes in cartons marked Pax, a registered mark, and would be likely to cause confusion and should not be registered.

An application to register a mark consisting of a crocodile in respect of clothing, including leather footwear, in *La Chemise Lacoste SA v Controller of Patents* (1978) was refused. The Supreme Court held that the crocodile in the mark was not so different from other crocodiles as to distinguish the goods, and the appearance of a crocodile on leather goods was likely to mislead purchasers into believing that the goods were made of crocodile leather. It was sufficient that a substantial body of the public, even a minority, was likely to be deceived. The High Court held, in *The Seven-Up Co. v Bubble Up Co. Inc.* (1990), that the mark Bubble Up was not likely to be confused with the mark 7-Up.

Registration of Trade Mark

A party claiming to be the owner of a trade mark in use, or proposed to be used, and desirous of registering it must apply in writing to the Controller for registration. The Controller may refuse the application or may accept it absolutely, or subject to such amendments, modifications, conditions or limitations as is thought proper. Where the Controller accepts the application it is advertised and opposition to the application may be entered.

The registration of a trade mark is, in the first instance, for a period of ten years, but it may be renewed from time to time for successive periods of ten years thereafter.

Register of Trade Marks

The Register of Trade Marks is maintained at the Patents Office and contains all registered trade marks together with names, addresses and description of their owners, notifications of assignments, disclaimers, conditions, limitations and other matters relating to registered trade marks as are required by law to be registered. The register is under the management of the Controller of Patents, Designs and Trade Marks and is open to public inspection.

Effect of Registered Trade Mark

The owner of a registered trade mark has, from the date of its registration, the exclusive rights in the trade mark and such rights are infringed by the use of that trade mark without the owner's consent and constitute infringements of the owner's rights.

Infringement of Trade Marks

Where a registered trade mark is infringed, the infringement is actionable by the owner of the trade mark. In an action for infringement all relief by way of damages, injunction, rendering of an account is available, and in certain circumstances an order may be made for the delivering up of the goods alleged to have infringed the trade mark. An action cannot be maintained for the infringement of an unregistered trade mark though an action for the tort of passing off (see page 216) may be taken.

Registration of Disclaimer

A person who applies for the registration of a trade mark or the owner of a registered trade mark may disclaim any right to the exclusive use of any specified element of the mark, or agree that the rights conferred by the registration shall be subject to a specified territorial or other limitation. In the application for the registration of a trade mark it appears that any particular element is not distinctive and the inclusion of that element could give rise to doubts as to the scope of protection of the trade mark the registration may be refused unless the applicant agrees to make a disclaimer in respect of that element.

In *Miller Brewing Co. v Controller of Patents* (1988) an application was made to register a beer mark which combined the word Miller in the form of a signature, the German words Meister Brau in block type with a square double border and a small, insignificant bird-like figure placed within the border above the words Meister Brau. The High Court ordered the registration of the mark, subject to disclaimers with regard to Miller, because it was a common surname in this country, and Meister Brau because these words had a phonetic and visual similarity to their English translation Master Brew.

Surrender and Revocation of Trade Mark

A registered trade mark may be voluntarily surrendered by the owner. Equally, the registration of a trade mark may, for example, be revoked if it has not been put to genuine use in relation to the goods or services for which it was registered within five years following the date of registration, and there are no proper reasons for non-use.

Invalidity of Registration

The registration of a trade mark may be declared invalid on the ground that it was registered in breach of the prohibition on the registration of certain trade marks, discussed earlier.

In *Beecham Group Ltd v Goodalls of Ireland Ltd* (1978) the registered owner of the trade mark Tango, in respect of an aerated soft drink produced in two flavours, ceased to market the product in 1968. In 1977 another manufacturer introduced a concentrated orange drink under the name Tang. Shortly afterwards Tango was again distributed. When the owner of Tang sought the removal of the mark Tango from the register, the registered owner claimed that the use of Tang was likely to deceive or cause confusion. The High Court held that for purchasers of a product the appearance of a word, or the sound when spoken, are more important than its dictionary definition. In such circumstances Tang was likely to deceive or cause confusion with Tango.

Part Nine
EMPLOYMENT LAW

Chapter 42

CONTRACTS OF EMPLOYMENT

Distinction between Employee and Independent Contractor

In legal terms an employee is a person employed under a contract of service as distinct from an independent contractor who is employed under a contract for services. The courts have found it difficult to devise hard and fast rules as to what constitutes an employee and believe that each case must be considered on its own facts. Having said that, in the Supreme Court, in *Henry Denny & Sons (Ireland) Ltd v Minister for Social Welfare* (1997), Keane J. suggested that 'in general a person will be regarded as providing his or her services under a contract of service and not as an independent contractor where he or she is performing those services for another person and not for himself or herself. The degree of control exercised over how the work is to be performed, although a factor to be taken into account, is not decisive. The inference that the person is engaged in business on his or her own account can be readily drawn where he or she provides the necessary premises or equipment or some other form of investment, where he or she employs others to assist in the business and where the profit which he or she derives from the business is dependent on the efficiency with which it is conducted by him or her.' In that case it was held that a demonstrator in a supermarket who offered passing shoppers free samples of goods was employed under a contract of service and was not an independent contractor. However, in *McAuliffe v Minister for Social Welfare* (1995), the High Court held that two persons who delivered newspapers to shops and other outlets for between five and seven days a week, and owned their own vehicles in which they could carry other goods, except newspapers, at the time they were carrying newspapers for the plaintiff, were held to be independent contractors. An employer may lend or hire employees to another, and it may be important, as in *Lynch v Palgrave Murphy Ltd* (1964) (page 206), to decide whether the 'new' relationship creates the relationship of employer and employee between them. Other cases in this regard are discussed on page 204, when considering whether an employer was responsible for the tortious acts of employees, and on page 391 when discussing whether a partnership existed.

Once the distinction is made between an employee and an independent contractor a number of consequences follow:
1. An employer is vicariously liable for the torts of an employee but not for those of an independent contractor.
2. The employer owes a duty of care to an employee but not to an independent contractor.
3. Employees pay income tax under Schedule E, with deduction of tax at source whereas the independent contractor is assessed under Schedule D.
4. The provisions of the *Unfair Dismissals Act 1977* apply to employees and not to independent contractors.
5. Under the *Industrial Training Act 1967* firms in certain industries may be required to pay a levy to FAS. The amount of the levy is based on the number of employees in a particular firm.
6. The *Redundancy Payment Act* applies only to persons employed under contracts of service.
7. The *Social Welfare Acts* distinguish between employed persons and the self-employed.

Relationship of Employer and Employee

The relationship of employer and employee is a personal one between the parties. The employer cannot assign a contract of service to another employer and an employee cannot delegate performance of the contract of service. In earlier times the employer and employee relationship was known as the relationship of master and servant. The employer was deemed to have a quasi-proprietary interest in the employee and could sue a third party who injured the employee, in the action *per quod servitium amisit* (whereby the services were lost) with the possibility of recovering damages where the services of the employee were lost. While this action survives, it is rarely resorted to.

The employer and employee relationship is essentially a contractual one between the parties though it must be recognised that in modern times the individual's freedom to contract is sublimated to the actions of trade unions by collective bargaining on the one hand, and the ever increasing body of protective legislation relating to employees on the other. This body of legislation dealing with wages, safety at work, health, welfare, discrimination on grounds of sex, holidays, leave, redundancy and unfair dismissal must be kept in mind when considering the individual contract of employment. These statutory protections are considered in the next chapter.

FORMATION OF THE CONTRACT OF EMPLOYMENT

No Particular Formality Required

A contract of employment may be evidenced by deed, be in writing or be created verbally. In this respect the employment contract is not any different from all other contracts. The general rules of contract law apply to contracts of employment. There are minor exceptions to this rule as to formalities, for example, a contract for the hire of a seaman and a true contract of apprenticeship must be in writing.

Statutory Requirement to Supply Information

The *Terms of Employment (Information) Act 1994* requires an employer to give detailed written information to an employee with regard to the terms of employment. A new employee must, not later than two months after commencing employment, be supplied with the following information:

1. the full names of the employer and the employee;
2. the address of the employer; the place of work or, where there is no fixed or main place of work, a statement specifying that the employee is required or permitted to work at various places; the title of the job or nature of the work;
3. the date of commencement of employment; in the case of a temporary contract of employment the expected duration thereof, or if the contract of employment is for a fixed term, the date on which the contract expires;
4. the rate or method of calculation of the employee's remuneration;
5. the length of the intervals between the times at which remuneration is paid, whether a week, a month or any other interval;
6. any terms or conditions relating to hours of work (including overtime);
7. any terms or conditions relating to paid leave (other than paid sick leave);
8. any terms or conditions relating to: (a) incapacity for work due to sickness or injury, and paid sick leave; and (b) pension and pension schemes;
9. the period of notice which must be given by both the employer and the employee for the termination of the employment contract;
10. a reference to any collective agreements which directly affect the terms and conditions of the employee's employment.

An existing employee may request the like information which must be supplied by the employer within one month. This Act does not apply to employees who normally work less than eight hours per week.

Capacity to Enter Employment Contract

The policy of both common law and statute law has been to protect minors against oppressive contracts. As a result, minors are only bound by contracts of service, or apprenticeship, where such contracts are on the whole beneficial. This topic is considered on page 102.

The *Protection of Young Persons (Employment) Act 1996* severely restricts, but does not completely prohibit the employment of children, persons under the age of sixteen years or the school-leaving age, whichever is the higher, and young persons, those who have reached sixteen years of age or the school-leaving age, whichever is the higher, and are less than eighteen years of age.

Legality of Employment Contract

An employment contract cannot be enforced if it is illegal by its nature or by its performance. The illegality may arise because the contract infringes the provisions of a statute, or because at common law the contract is contrary to the common good. A regularly litigated problem in employment contracts arises from clauses in restraint of trade (see page 116).

TERMS OF THE EMPLOYMENT CONTRACT

Express and Implied Terms

The parties agree the terms of the employment contract, subject to whatever terms may be implied by statute law or the common law. As with other contracts some terms of the employment contract will be expressed. In some cases the entire terms of the contract will be reduced into writing while in others only some of the terms will be actually agreed. The type of work to be done, the hours of attendance, payment, holiday leave, and the notice required to terminate the contract, will probably be expressly agreed. The remainder of the terms will be implied in that in many employment contracts not all of the terms will be expressly agreed between the parties. How the work is actually to be done, the procedures to be followed in the event of disputes, compassionate leave, and promotional procedures may not be expressly agreed but are implied terms.

Terms to be implied into an individual contract of employment may have their source elsewhere. In some instances collective agreements may imply terms into the individual's contract. For example, where a change in working hours is agreed between the trade union and the employer and put into effect the terms of this new arrangement become a term of the contract.

Statute law may imply terms into an employment contract. There are a collection of these, discussed in the next chapter, which grant considerable protections to employees and may, in appropriate cases, form part of the employment contract.

DUTIES OF THE EMPLOYER

Payment of Remuneration

An employer is only bound to pay remuneration where there is an agreement, either express or implied, to this effect. In the absence of an express agreement a right of remuneration may be implied where the party performing the service does so in circumstances where payment is expected. A stableman, in *McEvoy v Moore* (1902), was requested by the defendant's head groom to go to the premises and do some work. Nothing was said as to wages, or about the period of the employment. It was held that there was an implied contract to pay the ordinary rate of wages for such employment.

Amount of Remuneration

At common law the amount of remuneration payable is a matter of agreement between the parties. There has been limited statutory intervention in this regard. The *Industrial Relations Act 1946* empowers the Labour Court to establish joint labour committees for the fixing of minimum rates of remuneration, and conditions of employment, for the sector of employment in respect of which it has been established. For example, committees have been established to cover messengers, law clerks and certain hotel employees.

Statute law may determine how the rate of remuneration may be fixed. In *Transport Salaried Staff Association v CIE* (1965) statute provided that certain conditions of employment, including payment, of railway employees was to be regulated in accordance with agreements made between the employees' trade unions and the company. This was done with regard to clerical officers, who were represented by the plaintiff association. The company proposed to recruit university graduates at levels of remuneration above those agreed on. The association was granted an injunction to prevent any payment above those stipulated in the agreement which had been entered into in pursuance of the statute.

Statute law itself may attempt to regulate remuneration. The *Regulation of Banks (Remuneration and Conditions of Employment) (Temporary Provisions) Act 1975* enabled the Minister for Labour to regulate for a limited period the remuneration and conditions of employment of bank employees.

Method of Remuneration

The *Payment of Wages Act 1991* enshrines the right of every employee: (a) to a readily negotiable mode of wage payment, (b) to protection against unlawful deductions and (c) to a written statement of wages and any deductions.This statute provides the sole method of the payment of wages. The principle methods are: (a) cheque, draft or other bill of exchange, (b) credit transfer, and (c) cash. Where cash is the usual method of payment a different method can only be used by the agreement of the employee.

Every employee must be given a written statement of wages. Deductions are prohibited unless these are required by statute (income tax, social welfare) or a pension deduction is authorised by a term of the contract of employment. Other deductions are possible, such as a trade union deduction, where the employee consents in writing.

The *Juries Act 1975* provides that a person is to be treated as employed during any period when absent because of compliance with a jury summons. An employee must be paid by the employer when on jury service.

Provision of Work

The general rule is that an employer is not bound to provide work for the employee. It follows that where an employee is entitled to a period of notice on the termination of the employment contract, the employer can validly terminate it by handing the employee remuneration in lieu of notice.

There are exceptions to this general rule. Where the employee is paid wholly, or partly, by commission the employer must provide work in order that the commission can be earned. Certain contracts, such as those with actors and persons involved in sports, carry the duty to provide an opportunity for the employee to enhance a reputation. Where the employee is employed to perform a particular task, or to fill a particular post, the employer breaches the contract where the employee is prevented from carrying out the task.

Provision of Holidays

The provision of holidays is also a matter for contract between the parties. But again statute has interposed by laying down minimum holiday periods for certain employees. The parties may agree to greater holiday periods than the statutory minimum. The *Organisation of Working Time Act 1997* provides that an employee shall be entitled to paid annual leave equal to: (a) four working weeks in a leave year in which he or she works at least 1,365 hours; (b) one-third of a working week for each month in the leave year in which he or she works at least 117 hours; or (c) 8 per cent of the hours he or she works in a leave year but subject to a maximum of four working weeks. The annual leave of an employee who works eight or more months in a leave year shall generally include an unbroken period of two weeks.

The times at which annual leave is granted to an employee are determined by his or her employer having regard to work requirements, and subject to the employer taking into account the need for the employee to reconcile work and any family responsibilities, the opportunities for rest and recreation available to the employee, and the employer having consulted the employee or the trade union, if any, not less than one month before the day on which the annual leave is due to commence. Remuneration for annual leave must be paid in advance and, where an employee becomes ill while on annual leave, and furnishes medical evidence of that illness, the period so covered cannot be counted as part of the annual leave.

Employees are entitled to a number of public holidays a year: Christmas Day, St Stephen's Day, New Year's Day, St Patrick's Day, Easter Monday; the first Monday in May; the first Monday in June; the first Monday in August, and the last Monday in October. In the case of each of these public holidays the employee is entitled to a paid day on the holiday, or a paid day off within a month, or an extra day's annual leave, or an extra day's pay, as the employer may decide.

The provision of this Act applies to all employees except members of the Garda Síochána or the Defence Forces, sea fishers and others who work at sea, the activities of a doctor in training, and employees living with their relative employer.

An employee may be requested in emergency situations to return to work from holidays. An accountant while home on annual holidays, in *Hartery v Welltrade (Middle East) Ltd* (1978) was requested to return to Libya, where he was employed, when serious tax problems arose. This he did and returned home to continue his holidays. The matters were not resolved and he was subsequently called to London. He refused to obey and was dismissed. The High Court ruled that in view of the gravity and urgency of the problem it was not unreasonable for the employer to request the employee to interrupt his holidays. An employee was bound by the contract of employment to accede to such a reasonable request and failure to do so justified dismissal.

Safety Provisions

Apart from a substantial amount of statute law on the subject, an employer is under a common law obligation to take reasonable care for the safety of the employee. This duty was considered in detail on page 202 which discusses an employer's duty towards an employee in negligence. Some of the legislative measures which grant such protections are discussed in the next chapter.

Does the duty to take care for the personal safety of an employee extend to the employee's property? The answer it seems is no, at least as regards items which are independent of the employee when destroyed. For example, should an employee leave clothes in a locker it seems the employer is not responsible where these are stolen. However, should the employee suffer personal injuries as a result of the employer's negligence and the clothes worn at the time are damaged or destroyed the employee is entitled to reclaim their loss.

Medical Attention and Board and Lodgings

An employer is not bound to provide medical attention for an employee who becomes ill during the course of employment. An employer is not bound to provide board and lodging for employees even if an employee must live away from home while employed. The parties may contract differently. They frequently do in the case of domestic employees, hotel staff and teachers in boarding schools.

Indemnity

The employer receiving the benefit of the employee's service must indemnify the employee against all liabilities and expenses incurred in the proper performance of the employment. With regard to liability for contracts where the employee is the agent of the employer see page 206.

Right to a Reference

It was decided in *Lint v Johnston* (1894) that no action lies against an employer for a refusal to furnish a certificate of character to an employee leaving the employment. Where the employer gives a character reference a number of legal matters arise. If the reference contains anything defamatory of the employee, or a third party, and is given directly to a prospective employer an action may lie against the employer. An employer may be liable in deceit where a false reference is given and the employer knows it to be untrue. An employer may be liable for negligent misstatement. For example, an employer who states that an ex-employee is honest when that employee was dismissed for stealing might be successfully sued by a subsequent employer who relies on that statement and suffers loss.

DUTIES OF THE EMPLOYEE

Duty to Act Reasonably Using Appropriate Skill

An employee must perform the employment contract in a reasonable manner and is in breach of contract where any act is done which frustrates its commercial object. An employee must use the requisite amount of skill in carrying out the employment. It was held, in *Harrington v Gleeson* (1897), that an employee had been properly dismissed when, having been placed in charge of a thrashing machine, his lack of skill in its operation led to the loss of customers by the employer.

Duty to Render Personal Service and Follow Instruction

Since the relationship of employer and employee is a personal one the employee cannot, without the employer's permission, delegate the performance of duties to another. An employee is bound to follow the instructions given by the employer provided these come within the ambit of the employment contract. An employee can never be compelled to obey an unlawful instruction, or an instruction which places the employee in personal danger.

Duty to Act in Good Faith

An employee is bound to act in good faith when dealing with the business of the employer and third parties. For example, an employee may not be allowed by the employment contract to engage in work outside the employment. While such a broad term could hardly be enforced an employee will not be acting in good faith should activities be engaged in which may harm the employer. To sell the trade secrets to a competitor is not an act of good faith.

Duty to Disclose Breaches of Duty

An employee is under no obligation to disclose to the employer breaches of duty which that employee commits. Whether or not the employee must disclose the breaches of duty on the part of fellow employees will depend on the status of that employee. For example, a supervisor is bound to report the breach of duty of employees.

Indemnity

An employee is bound to take reasonable care in the performance of the duties of the employment. Where that duty is breached, and should a third party suffer damage or injuries which must be compensated, because of the principle of vicarious liability (see page 204), the employee may be called on to indemnify the employer. In practice, an employee is rarely called upon to indemnify the employer.

TERMINATION OF EMPLOYMENT CONTRACT

Various Ways of Terminating Employment Contract

A contract of employment may be terminated in a number of ways. The rules discussed here are the general principles of contract law applied to the contract of employment. These common law rules have been supplemented by statute.

Efflux of Time

Where an employee is engaged for a set period of time, or for a particular task, when that period of time has expired or the task is completed, the employment is at an end. There are many types of short-term or casual employment.

Death of the Employer or Employee
An employment contract is discharged by the death of either party unless there is an express or implied term to the contrary. This rule has no significance where the employer is a registered company which may have perpetual existence though the granting of a winding-up order terminates the employment contract. While the death of the party extinguishes the employment contract, it does not extinguish any liabilities arising thereunder. Payment of outstanding remuneration must be made to the employee's estate.

Termination by Frustration
Should performance of the employment contract become impossible owing to some intervening action which is not caused by either party, the contract may be terminated under the well established rule relating to frustration. The problem of an employee who becomes ill during the continuance of the employment contract was considered in *Flynn v Great Northern Railway* (1955) (page 123), where it was decided that the permanent incapacity of an employee is sufficient to frustrate the business object of the employment contract.

Termination by Insolvency
The bankruptcy of either party to an employment contract does not automatically determine the contract, though it may expressly be provided that such an event does terminate it. In practice, an employer who becomes a bankrupt will be unable to pay the employee's remuneration. The employee can submit a claim in bankruptcy for remuneration owed, and for wrongful dismissal where the proper period of notice has not been given. A redundancy claim may also be lodged. As already mentioned an employee is discharged when a winding-up order is made, or when a company is voluntarily liquidated.

Termination by Notice
The termination of an employment contract by notice can be examined under four headings: (1) statute; (2) express terms; (3) implied terms; and (4) custom. When considering this problem of termination by notice the concept of unfair dismissal, discussed in the next chapter (page 454), must be borne in mind. For example, an employee may be unfairly dismissed despite being given the proper notice.

1. *Statute:* Where an employee has completed thirteen weeks' continuous service with an employer, the employee becomes entitled under the *Minimum Notice and Terms of Employment Act 1973* to receive a minimum period of notice before the employer can exercise a right of dismissal. The required period of notice varies according to the length of the employee's service in

accordance with the following scale:

(a) Where the service has continued for over thirteen weeks, but is under two years, the minimum notice is one week; where the service has continued for over two weeks, but is under five years, the minimum notice is two weeks.

(b) Where the service has continued for over five years, but is under ten years, the minimum notice is four weeks; where the service have continued for over ten years, but is under fifteen years, the minimum notice is six weeks.

(c) Where the service has continued for over fifteen years, the minimum notice is eight weeks.

A clause in an employment contract providing for shorter periods of notice than the statutory minimum periods is void. However an employee, or an employer, may waive the right to notice, or may accept payment in lieu of notice. The Act provides that these provisions as to minimum notice do not affect the right of an employer, or an employee, to terminate an employment contract without notice due to misconduct of the other party.

Where an employee proposes to terminate the employment contract and has been in that employment for at least thirteen weeks, the employee must give at least one week's notice to the employer. This Act does not apply to: employees who normally work for less than twenty-one hours per week; close relatives of the employer; established civil servants and local authority officials; members of the Defence Forces and Garda Síochána; or seamen.

2. *Express Terms:* An employment contract can be determined by notice should its terms so provide. Of course, it cannot oust the provisions of the *Minimum Notice and Terms of Employment Act 1973* already noted. Where an employer wishes to reserve an express right of summary dismissal, the contract must do so in clear and certain language. Where the contract specifies grounds for dismissal these may be construed as exhaustive and the employer cannot invoke any other ground not specified in the contract.

3. *Implied Terms:* Where the subject of notice is not regulated by express terms the courts may imply such a term into the contract. The outcome of the case will depend on whether the employment is for a fixed term or for an indefinite term. In an employment contract for a fixed term there is no implied right to determine it by notice before the end of the term.

Where the employment is for an indefinite period, then subject to the minimum period laid down by the *Minimum Notice and Terms of Employment Act 1973*, which does not apply to all employees, the contract is terminated by reasonable notice given at any time by either the employer or employee. What is reasonable notice depends on factors such as the nature of the work, the method of payment and any relevant trade custom. The more important, or unique, the position, the longer will be the period of notice. In *McDonald v Minister for Education* (1940) a lecturer in a teacher training college on her marriage was given three months' notice. In an action for wrongful dismissal the Supreme Court held that the contract was for an indefinite period and that six months' notice in the circumstances was reasonable.

The fact that a post is described as permanent and pensionable does not remove it from the general rule that the employment contract can be terminated by reasonable notice. In *Walsh v Dublin Health Authority* (1964) a carpenter obtained employment which was described as permanent. After serving a probationary period he was placed on a register of pensionable servants. Six years later the employment was terminated. The High Court rejected the claim that the employment was permanent in the sense of being continuous for life or until he had attained full pensionable age, subject only to termination for misconduct, neglect or unfitness for employment. It was decided that employment was permanent only in the sense of being for an indefinite period and was therefore terminable by reasonable notice.

4. *Custom:* Occasionally, the length of notice is fixed by a custom prevailing in a particular employment. In *Ó Conaill v Gaelic Echo* (1958) it was decided that, in accordance with the prevailing practice within the journalist profession, a member of the editorial staff of a monthly magazine was entitled to at least one month's notice. Needless to remark, the prevailing custom can only be invoked in the absence of express agreement, or in the absence of the application of the 1973 Act.

Dismissal Without Notice

At common law an employer may terminate an employment contract by dismissing an employee without notice, provided the contract expressly grants such a right. Having regard to the intervention of statute, already explained, this right of dismissal without notice is severely curtailed. But there remains one situation in which this pre-emptory right of dismissal survives and that is where the employer is guilty of serious misconduct. Such conduct must be of a kind which has the effect of acting as a repudiation of the contract. What amounts to misconduct in the eyes of the law? A quotation from a judgment on this topic explains what circumstances suffice to justify a dismissal without notice: 'An employer is justified in dismissing his employee without notice if the conduct of the employee is inconsistent or incompatible with the due, or faithful, discharge of his duty to his employer; or if the employee unlawfully disobeys any lawful order of his employer, or is guilty of such moral misconduct, or such a violation or non-performance of any express or implied obligation, undertaking, or duty imposed upon him by, or involved in, his contract of service, as is either prejudicial to his employer, or is likely to render his continuance in the service prejudicial to his employer.'

The Supreme Court decided, in *Carvill v Irish Industrial Bank Ltd* (1968), that an employer, in defending an action for wrongful dismissal, cannot rely on misconduct which was unknown to the employer at the time of dismissal, unless the misconduct constitutes a breach by the employee of a fundamental term of the employment contract which amounts to a repudiation. In that case the employee's dismissal without notice was sought to be proved by an act of misconduct which took place before, and which was unknown to the employer, when the dismissal took place. The misconduct alleged was that the employee obtained a carpet for his home and had the old carpet lifted and fitted in the employer's premises while the employer paid for the new carpet.

Nothing in the *Minimum Notice and Terms of Employment Act 1973* restricts the right of an employer, or an employee, to terminate an employment contract without notice, due to the misconduct of the other party. There are very few cases of wrongful dismissal taken in the courts because the more informal, and less expensive, procedures relating to unfair dismissal are generally resorted to (see page 454).

REMEDIES FOR BREACH OF EMPLOYMENT CONTRACT

Remedies of Employer

An employee may be dismissed summarily for misconduct and the employer incurs no further liability though the employee must be paid up to the dismissal date. Where an employee has been guilty of a breach of duty, and the employer suffers loss, the employer may be sued though this is rarely done. An employer may seek an injunction against a former employee to restrain the performance, or to compel the performance, of some agreed act. In the case of *Arclex Optical Ltd v McMurray* (1958) an employer obtained an injunction to prevent a former employee from canvassing orders from clients of the employer whom the employee had dealt with during the course of employment. This case, and others, are considered on page 116 under the doctrine of restraint of trade. Where an employee has made a secret profit, for example by selling goods stolen from the employer, the employer may sue for the proceeds.

Remedies of Employee

Where an employer repudiates the employment contract the employee can leave without notice and is discharged from further obligations. In theory, an employee dismissed wrongfully may seek an injunction to restrain the employer from acting on the dismissal though the courts, in practice, tend not to grant such relief. The reason is that the law will not force an employer to employ a particular employee nor force a particular employee to work for a particular employer. But as will be seen in the next chapter the remedies of reinstatement and re-engagement are statutory reliefs available to the unfairly dismissed employee. Where an employer repudiates the employment contract the employee can claim a *quantum meruit* for services rendered, or sue for remuneration due and unpaid.

Where the employee is an office holder the employee may claim that the purported dismissal is null and void because the rules of fair procedures, considered on page 74, have been infringed. It was decided in *Glover v BLN Ltd* (1973) that a technical director, removed from office after an inquiry, was wrongfully dismissed because he should have been given prior notice of the charges and an opportunity to refute them. Other cases with the same result are *The State (Gleeson) v Minister for Defence* (1976) and *Garvey v Ireland* (1979) discussed on page 75.

CHAPTER 43

PROTECTIVE LEGISLATION

Statutory Protection of Employees

It is obvious from the previous chapter that the Oireachtas has enacted legislation for the protection of employees. This has been necessary because the free market and the common law, loyal to the freedom of employment tradition discussed in the next chapter, proved unable to offer employees any measure of real protection against unscrupulous employers though most employers tended, insofar as economics allowed, to treat employees fairly. The development of the trade union movement greatly enhanced the status and employment conditions of employees. Political power has resulted in the enactment of a code of protective legislation which grants employees rights and entitlements independent of the employment contract. The major areas of such legislation are discussed in this chapter.

UNFAIR DISMISSAL

Concept of Unfair Dismissal

The *Unfair Dismissals Act 1977*, as amended, introduced into law the radically new concept of unfair dismissal, which is based on the principle that employees are entitled to security of employment. The unfair dismissal procedure negatives the traditional common law principle of freedom of contract. The concept that a dismissal may be unfair though an employer has complied with contractual obligations as to notice, even the statutory obligation as to notice contained in the *Minimum Notice and Terms of Employment Act 1973*, discussed on page 449, has been introduced into law. A procedure has been established whereby the cause of dismissal can be examined and adjudicated on as to its fairness.

Scope and Intent of the Statute

The 1977 Act states the principle that every employee has the right not to be unfairly dismissed by an employer. The Act applies to every employee who, at the date of dismissal, has at least one year's continuous service with the employer. The following are excluded: (a) employees who have reached the old age pension age or those who have reached the normal retiring age of their firm; (b) persons employed by a close relative in a private house or on a farm where both reside; (c) members of the Defence Forces and the Garda Síochána; (d) FAS trainees and apprentices; (e) civil servants, other than various industrial grades; (f) officers of local authorities, health boards, vocational education committees and committees of agriculture.

The Act lays down criteria by which the fairness of dismissals is to be judged. It establishes adjudication machinery and provides redresses where the dismissal is held to be unfair. Special rules are stated to govern fixed-term contracts, probation and training contracts, and dismissal arising from lock-outs, strikes and trade union membership.

What Amounts to Dismissal?

An employee has been dismissed where any of the following situations occur: (a) where the employer terminates the employment contract with or without notice; (b) where the contract is for a fixed term and is not renewed on termination; (c) where the employee, with or without notice, terminates the employment contract because of the employer's conduct, this is known as constructive dismissal.

It is clear from these three situations, which are exhaustive, that an employee cannot claim to have been dismissed where the employee resigns, or where the contract has been mutually terminated. For example, an employee terminates the contract by refusing to work out the period of notice given by the employer. In such situations the employee, by acting precipitously, excludes the protections given by the Act.

When Does Dismissal Occur?

Ascertaining the dismissal date is imperative because it affects such issues as age limits and the length of continuous employment. Where the contract is terminated by notice the dismissal date is the date on which the notice expires. Where no notice is given the dismissal date is the date on which the termination takes effect. Where the contract is for a fixed term the dismissal date is the date on which the term expires.

Is the Dismissal Fair?

The 1977 Act provides that a dismissal is presumed to be unfair unless and until the employer proves to the contrary. The onus of proof rests with the employer to show the dismissal was fair and not with the employee to prove it was unfair.

The Act provides a number of reasons which make a dismissal fair. Apart from proving one, or more, of these grounds the employer may be able to show that in all the circumstances of the case the employer acted reasonably in treating that ground as a sufficient reason for dismissing the employee.

It is fair dismissal to dismiss an employee shown to be incapable, incompetent, or lacking the necessary qualification to perform the tasks he or she was employed to do. Lack of capacity may be on the grounds of lack of skill, or physical or mental ability, or adequate health, or such formal professional or technical qualifications as are appropriate to the employment. In practice, this is rarely a ground for dismissal because the employer has one year to measure the competency of the employee.

The employee's conduct is the second most frequent ground relied on by employers when dismissing employees. To be effective the conduct must be of such a serious or continuing nature as to amount to serious misconduct. Isolated acts, or behaviour, which have not warranted a warning by the employer, are not sufficient.

An employer is entitled to dismiss on the ground of redundancy, a topic more fully discussed later in this chapter.

An employer may dismiss an employee where the continued employment amounts to a contravention of the law. For example, to continue to employ a driver following a disqualification from driving is a contravention of the law.

Dismissal may be for a substantial reason. The employer must have more than a trivial excuse, that is, the ground for dismissal must be of a serious nature. For example, in *Cox v Genfitt* (1978), it was held to be fair dismissal where the employer discovered that the employee had established a business in direct competition with the employer. Such an action was considered serious misconduct.

Unfair Dismissal as an Automatic Consequence

The *Unfair Dismissals Act 1977*, as amended by the *Unfair Dismissal (Amendment) Act 1993*, provides that a dismissal in a number of stated situations is always automatically unfair, and can never be justified. These are:

1. trade union membership or activities, either during or outside working hours;
2. the religious or political opinions of the employee;
3. the race, colour or sexual orientation of the employee;
4. the race or colour of the employee;
5. the age of the employee;
6. the employee's membership of the travelling community;
7. participation by the employee in legal proceedings against the employer;
8. the pregnancy of the employee, unless the pregnancy prevents the carrying out of the duties properly, and the employee has refused the offer of a suitable alternative job, or there was no suitable alternative job available.

Lock-Outs and Strikes

An employee's dismissal by way of lock-out is not considered to be unfair, provided reinstatement, or re-engagement from the date of the resumption of work is offered. A lock-out takes place where the employer shuts down and dismisses all employees, or suspends operations or suspends all or any of the workforce, or excludes employees from the workplace.

Where an employee is dismissed while engaged in lawful industrial action, the dismissal is unfair unless an offer of re-employment is made when the strike has ended, and the dismissal contains some element of selection. Where one other employee who took part in the strike is not dismissed, or where some or all of those engaged in the strike are dismissed and at least one is offered re-employment, the dismissal is unfair. It follows that where no member of the original workforce is re-engaged there is no unfair dismissal.

Statement of Reasons for Dismissal

An employee may request from the employer a written statement of the reasons for dismissal which must be supplied within fourteen days.

Time Limit on Bringing Claim

A claim for unfair dismissal must be brought within six months of dismissal. There is no procedure under the Act whereby this time limit can be extended. In *The State (IBM Ireland Ltd) v Employment Appeals Tribunal* (1984) the High Court held that once the notice was served on the employer within the time limit it does not matter whether the notice is served by the employee or by the tribunal.

Adjudication Machinery

The Act provides three possible stages of adjudication on claims for unfair dismissal. These include process by a Right Commissioner, or the Employment Appeals Tribunal, an appeal to the Circuit Court and a further appeal to the High Court. An employee can initiate the claim before a Rights Commissioner, or should the employee prefer, written notice can be given to the Employment Appeals Tribunal. The Rights Commissioner is a civil servant, whereas the Employment Appeals Tribunal, consisting of three persons, is composed of a chairman, a representative of the trade union movement, and a representative of employers' organisations.

Where the claim is heard by a Rights Commissioner a dissatisfied party may appeal to the Employment Appeals Tribunal within six weeks. The Employment Appeals Tribunal will determine a claim coming before it either by way of appeal or by original claim. At their own initiative and expense either party may appeal within six weeks to the Circuit Court and a further appeal lies to the High Court. Few cases traverse each of these stages.

Remedies for Unfair Dismissal

Where the adjudicating body finds that an employee has been unfairly dismissed it may order any of the following remedies:

1. the reinstatement of the employee to the former position;
2. the re-engagement in that position, or in a suitable alternative position;
3. if the employee incurs financial loss attributable to the dismissal, payment of compensation for such loss not exceeding 104 weeks' remuneration; or
4. if the employee incurs no financial loss attributable to the dismissal, payment of compensation not exceeding four weeks' remuneration.

Enforcement of Remedy

Where the employer fails within six weeks to comply with the award made by the Rights Commissioner or the Employment Appeals Tribunal the Minister for Labour may take the case to the Circuit Court on the employee's behalf to enforce the remedy obtained.

Alternative Remedies

An employee is not obliged to process a claim for dismissal in accordance with the procedures laid down in the 1977 Act. A common law action for wrongful dismissal, with the single remedy of compensation, remains an option. However, the employee must choose between an action for wrongful dismissal in legal proceedings or the unfair dismissal process. An employee cannot seek both remedies.

REDUNDANCY

Employees Entitled to Benefit

To mitigate the real hardship of losing employment, particularly for older employees or those possessed of dying skills, the *Redundancy Payment Acts 1967–90* provides for the making of redundancy payments in certain situations.

Every employee, over the age of eighteen years and under the old age pension age limit, who is employed for at least eight hours per week, by the one employer, is entitled to redundancy. A wide range of persons, such as those holding permanent and pensionable civil service and local government posts, are excluded. To be eligible to claim, the employee must prove that he or she had worked continuously for the same employer for at least two years by the date employment was terminated due to redundancy.

Should the business be sold and the employee's contract be renewed by the purchaser, the period of employment is deemed to be unbroken. The following interruptions do not constitute a break in continuous service: (a) sickness or injury lasting up to eighteen months; (b) service in the Reserve Defence Forces; (c) the period of maternity or adoption leave; (d) a lay-off; (e) holidays; (f) other causes authorised by the employer which did not last longer than twenty-six weeks; or, (g) a lock-out or a strike for any period.

Dismissal by Reason of Redundancy

A dismissal of an employee is deemed to have been by reason of redundancy if it was due wholly, or mainly, to the fact that the employer has ceased, or intends to cease, to carry on the business, or to the fact that the need for employees for work of a particular kind is expected to diminish, or has diminished.

A dismissal is presumed to have been by reason of redundancy, unless the contrary is proven, which burden lies on the employer. The employee will not have a claim if the contract of employment is renewed, or, if the employee unreasonably refuses a suitable offer of alternative employment. Whether the alteration of the work-place amounts to dismissal is a question of degree.

Calculation of Redundancy Payments

The Act establishes a minimum lump sum which must be paid on redundancy. The amount depends on the age of the employee, length of service, and gross weekly pay.

Duty to Notify Redundancies

Under the *Protection of Employment Act 1977* an employer who purposes to dismiss an employee for redundancy is under a duty to notify that employee's trade union at least one month in advance of the redundancy. The employer must also in certain cases of mass redundancies notify the Minister for Enterprise, Trade and Employment.

EMPLOYMENT EQUALITY

Principle of Equality

The *Employment Equality Act 1998* makes provision for the promotion of equality and deals with issues of discrimination in the workplace, with regard to education or training, and with regard to the membership of a trade union, an employers' organisation, a professional or trade organisation and bodies which control the entry to a profession, vocation or occupation.

Discriminatory Grounds

For the purposes of the *Employment Equality Act 1998* discrimination occurs where one person is, has been or would be treated less favourably than another on any of the following grounds:

1. *Gender*: that one is a woman and the other is a man.
2. *Marital status*: that they are of different marital status. Marital status means single, married, separated, divorced or widowed.
3. *Family status*: that one has family status and the other does not. Family status means responsibility as a parent or as a person *in loco parentis* in relation to a person under eighteen years of age, or as a parent or the resident primary carer in relation to a person over eighteen years of age with a disability which is of such a nature as to give rise to the need for care or support on a continuing, regular or frequent basis.
4. *Sexual orientation*: that they are of different sexual orientation. Sexual orientation means heterosexual, homosexual or bisexual orientation.
5. *Religion*: that one has a different religious belief from the other, or that one has a religious belief and the other has not. Religious belief means religious background or outlook.
6. *Age*: that they are of different ages. Treating persons either over sixty-five years or under eighteen years more or less favourably than other persons shall not be regarded as discrimination on the age ground.
7. *Disability*: that one is a person with a disability and the other either is not or is a person with a different disability.
8. *Race*: that they are of different race, colour, nationality or ethnic or national origins.
9. *Traveller community*: that one is a member of the traveller community and the other is not.

Discrimination by Employers

An employer must not discriminate against an employee or prospective employee on any of the discriminatory grounds set out above in relation to:
1. *Access to employment*: Discrimination occurs where the employer, in making arrangements for deciding to whom employment should be offered, or by specifying, in respect of one person, entry requirements for employment which are not specified in respect of other persons where the circumstances in which both such persons would be employed are not materially different.
2. *Conditions of employment*: Discrimination occurs where the employer does not offer or afford to an employee or prospective employee the same terms of employment, other than remuneration and pension rights, and the same working conditions, and the same treatment in relation to overtime, shift work, short time, transfers, lay-offs, redundancies, dismissals and disciplinary measures.
3. *Training or experience for or in relation to employment*: Discrimination occurs where the employer refuses to offer or afford to an employee the same opportunities or facilities for employment counselling, training, and work

experience as the employer offers or affords to other employees, when the circumstances in which that employee and those other employees work are not materially different.

4. *Promotion or re-grading*: Discrimination occurs where the employer refuses or deliberately omits to offer or afford the employee access to opportunities for promotion in circumstances in which another eligible and qualified person is offered or afforded such access, or the employer does not in the circumstances offer or afford the employee access in the same way to those opportunities.

5. *Classification of posts.*

Equal Payment for Like Work

The *Employment Equality Act 1998* provides that equal remuneration must be paid for like work where:

1. one employee is a man and another employee is a woman;
2. one employee has marital status and another employee has a different marital status;
3. one employee has family status and another employee has a different family status;
4. one employee has a sexual orientation and another employee has a different sexual orientation;
5. one employee has religious beliefs and another employee has different religious beliefs or no religious beliefs;
6. one employee is of one age and another employee is a different age;
7. one employee has a disability and another employee has not, or that other employee has a different disability;
8. one employee is of one race, colour, nationality or ethnic or national origins or any combination of these and another employee is of a different race, colour, nationality or ethnic or national origins or any combination of these;
9. one employee is a member of the traveller community and another employee is not of the traveller community.

Two persons are employed on like work where:

1. both perform the same work under the same or similar conditions, or interchangeable with the other in relation to the work;
2. the work performed by one is of a similar nature to that performed by the other and any differences between the work performed or the conditions under which it is performed are of small importance in relation to the work as a whole or occur with such irregularity as not to be significant to the work as a whole; or,

3. the work performed by one is equal in value to that performed by the other, having regard to such matters as skill, physical or mental requirements, responsibility and working conditions.

Harassment in the Workplace

The *Employment Equality Act 1998* prohibits certain types of harassment in the workplace or in the course of employment. Sexual harassment amounts to discrimination on the gender ground and consists of any act of physical intimacy, or any request for sexual favours, or any act or conduct including spoken words, gestures, or the production, display or circulation of written words, pictures or other material if the act, request or conduct is unwelcome and could reasonably be regarded as sexually offensive, humiliating or intimidating to the man or woman at whom it is aimed. Sexual harassment can only be committed by a man against a woman or a woman against a man. It appears that sexual harassment cannot be committed by a man against a man or a woman against a woman.

Harassment is any act or conduct, including spoken words, gestures, or the production, display or circulation of written words, pictures or other material if that action or conduct is unwelcome and could reasonably be regarded as offensive, humiliating or intimidating by the person at whom it is aimed. Harassment can be committed on the various other discriminatory grounds set out above.

Exemptions

Certain acts are exempt from the provisions of the *Employment Equality Act 1998*. In the area of family and personal matters an employer may provide treatment which confers benefits on women in connection with pregnancy and maternity or adoption. Where the employment consists of the performance of services of a personal nature, such as the care of an elderly or incapacitated person in that person's home, the employer may discriminate on the gender ground. Measures which are intended to reduce or eliminate the effects of discrimination and which facilitate the integration into employment of persons over fifty years of age, or persons with disabilities, or members of the traveller community are permitted.

A religious, educational or remedial institution which is under the direction or control of a body established for religious purposes, or whose objectives include the provision of services in an environment which promotes certain religious values, shall not be taken to discriminate if it gives more favourable treatment, on the religion ground, to an employee or a prospective employee where it is reasonable to do so in order to maintain the religious ethos of the institution. Nor shall it be taken to discriminate if it takes action which is reasonably necessary to prevent an employee or prospective employee from undermining the religious ethos of the institution.

Adjudication Machinery

A person who claims to have been discriminated against may seek redress by referring the matter to the Director of Equality Investigations. If the case can be resolved by mediation, the Director refers the case to an equality mediation officer. If mediation is not possible, the Director hears and determines the complaint. A person who claims to have been dismissed because of discrimination seeks redress by referring the matter to the Labour Court.

Equality Authority

This body was established by the *Employment Equality Act 1998* to work towards the elimination of discrimination in relation to employment, to promote equality of opportunity in relation to employment and to provide information and to keep under review the working of the *Employment Equality Act* itself, the *Maternity Protection Act 1994* and the *Adoptive Leave Act 1995*, which are both discussed below.

WORK LOCATION

Safety at Work

It shall be the duty, according to the *Safety, Health and Welfare at Work Act 1989*, of every employer to ensure, insofar as is reasonably practicable, the safety, health and welfare at work of all employees. It shall be the duty of every employee while at work to take reasonable care of his or her own safety, health and welfare and that of any other person who may be affected by his or her acts or omissions.

Every employer must prepare a statement in writing, to be known as a safety statement, which shall specify the manner in which the safety, health and welfare of employees shall be secured at work. An employer must consult his employees for the purpose of making, and maintenance of, arrangements which will enable the employer and the employees to co-operate effectively in promoting and developing measures to ensure their safety, health and welfare at work. Towards that end, employees, known as safety representatives, may be appointed.

Offices

The *Office Premises Act 1958* provides for the protection of the health, welfare and safety of persons employed in offices, and contains provisions concerning cleanliness, overcrowding, lighting, ventilation, temperature, sanitary arrangement and fire escapes. The Act applies to all offices in which more than five persons are employed on clerical work, and all parts of a building in which persons are employed on clerical work are taken as forming one office. A person is not regarded as employed on clerical work if such work is merely incidental, or subsidiary to a main occupation.

Factories

The *Factories Act 1955*, as amended by the *Safety in Industry Act 1980*, sets out requirements for ensuring the safety, health and welfare of persons employed in factories.

A factory is defined as premises at which persons are employed in manual work in any process relating to the making, cleaning or adapting any article for sale. Certain parts of the Acts are applicable to electrical stations, docks, wharves, quays, warehouses, building operations, and works of engineering construction.

Mines and Quarries

The *Mines and Quarries Act 1965* contains provisions for protecting the lives, health and welfare of workers in mines and quarries. The Act applies to mines and quarries, including those belonging to the State. A mine or quarry is defined as excavations for, or in connection with, the getting of minerals or mineral products. Minerals include stone, slate, clay, sand and other natural deposits, except peat.

National Authority for Occupational Safety and Health

The *Safety, Health and Welfare at Work Act 1989* established the National Authority for Occupational Safety and Health whose function it is to make adequate arrangements for the enforcement of the relevant legislation, to promote and encourage the prevention of accidents and injury at work, to provide information and advice on matters related to safety, health and welfare at work, and to undertake, promote and sponsor relevant research.

STATUTORY LEAVE

Maternity Leave

The *Maternity Protection Act 1994* entitles pregnant employees to a period of maternity leave. The leave is of at least fourteen continuous weeks. The exact dates of the leave can be chosen by the employee, but the period must cover the four weeks before and the four weeks after the confinement. This period may be extended to eighteen weeks in certain circumstances. Where the mother of the child dies before the expiry of the fourteen weeks the father of the child may be entitled to take the remainder of the leave.

Adoptive Leave

The *Adoptive Leave Act 1995* applies many of the provisions of maternity leave to adoptive mothers and, in very limited circumstances, to adopting fathers. These include adoptive leave of ten consecutive weeks and a future period of unpaid leave of four weeks. A sole male adopter has similar rights. An adopting father may take leave where the adopting mother has died either before or during her period of leave.

Parental Leave

The *Parental Leave Act 1998* provides that an employee who is the natural or adoptive parent of a child shall be entitled to take unpaid leave for a period of fourteen weeks to enable him or her to take care of the child. Fathers and mothers are each entitled to this leave. The child must have been born or adopted after 3 June 1996. The leave must be taken before the child is five years of age, though in certain adoption cases this age is extended. The leave may be taken as a continuous block or in separate blocks or by reduced working hours.

Force Majeure *Leave*

The *Parental Leave Act 1998* provides that where for urgent family reasons, owing to an injury or an illness to a child, spouse, a person with whom the employee is living as husband or wife, a brother or sister, a parent or grandparent, the immediate presence of the employee is indispensable at the place where the person is, the employee shall be entitled to *force majeure* leave. This paid leave amounts to a maximum three days in twelve consecutive months or five days in thirty-six consecutive months.

PART-TIME WORKERS

Statutory Protection

In broad terms, the purpose of the *Worker Protection (Regular Part-time Employees) Act 1991* is to ensure that regular part-time employees will enjoy the same protections under the law as full-time workers. A regular part-time worker means an employee who has been in the continuous service of the employer for not less than thirteen weeks and is normally expected to work not less than eight hours a week for that employer.

WORKING TIME

Weekly Working Hours

The *Organisation of Working Time Act 1997* makes provision for the organisation of working time. In general, an employer shall not permit an employee to work, in each period of seven days, more than an average of forty-eight hours, that is to say an average of forty-eight hours calculated over a period that does not exceed four months, or in certain cases six months.

Nightly Working Hours

In general, an employer shall not permit a night worker, in each period of twenty-four hours, to work more than an average of eight hours, calculated over a period that does not exceed two months or where a collective agreement permits a greater length of time. A night worker is an employee who normally works at least three hours of his or her daily working time between midnight and 7 A.M. on the following morning, and the number of hours worked during night time, in each year, equals or exceeds 50 per cent of the total number of hours worked by him or her during that year. Where the night worker is a special category night worker, an employee whose work involves special hazards or a heavy physical or mental strain, the employer shall not permit such worker to work more than eight hours in each period of twenty-four hours.

Daily Rest Period

An employer shall be entitled to a rest period of not less than eleven consecutive hours in each period of twenty-four hours during which he or she works for his or her employer.

Rests and Intervals at Work

An employer shall not require an employe to work for a period of more than four-and-a-half hours without allowing him or her a break of at least fifteen minutes. When the employee works for a period of more than six hours the break must be at least half an hour.

Weekly Rest Periods

In general, an employee shall, in each period of seven days, be granted a rest period of at least twenty-four consecutive hours. In lieu of this, an employer may grant an employee in the next following period of seven days, two rest periods, each of which shall be a period of at least twenty-four consecutive hours.

CHAPTER 44

TRADE UNIONS

Nature of a Trade Union

A trade union is an association of employees established for the protection of their interests and the improvement of their incomes and employment conditions.

The Common Law and Trade Unions

At common law a trade union had no legal status. It was a cardinal principle of the law that every person had the right to dispose of his or her labour according to his or her wishes. Any combination of employees formed for the purpose of seeking wage increases, and the threat to withdraw labour if these increases or betterment in working conditions were not forthcoming was regarded by the law as a criminal conspiracy. A contract or bargain made by a union which imposed restrictions on the freedom of trade, or on the right of a person to sell his or her labour as he or she pleased, was outlawed as being contrary to public policy. Not alone was the agreement between the employees unlawful but the trade union, if formed for the express purpose of making collective bargains, might also be declared illegal.

Statutory Recognition of Trade Unions

The fact that the common law failed to recognise trade unions did not mean that trade unions did not exist. When it became obvious that trade unions had a beneficial role to play in society the common law was unable, because of its continued hostility to such organisations, to find a place for them within the law. The task of legalising trade unions fell to statute law.

The *Trade Union Act 1871* granted, for the first time, legal recognition to trade unions and this statute remains the principle statute in this regard. This 1871 Act had three objectives. Firstly, it relieved trade unions from some of the civil and criminal liabilities under which they had laboured. Secondly, trade unions were to be protected from legal actions by their members, or from another trade union, in regard to some matters. Thirdly, a system of voluntary registration of trade unions was established, which provided that registered trade unions had the right to exclusive use of the registered name.

THE CONSTITUTION AND TRADE UNIONS

Freedom of Association

Article 40 of the Constitution guarantees to the citizen, subject to public order and morality, the right to form associations and unions. This express right to form unions and associations must include the implied right to join associations and unions, though this right, like all other constitutional rights, is not absolute.

Right to Dissociate

Can an employee be compelled, either by an employer or fellow employees, to join a trade union? The answer may depend on when that demand is made. Where an employee is already in employment and trade union membership was not a condition of employment the answer seems to be no. This was decided by the Supreme Court in *Educational Co. of Ireland v Fitzpatrick* (1961) where employees, members of a trade union, in order to force their employer to solely employ trade union labour, picketed the premises in an attempt to force all the employees to join the union. The picketing was prevented by injunction because, as Budd J. explained: 'The dispute is concerned with an attempt to deprive persons of the right of free association or free dissociation guaranteed by the Constitution.'

As a result of the recognition of this right it follows that an employer who dismisses an employee for the failure join a trade union is liable in damages to that employee for breach of this constitutional right to dissociate. In *Meskell v CIE* (1973) a scheme by the employer and trade unions whereby employees would be dismissed and re-employed on condition that they joined and remained members of a particular trade union was held to be a conspiracy to deprive an individual of the constitutional right to dissociate. The Supreme Court held that the dismissed employee was entitled to damages. Walsh J. explained: 'To exercise . . . a common law right of dismissal as a method of compelling a person to abandon a constitutional right . . . must necessarily be regarded as an abuse of the . . . Constitution.'

Union Membership or Non-Membership as a Condition of Employment

The closed shop is a feature of our industrial practice. A closed shop exists where all the employees of a particular grade in a particular business belong, or agree to belong, to a particular trade union with the employer agreeing with that union to exclusively employ persons who agree to join, and remain, a member of that union during the continuance of the employment. Is it constitutionally permissible to make it a condition of employment to (a) join and remain in any trade union; (b) join and remain a member of a particular trade union; or, (c) not to join a trade union and to suffer lawful dismissal for a breach of such a condition?

There is no judicial decision on any of these possibilities. In *Becton, Dickinson Ltd v Lee* (1973) the employees pre-empted dismissal by withdrawing their labour leaving to the courts the sole issue of deciding whether a trade dispute existed. The employer agreed with a particular union that all craft employees would join and remain members of that union. Craft employees on entering employment signed an agreement to this effect, but once in employment refused to join that union because they already belonged to a different union. When the employer refused to negotiate with the employees' existing union, the employees went on strike and the employer sought an injunction to prevent the picketing, which was refused.

Obligation of a Trade Union to Accept Members

A trade union is not obliged to accept those who apply to it for membership. The High Court refused, in *Tierney v Amalgamated Society of Woodworkers* (1959), to direct a trade union to accept an application, which it had refused because the applicant was not a genuine carpenter. Budd J. explained: 'It has heretofore been of the essence of a voluntary organisation that the members, and they alone, should decide who should be their fellow-members.'

Conversely, if it were impossible to obtain work without belonging to a trade union, and membership was denied, a different attitude might be adopted by the courts. In *Murphy v Stewart* (1973), which involved persons attempting to transfer from one union to another, Walsh J. in the Supreme Court said: 'If the right to work was reserved exclusively to members of a trade union which held a monopoly in this field and the trade union was abusing the monopoly in such a way as to effectively prevent the exercise of a person's constitutional right to work, the question of compelling that union to accept the person concerned into membership (or, indeed, breaking the monopoly) would fall to be considered…'.

Right of Trade Union to Negotiate on a Member's Behalf

The courts will not compel an employer to negotiate with a union of the employee's choice. This was decided in *Abbott v ITGWU* (1980) where the employee first belonged to the ITGWU but resigned and joined another union. When this latter union had recruited about half the employees it wished to enter into negotiations with the employer. The employer refused to deal with any union except the ITGWU for fear that the latter would initiate strike action. The employee sought an order to compel his employer to negotiate with the trade union of his choice. The High Court refused the order on the ground that there was no constitutional right of negotiation.

Restrictions on Trade Unions

Citizens can form unions and associations subject to public order and morality. There are a number of restrictions contained in statute law on the right to form unconstitutional and illegal associations. In the trade union field there are some restrictions on the right, particularly for those involved in the security of the State, to form trade unions. Such limitations are restrictively interpreted and the Garda Síochána and Defence Forces are permitted, by statute, to form representative associations.

How far can the Oireachtas regulate the number of trade unions? The argument is often made that there are too many unions and that legislation should limit their numbers though in recent years there have been a number of amalgamations of unions. Some attempt was made to restrict the number of trade unions by the *Trade Union Act 1941*. This statute established a tribunal which could determine that where a majority of the workers of a particular grade, in a particular employment, were organised by a particular union no other union could accept as new members any workman of that grade in that employment. The Supreme Court, in the *National Union of Railwaymen v Sullivan* (1947), declared this procedure to be unconstitutional on the ground that it deprived citizens of the choice of persons with whom they might associate.

PICKETING IN FURTHERANCE OF A TRADE DISPUTE

Right to Picket

The mere withdrawal of an employee's labour, particularly if done collectively, is usually sufficient to totally disrupt the employer's business. It may, or may not, lead to a settlement but while the employee is without wages, the employer is without profit. However, in many cases the mere withdrawal of labour is not sufficient to achieve the employees' object, which is the bringing of the business to a halt.

In general, it is a criminal offence to watch and beset the premises of another. But section 11 of the *Industrial Relations Act 1990* provides: 'It shall be lawful for one or more persons, acting on their own behalf, or on the behalf of a trade union in contemplation or furtherance of a trade dispute, to attend at, or where that is not practicable, at the approaches to:

(a) a place where their employer works or carries on business, if they so attend merely for the purpose of peacefully obtaining, or communicating information or of peacefully persuading any person to work, or to abstain from working; or

(b) a place where an employer who is not a party to the trade dispute works or carries on business if, but only if, it is reasonable for those who are so attending to believe at the commencement of their attendance and throughout the continuance of their attendance that that employer has directly assisted their employer who is a party to the trade dispute for the purpose of frustrating the strike or other industrial action, provided that such attendance is merely for the purpose of peacefully obtaining or communicating information or of peacefully persuading any person to work or abstain from working.'

The protection conferred by section 11 is confined to authorised trade unions holding a negotiation licence under the *Trade Union Act 1941* and to members and officials of such a trade union.

Two points must be emphasised. First, there must be a trade dispute, and second, the picketing must be peaceful and must not be for an unconstitutional purpose.

Meaning of Worker

The 1990 Act defines worker to mean any person who is or was employed whether or not in the employment of the employer with whom a trade dispute arises, but does not include a member of the Defence Forces or the Garda Síochána.

Meaning of Strike

The 1990 Act defines a strike as a cessation of work by any number or body of workers acting in combination or a concerted refusal or a refusal, under a common understanding, of any number of workers to continue to work for their employer, done as a means of compelling their employer, or to aid other workers in compelling their employer, to accept or not to accept terms or conditions of, or affecting, employment.

Meaning and Existence of Trade Dispute

A trade dispute is defined by the 1990 Act as any dispute between employers and workers which is connected with the employment or non-employment, or the terms or conditions of, or affecting, the employment of any person.

The courts have had to decide in many instances whether a trade dispute existed. The consequence of an affirmative decision is that peaceful picketing is permitted. Where the court decides in the negative the picketing is unlawful and may be restrained by injunction.

Where a party with whom the employees, or the union, have a dispute is not the employer the dispute is not a genuine one. This was decided in *Roundabout Ltd v Beirne* (1959) where a company, which operated a licensed premises, closed down and leased the premises to another company, which commenced the same business in the premises three weeks later. That company sought an injunction when the premises were picketed by the employees of the former company. The High Court granted the injunction holding that a picket could not be placed on the premises of the new owners by reason of the dispute with the previous owner.

However, a trade dispute was acknowledged to exist in the *Silver Tassie Ltd v Cleary* (1958) where a barman in a public house was dismissed because the managing director of the company owning the premises wished to enter the business and there was no place for them both. The Supreme Court, in holding that a trade dispute existed, decided that the genuineness of a dispute did not depend on the actual facts of the dispute but on the *bona fide* of the parties.

Where an employer dismisses an employee on the ostensible ground of misconduct but in reality because of the suspicion that the employee is about to join a trade union, as happened in *Maher v Beirne* (1955), it constitutes a trade dispute, and picketing in demand of reinstatement is lawful. A trade dispute exists where employees picket the premises of the employer for the purpose of having their union recognised see *Becton, Dickinson Ltd v Lee* (1973), page 469.

A dispute between a trade union and the employer, which is confined to the hours of trading of that employer and which is not related in any way to the terms of an employee's employment, is not a trade dispute. This was decided in *Esplanade Pharmacy Ltd v Larkin* (1950) where it was decided to open the premises on a Sunday but did not require the employee, a member of a union, to work. The union argued that this extension of opening hours would worsen conditions of employment of union members working in competitors' premises in the area because the added competition would compel competitors to require their employees to work on Sundays. The Supreme Court held there was no trade dispute. The union was attempting to enforce an agreement as to trading hours, which was a matter concerned with the employer's business and not with the employee's conditions of employment.

The Supreme Court held, in *Nolan Transport (Oaklands) Ltd v Halligan* (1998), that a trade dispute exists where workers have good grounds for believing themselves to have been dismissed by their employer.

Rules Governing Picketing

The 1990 Act permits peaceful picketing at, or where that is not practicable, at the approaches to, a place where the employer works or carries on business. A farm belonging to the managing director of a business was picketed, in *Ellis v Wright* (1976), in furtherance of a trade dispute in the business. It was proved that, while the business and the farm were completely separate, some activities of the farm such as the collection of milk, were performed by employees of the business. The High Court refused to injunct the farm's picketing.

The immunity to picket is only available where it is done peacefully. Picketing which is not peaceful is unlawful. A union, in *Ryan v Cooke* (1938), with the consent of the employer, canvassed the employees to join the union. When none joined the union requested the employer to exclusively employ trade union labour. When this request was ignored the employer's premises were picketed with placards which read: 'This firm refuses to employ trade union labour' and 'Support fair traders'. The High Court granted an injunction to prevent the picketing because it was not peaceful to disseminate a falsehood or to persuade the public to trade with competitors. In *Brendan Dunne Ltd v Fitzpatrick* (1958) the employer agreed with its employees to open the premises later on occasional evenings. Members of a trade union, objecting to the late openings, picketed the premises and paraded in adjacent streets with placards. The High Court injuncted the picketing because the number of pickets were unduly large which frightened and overawed those picketed, and because some of the placards invited the public to support concerns other than that of the employer.

Peaceful picketing, even in furtherance of a trade dispute, is unlawful where its purpose is the interference with constitutional rights. We have seen in *Educational Co. of Ireland v Fitzpatrick* (1961) (page 468) that the courts will injunct picketing which has as its purpose the deprivation of the constitutional right to dissociate. There was a demand, in *Murtagh Properties Ltd v Cleary* (1972), backed by a threat of a picket, that women should not be employed. An injunction was granted by the High Court because the purpose of the picket was to compel the employer to dismiss the women solely because they were women, which was a breach of their constitutional rights.

TRADE UNION IMMUNITIES

Immunity for Inducing a Breach of Employment Contract

Section 12 of the 1990 Act provides that an act done by a person in contemplation or furtherance of a trade dispute shall not be actionable on the ground only that it induces some other person to break a contract of employment, or that it consists of a threat by a person to induce some other person to break a contract of employment, or a threat by a person to break his or her own contract of employment, or that it is an interference with the trade, business, or employment of some other person, or with the right of some other person to dispose of his capital or labour as he or she wills.

Thus, a party who interferes with the contractual relations between an employer and an employee during a trade dispute is immune from action which is otherwise tortious: see page 219.

This protection, legal in nature, may not extend to the breach of a constitutional right. For example, if in the course of a trade dispute a trade union interfered with an employee's right to dissociate, the trade union might not escape liability under this section because the breach was of a constitutional right, see *Meskell v CIE* (page 468). Where illegal means are adopted to procure the breach of contract the section offers no protection. Some employees, in *Riordan v Butler* (1940), objected to the employment of a non-union employee and informed their employer that should this employee start work they would cease work immediately. The employer dismissed the non-union employee who successfully sued his former fellow employees. The High Court held that the threat to cease work without giving notice was illegal and, although a trade dispute, did not gain the protection. This protection is only available where a breach of the employment contract is procured and not other contracts. A trade union wrote to the employer, in *Sherrif v McMullen* (1952), stating it understood that the employees' wages would be increased should they resign from union membership. The union intimated that if this were so it would not allow its members in any part of the country to handle the employer's products. As a consequence a buyer who had purchased a quantity of timber from the employer refused to take delivery because his employees refused to handle it. The Supreme Court decided that the section offered no protection because the contract of which the union had procured a breach was a contract for the sale and delivery of goods and not a contract of employment as laid down by the section.

Immunity from Tortious Liability

Section 13 of the 1990 Act provides: 'An action against a trade union . . . or against any members or officials thereof on behalf of themselves, and all other members of the trade union, in respect of any tortious act alleged to have been committed by, or on behalf of the trade union in contemplation or furtherance of a trade dispute, shall not be entertained by any court.' This amounts to a statutory prohibition on courts from entertaining certain actions in tort against a trade union. The section does not suggest that a union cannot commit a tort; it simply protects the trade union from the consequences of such an act. This immunity is given to a trade union, whether of employers or employees, and to no other body. The purpose of this immunity is to protect the union funds. This immunity is restricted to a trade union which is the holder of a negotiation licence under the *Trade Union Act 1941*.

This immunity does not apply to contracts entered into by trade unions nor to other areas of legal regulation. For example, in *Connolly v McConnell* (1983) the Supreme Court ruled that the decision by a trade union to dismiss an official breached the constitutional right to fair procedures on the ground that those with a financial interest in the outcome of the decision should not have taken part in the decision making process (see page 74).

Industrial Action and Secret Ballot

According to section 14 of the 1990 Act, 'The rules of every trade union shall contain a provision that: a trade union cannot organise, participate in, sanction or support a strike or other industrial action without a secret ballot, entitlement to vote must be accorded equally to all members whom it is reasonable at the time of the ballot for the union concerned to believe will be called upon to engage in the strike or other industrial action.'

The immunities granted by sections 12 and 13 of the 1990 Act shall not apply in respect of proceedings arising out of or relating to a strike or other industrial action by a trade union or a group of workers in disregard of or contrary to, the outcome of a secret ballot relating to the issue or issues involved in the dispute. The Supreme Court ruled, in *Nolan Transport (Oaklands) Ltd v Halligan* (1998), that the participation by a trade union in, or its support for, a strike or other industrial action without the authority of a secret ballot of its members was a matter of internal management of the affairs of the union and constituted a breach of contract between the union and the membership and, very importantly, did not give rise to a cause of action by any person affected by the industrial action. In such circumstances the trade union did not forfeit the immunities contained in sections 12 and 13 but merely risked the loss of its negotiating licence.

Injunctions and Industrial Action

Section 19 of the 1990 Act provides that where a secret ballot has been held in accordance with the rules of a trade union and the outcome favours a strike or other industrial action and the trade union gives notice of not less than one week to the employer of its intention to do so, the court shall not grant an injunction restraining the strike, or other industrial action, where the trade union establishes a fair case that it was acting in contemplation of, or furtherance of, a trade dispute. The Supreme Court upheld the granting of an injunction against picketing, in *G. & T. Crampton Ltd v Building & Allied Trades Union* (1998), on the ground that there was a fair question to be tried whether, in the conduct of a secret ballot the nature of the industrial action proposed should be particularised, and also whether the ballot was inadequate in that members who were likely to be affected by it were not balloted or given an opportunity of voting on the proposals. The court also seemed to suggest that the onus lay on the party resisting the injunction to show that a properly conducted secret ballot had been held.

INDEX